HENRY CHADWICK

Selected Writings

HENRY CHADWICK

Selected Writings

Edited and introduced by

William G. Rusch

WILLIAM B. EERDMANS PUBLISHING COMPANY

GRAND RAPIDS, MICHIGAN

Wm. B. Eerdmans Publishing Co.
2140 Oak Industrial Drive NE, Grand Rapids, Michigan 49505
www.eerdmans.com

23 22 21 20 19 18 17   1 2 3 4 5 6 7

ISBN 978-0-8028-7277-7

Library of Congress Cataloging-in-Publication Data

Names: Chadwick, Henry, 1920–2008 author. | Rusch, William G., editor.
Title: Henry Chadwick : selected writings / edited and introduced by William G. Rusch.
Description: Grand Rapids, Michigan : Eerdmans Publishing Company, 2017.
Identifiers: LCCN 2015042533 | ISBN 9780802872777 (hardcover : alk. paper)
Subjects: LCSH: Theology. | Church of England—Doctrines. | Church history.
Classification: LCC BX5199.C43 A25 2017 | DDC 230/.3—dc23
    LC record available at https://lccn.loc.gov/2015042533

Credits for previously published articles can be found on pp. 318–20.

Contents

Contents

Foreword

Throughout his lifetime Henry Chadwick was, by common consent, the most distinguished scholar of the early Church in the English-speaking world. Magisterially comprehensive books on the whole period were complemented by brilliant monographs on particular figures or texts. There can be few books on early Christianity in the last few decades that do not somewhere contain a reference to his work or at least a trace of conclusions that he had pointed to. The books and monographs, however, were accompanied in turn by a number of exceptional articles or essays, many of which, despite their relative brevity, succeeded in changing the scholarly landscape in respect to some particular question — which is why it is a great help to have some of the most important of these collected in accessible form as they are in this welcome volume. Pieces like the study of the role of the bishop, of the origin of the term 'ecumenical' as an adjective for councils, of the sacramental and devotional issues around in the background of the Council of Chalcedon or of the borderlands between classical and Christian ethics have all been landmarks in the understanding of early Christianity, and remain indispensable even when later and more detailed work has further filled out the picture.

Very broadly, most of these essays deal with three kinds of topic. There are studies of how the early Church actually worked; studies of the complex interaction of Christian thinking with pagan philosophy and culture; and a clutch of essays on aspects of Augustine. Chadwick published a short but invaluable book on Augustine, and the essays reproduced here show something of the depth of specialist learning that underlay every page of it. There were also books on the classical/Christian interface, but many will regret that he never produced the longer study of early Christian ethics that he was uniquely equipped to write; we are fortunate to have some of the raw materials he would have been building into such a book, in the shape of the articles in this area reprinted here. And the close-focus discussions of the Church's workings and on the councils and their hinterland informed the ample surveys he wrote of the development of the Church throughout the early period (and indeed beyond, bearing in mind his comprehensive book on the developing divisions between Eastern and Western churches).

Henry Chadwick was never a voluble commentator on contemporary ecclesiastical issues (though he had some strongly defined views on some of them); but he believed as firmly as he believed anything that the Church suffered enormously when it allowed itself to forget its past. This past was for him not a repository of finished business but a record of continually intriguing and engaging arguments, internal and external; and so what we learned from it was not simply a set of orthodox conclusions — though he was entirely happy to accept conciliar orthodoxy as his spiritual and intellectual home. At best it was a sense of the way these conclusions remained alive because of the lively and complex processes by which they had been formulated. Neither a revisionist nor a mechanical traditionalist, Chadwick conveyed to generations of students and colleagues something of this sense of a living past, deserving of our best efforts of intellect and imagination in mapping and interpreting it. In his unique contribution to Anglican–Roman Catholic dialogue (recognised by the gift of a priestly stole from Pope Paul VI), he deployed his own best efforts in this task for the good of the Church, as he had always done for the good of honest academic endeavour. He was unusual in the degree of respect he earned equally from entirely secular scholars of the ancient world and from church leaders and hierarchs of all confessions.

As many have said, he represented for countless people the essence of a particular kind of Anglican identity, learned, irenic but not bland. These studies show something of the rare stature of the man — occasionally but unmistakeably also showing the wry wit that was so typical of him. His authoritative presence is still missed, but his legacy is not in doubt. My hope is that this book will make him better known to a new generation of students of early Christianity and of the endlessly fascinating thinking of Augustine and others. He remains one of those giants on to whose shoulders we lesser mortals of the scholarly world scramble to get a view, and this collection demonstrates why that debt is so great.

Rowan Williams
Cambridge, Lent 2016

Introduction

The following pages offer the reader a selection of the scholarship of one of the premier church historians and students of the early church in the twentieth century — Professor Henry Chadwick. To understand the contribution of Professor Chadwick's life and work, some comments are in order about the area of his endeavors — the history and thought of early Christianity.

For Christianity, history has never been an option. Because of this fact, those individuals throughout the centuries who have put their faith in Christianity, or who sought to understand its nature and significance, have grasped this insight.

Christianity not only has a history; its historicity has been essential to its existence. The nature of the Christian faith is not expressed in timeless abstractions, but in the claim of the historical incarnation and revelation of Jesus Christ as fully human apart from sin and fully divine. This foundational understanding means that the Christian faith is embodied in human history. The story of Christianity for its adherents exists in a tension between the entry of the Triune God into human history, already foreshadowed in the earlier events of Israel and the Jewish people, and the human situation with its ambiguities in every age. Finally the Christian faith must be seen both as historical and as an object of faith, involving both history and theology. Therefore, the Christian faith demands a "factual" account of its story and a need to see beyond the facts.

In view of this characteristic of Christianity, attention to its history is not surprising but expected. History looms large in the scriptural and primary texts of Christianity. From the earliest days of the expansion of the Christian faith, its narrative in history was regarded as significant. Not only major figures such as Eusebius of Caesarea and Augustine of Hippo concerned themselves with the history of their faith. A survey of the literature of the first several centuries of church history reveals many others with the same concern, if not with the identical depth of perception to comprehend this history.

The same preoccupation continued in the medieval church when the history of Christianity was often portrayed as the story of salvation, sometimes with little regard for the accuracy of details of the account. In this period, many in addition to Bede, Dietrich of Nieham, and Procopius occupied themselves with a historical account of Christianity.

The sixteenth-century Reformation(s) challenged many of the presuppositions of the former narratives. There was a call for a return to the early church, but this very appeal became a matter of polemics and debate. Catholics such as Jerome Emser and Johann Cochlaeus in part sought an invocation of history to support Catholic views, as did other authors in the *Corpus Catholicorum.*

On the Protestant side there were individuals like Philipp Melanchthon and Matthias Flaccius, especially in his *Historia Ecclesiastica,* who claimed the affirmation of the previous history of the church for Protestant views. The *Corpus Reformatorum* provides considerable documentation for this concern. Much of the debate centered on the question: who had the accurate story and correct comprehension of the early church?

During the Enlightenment in the following centuries the notion of a theological interpretation of the Christian faith was rejected and a secularized version of the narrative was sought. Such views found expression in the writings of René Descartes and Immanuel Kant among others.

A reaction against this point of view began in the nineteenth century. Specialization developed. Hagiography, archaeology, iconography, liturgy, and dogma were acknowledged as independent areas of study with their own literature. The many complex dimensions of the historical narration and of the doctrinal development of Christianity were recognized. There was also a blooming of the historical sciences. Impressive collections of source material from the early and medieval churches became available to scholars. These included not only J. P. Migne's *Patrologia Latina* and *Patrologia Graeca,* but the *Corpus Scriptorum Ecclesiasticorum Latinorum* and *Die griechischen christlichen Schriftsteller der ersten drei Jahrhunderte.* Surveys of the writings of early Christian authors and of movements in the early church were published by such outstanding experts as Otto Bardenhewer, Adolf von Harnack, both of the nineteenth and twentieth centuries, and John Henry Newman of the nineteenth century.

All these advances served as resources and motivation for the telling of the Christian story in the twentieth century. As that century unfolded, a movement occurred away from the positivism of the previous hundred years with its stress on empirically tangible datum. A new appreciation for a theological-historical-ecclesiastical orientation became obvious. The new goal was to move beyond the mere presentation of historical facts to grasp the significance of these events in terms of the history of ideas and to interpret them theologically. As the years of the twentieth century passed, there was a shift from "Patrology" (narrowly conceived as the study of ancient Christian writers down to Gregory the Great or Isidore of Seville in the West, and John of Damascus in the East) to "Early Christian Studies," perceived as a vast area of intellectual pursuit with considerable diversity. It included in part a discussion of geography, the role of women, and a debate about the accuracy of specific labels such as "orthodoxy," "heresy," and "Arianism." Social factors were taken into account in the description of movements like Donatism. The porous boundary, once regarded as almost air-tight, between the New Testament period and the early church was newly appreciated.

In this last century of tremendous energy devoted to the investigation of the ancient church and its theology, Henry Chadwick emerged as a major contributor and authority whose work and influence has continued into the twenty-first century. His impact and status have placed him in the first rank of his contemporary savants of early Christianity.

Henry Chadwick was born in Bromley, England, on June 23, 1920. After his years at Eton, he won a music scholarship to Magadalene College in Cambridge. His interest soon turned to Christianity, and in 1943 he was ordained a priest in the Church of England. For a short time he served a parish and then was a schoolmaster. In 1946 he was named a fellow and chaplain at Queens College, Cambridge. The publication of his edition of *Contra Celsum* in 1953 brought him prominence as a scholar. In 1959, Dr. Chadwick was appointed Regius Professor of Divinity at Oxford, and in 1969 he became Dean of Christ Church at Oxford. From 1979 until 1983 he was Regius Professor of Divinity in Cambridge. In 1987 he left retirement to be Master of Peterhouse in Cambridge. In 1989 he was knighted. His final retirement began in 1993, and he spent his later years in Oxford, dying at the age of 87 in 2008.

Professor Chadwick, no doubt, would have described himself as a historian, but he has equal claim to being appreciated as an ecumenical theologian of the first rank. A prominent aspect of his life and work was his commitment to ecumenism, and especially to assist Anglicanism and Roman Catholicism to resolve their historic divisions. Dr. Chadwick believed progress could be made in this area by agreement over those items shared by most early

Christians. In the 1970s he was an active and influential member and drafter in the Anglo-Roman Catholic International Commission.

Dr. Chadwick's interests and contributions in the examination of early Christianity were wide-ranging. They included the emerging faith's relationship to classical culture; the interaction among piety, politics, and theology; attention to groups on the margins of what was to become mainstream; "Orthodox" Christianity; and respect for newly discovered texts. Such productivity made Henry Chadwick an ultimate authority on early Christianity in the English-speaking world.

His scholarship found expression in substantial works such as an edition of *Contra Celsum,* two monographs, *Early Christian Thought and the Classical Tradition* and *The Early Church,* as well as an edition of Ambrose's *De Sacramentis.* Priscillian of Avila, Boethius, and Augustine were topics of his ongoing publications. His later works included *The Church in Ancient Society: From Galilee to Gregory the Great* and *East and West: The Making of a Rift in the Church.*

Much of Dr. Chadwick's groundbreaking work circulated in articles on a great variety of subjects in a plethora of journals and in independent pamphlets. In some cases his work was never published. For years he was an editor of the *Journal of Theological Studies,* where he regularly published articles. The vast majority of these lectures and articles are as relevant for the study of early Christianity today as when they were first written. His scholarship continues to be a resource to understand the present-day church and to enlighten ecumenical problems that keep Christians in the twenty-first century visibly divided. Some of these works are scattered in numerous periodicals; others are available in expensive reprint collections of Dr. Chadwick's articles and reviews.

The essays selected for this volume fall under themes that were important throughout his scholarly life. It includes his work on topics such as ministry and councils in the early church, the Church of Rome, music, St. Augustine's influence on the early church, Christian living in the early church, and the early church in the Roman world.

Ministry in the Early Church

From its earliest days the church confronted the subject of leadership in the community. Questions about the structuring of leadership and how such leadership was to function in relationship to the entire community were paramount. Answers to such questions not only led to a more accurate portrayal of the early church but offered assistance in answering pressing ecumenical questions facing the contemporary church of the twentieth and twenty-first centuries. Because of the importance and urgency of such topics, Dr. Chadwick addressed these issues or, in some cases, was requested to offer his insights on them.

Ministry and Tradition

Chapter one, originally given as a lecture in Spanish at the University of Burgos, is a presentation devoted to a topic of interest not only to students of the early church but also to ecumenists. It has a dual focus on ministry and tradition. Dr. Chadwick begins the lecture by reminding his audience of Augustine's view that the whole people of God are ministers. Ministry is rooted in the continuing life of the church and so related to tradition. Tradition, according to Dr. Chadwick, means the memory of the community, which gives the people of God their self-understanding. With this meaning, tradition is connected with the apostolic succession of pastors. Dr. Chadwick insists that this view does not mean an imprisonment to the past. It is also a mandate to proclaim the gospel in a changing situation. He points out how ministry and tradition can help to secure the church in a time of debate about change. He also indicates that uniformity has been a topic of contention throughout church history.

Episcopacy in the New Testament and Early Church

Chapter two, composed for the bishops of the Anglican Communion, is evidence of the ecumenical interest in this subject in the late 1970s. It was written for the Lambeth Conference of 1978. Dr. Chadwick recalls for his hearers that all ministry is a charism from the Spirit and a service within the church. Ordained ministry is given a role of oversight to assist the unity of the local and universal community. Pastoral ministry in the New Testament in a variety of forms is a gift of God for the church's mission. Dr. Chadwick notes that the apostles had a unique role in this process. He recognizes both the place and importance of continuity and the constant need for some permanent structure of ministry amid the diversity in the emerging church.

Dr. Chadwick points out in a varied and complex set of situations that local churches show evidence of a presiding minister with leadership in the local settings and links to other churches. He notes how the centralized function of the bishop became a safeguard against heretical and schismatic forces. In this role of the bishop, the idea of apostolic succession gains in importance. The lecture closes with some comments on the question of the defect of orders and on the recognition and reconciliation of ministry.

The Role of the Christian Bishop in Ancient Society

Dr. Chadwick offers a description of the functions of the bishop of a Christian community in the context of ancient society, including many examples of the conduct of the episcopal office. He begins with an account of the bishop's authority within the church. Because there is a correspondence between the church in heaven and the church on earth, the bishop is viewed as a counterpart of God.

Each city is to have one bishop; the local bishop's authority by the fourth century was rooted in the local community. The ideal of consecration by three bishops with the consent of the faithful was evident by the fourth century. The bishop's power-base was the allegiance of the local flock. This allowed the bishop to play a role in secular society. The bishops became more and more involved in financial matters, arbitration of disputes, the care of the poor, hospitality to traveling missionaries, and granting asylum.

In view of all these factors, Dr. Chadwick points out that it is not surprising that episcopal elections could be times of unrest. By the fifth century, he notes, important sees had bishops who were former senators. Such figures became involved in the redemption of prisoners of war and filled the role of ambassadors. The frequent function of the bishop was to pray for the emperor and for peace. The chief critics of this expanding social role of bishops were often monks.

Nevertheless, there were links between the ascetic movements and some bishops, as Athanasius of Alexandria illustrates. This unfolding narrative discloses for Dr. Chadwick the emergence of a new type of leader in a Christianized Roman empire. This leader with permanent tenure for life, chosen by a local community, linked to a worldwide fellowship, was harnessed by emperors for social purposes in ways without earlier parallels.

Bishops and Monks

Here Dr. Chadwick takes up a topic to which he made allusion in his other writings. He presents a picture of the emerging and critical functions of the bishop with his own people in the early years of the church and also of the counter-tendency in the church: an ascetic movement. If the bishops helped the church in the world, the monks assisted the church to get out of this world. Because of their differing emphases, bishops and monks were not always in agreement on crucial matters.

The office of bishop took on more social and juridical functions by the third century. (See chapter three.) The episcopal office dispensed legal decisions, assumed the role of an ambassador, and aided the poor. Such functions at times complicated the relation of bishops to civil authority. The selection of bishops could often be untidy. Bishops could also be irate at government officials. Bishops did establish small monastic communities, but bishops and monks also could clash on occasion. Still, Dr. Chadwick cautions against overstating the case of conflict.

Celibacy for clergy arose in the fourth century. The Eastern and Western churches were in agreement about its value, but they had distinctive positions on the issue of making celibacy a requirement for the clerical life.

Already in the fifth century there are examples of bishops who were chosen for their high culture and good education. By the time of Gregory the Greet, monasteries had become a major factor in the creation of a class of literate bishops, who were exercising practically every secular activity of leadership.

Councils in the Early Church

Councils or synods soon became a standard feature in the life of the church in its early centuries. A true picture of the role and function of these episcopal gatherings is a resource to help comprehend the content and method of doctrinal teaching in the emerging church. For Dr. Chadwick, greater clarity about how the early church came to express its faith and to teach authoritatively had the potential of being an ecumenical asset.

The Origin of the Title 'Oecumenical Council'

This chapter raises the question of the origin of the expression "oecumenical council." Professor Chadwick observes that the Council of Nicaea recognized itself as a particularly significant event; however, it is not known if the Council of Nicaea ever described itself as "oecumenical." Rather, this description of Nicaea appears in documents from the year 338 dealing with

Athanasius and Eusebius's *Life of Constantine*. In both cases "oecumenical," according to Dr. Chadwick, seems to have had no theological overtones. What was stated is that Nicaea was a "worldwide" event. Christians borrowed the phrase "oecumenical synod" from long-held usage, especially in regard to a worldwide association of athletes and Dionysiac artists. Only later, and largely because of the efforts of Athanasius, would "an oecumenical council" designate a special category of council.

Faith and Order at the Council of Nicaea: A Note on the Background of the Sixth Canon

In this chapter Professor Chadwick takes up the question of how the Council of Nicaea influenced both the faith and order of the fourth-century church. He points out the significant achievement of the creed of Nicaea with its all but unanimous approval of the bishops in attendance.

The letter of Eusebius of Caesarea to his church after the conclusion of the council is described and recognized as a statement of a general theological platform for a coalition of diverse standpoints. Eusebius was caught in a somewhat embarrassing situation in the debates at Nicaea.[1] His support for the creed was not total; his endorsement could be viewed as lukewarm.

Professor Chadwick indicates that since the creed of Nicaea did not disturb the order of the churches and was highly ambiguous about the faith of the church, many bishops could sign it. In fact, it is somewhat puzzling that there were even a few holdouts. The explanation of this situation may be in part the popularity of Arianism in Libya. According to Dr. Chadwick, this state of affairs may provide the background to the sixth canon of Nicaea, whose manuscript tradition he reviews. It seems that the wording of the canon became obscure. Its real concern was Alexandria's privileges in Libya. The debates involved the situation in the See of Antioch and the status of Jerusalem. The influence of all the canons of Nicaea was great, and the Roman Church would quote the sixth canon in particular against the claims of the church of Constantinople. The internal church disputes about order may have been influenced by early secular decisions like Diocletian's reform of provincial organization

---

1. Since Dr. Chadwick published this article in 1960, continuing attention has been given to the status of Eusebius at Nicaea and the role and purpose of his letter to his home diocese. E.g., see R. P. C. Hanson, *The Search for the Christian Doctrine of God* (Edinburgh: T & T Clark, 1988), 140, 159–67, and Lewis Ayers, *Nicaea and Its Legacy: An Approach to Fourth-Century Trinitarian Theology* (Oxford: Oxford University Press, 2004), 96–97.

in the empire. With all this maneuvering, the question remains: How did the sixth canon affect the state of the church in Libya? Dr. Chadwick concludes that the evidence renders a final answer impossible. Yet it is clear that, by the time of Cyril, Libya's bishops were Orthodox and not Arian.

Ossius of Cordova and the Presidency of the Council of Antioch, 325

In chapter seven, Dr. Chadwick explores the Syriac text of a synodical letter of the year 325, discovered by Edward Schwartz. He describes the chance discovery of this text. The letter comes from a council at Antioch held before the Nicene Council of the same year. Dr. Chadwick sees the debate about the authenticity of the letter as now largely resolved in favor of the document being genuine, but the question remains about the identity of the presiding bishop at the synod.

Dr. Chadwick surveys the evidence and offers an emendation to the text that would give the presidency not to the relatively unknown Eusebius but to Ossius, a well-known bishop and advisor to Constantine. Professor Chadwick relates his discovery of another Syriac manuscript that would support the reading of Ossius. He connects Ossius to a bishop named Paulinus, whom scholarship now concludes was Bishop Paulinus of Adana.

Dr. Chadwick points out that the composition and purpose of the council are still matters of speculation, as are the factors that led to its location. The efforts of the Council at Antioch to prejudge issues before the churches ended in failure. Ossius tried to close the ranks of the Eastern Church before a larger council could meet. In this attempt, Dr. Chadwick suggests Ossius may well have determined by a strange set of circumstances that when this group finally gathered it was not at Ancyra but Nicaea.

The Chalcedonian Definition

In this chapter, Dr. Chadwick addresses the significant status of the Council of Chalcedon. He raises the question whether the Chalcedonian consensus is real and adequate for the task at hand. The context is two competing Christologies, both of which had critical insights to preserve for the church. For it is both the Alexandrian and Antiochian Christologies as rival reactions to the Arians that provide the background for the Council of Chalcedon, which understandably endeavored to address the issues of the debate in fifth-century language and concepts. Dr. Chadwick offers an account of the detailed and intense dispute between Cyril of Alexandria and John of Antioch, as well as Pope Leo's interjection into the discussion with his Tome. The reader is reminded of the importance of the political setting for this theological discussion.

In this context, the Definition of Chalcedon was drafted while the permanent status of Nicaea (325) and Constantinople (381) continued to be recognized. Although ambiguities exist in the Chalcedonian Definition, its purpose was to bring peace and to end dissension in the church. As Professor Chadwick indicates, it sought to do this by making a distinction between "nature" and "person" in Christology and by accepting (under political pressure) the less than clear expression, Christ is "known in two natures." Thus Dr. Chadwick concludes that the Council of Chalcedon with its use of technical philosophical terms and negative adverbs did not adequately express the Christology found in the Bible. Nevertheless, the Definition is more than a mere juxtaposition of teachings from two incompatible schools. It wishes to state that behind the warring formulas of Alexandria and Antioch there is an underlying agreement reflecting two patterns of Christology from the New Testament.

The Church of Rome in the Early Church

One of the most consequential subjects in the study and understanding of the early church is the place and growing impact of the church at Rome. The topic raises issues of authority and structures in the life of the church. Professor Chadwick devoted considerable attention to the church at Rome in the early centuries of Christianity, not only because of his interests in early Christian studies, but also because of his commitments as an ecumenist. His hopes were that a better and more accurate grasp of this early history could be a resource to resolve present ecumenical claims.

The Circle and the Ellipse:
Rival Concepts of Authority in the Early Church

This chapter is comprised of the text of Professor Chadwick's inaugural lecture as Regius Professor at the University of Oxford. With the intriguing title of "The Circle and the Ellipse," Dr. Chadwick takes up the subject of authority in the early church and especially the question of how the Church of Rome became so important in the early centuries of the ancient church.

Primitive Christianity was a circle with Jerusalem at its center. This fact created a tension with the Gentile mission, as Paul's writings indicate. Jerusalem remained at this pivotal point even after two revolts and the destruction of much of the city. A Jerusalem-mystique remained beyond those events, and it was encouraged by Constantine.

However, a parallel story simultaneously existed—that of the Rome idea. Rome had claim to two eminent apostles, Peter and Paul. Monuments in Rome were constructed to them, and early Western churches looked to Rome. The idea that Christianity is a circle with its center in Rome took root with the encouragement of Rome. To counter this view, Eastern churches started to think of an ellipse with two foci.

Thus Eastern bishops regarded the Bishop of Rome as Patriarch of the West, bishop of the world's great city. Bishops of Rome took it for granted that they were the center of the circle, successors of the prince of the apostles. Different liturgical patterns developed in the East and in Rome, along with other differences that caused tensions.

Dr. Chadwick points out that the original primacy of Jerusalem became a sensitive issue. He sees the beginnings of this tension already in the New Testament with the missions of Paul and Peter. He believes that the circle was already becoming an ellipse. Paul expressed a duality in the idea of the church. There is a need for the recognition of the church in Jerusalem. There is an additional need for an acknowledgment of the equal status of Gentiles in the one church. The apostle Paul became the creator of a quasi-independent Gentile Christendom. This is the context in which Paul's journey must be seen. For the book of Acts, the preaching of the apostle of the Gentiles in the capital of the Gentile world was a supernatural fact.

Therefore, Professor Chadwick concludes, although relatively neglected in the Roman tradition, it was Paul more than Peter who may be regarded as the founder of the papacy.

St. Peter and St. Paul in Rome:
The Problem of the Memoria Apostolorum Ad Catacumbas

In the tenth chapter, Professor Chadwick addresses the topic of the presence of Peter and Paul in Rome by pointing out a piece of literary evidence often overlooked—an inscription by Pope Damasus. He thus explores the question of the locations of the graves of the two apostles.

An adequate account of the memorials of Peter and Paul in Rome must explain the double shrine on the Via Appia and its relation to the two other memorials, one on the Vatican hill and the other on the Via Ostiensis. The double memorial on the Via Appia probably dates from the mid-third century. Yet the question remains: Why the establishment of the site? The answer appears to be, according to Professor Chadwick, that this was the third milestone of the Via Appia and the actual location of the remains of both apostles. At one time, this place did possess the remains of the apostles.

Dr. Chadwick examines the inscription of Pope Damasus that deals with this issue. The epitaph is in agreement with the graffiti at the Via Appia—once the remains of the apostles were there, and subsequently they were moved to the Vatican and the Via Ostiensis. Dr. Chadwick wonders whether the wrong question has been asked of the memoria. He observes that a number of theories have been put forth, but they have little to support them. He proposes the idea that an aetiological myth might be operative to explain two rival and antithetical traditions. He recognizes that there is not a final answer to the question of whether the aedicule in the red wall on the Vatican hill did mark the apostles' grave. He describes the shifting evidence, including the theory that at one point the memoria was a cult-center for a dissentient group. There may have been tension between those who favored the site on the Via Appia and the official Roman community. In these circumstances, a story could have been put forth to explain the translation of the apostles from an original burial site.

Evidence in the Decretum Gelasianum points to differing views of the days of the martyrdom of Peter and Paul. If this account is accurate, there is a twofold tradition not merely about the place of burial but also about the date. Then the single commemoration of both apostles on June 29th would be connected with the shrine on the Via Appia, where both bodies were believed to be. Separate commemorations would favor two individual shrines at the Vatican and the Via Ostiensis. Dr. Chadwick sees the solution in the work of Pope Damasus. Both apostles' martyrdoms were celebrated on the same day, June 29th. The shrine on the Via Appia was dropped, and the proceedings on June 29th were conducted at only two places, the Vatican and the Via Ostiensis. The poem of Damasus told inquiring pilgrims on the Via Appia to look elsewhere for the two apostles. All this confusion, Dr. Chadwick believes, indicates that Christians in Rome during the second and early third centuries were no more certain about the location of the apostolic graves than we are today.

Music in the Church

At first glance, the following chapter could appear incongruous with the preceding several chapters. However, this is not the case. Throughout his career Henry Chadwick had an intense love for and interest in music for its own sake, as well as for its relation to religion and especially Christianity. This chapter is further evidence of the scope and depth of Professor Chadwick's learning.

The Power of Music

Chapter eleven is a previously unpublished essay by Professor Chadwick. It reflects his profound knowledge of and interest in music, his first academic interest. Dr. Chadwick analyzes the role of music both as a vehicle and support for the assertion of power and also as an art to place constraint on individuals. He notes that physics can aid in the understanding of music, but music remains an ancient and mysterious activity. The essay offers numerous examples to illustrate the various points that the author makes.

Music has played the role of enriching and ennobling ceremonial solemnities for communities. It has expressed emotional power, and it has sociological implications. This can be shown throughout history, as Dr. Chadwick asserts. He also addresses the contemporary situation. He indicates the evidence for the abandonment of tonality in contemporary music and questions whether the public will accept such developments. Dr. Chadwick also speaks of the relation of music to the political scene, observing the rise of vulgar music in Stalinist Russia. In addition, Dr. Chadwick makes comments about pop music and jazz, expressing an appreciation for the freshness and originality of the music of the Beatles. He reminds his audience that music has the power to tame wildness and excess.

The religious community gives intense value to music because it compels its hearers to listen, but the religious community has fear and misgivings about music for precisely the same reason. Somewhere in the mysterious and profound region of the psyche resides the power of music. Dr. Chadwick's concluding word is an acknowledgment that music can do much for the therapy of the human soul, but it has two limits. It cannot easily cope with death, and it cannot heal the conscience haunted by shame and guilt. Here religion still fills its need.

Saint Augustine in the Early Church

Professor Chadwick had a long and continuing interest in and appreciation for Bishop Augustine of Hippo. He recognized this North African bishop of the late fourth and early fifth centuries as the major influence in the development of numerous areas of theology of the Western church and as a figure claimed by all sides of the sixteenth-century Reformation. Over the years, Dr. Chadwick published monographs on Augustine and an abundance of articles dealing with countless aspects of Augustine's life and thought.

New Letters of St. Augustine

In this chapter, Dr. Chadwick describes the discovery by Johannes Divjak of a large group of previously unknown and unprinted letters by Augustine. These letters were first published in 1981. Chadwick's essay, published in 1983, makes available a summary of the collection of letters. Dr. Chadwick reviews the manuscript evidence for the collection and concludes that the authenticity of the new texts is beyond question. The chief value of the letters is their insights into the life of the church and society of their time and their role as a resource for Augustine's biography. Professor Chadwick acknowledges that the letters tell little about Augustine's theology that was not already known. Yet the letters do supply information about Donatism, Pelagianism, Priscillianism, and Roman law on slavery.

The chapter offers a picture of the contents of the twenty-seven letters. Among the noteworthy letters are 4* and S*. Both deal with the Pelagian controversy. Letter 4* is addressed to Cyril of Alexandria. Letters 7* and 8* provide insight into the tangled complexity of church finances and property even in the fifth century. Letters 9* and 10* are to Alypius of Thagaste and deal with church problems. Letters 11* and 12* are not authored by Augustine, but are addressed to him by a Constentius; they take up the doctrine of the Trinity and Priscillianism, among other matters. Letters 13* and 18* speak of moral lapses among the clergy. In letter 16*, Augustine conveys to Aurielius of Carthage some of his Christmas and Epiphany sermons. Letter 19* is sent to Jerome and speaks of the acquittal of Pelagius. Letter 20* is an exceptionally long epistle on the subject of the Priscillianists. Letter 21* replies to landowners of a church. Letter 24* addresses a lawyer, Eustochius, regarding the law on children sold into slavery. Letter 27* is unusual in the collection as it is a letter from Jerome to Aurelius on the occasion of Aurelius being ordained Bishop of Carthage. And, finally, letter 29* is to Paulinus, a deacon in Milan and the biographer of Ambrose. Dr. Chadwick's concluding word is an expression of appreciation to Johannes Divjak as the discoverer and editor of this epistolary collection that for too long escaped the attention of Augustinian scholars.

New Sermons St. Augustine

In chapter thirteen Dr. Chadwick deals with twenty-six newly discovered sermons of Augustine. Some thirteen years after Professor Chadwick drew the scholarly world's attention to letters of Augustine that had previously been unknown, he had the opportunity to share with that same world newly uncovered sermons of the Bishop of Hippo. The primary purpose of chapter thirteen is to underline the significance of this discovery by François Doibeau. Dr. Chadwick admits that the sermons disclose no scandals, but they do provide some domestic drama and new evidence on how Augustine sought to convert pagans in Proconsular Africa. Dr. Chadwick concentrates on the content of the new sermons and some of their distinctive characteristics in comparison with other Augustinian writings. Most of the sermons are evidence that Augustine preached extempore. The sermons contain a few attacks on the Manichees but devote more of their attention to the Donatists. On several occasions, Augustine attacks Donatist views of the universal church.

In this sermon collection, Augustine often returns to two themes: first, true religion is a matter of the heart and inward; and second, true faith will issue in a reformed moral life. He also addresses the need for private Bible study and the place of the defense of Christianity against educated pagan criticism.

Augustine stresses the essential human goodness of procreation against the opinion of the Manichees. At the same time he encourages ascetic renunciation. Augustine tells his congregation that pagan practices carried over into Christian conversion must be rejected. He also describes the tenacity of pagan landowners in maintaining aspects of the old religion. The sermons reveal the need for the reeducation of many individuals who were now coming into the church. Clearly in Augustine's opinion paganism was not dead. In society, the temptations and dissensions of the amphitheater were still present. In brief, Dr. Chadwick concludes that this new material enriches our knowledge of Augustine and his times.

On Re-Reading the Confessions

Here Dr. Chadwick tells in a picturesque and attractive manner the story of Augustine as the main figure in the *Confessions*. He observes that Augustine's ordination to the presbyteral office was not unusual for the times. It was also something that Augustine did not desire.

While practices regarding ordination differed between the Eastern and Western churches, a reluctance to accept such ordination was not uncommon, but also not universal. Some individuals saw the earthly benefits of ecclesial offices. Over time, the office of bishop in particular gained perquisites.

Augustine's *Confessions* relate the early stages of his journey from a bookish, highly sexed man to a contemplative ascetic, and finally a pastor and defender of the Christian faith. Dr. Chadwick notes that the *Confessions* is an essay in self-defense. It is not a simple autobiographical record. The former Manichee, skeptic, pagan professor, and Neo-Platonist who was now a presbyter had some explaining to do to those who had questions about his conversion.

As Professor Chadwick indicates, Augustine's letters and sermons show the Bishop of Hippo involved in arbitrations, property issues, and matters of asylum. As bishop, Augustine entered into disputes with Manichaeism, Donatism, and Pelagianism. The *Confessions* offer a selective portrait of the individual who became involved in all these activities. This situation changes only in the last four books of the *Confessions*, where Augustine, the teaching bishop, is encountered.

Dr. Chadwick's reading of the *Confessions* leads him to the conclusion that no work of Augustine discloses more of Augustine's understanding of the high calling of the priesthood, although interestingly enough the subject of ordination is never mentioned.

Providence and the Problem of Evil in Augustine

Dr. Chadwick pursues in chapter fifteen two key issues that occupied Augustine throughout life—providence and evil. He remarks that in Augustine's world there was a widespread assumption of divine providence on a large scale and in individual lives. Neo-Platonism provides the context for such views. Augustine himself held these opinions even in his skeptic period. He looked at his own life for the substantiation of this position. Professor Chadwick believes that in spite of recent scholarship it is still uncertain what attracted Augustine to Manichaeism for so many years.

Finally Augustine could no longer accept the weakness of the Manichees' view of light-power, imprisoned in matter and unable to act without serious restriction. Augustine's conversion to Christian Platonism meant that he would uphold the absolute, unlimited power of God, which also meant that evil was either non-being or really not evil. Dr. Chadwick points out that Augustine's reading of Cicero and the Platonists, especially Plotinus, shaped his thinking. Years later, as a bishop, Augustine would warn his flock against thinking that the Christian faith was to insure secular success; life is uncertain. Still, as his letters reveal, Augustine was concerned about social issues. He cautioned that success is transitory. Adversity can even be good for the wise soul. Augustine's debt to Stoicism in such advice is obvious, although his attention to Plotinus's metaphysic also informed his discussion of such matters. He was also influenced by Plotinus's notion that evil is a necessary counterpart to good.

Dr. Chadwick comments that the Bishop of Hippo's views hardened with the passage of life. There is no undeserved suffering in the world, but it can be transformed by grace. He gives a summary of Augustine's view of evil, the Stoic and Platonic elements it contains, and the influence of the Bible.

Scripture led Augustine to place considerable stress on the penal nature of human distress. Human beings suffer because they deserve it. Nevertheless, Augustine's writings reveal sympathy for the idea of purification after death and an advance of sanctification, where evil is purged away.

The Attractions of Mani

This chapter, originally a contribution to a Festschrift, offers an explanation for the appeal of Mani and his religion. Professor Chadwick explains that the Orthodox and Gnostics held many attitudes in common. Yet Gnosticism furnished answers to questions that the Catholic Tradition seemed unable to address convincingly. Gnostics and Manichees were not simply uneducated individuals. As a convert from Manichaeism, Augustine had a number of questions to answer for his co-religionists in Numbia. Some of these African Christians were not convinced that Augustine had truly left Manichaeism.

As Professor Chadwick indicates, Augustine's challenge was to show that Manichaean practices were ridiculous, incoherent, and irrational. At the same time he had to explain how he could be an adherent for decades.

Manichaeism presented itself as the authentic form of Christianity. Thus the central thrust of Manichaean mission was toward members of the church. Manichaean life for the elect and non-elect (hearers) was rigorous, though Augustine would argue that these standards were not always kept, including in matters of sexual conduct. Manichaean openness to astrology was an attraction to the young Augustine. Later, Manichaean explanations of eclipses and cosmic battles disillusioned Augustine, but in his early years Manichaean scientific explanations of natural phenomena were a positive force.

Manichaean views of the sacraments of baptism and the Eucharist were in decided opposition to Catholic views. The area of clearest distinction was the Manichaean position on the Old Testament. Manichees asked repeatedly how the Old Testament could be regarded as divinely inspired. Catholics also appeared to the Manichees as "Pharisees" with their external rites. Manichees put the question to Catholics: What is the source of evil? They considered the Catholic response inadequate.

Yet, as Dr. Chadwick points out, the Manichaean answer to this question had its own inconsistency. They resolved the problem of evil by denying divine power rather than divine goodness. The God of the Old Testament seems to the Manichees as seriously deficient in power and goodness. Manichees tried to substantiate their claim of being Christian. Their ethic stressed the duty to love God and one's neighbors, but they denied that this was taught in the Old Testament.

Manichaeism taught prohibition against meat, wine, lying, and blasphemy. They rejected any view of the resurrection. At some point, Manichaean missionaries developed a canon of sacred texts to support their views.

Dr. Chadwick believes that Augustine's son, Adeodatus, in his brief life was brought up by his Catholic mother and grandmother, not by Augustine, his Manichaean father. Professor Chadwick also indicates, on the basis of careful examination, that obviously for many Manichees the tenets of their religion were not as ridiculous as Augustine suggested. Acceptance of the Old Testament by Christians and arguments about the fulfillment of its prophecies did not convince all, and these were topics Manichees would exploit.

Both Manichaean ethics and its rule of celibacy found a response. In addition, similarity of Manichaean belief to Catholic orthodoxy (e.g., Scripture, liturgy, and moral life) made local churches a hunting ground for Manichaean mission efforts. Dr. Chadwick concludes that Augustine did move away from Manichaean mythology, but aspects of Manichaean ethics, especially sexual ethics, would remain with the Bishop of Hippo his entire life.

Augustine's Ethics

Chapter seventeen deals with Augustine's ethics. Professor Chadwick remarks that Augustine's ethical teaching is scattered throughout his works. The Bishop of Hippo speaks of ethical issues in his writings against the Manichees, in his sermons, in his advice on marriage, and in his texts dealing with faith and works. In the tradition of both Plato and Cicero, Augustine employs the distinction between means and ends. Friendship was an extremely important relation for Augustine, but he found in his life that friends can disappoint. Augustine notes that Plato and Seneca remind their audiences that good things are ambivalent. Dr. Chadwick points out that Augustine often stresses that the moral value of an act is never independent of the intention and the circumstances.

For Augustine, the responsibility for fidelity in marriage applies to both partners. Dr. Chadwick refers to Augustine's comment in *De Bono Conjugali* that a husband and wife should walk side by side in the street—a remark probably referring to a custom still in force in Arab countries where the wife walks a few yards behind her husband with the children. Dr. Chadwick dryly comments that if you see the wife walking five yards in front, that might be a sign that landmines are suspected!

The marriage state is good, but Augustine insisted that the ascetic vocation is superior. Augustine did not think that usury or war were right. Even though he considered war wrong, he allowed that it might be necessary in order to recover peace.

Finally, as Professor Chadwick notes, for Augustine the only proper end is God. The incarnation is the assertion by God of human values. Yet many within the church lead evil lives, while outside the church virtuous pagans feed the hungry. Whether such upright people can be saved is a question that caused Augustine great pain. Dr. Chadwick concludes that it seems there are thinkers and heroes for whom Augustine can find no place in the city of God.

Living in the Early Church

Professor Chadwick was interested not only in the development of Christian doctrine and the structures of the church for their own sake as well as their ecumenical implications; his concern was also to describe accurately how Christians in the early church lived out their lives of faith in their contemporary world. Dr. Chadwick believed that there were lessons in that record for his own time. His attraction to Christian ethics is evident in many of his published writings, even though some of these lectures and articles do not have ethical concerns at their center. This section contains two essays that deal directly with ethical issues.

The Originality of Early Christian Ethics

Chapter eighteen was written for the Bryce Memorial Lecture Series. Thus part of its contents rehearses Lord Bryce's many accomplishments. It is a story probably unknown to most American readers.

Dr. Chadwick notes the complexity of the topic of early Christian ethics. He cautions that at the outset two views must be put aside: that Christian missionaries brought light to a darkened pagan world and that Christian ethics had nothing new to say. In regard to the former, the general human condition before and after the introduction of Christianity must be recognized. In regard to the latter, similarities and borrowings in Christianity from Platonism or Stoicism should not overshadow the fact that Christian belief did add something new to the discussion.

As Dr. Chadwick indicates, Christianity, for example, moved the discussion from individual concerns to social questions. John Chrysostom's advice on slavery, wealth, and class divisions is a good example. Chrysostom often took up themes found in pre-Christian writers and placed them in a Christian framework for discussion. Another example suggested by Professor Chadwick is Ambrose's work *On Duties* (*De Officiis*). He highlights the similarities and differences with Cicero's work of the same title.

In the lecture, Dr. Chadwick takes up the question of whether or not Christianity improved the condition of women. His conclusion is that by and large it did ameliorate their situation. The early church also engaged in such activities as the ransoming of prisoners and the emancipation of slaves in households where their conditions were harsh.

Nevertheless, significant differences remained between Christian and Greek/Roman ethics. Part of the explanation for this situation is the Jewish matrix out of which Christianity arose. Yet ultimately the distinctiveness of early Christian ethics comes from the call to imitate Jesus Christ. Christianity declares that the good is the revealed will of God. Platonism's ethic depends on a hypothetical imperative. The Christian imperative is categorical. Also, Professor Chadwick declares that Greek/Roman ethics, especially Neo-Platonic ethics, focuses on individualism. In contrast, Christianity expresses its moral conviction on social topics.

Pachomios and the Idea of Sanctity

Chapter nineteen is a lecture that Professor Chadwick delivered at a symposium on Byzantine studies. At the outset he confessed that "sanctity" is a difficult topic to discuss in the present context. Silence is attractive on this subject, for the forgoing of natural goods is never a simple decision. Dr. Chadwick reminded his listeners that the famous Roman historian, Edward Gibbons, had a low view of monasticism. The lecture points out that what needs to be examined, among other items, is the religious presuppositions that underlie the ascetic's role. A significant factor is that, even before Constantine, the church experienced a shift from a tiny, persecuted body to a mixed society of committed and less committed Christians.

Dr. Chadwick sees the role and influence of Pachomios in these developments as considerable. Pachomios made the "monk" (originally a "solitary") into a member of a community. Pachomios strove to incorporate large numbers of monks within a society and to impose a strict discipline. Part of his creative contribution was literally the enclosure wall of the monastery. Within that enclosure, buildings for various purposes, including a library, were to be found. There have been many debates about the complex sources of Pachomian foundations.

Dr. Chadwick quickly reviews the evidence and shows how interests changed in the Pachomian tradition. The Pachomian monks had warm and cordial relations with Athanasius, but the Alexandrian bishop may have been less than pleased with the monks' choice of reading material. The niceties of Orthodox doctrine were not the monks' highest priorities. What was a matter of great concern was the Pachomian Rule. Dr. Chadwick notes that Pachomios's community grew rapidly and the number of monks increased. Problems arose after Pachomios's death, resulting in a crisis of leadership. This situation was not solved easily even in a context that stressed obedience to the superior.

Professor Chadwick outlines Pachomios's achievements, which included identification with the poor and the restraint of lust for power and clerical domination. Pachomios did this by creating rules and wise customs for good order in a religious community.

Pachomios's erection of the enclosure wall brought many benefits. Yet Dr. Chadwick notes in conclusion that the wall came to symbolize the separateness of the community from the world and thus accentuated the secularization of the created order.

Introduction

The Early Church in the Roman World

Professor Chadwick's interests in early Christianity were never merely pedantic. He was motivated by his scholarship to understand the primitive church and its faith in relationship to the greater world. He was concerned to see what such understanding could contribute to a church engaged in the struggle to grasp its place in the world of the twentieth and twenty-first centuries. On a number of occasions, Dr. Chadwick sought to probe the evolving interaction of the early community of followers of Christ and the worldwide empire of its day. The last two chapters in this volume take up questions about that ancient church-state relation.

Christian and Roman Universalism in the Fourth Century

In chapter twenty, Professor Chadwick offers a description of how Constantine quickly moved to the heights of power. He explores the reasons for Constantine's allegiance to Christianity when the church could not give him a wider recognition of his legitimacy. Using a panegyric of an anonymous orator, Dr. Chadwick suggests that Constantine was viewed as a person for whom the highest deity had a grand purpose. Such a position would be in harmony with a general pagan acceptance of the notion that all religions follow different roads but aspire to the same destination. Such an attitude was not something that was considered kindly by Christians, whom Constantine came to regard as an internally quarrelsome community. Constantine, according to Professor Chadwick, had a strong consciousness of a mission from the highest god. Yet, by adhering to the church, Constantine had identified himself with a society that did not think of itself as bound to the particularities of the Roman empire. Nevertheless, Constantine came to see an agency for imperial internal order in the episcopate as focused in the great patriarchates, especially Rome. The church was free from ethnic divisions, but the Donatist schism, Dr. Chadwick points out, revealed that civil war was possible within the church.

Constantine found the background for his self-vision in the earlier attitudes of the church. Yet those attitudes included an idea of unity that Christians had not found easy to preserve, as Celsus would demonstrate for them. Celsus, however, also observed that Christians could transcend the usual barriers of ethnicity and differing social ranks. Thus Celsus feared the possibility of a Christian emperor. He disclosed that, even in the second century, there was a plan in the church for a "Constantinian" kind of revolution. In the middle of the third century, Origen, in response to Celsus, held that Christian unity was not merely the result of external hostility. Constantine's concern for unity and mission had a long backdrop.

These two concerns are evident in the writings of Eusebius of Caesarea. Eusebius portrays the emperor as one who has a mission from God to convert the empire to the right faith. Monarchical government is the image of God's heavenly monarchy. Dr. Chadwick believes that Eusebius is correct in picturing Constantine as moving toward the opinion that his empire should have one law and religion. Yet it was an empire that came under more and more external pressure even as it made possible the spread of the gospel beyond its own frontiers. For at least the Greek East, the emperor at Constantinople was the linchpin of order and the embodiment of unity. The Latin West had more hesitations in regard to the role of the government in the church. This hesitancy provided space for a growing authority of the Roman See. Therefore Dr. Chadwick concludes that the Eusebian and Constantinian ideal of a universal society became a reality in the West and the East, but in distinctive ways.

Oracles of the End in the Conflict of Paganism and Christianity in the Fourth Century

In this final chapter, Dr. Chadwick pursues an issue that caused conflict between paganism and Christianity in the early church. He shows that interest in futurism has had a long history. In the struggle between paganism and Christianity, the place and usefulness of demons or lower gods became an issue.

Christians were convinced that pagans were paying homage to inferior and evil demons, who were malevolent spirits. Pagans, on the other hand, had many hopes and calculations that Christianity would end. A suggested year for such a termination was in the 390s. Professor Chadwick sketches out the resources for these views. Such opinions were not particularly foreign to Christians with their teaching about the anti-Christ and the end. The political disasters of the 370s and the 380s gave both the pagan and the Christian an impending sense of the end of the empire. The exegesis of texts from the Book of Daniel and the Apocalypse of John in certain circles encouraged some to see prophecy being fulfilled before their eyes. Times and numbers in Scripture held a fascination for many, as can be seen in the writings of Tyconius, who believed in the millennial reign of Christ with his saints. Even Augustine reflected on millenarianism and believed that he saw prophecy being acted out and fulfilled in edicts of the Emperor Theodosius.

Dr. Chadwick sums up the situation. Many persons in the fourth century believed that the end would come. They looked to oracles or to Scripture to tell them when it would be. Augustine gave his contemporaries a word of caution: adventist expectations are productive of excellent devotion, yet they run the risk of mockery when the hope is not realized. Therefore Augustine suggested that it is wise to believe that the Lord will come, but not soon. As Augustine puts it, it is better to be surprised by joy than humiliated and disappointed, a word that could have benefitted a number of groups in the course of Christian history.

*   *   *

The purpose of this volume is to offer a means by which the considerable contribution of Henry Chadwick to the comprehension and appreciation of early Christianity and its contemporary consequence may be accessible in a convenient form, primarily to students and others interested in the topic. The selection provided here could indeed be viewed as arbitrary given the huge treasure that could be mined. Yet it is the hope that this collection reveals the extensive erudition of the churchman, scholar, historian, teacher, and ecumenist who was Henry Chadwick and that it allows us to encounter again the picturesque and engaging manner of Dr. Chadwick's scholarly presentation.

This publication reminds us of the consequential debt we continue to owe to him. It is now fitting to allow him to speak for himself in this collection of studies.

WILLIAM G. RUSCH

Ministry and Tradition

The term 'ministry' is one which Christians associate with ordination. That association was already fixed for Latin-speaking Christians by the time of Augustine. In one of his sermons on St. John's Gospel (51:12–13) he warns his people against supposing that only bishops and presbyters are Christ's ministers. All lay people who live rightly, who are generous in alms to the poor, who proclaim the name and teaching of Christ to everyone, are ministers of Christ. Every paterfamilias exercises a kind of episcopal office in his own household. And the majority of martyrs in the calendar are lay people, men and women, old and young. Clergy are a minority.

Spiritual discernment is given by God to both the clergy and the laity; it is no monopoly of the clergy (*Confessions* 13, 23, 33). The evangelists of the Church are laity: 'Because of the witness of lay people, many with whom I have had no contact are coming to me wishing to become Christians' (*Enarr. in Ps.* 96:10).

More than one passage in Augustine speaks of the priesthood of the entire body of the Church. A clericalised conception of the Church seemed to him characteristic of the Donatist community, for whom the authenticity of the Church was exclusively located in the episcopal succession. So, in his stress *on* ministry as an activity shared by the laity, there may be an underlying anti-Donatist motive. However, the passage from the sermons on St. John's Gospel makes it certain that his people ordinarily associate ministry with the functions and offices of bishop, presbyter, and deacon.

In this lecture I shall assume that the term 'ministry' primarily concerns the ordained members of the Church, but without forgetting Augustine's warning.

The gift of Christian ministry is a spiritual charism for the building up of

1

the Church (Eph. 4:7–16). Because it is rooted in the continuing life of the Church, it is deeply related to tradition.

'Tradition' is a word with many meanings, and with many implicit evaluations. Sometimes we speak of 'mere tradition', meaning a conventional way of thinking or acting which has not been subjected to scrutiny. Unexamined theology is not worth doing. During the baptismal controversy of the third century between Stephen bishop of Rome and Cyprian bishop of Carthage, one of the questions at issue was precisely whether immemorial tradition is or is not binding. To Cyprian and the African bishops, there was no force in the Roman principle 'Nihil innovetur nisi quod traditum est'. That was nothing more than 'consuetudo', custom or convention which was to be contrasted with *veritas,* and the 'truth' for Cyprian is that all sacramental acts performed by heretics or schismatics are not only invalid but the devil's deceit, a counterfeit for the divine reality. Cyprian's sacramentology was not accepted in Rome, but was welcomed in the East by Greek bishops.

The consequent debates on the relation of ministry and sacraments have remained a lasting source of divergence between East and West. The Orthodox Churches of the East are deeply resistant even today about the possibility of recognising the baptism of any Christian community which does not wholly share the right faith, *orthodoxia:* Baptism is initiation into the Church, and no heretic can admit anyone to the Church. At the first ecumenical Council of Nicaea a distinction was drawn. The followers of Novatianus were schismatics but orthodox in the doctrine of the Trinity and of the Person of Christ. Their baptism could stand, but individuals returning to the Catholic Church must be admitted by imposition of hands. On the other hand, the adherents of Paul of Samosata at Antioch must be baptised in water. Later Greek canons tend to become more rigorist. The Apostolic Canons (46–50) eliminate all distinctions, and declare heretical baptism to be invalid without distinction. In accordance with the rigorism, at Constantinople in 1755 it was decreed that the baptism of the western churches is null and void (Rhalles-Potles, *Syntagma* 5, 614–616), and, although the decree did not receive unanimous support, it was printed and diffused.[1] It has remained a difficulty in ecumenical conversation that the Greeks do not recognise Cath-

---

1. For a clear account of the controversy see Timothy Ware, *Eustratios Argent* (Oxford University Press, 1964) chapter 3. A brief summary in F. Kattenbusch, *Lehrbuch der vergleichenden Confessionskunde* I (1882), 404. Rejection of Roman (Catholic) or 'Latin' baptism is sharply formulated in 1054 by the patriarch Michael Cerullarius: See Anton Michel, *Humbert und Kerullarios,* Paderborn, 1930, II 144-151, text at 277, and in C. Will, *Acta et Scripta* (1861), 182.

olic baptism, while the Russians accept it. From the baptismal controversy of the third century there flows the difference between East and West in attitude to the ecumenical movement. If the Roman Catholic Church, the Anglican Communion, and the Lutherans recognise each other's baptism, which also implies recognition of right faith concerning Christ and the Holy Trinity, then they are in a state of imperfect communion. And this partly positive appreciation of the churches from which one is separated goes with a western attitude of continual striving after a not yet attained truth, a not yet attained grasp of salvation. The continuity of tradition in the West is intensely important, as also in the East. But unlike the Orthodox Churches of the East, the West characteristically wishes to be forever questioning, forever seeking to get back to first principles.

We speak of tradition, first, in the sense of the Gospel, the word of God which is the content of what is transmitted. But the Gospel requires a preacher who is a primary organ of the process of transmission. Moreover, the context in the community within which he transmits the Gospel provides an interpretation of the text which the preacher is expounding. The biblical text, the interpretation in the community (which may be contrasted with that found among the Rabbis), and the interpreting preacher are all included in the transmitting of tradition. The ministry of ordained bishops and priests is never independent either of the sacred text or of the community within which the text is received.

We often speak of 'tradition' in the sense of the way in which we worship, or of the characteristic ethic of the Church, that is 'our moral tradition'. Not all of these features of Christian liturgy and action are explicit in scripture. Nevertheless it is not today controversial to say that tradition is not really a second source besides scripture from which we can produce truths of a different kind and content. At the same time, the principle that definitions of dogma need to be consonant with scripture is not to be understood to mean that scripture is the sole source or means by which we can know anything of the will of God. The divine will is also mediated and declared to us through the glory and wonder of the created order and through the experience of the worshipping community in the fellowship of the mystery. Tradition, then, means the memory of the community which gives the people of God their self-understanding.

We feel deeply sorry for elderly people who have lost their memory. It is a rich treasury of experience for them and for all who have conversation with them. Augustine liked to say that the memory is the stomach of the mind (*Conf.* 10:14, 21 and elsewhere). The tenth book of the *Confessions* is a study of the way in which the memory of the past is decisive for interpreting the present. In the community, tradition is the memory of the Church's foundation and origins, and a continuing story to determine the present. To speak of tradition is to recognise that the prophetic and apostolic witness of the biblical record can become revelation for us now because of the experience of grace in and through the Church which is Christ's Body. In the life of the Church we are anchored to the past because, by faith and baptism, we are members of a society with a continuing history, linking us to St. Peter, to the Twelve, to Mary the mother of Jesus, to St. Paul and the Gentile mission, to the emerging ministry with apostolic commission which would become the visible and concrete sign and instrument of continuity and of the links in a historic chain. The concept of a sacred tradition of teaching antedates the concept of an apostolic succession of pastors, but the second became necessary to safeguard the first. This should not mean that the visible succession of ordinations is the only factor to be considered. In the course of history the Church has observed groups of bishops and individual bishops whose juridical succession could hardly be faulted. Yet they have not been reckoned to share in the apostolic succession because they have not been seen to share in the tradition of Catholic teaching and in the universal communion of the local churches. Teaching and communion are not less significant than the visible manifestation by which legitimation is put beyond controversy.

If the juridical succession is regarded as providing everything necessary and sufficient, the normal and natural consequence is to produce individualism among bishops. Because the sharing in a common inheritance of doctrine and universal fellowship has not been stressed as having no less importance, each bishop can easily come to think that he can disregard his colleagues. He may come to have little respect for the exhortation in the Pastoral Epistles (2 Tim. 3:14) that he should 'teach what he has been taught'.

Transmitter of a sacred trust, the mediator of a tradition, the bishop shares in a common pastorate whose commission lies in the past.

Nevertheless, this does not mean imprisonment in the past. A Church which is imprisoned in its own past will end by betraying the deposit of faith entrusted by God. A society 'without the means of change is without the means of its conservation' (Edmund Burke, 1790). 'To live is to change' (John Henry Newman, 1845). And so the ordained ministry with apostolic commission does not exist exclusively to mediate and to transmit faithfully what has been received from a sacred past. It is also called to proclaim, to utter prophecy in the Spirit, speaking to a changing situation. It must teach;

and that teaching must imply far more than an unreflective repetition of formulas of a distant past shaped in utterly different circumstances and with philosophical presuppositions that later generations cannot share. The ministry exists to serve the pastoral needs of the community, some of which are astonishingly unchanging, but others (especially in our modern world) change fast, and somehow we have to move at the same speed to stay in the same place.

In the second century Irenaeus of Lyon pronounced orthodoxy to be unchanging, while it was a characteristic of heretics that they were continually changing. To Irenaeus orthodoxy is uniform, heresy marked by variations. Eighty years before his time, during the generation which followed the death of the last of the twelve apostles and which had to come to terms with the fact that the Lord had not returned and so the Church would have a historical future, the Church experienced a degree of diversity which was traumatic. There was near-anarchy, whether in ministerial order or in moral practice or in central matters of faith. Therefore, at a very early stage as the apostles passed from the scene, the Church found it necessary to establish frontiers and standards, criteria of authenticity. Three norms of reference appeared, very familiar to every elementary student of the subject: first, a ministry in visible and tangible continuity with the apostolic community and possessing an apostolic commission; secondly, a baptismal confession of faith, structured round the affirmation of belief in God the Father, Maker of heaven and earth (by familiarity we forget how contentious and controversial these words were early in the second century); belief in Jesus his unique Son, so truly human that he was born and crucified, yet experiencing both in such a way that the birth and the crucifixion were divine wonders; and belief in the Holy Spirit in the Church. Thirdly and last in chronological order, but greatest in weight, the formation of the biblical canon.

In much later debate the formation of the canon became a sensitive issue. Were the books admitted to the lectionary because their content was self-evidently authoritative and apostolic, so that the acknowledgement of their inherent quality of authority was a purely passive act of submission by the community? Or did the Church have an active and creative role in forming the canon in response to Marcion and Montanism? The historian finds it easier to give a positive answer to the second question than to the first. But in the formation of the canon of scripture, the second-century churches were right to discern in these books the record of the oldest and most original witness to their faith and practice. Until the middle years of the second century, Christians appear to have drawn more upon oral tradition than upon authoritative books. The words of Papias about the superiority of oral tradition are famous. Irenaeus is the first to possess a canon of the New Testament.

It is a safe generalisation that there is friction in the Church when someone wishes to modify or even discard one of the three norms which evolved in the second century. The continuing Church on earth needs to affirm its faith, needs to acknowledge the witness of scripture, needs to admit to its community by baptism in the name of Christ, and, in obedience to his command, to renew its life by the eucharistic memorial. Moreover, for the sake of its own coherence, it needs a ministry generally accepted as possessing a commission, given by Christ in his Church, to serve and to safeguard the word and the sacraments. In these areas of Bible, Creed, Sacraments and Ministry, the Church understands itself to have received divine gifts (as in Ephesians 4), *dona data,* touching the deepest roots of Christian existence, and therefore needing to be handled with sensitivity.

Uniformity in respect of the canon of scripture, the apostolic ministry, the essentials of the faith, and the sacraments does not necessitate uniformity in liturgy. In forms of worship the tradition allows for wide diversities, at least between different regions. The desire for liturgical uniformity has pastoral roots. But such uniformity has normally been imposed more by secular than by ecclesiastical authority, more by Charles the Great than by medieval Popes.[2] In the time of Augustine, there were different translations of the old Latin Bible in Africa and Italy, and different customs. One letter complains of the bewilderment caused to congregations when the clergy introduced liturgical customs which they had seen abroad (*Ep.* 54, 3; 55, 35). He recalled the advice given by Ambrosius to his mother Monica to keep Roman customs in Rome, but not when not in Rome (*Ep.* 36, 32; 54, 3). Liturgical variety is compatible with one faith (*Ep.* 36, 22). Admittedly, Augustine was in favour of reasonable uniformity in a single region, and warns his correspondent Januarius (who seems to have been confronted by people wanting total uniformity in a single rite) that there are limits to diversity (*Ep.* 55, 35). The Lord imposed certain minimum obligations; these are whatever is commanded in the Bible, baptism, eucharist, what has apostolic sanction or is agreed by plenary councils of the Church; but there can be regional

---

2. Social instability comes when a ruler reigns over a multiplicity of kingdoms or ethnic regions, as in Britain or in the Iberian peninsula, mainly because the most powerful partner often forgets the weaker partners in making decisions. If (as in 17th century Britain, where England is Anglican, Scotland Presbyterian, and Ireland Roman Catholic — but Wales not yet Baptist) religion is added to this multiplicity, serious civil war can follow.

diversity beyond these (*Ep.* 54, 1). Tolerable diversity does not, however, include heretical prayers (*Bapt.* vi, 25, 47).

One of the grounds on which Cardinal Humbert excommunicated the ecumenical Patriarch Michael Kerullarios in the year 1054 was that by using leavened bread the Greeks rendered their mass invalid. A dissenting view was recorded by St. Anselm of Canterbury. Anselm thought the Greeks wrong not to use azyma, unleavened bread; and that mistake was for him no adiaphoron. Nevertheless what they used was bread. Therefore, *substantialiter* there was agreement. (*Ep. de sacrif. azymi* 1, Schmitt II 224). The passage is the earliest instance known to me of a claim that in ecumenical conversation there can be differences of language or custom within an essential agreement. Anselm was writing to a man who thought that all recognised Catholics must use a single eucharistic rite. Uniformity in rite was for that man a mark of catholicity.

In the Church of our own time, the link between ministry and tradition has become problematic because of the question precipitated by the feminist revolution in the West. In antiquity priestesses were associated with the temples of goddesses. Epiphanius (*Panar.* 78, 3; 79, 1–8) rejected priestesses because he rejected goddesses, and argued that the first could lead to the second. Outsiders would mock the Church if it had women as priests or bishops. In the West of the twentieth century, outsiders mock the Church because it has none.

Episcopacy in the New Testament
and Early Church

All Christian ministry is a gift of the Spirit, a charism. It is neither an end in itself, nor an entity independent of the community, but rather a service for the building up of the Church (Eph. 4:7–16). As a supernatural call, a charism belongs to the transcendent, divine order. As a service within the community, its action is seen in the visible historical order, in the society grounded in the discipleship of Jesus Christ and rooted in the continuing life of the Church. This society is ever vulnerable to temptations and to secularising pressures; the treasure may be contained in very earthen vessels. Nevertheless, if the revelation of God in Christ is rightly seen not only as a word of justifying grace in mercy to the ungodly, but also as a sanctifying power mediated in, with, and under the means of grace in word and sacrament and shared worship, the role of an ordered ministry in relation to these means of grace is of essential importance to the maintenance of the Church in the truth of the gospel and the life of the Spirit. For in these words and acts, done in obedience to the Lord's command, the presiding minister is called to act in the name of Christ, the head of the body. He is not merely carrying out a function which the community delegates to him. Himself a man under obedience, he calls those whom he serves to a like obedience.

Charisms differ (1 Cor. 12:4–13). The ordained ministry is one of the Spirit's gifts to the Church, by which ministers are specially appointed to an office and authorised both for the proclamation and guarding of the word and for the due administration of the sacraments. They are not to lord it over the community they serve (1 Peter 5:3), but to protect the means of grace upon which the community as a whole depends for its life. Among the Spirit's gifts, this ministry is called to ensure that the very diversity of charisms does not endanger the essential unity of the one fellowship of Christ's flock.

Accordingly, the oversight given by the ordained ministry always has a dual role or relationship—on the one hand, in service to the local Christian community; on the other hand, in relation to other churches in the federation of local communities bonded together in love and constituting the visible universal Church.

The New Testament does not show a precise form or single structure of ministry which can be seen to be there from the day of Pentecost and can in the simplest sense be claimed as a direct and express institution by Jesus. The primary ministry in the apostolic age is that of the apostles themselves; and we have to look partly beyond the first-century documents to see what forms of ministry the Church developed as and after the apostles passed from the scene. In fact the later books of the New Testament provide a substantial body of historical evidence for the earlier stages of this development. One essential principle, however, remains constant from the start through all variations of form, namely that the pastoral ministry is not a human invention but a gift of God to his Church to enable it to be what he intends in mission, unity, and holiness.

The *apostolate* was strictly no doubt neither a charism nor an office in so far as the latter concept would imply a more constitutionally structured society than the earliest Christians possessed. The apostles are witnesses to the resurrection of the Lord and from their glorified Master receive a commission to preach the gospel. But they are not an authority only in the sense of good historical testimony for the events of Christ's coming and triumph. In the communities which their mission founded they also become a source of contemporary jurisdiction. The power of the keys is a dominical commission to decide points in dispute as well as a discretion to give rulings concerning the position of erring individuals within the society of disciples.

In respect of their witness to Jesus Christ (both of his words and deeds 'in the days of his flesh' and as to the fact of God's triumph in his rising again) there is an obvious sense in which the apostles had and could have no successors. What they said and did in their generation no one else can say or do at a later time. The refusal of the Church to add to the canon of the New Testament (i.e. to admit later Christian writings to the lectionary) is a way of making this point, that in the apostolate certain essential functions are not transferable or transmissible, and that primary apostolic authority is permanently contained in the written records of apostolic literature. At the same time the historical continuity of the Church means that in another sense there are responsibilities and powers of the apostolate which have not died with them. Not only does the Church as a whole have an apostolic mission and character. The authenticity of the tradition about Jesus needs to be preserved in the process of transmission. The local families of Christians gathered in scattered communities need pastoral leadership for decisions on questions of right training and practice in obedience to the revealed will of God. As the early Church came to understand that history was not coming to an immediate end, they also came to see that some permanent structure of ministry was required.

In the earliest stage of pioneer missionaries, the ministers will often have been itinerant 'prophets' or teachers, not tied to any single congregation, but going about from place to place encouraging and correcting, and receiving hospitality (according to the Didache, up to a limit of three days). But the congregations will also require resident shepherds to guide and protect the flock. Accordingly there come to be those 'set over' the congregation whose position of authority (1 Thess. 5:12f.; Heb. 13:17) derives sanction and lifelong tenure from the sacred nature of their functions.

During the first century some diversity in structure between different regions and local churches seems to have been characteristic. In some churches spiritual leadership was in the hands of a group of elders or 'presbyters', as at Ephesus (Acts 20:17), under the overall authority of the apostle. On the other hand, the mother church at Jerusalem had a single head in the person of James, the Lord's brother. This 'monarchical' and apparently earliest form of pastorate could easily be fused with a presbyteral council, in which it would be natural for one man to be held as first among equals if he possessed special charismatic powers or seniority in years and wisdom, or, like Stephanas at Corinth (1 Cor. 16:15–16), was the first convert who then devoted himself to forming a community round him.

At Philippi Paul sends greetings to the 'bishops and deacons' (Phil. 1:1). This reference is the only Pauline allusion, outside the late Pastoral Epistles to Timothy and Titus, to permanent ministerial offices in a local church. In Paul's letters the overwhelming emphasis lies upon the Spirit as the creator of both vitality and order in the Church (as in 1 Cor. 12–14, order at Corinth being less evident than vitality); and the only controversy about 'office' revealed in the epistles concerns Paul's own standing as an apostle. The Gentile churches he has founded are themselves the living vindication of the Lord's call to him to be apostle to the Gentiles; and their membership and acceptance in the one universal Church, with its focus and touchstone of communion in the mother church of Jerusalem (Gal. 2:1–10), depend upon the authenticity of his apostolate (1 Cor. 9:1–2). While Paul has much to say of the principles and nature of Christian authority, e.g., that its function is to set free, not to enslave (2 Cor. 1:24; 10:8), he has nothing to say about the practical provision of a formal constitutional structure for his missionary churches, for whom he himself, through his letters and his helpers such as Titus, is the focus of loyalty under Christ. The reference in Philippians 1:1 shows that in time the general itinerant care exercised by Paul and his helpers is being supplemented by resident officers. Although one cannot be sure just what functions the Philippian bishops and deacons had, the subsequent development suggests that the deacons helped on the administrative side, while the spiritual leadership of the community would be in the hands of the 'bishops' with pastoral oversight, subject to Paul himself. The Didache (15) shows how there was a natural tendency for local churches at first to value their resident bishops and deacons much less than itinerant prophets and teachers, perhaps not only because they seemed less obviously charismatic, but also because of the limited and local character of their responsibilities.

The twofold designation of 'bishops and deacons' attested in Philippians 1 appears both in the early (probably first-century) church order, the Didache (chap. 15), which never mentions presbyters, and also in the epistle written by Clement in the name of the church of Rome to the church of Corinth about the end of the first century (1 Clement 42). In the Rome of A.D. 100 the name 'bishop' may be applied to church leaders who are also called 'presbyters'. At least, therefore, the presbyterate is a function and office in which bishops also have a full share. A similar pattern of terminology appears in the Pastoral Epistles to Timothy and Titus, where presbyters are generally plural, the bishop is singular, suggesting the probable conclusion that already among the college of presbyters exercising *episkope,* or pastoral oversight, one is the commonly accepted president. Of the bishop the highest qualities are required, and they are not only spiritual or supernatural but include natural qualities of leadership and common sense (1 Tim. 3:3–7; Titus 1:6–9). The likelihood is that in some local churches an initially single pastor subsequently became joined in authority by a council of presbyters, while in others the development went the opposite way; i.e., among a group of equal 'presbyter-bishops', one became distinct as presiding bishop without losing the sense of fully sharing a common pastorate and liturgical duty with his presbyteral colleagues, sitting with them in common council much like the 24 elders of the Revelation of John of Patmos (Rev. 4:4). In a relationship of primacy among equals, it is likely enough that in some places the primacy was more apparent than the parity, and elsewhere the other way round. In the first epistle of Peter addressed to the Gentile churches of Asia Minor the 'presbyters' are instructed to be shepherds after the pattern of Christ who is the Chief Shepherd, and are therefore to be living examples to their flock (1 Peter 5:2–4). The author of the second and third Johannine epistles, 'John the Presbyter', exercised authority not only as a local teacher but as a shepherd of a region in which there were a number of churches. Like Timothy and Titus in the Pastoral Epistles, John the Presbyter probably had special responsibilities in ordinations of local clergy, since at ordinations the choice of local congregations would need to be guided and even in some measure controlled to maintain the fellowship of churches with each other. As the local churches grew in strength and independence, the authority of the ministry of local congregations became more securely recognised. It was then natural for the presiding minister in each local church to play a principal role in, and to bear ultimate responsibility for, ordinations of presbyters and deacons in his church, though always with the consent of the people. Likewise this presiding 'bishop' or 'presbyter' was responsible for correspondence with other churches, for hospitality to travellers, for going to represent his own people at the ordination of the ministers of neighbouring churches. He was therefore the person through whom the local church realised its links with others in the worldwide fellowship of churches.

Each local church is to be a self-sufficient fellowship, in which all the elements of the universal Church are present. Yet its independence is simultaneously limited by the mutual care that local churches have for each other or by the leadership given particularly by prominent churches looking back to an apostolic foundation (a feature exemplified in the epistle of Clement of Rome to Corinth). The synodical idea imposes a restriction on what any individual bishop or church may do. At the same time the second-century Church found in churches of apostolic foundation (in the West, in Rome as the city where St. Peter and St. Paul died) a touchstone of authentic communion. Accordingly, frequent contacts between churches act as a check upon private idiosyncrasies in teaching, at the same time as they help the realisation of catholicity. Through their fellowship with one another, at first expressed in informal ways and without formalised patterns of conciliarity, the presiding clergy of local churches are a living embodiment of the sacred tradition about Jesus Christ. This special ministerial responsibility for safeguarding what is taught in the churches goes back to an early stage. In Paul's discourse to the presbyters of Ephesus (who are called 'bishops': Acts 20:24–28) these leaders of the church are warned to be guardians of the true tradition against the false doctrine that threatens the very existence of the Church of Christ's redemption. (It is not thereby implied that laymen have no responsibility to interpret the faith.) This protective, guarding role comes to be especially carried out by synods, in which the bishop is the sacramental representative of his local community.

Of the manner of the making of clergy in the New Testament period, the Pastoral Epistles and Acts 13:3 mention the laying on of hands, the rite associated with the giving of the power of the Spirit in the sacrament of baptism: 'Do not neglect the spiritual endowment you possess, which was given you, under the guidance of prophecy, through the laying on of the hands of the elders as a body' (1 Tim. 4:14 NEB). 'I now remind you to stir into flame the gift of God which is within you through the laying on of my hands' (2 Tim. 1:6). Ordination is here understood to be a sacramental act conferring a charismatic gift of grace appropriate to the office. There is or should be no antithesis of office and charism, because the laying on of hands with prayer, in a solemn act by the council of 'presbyters', is at the same time a recognition of the prophetic call and a sign of the Spirit's gift. The gift can be nullified, or Timothy would not need to be warned to take good care to act according to the charism bestowed (1 Tim. 1:18–19; 2 Tim. 4:10). At the same time the gift and call in ordination are to be the ground of his confidence as a minister, and the commission of ordination is apparently accompanied by a most solemn charge to keep 'the good confession' (1 Tim. 6:11–16). So also St. Paul tells the presbyters of Ephesus that their appointment to exercise episcopal oversight comes from the Holy Spirit (Acts 20:28). Hence the ancient Church's conviction that in ordination God's call is irrevocable; the shepherd of the flock is to represent the Chief Shepherd whose constancy is unfailing.

The ancient Church understands ordination as more than a local authorisation limited to the local community where the ordination has taken place. The orders of episcopate, presbyterate, and diaconate are universally extended orders; that is to say, a presbyter ordained at Corinth needs only a letter of recommendation by his own bishop to be accepted, without reordination, in, say, Rome or Ephesus, and allowed to officiate there with the agreement of the local bishop. The priesthood in which he shares belongs to the universal Church and at his ordination other presbyters join the bishop in the laying on of hands. A newly elected bishop, chosen by his flock, is duly entrusted with the charism of episcopal office by other bishops, who represent, therefore, this universal recognition. This is in line with the New Testament records in which all those commissioned to exercise pastoral oversight are appointed by those who themselves have previously received such a commission. Nevertheless, the ancient Church had a deep sense of the intimate bond between a bishop and his own flock. He is, or ought to feel himself, married to his church. Hence their censures of episcopal translations from a small see to a greater as a secularising concession to worldly ambition.

This bond was inevitably weakened by the success of the Christian mission, which so enlarged the size of local churches that at least in large cities it soon became impossible for the bishop to know each of his sheep personally. It then became common to assign suburban or rural parishes to one or, in Rome, two presbyters. This increase in the number of presbyters, and the growth during the fourth century of the notion of grades of ordained ministers constituting a ladder of honour, like a civil service, came to erect a barrier between the laity and the president of their diocesan family. By the fourth century the clergy came to play a more prominent part than the laity in the election of a new bishop. Even so, the rule (expressed by Cyprian and enacted at Nicaea, 325) that each city may have only one bishop continued in force.

The early Church learnt by experience that the diocesan family needs to have one man rather than a committee as the focus of unity both in the local church and in his fellowship with the college of bishops. Despite the strong language of Ignatius of Antioch, the 'monarchical' character of the episcopate is not, as such, a matter of fundamental juridical or dogmatic principle, essential to the Church in the sense that if the episcopate were shared and not monarchical the Church would be amputated, but is a practical need for the expression of unity. Nevertheless, Ignatius is surely right in seeing the bishop's central authority as linked to his presidency at the eucharist, in which he stands in a sacramental relation to Christ. He is there a focus of 'harmony' (Ignatius does not say unison) in the family of God. Ignatius never alludes to a historic succession as the ground of episcopal authority. But he simply assumes that what orthodox bishops are teaching is what the apostles taught; he holds office in a society that is continuous with that of Peter and Paul.

Ignatius is the earliest writer to attest a threefold ministry in which bishop, presbyters, and deacons are distinguished as separate grades, 'without which a community cannot be called a church' (*Trall.* 3). This three-tiered structure is well attested (and taken for granted) by later writers, and must quickly have become universal without trace of controversy. The three grades were seen to correspond to the three grades of Old Testament ministry, high priest, priest, and levite. It cannot, however, be this correspondence which made it seem natural to use the Greek *hiereus* or the Latin *sacerdos* of the Christian minister (attested from the beginning of the third century in both East and West), since these words were already being traditionally used of the bishop rather than of the presbyter. The Old Testament hierarchical typology did not create the threefold Christian ministry, a structure which owes its origin to the second-century Church's inheritance from the sub-apostolic generation in which an originally two-tiered local ministry, under general apostolic oversight, passed into a three-tiered ministry, with the presiding bishops representing apostolicity. The earliest deacons were needed primarily for administrative duties; male deacons gradually acquired limited liturgical functions, especially reading the gospel (power to celebrate the eucharist being expressly denied to them), but remained the bishop's personal staff. As the congregations grew in size and number, presbyters also acquired wider duties. From being a council, sharing the pastoral and teaching responsibility with the bishop, they began to look after suburban parish churches for which they performed all functions shared with the bishop other than ordination and (except in Egypt) confirmation; these the bishops kept in their own hands, ordinations being among their most solemn responsibilities, and confirmations being a direct link with the lay members of their flock. In the fourth century the extension of presbyteral duties was given a theological justification by the presbyter Jerome (letter 146), who argued from New Testament texts that bishops and presbyters belong to a single order of ministerial priesthood, sharply distinct from the diaconate. Jerome regretted the performance by deacons of certain liturgical functions as obscuring their distinction from the pastoral and priestly order of presbyters and bishops, and so encouraging mistaken pretensions.

In the conflict with gnostic dualism, perhaps the gravest crisis of the Church's history, the early Church found the centralising of authority in the bishop a necessary safeguard against centrifugal forces, whether heretical or schismatic. Formal institutions in the ministry, in the pattern of baptismal confessions of faith, and finally in a fixed canon of the New Testament were developed in the course of the second century. Clement of Rome sees the duly ordained ministry as the embodiment of the principle that God wills order in his Church, so that a local church like Corinth cannot simply get rid of its clergy without satisfying other churches in the universal fellowship that the deposed clergy have been unworthy of their holy office. This principle of order is linked for Clement with the idea of apostolic succession. The fact of a succession in ministerial commission is not asserted by Clement in controversy, but an agreed datum from which he argues for the security of tenure of worthy ministers. Against the gnostics' claims that their bizarre theosophical speculations represent a secret tradition handed down from the apostles, the second-century Church pointed to the publicly verifiable succession of bishops in the churches, especially in those of known apostolic foundation, and to the consensus of all the churches that authentic Christianity does not include these gnostic fantasies. The second-century bishops stand in the apostolic succession not merely (or even mainly) because of those who laid hands on them, but because the churches over which they preside do so in universal communion with each other. There is no question in the early period of an authentic ministerial succession having a career apart from the one holy catholic and apostolic Church and being empowered independently to minister the word and sacraments according to the mind of the Spirit. The local churches together with their clergy are authentic because they stand in the true and universal succession, which is accordingly a transmission of faith together with that recognized order of ministry which serves it. So Irenaeus excludes from the apostolic succession heretics, schismatics, and orthodox bishops of evil life.

The Donatist schism in fourth-century North Africa moved Augustine to find reasons to dissent from the general patristic view that outside the catholic Church there can be no authenticity; but his argument that if valid baptism can be received outside catholic unity, the same holds good for orders, was not generally accepted and acted on in the West until medieval times. The generous intention of Augustine's doctrine was to make reconciliation with the Donatists easier by allowing the unconditional validity of their orders. The form of his argument, however, had an obverse side. It unhappily encouraged men to think of ordination by a bishop in apostolic succession as if this were the exclusive and sole test of ministerial and ecclesial validity. The early Church did not think in this way. When the Council of Nicaea in 325 decreed that a bishop should be consecrated by the metropolitan with, if possible, all the bishops of the province or, if not all, a minimum of three, the Council understood its minimal three to be representing the wider fellowship. The Nicene bishops would never have thought that a person consecrated by any three bishops in any circumstances whatever had claims to catholic recognition.

The recognition of the orders of separated ecclesial bodies is invaluable as one element in a total reconciliation but useless if taken in isolation. When it becomes treated as a technical way of 'foot-faulting' other communions, argument about ministerial validity quickly comes to look trivial and pedantic, and can carry more than a suggestion (which would be alien to the thought of the early Church about apostolic succession) that the transmission of sacramental grace through the apostolic ministry is mechanical. On the contrary, for the early Christians the participation of bishops of other local churches in the consecration of a bishop is a sign and instrument of the continuity of both the new bishop and his church with the apostolic communion extended through time and space; and this is the nerve-centre of the concept of apostolic succession. It is a positive doctrine which has also a negative side in that it presupposes the presence of some defect of order in a separated ministry which is 'self-made' or is dependent on the private enterprise of a particular congregation. Such an independent pastorate may indeed be blessed by God as an efficacious means of proclaiming the gospel; but if it rejects communion with the apostolic and catholic tradition, something is lacking; it may assume a radical disjoining of charism and office which is out of line with the New Testament and the early Church; its authority and recognition are restricted; and ultimately the comprehension of the faith becomes one-sided and partial. Accordingly, the defect is one of universality: that is, it is not a technical fault of pedigree, but an isolation from the organic spiritual life of the one holy catholic and apostolic Church, in which the pastoral ministry has received its commission in a succession of order that goes hand in hand with a succession in faith and life.

The Role of the Christian Bishop in Ancient Society

1. The Bishop's Authority Within the Church

The early Christian bishop emerges as the leader of the local Christian community based upon the town. The first missionaries had concentrated upon the urban population, and almost all the evidence concerning the shape of second-century Christianity shows the churches to be organised round the towns. Ancient towns were, for the most part, small by our standards. Rome, Antioch, Alexandria, and Constantinople were large enough for an individual to be lost in the crowd; but most "cities" of antiquity are quite small communities in market towns, provided with a defensive wall in case of trouble. It was therefore possible for the bishop to know, and to be known personally by, his flock. To his people he has the authority of a shepherd, called to model himself upon the example of Christ the Chief Shepherd (1 Peter 5:2–4). His authority is acknowledged in the consent of the plebs to his consecration.[1] But the plebs, as experience showed, was vulnerable to faction, and soon an increasingly important role in the selection of a bishop was played by the bishops of neighbouring churches who came to lay hands upon the candidate at his consecration, and who represented not only their own churches but also the universal Church. No small part of the aura attaching to the local bishop depended upon this catholicity of recognition. In

---

1. The consent of the plebs: see Hippolytus, *Apostolic Tradition* 2: "let the bishop be ordained who is elected by all the people. . . . With the agreement of all let the bishops lay hands on him and the presbyters stand by in silence." For the late fourth century see Basil, *Ep.* 230, telling the magistrates of Nicopolis, who evidently thought otherwise, that the appointment of bishops is in the hands of the clergy though their choice requires ratification by the laity; now the bishops have selected their man, it is for the magistrates to support them.

synod he represented his people. To his people he represented the "synod"; that is, he was a sign of unity and universality among the federation of local churches bonded together in eucharistic communion, spread through the Mediterranean world of the Roman empire. Accordingly, while each local church felt itself to be a self-sufficient fellowship in which all the essential elements of the universal Church are present, yet the independence and autonomy of this local community is limited by the mutual care that local churches must have for each other. When at the end of the first century the church at Corinth decided to sack its clergy and to install a new lot, their brothers in Rome were much distressed and, apologising not for intervening but for not having interfered more quickly, wrote to admonish the Corinthians for having supposed the authority of their pastors to rest exclusively upon their consent. Rather must they understand that the shepherds of the flock derive their tenure from the succession from the apostles themselves and from the inherent nature of their sacramental functions as ministers of the word and sacrament. The Roman church accordingly invites the Corinthian church to reinstate the dispossessed clergy and so to submit "not to our will but to God's," knowing that if they refuse they must answer for it at the Last Judgement. The Corinthian Christians have failed to realise that the ordering of the community of the new covenant is no less precise, and no less divinely given, than the hierarchical priesthood of the Old Testament with its clearcut distinctions of function between priest and layman. The New Testament principle of obedience to the pastors who must give account for the souls of their flock (Heb. 13:17; 1 Thess. 5:12f.) is already being given a powerful reinforcement from Old Testament typology.

The schism in the community at Corinth was particularly embarrassing because it became generally discussed in the town: dirty linen was being washed in public, and pagan insult added to Christian injury (1 Clement 47). The existence of competing groups caused problems for visitors who could find that they had caused great offence by accepting hospitality from the wrong body of clergy (hence 1 Clement's emphasis on the virtue of hospitality exemplified by Abraham, Lot, and Rahab the harlot, "saved by faith and hospitality"). In short, the internal organisation of the Christian community at Corinth was not, and could not be, a purely private domestic matter; it affected other people elsewhere, and had immediate impact upon the standing of the church in the "secular" community. Clement of Rome tells them that the local church is to be the earthly counterpart of the heavenly: let the Corinthians imitate the angelic chorus which, though numbering ten thousand times ten thousand (and therefore liable to find it hard to keep together), nevertheless chant in unison and on the beat: "Holy, holy, holy. . . ."

This concept of a correspondence between the church in heaven and the church on earth goes back to the very roots of the earliest eucharistic theology. It provides Ignatius of Antioch with his principal argument for concentrating the local church in communion with the bishop, who is, according to Ignatius, the counterpart (*typos*) of God. Hence his monarchical presidency. The early Christian communities had deep feelings against having two bishops in one city.[2] Parallel jurisdictions in the same geographical area were very uncongenial. The eighth canon of the Council of Nicaea, 325, legislates for the full recognition of the orders of Novatianist clergy on the reconciliation of their flocks to the *ecclesia catholica* (subject to their willingness to accept to communion digamists[3] and those who have served their penitential term after lapse in time of persecution), except that the Novatianist bishop is to rank as a presbyter under the authority of the sitting catholic incumbent, even if he may retain the episcopal title with the consent of the catholic bishop. Alternatively he may become a "country bishop" or *chorepiskopos;* that is, a bishop with wholly rural responsibility which was in process of being subordinated to the city bishop. (A decade before Nicaea a council at Ancyra [Ankara] had restricted the powers of country bishops in ordinations. A council at Neocaesarea shortly afterwards explained that while city bishops are successors of the twelve apostles, country bishops are successors of the seventy sent out by the Lord according to Luke 10; they may concelebrate the liturgy in recognition of their ministry to the poor. A council of Antioch four or five years after Nicaea insists on their subordination to the city bishop of their region. Basil's *Epp.* 53–54 illustrate the problem: the city bishops did not trust the country bishops to be strict against simony and against nepotism.)[4] The Nicene canon about the Novatianists exemplifies a conviction that the Church has "one God, one Christ, one bishop," a Roman slogan of the time of the Novatianist schism in Rome in 251 (Eusebius, *H.E.* VI 43, 11; Cyprian, *Ep.* 49, 2) which was shouted as an acclamation by the crowd in the Circus Maximus

---

2. Evidence for the principle of not having two bishops in one city is collected in Joseph Bingham's *Antiquities of the Christian Church* II, 13 (1708 and later editions).

3. Novatianists were not agreed among themselves about the admission of digamists to communion, the Phrygians being rigorist: Socrates, *H.E.* V 22, 60. All agreed that digamy was a bar to ordination.

4. *Chorepiscopi:* a good survey by H. Leclercq in *Dict. d'arch. et de liturgie chr.* III/1, art. "Chorévêques."

in 358 when Constantius agreed to allow Pope Liberius to return from exile (Theodoret, *H.E.* II 17, 6).

If to us it may seem a little extravagant to hold that it inheres in the logic of monotheism that in one city there may be only one bishop, to the ancients the argument would have had a familiar ring. At the end of the third century an imperial panegyrist buttressed the authority of Diocletian and the tetrarchy with the reflection that, with four winds, four elements, etc., fourness corresponds to the essential nature of things. A few years later Eusebius of Caesarea suggested that Constantine's elimination of successively superfluous colleagues until he was sole emperor was a providential arrangement to provide an earthly counterpart for the divine Monarch. No doubt there were also less mystical reasons for thinking it right to establish a monarchical episcopate. The conflict with heresy made it a practical necessity to make one presiding figure the personal focus of ecclesial unity in the local congregation. The second-century conflicts with gnostic heresy, with the consequent movement towards greater standardisation and uniformity of expression, surely strengthened rather than weakened the authority of the bishop in relation to his flock. At the same time, however, the pressure of other churches on a dissenting community, or other bishops on a dissenting colleague, tended to diminish the autonomy of a local church and its bishop. Cyprian might indeed declare boldly that every bishop is equal, as every apostle was, and is answerable to God alone. But one hardly needs to read between the lines of his writings to see that in his opinion the episcopate ought to be unanimous, that decisions in synod are not reached by majority votes that preserve the conscientious dissent of the minority, and that the individual bishop has a duty to discern and bring himself into line with this unanimity. *Episcopatus unus est, cuius a singulis in solidum pars tenetur* sounds like a trained lawyer's way of affirming a truth dear to Cyprian's heart, that each local church possesses all the essential elements of the universal Church. But it does not mean for Cyprian that every bishop is allowed to be "a law unto himself," or that the principal function of the Holy Spirit in the fellowship of the Christian society is to foster mutual tolerance amid the continual dissension.

The diminution of the autonomy of the local bishop was increased still further early in the fourth century by the Nicene canons which created the authority of the metropolitan of the civil province. The fourth Nicene canon gives the bishop of the civil metropolis a power of veto over episcopal elections (it does not yet go so far as to make him always the principal consecrator). St. Matthew's Gospel (18:20) preserves a saying of the Lord,

"Where two or three are gathered in my name, there am I in the midst of them," which was interpreted as defining the quorum for a valid episcopal election. In case of any controversy or division it was prudent to have three bishops as one's consecrators, as Novatian did at Rome (Cornelius in Eusebius, *H.E.* VI 43, 8). In the same decade Cyprian claims that in North Africa and "in almost all provinces" the custom was for a new bishop to be chosen from among members of the local congregation and ordained by neighbouring bishops of the same province (*Ep.* 67, 5). In 314 the Council of Arles protested against consecrations carried out by only one bishop, and desired seven, while allowing three as the minimum (canon 20). At Nicaea the attendance of all bishops of the province was recognised as the ideal; but it is granted that a quorum of three may act, subject to the written consent of their absent colleagues and the metropolitan's veto (canon 4). However, the Arian author of the *Apostolic Constitutions,* and of the *Apostolic Canons* appended thereto, was reflecting an older usage when he allows the validity of consecrations by "two or three" bishops (*AC* iii.20; viii.27 and 47, 1 = *Ap. Can.* 1); he is writing in Syria, perhaps at Antioch, about 360, mainly revising older material. (The set of Apostolic Canons looks like the Constitutor's personal creation.)[5] Episcopal consecrations by only two bishops were almost always partisan. Their validity was sure to be questioned by the opposing faction and upheld by faithful supporters. In Spain, where the metropolitical structure was slow to develop, Priscillian could be ordained at Avila by only two bishops in 381, with the consent of the plebs.[6] When in 457 the news of the emperor Marcian's death reached Alexandria, the mob, hostile to their Chalcedonian bishop Proterius, rushed to the Caesareum to have Timothy the Cat installed as their true (monophysite) bishop, but could find only one bishop ready to lay hands upon him. The hermit bishop Peter the Iberian had to be dragged from his sickbed to make a second; and later anti-Chalcedonian writers claimed that he was actually the third, thereby complying with the Nicene minimum, and eliminating a source of grave embarrassment in controversy. That Timothy had the consent of the plebs was certain: his elevation led to the murder of poor Proterius.[7]

5. On the *Apostolic Canons* see F. X. Funk, *Die apostolische Konstitutionen* (1891); E. Schwartz, *Gesammelte Schriften* 5 (1963) 2–4–45; above all, C. H. Turner in *JTS* 16 (1915) 523–538.

6. Priscillian's consecration: see H. Chadwick, *Priscillian of Avila* (1976), 33.

7. Timothy Aelurus's consecration is grippingly narrated in the *Life of Peter the Iberian* (ed. and trans. Raabe, 1895) where Peter is the second bishop specially brought in, not the third as in Zacharias Scholasticus IV 1. Severus of Antioch (*Select Letters,* ed. Brooks, ii 3,

Accordingly, there was much good sense in the Nicene provision for control by the metropolitan. The metropolitical structure in turn came to be felt to be inadequate, and to need guidance from above by the creation of patriarchates. At Nicaea a desire on the part of Libya to be independent of Alexandrian control was crushed by the sixth canon, which lays down that the supra-provincial authority of Alexandria is justified by analogy with that exercised also by Rome and Antioch.[8] The patriarchate of Antioch was reduced by the achievement of Juvenal of Jerusalem in the mid-fifth century, who created a patriarchate for the mother see of Christendom at the expense of the jurisdiction of Antioch.[9] Antioch also lost control of Cyprus, where the church asserted itself to be autocephalous. The great see of New Rome at Constantinople was in time to become the dominant patriarchate in the Greek East, eventually "the ecumenical patriarchate" (the title, later to cause much offence to Pope Gregory the Great, was in use from the middle of the fifth century).[10] The patriarchs of Constantinople had grave initial difficulties in establishing their authority, partly because of a desire by metropolitans in Asia Minor to retain their independence, partly because of political rivalry between Alexandria and the upstart capital on the Bosphorus. The imperial government in the fourth century liked dividing provinces, but simultaneously grouping them under larger units called "dioceses." At the time of the Council of Constantinople of 381, the second "ecumenical council," some were inclined to expect the bishop at the administrative centre of the civil "diocese" to exercise leadership and some appellate jurisdiction over provincial metropolitans. In practice, the older order continued to assert itself. To the distress of the bishops of Alexandria the see of Constantinople slowly came to exercise considerable authority not only in Thrace but also in Asia Minor. But no patriarch of Constantinople ever exercised the power enjoyed in Egypt by the see of Alexandria, whose bishop had the traditional right to consecrate every bishop under his jurisdiction. The imperial court sought to

---

transl. I 224–5) rejects as a lie the story that Timothy was ordained by only two rather than by three bishops. Pope Pelagius I, 556–61, whose election was highly controversial, could only find two bishops to consecrate him, and the third was in presbyteral orders: *Liber Pontificalis* I 303 Duchesne.

8. On the sixth canon of Nicaea there is a justly famous paper by Schwartz in the *Berlin Academy Sitzungsberichte,* 1930. I have tried to take the story further in *Harvard Theological Review* 53 (1960) 171–195.

9. On Juvenal of Jerusalem see Honigmann in *Dumbarton Oaks Papers* V.

10. On the rise of the patriarchate of Constantinople see now the last section of Gilbert Dagron's admirable book on the origins of the city, *Naissance d'une capitale* (1974).

sweeten Theophilus of Alexandria by inviting him to be the principal consecrator when John Chrysostom was brought from Antioch to Constantinople in 398. But Theophilus soon had reason to resent John's very active exercise of jurisdiction, e.g. in the investigation of the consecration fee that bishops in the province of Asia had been paying to the metropolitan of Ephesus, a scandal which John dealt with in a most unbending manner (like a man with no knees, they said of him). In the Nestorius affair, the see of Alexandria triumphed over New Rome apparently decisively. The patriarch of Constantinople was branded as a heretic and eventually exiled to the Egyptian desert. Even so, each successive conflict between Alexandria and Constantinople left the new patriarchate at the capital in a stronger position than before. As long as Cyril presided at Alexandria, Alexandrian influence remained predominant. His successor Dioscorus was a much less political animal than Cyril; a zealot who disliked theological compromise and preferred to stand on principles, Dioscorus of Alexandria took the first and fatal step towards detaching the Egyptian church to become a separated body. He and his suffragans broke with Rome and the West as well as with Constantinople, and thereby shattered the traditional standing of the Alexandrian patriarchate.

One might expect the consequence to be the acquisition by Constantinople of powers in the Greek churches comparable to those exercised in the West by the bishops of old Rome. That it was not so is evidence of the deep strength of feeling in the Greek churches that authority grows "from the bottom upwards," and that the eucharistic communion of the local churches is the foundation of all communion. In the West, on the other hand, communion with the see where St. Peter and St. Paul taught and died a glorious death was instinctively felt to be the criterion and touch-stone of authentic ecclesiality. Even the churches in North Africa, which held the most Cyprianic views on the equality of all bishops as brothers in the Lord and reacted with vehemence against any suggestion that there could be an *episcopus episcoporum,* nevertheless assented without reservation to the concept of the see of Peter and Paul as the focus of unity and universality.

Without the internal structure of authority within the Church there could have been no wider role for bishops to play in "secular" society. The bishop's power-base, so to speak, lay always in the allegiance of his flock to the ministry of word and sacrament and pastoral care of which he is the focus. To the faithful he represented not merely a properly constituted officer of the community but an instrument of divine grace, inasmuch as his ordination is a sacramental act conferring a charismatic gift of grace appropriate to the office (1 Tim. 4:14; 2 Tim. 1:6).

2. The Bishop's Social Role Within the Church

The bishop's responsibility for hospitality has already been alluded to above. In the first instance, it was a responsibility for travelling missionaries; then for *peregrini* generally (Ambrose, *de officiis* ii 103). His share (normally a quarter of the offerings of the faithful) of the church treasury was also the resource on which he called for supporting the poor, the protection of whom was one of his prime responsibilities. In the fifties of the third century the community in Rome had on its payroll one bishop, 46 presbyters, 7 deacons, 7 sub-deacons, 42 acolytes, 52 exorcists, readers, and door-keepers, and more than 1500 widows and distressed persons, "all of whom were fed by the grace and kindness of the Lord" (Cornelius in Eusebius, *H.E.* VI 43, 11). The distribution of alms to the poor was a plentiful source of discontent among the recipients. Augustine confesses that he finds the problems of the administration of church finance altogether hateful (*Ep.* 126, 9), so numerous are the resentments created over money matters. On the anniversary of the bishop's ordination, his *natalis* or birthday, he was expected to give a general dinner for the poor on the church roll (Augustine, *S Frangip.* 2 p. 189). The bishop would also be entrusted with young children made wards of the church (Augustine, *Epp.* 252–255), a responsibility not very easy for the clergy to discharge when their wards turned out to be turbulent teenage girls (see a classic papyrus document from Egypt on this subject in Mitteis-Wilcken, *Chrestomathie*). Orphans would be taken into the bishop's household (Augustine, *S.* 176, 2). This special care for the poor, for waifs and strays, is often mentioned in epitaphs of bishops besides the excellence of their instruction—"teaching apostolic doctrine so as to make all his congregation weep for their sins" (*ILCV* 967; cf. 989 on generosity to the poor). The church's financial needs naturally imposed on the bishop and his staff a care for church property, after the advent of Constantine made it legally possible for bequests to be made. The church's property interests sometimes needed to be defended in the courts (Augustine, *Ep.* 21, 5); Augustine, *Ep.* 99, records an uncomfortable dispute about the property of his church at Hippo. By A.D. 400 it was common practice for the more devout in Syria and Asia Minor to bequeath to the church a third of their estate (Basil the Great, *Or.* 7, *PG* 31, 299; Greg. Nyss. *de pauperum amore, PG* 46, 466B; Chrysostom, *de eleemos. et hospit. hom.* 23, *PG* 63, 725; *in Matt.* 88, *PG* 57, 779). In the West the expected benefaction was the share that an additional child would have received (Jerome, *Ep.* 120, 1; Augustine, *en. ps.* 38, 12; *S.* 86, 11–14, and esp. 355 rejecting as wrong the bequeathing of all one's property to the church in disregard of any family claimants).

The apostle Paul told the Corinthians that they must not take their grievances against one another to the lawcourts but settle disagreements by asking members of the congregation to arbitrate. Arbitrations became a major preoccupation of bishops.[11] In third-century Syria it was the rule for the bishop to set each Monday to hear cases, and to be assisted by his presbyters and deacons; the court sat on Mondays to give time for negotiation towards reconciliation in time for the eucharist on the following Sunday (*Didascalia* ii, 47 p. 111 Connolly = *Apost. Const.* ii, 47, partly taken over by *Statuta Ecclesiae Antiqua* 14). Constantine even allowed a civil case to be transferred, at the request of either party, to the bishop's court and enacted that in that event there should be no appeal from the bishop's decision (*C.Th.* i, 27, 1). It is important that the earliest evidence for the operation of the episcopal court or *audientia* shows an overriding concern for the amicable reconciliation of the parties, and that "justice" is a secondary matter. A striking illustration of the same point may be found in Gregory of Nyssa's *Life* of the third-century missionary in Pontus, Gregory Thaumaturgus (*PG* 46, 925). Augustine found that his duties as arbitrator and judge were in general distasteful, certainly a major distraction from his spiritual duties. In his experience those who brought cases before the bishop were not the good faithful members of his congregation, but persons with a consistent record for being tiresome and contentious (*en. ps.* 118; *S.* 24). Moreover, it brought the bishop into some *odium* if, as was often the case, the contention was between rich and poor: to decide in favour of the rich man was to invite accusations of upholding a class interest and toadying the powerful, and to decide in favour of the poor man was to invite accusations of bribery (*en. ps.* 25, 13; Ambrose, *off.* ii, 125).

Constantine was asked by an incredulous high official whether he

---

11. On the bishop's court, *audientia episcopalis,* see J. M. Bakhuizen van den Brink in *Mededelingen d. Akad Wet. Amsterdam* 19 (1956) 145–301. On Byzantine Egypt, H. I. Bell in *Byzantion* 1 (1924) 139; Steinwenter, *BZ* 30 (1929) 660; his article in *Reallexikon für Antike und Christentum* I, s.v. *Audientia episcopalis,* is a disappointment. On transfer to the bishop from civil process, see, e.g., Ambrose, *Ep.* 82 (an arbitration); for a criminal case, Basil, *Ep.* 286, asking the civil authority to leave to him the discipline of some thieves caught stealing clothes at a large church festival. Synesius, *Ep.* 105, mentions *scholastikoi* of the Alexandrian church. The intimate cooperation between bishops and magistrates in keeping down the poor is bitterly attacked by Jerome, *in Mich.* I 2, 9–10, p. 457 Vallarsi, as fatal to the bishop's plausibility in his prime duty to act as protector of the poor against the powerful.

really meant to make the bishop's decision final, and replied that he did, that it was the secular judge's duty to see that the bishop's decision was strictly enforced, and that, because of the freedom from restriction in the admissibility of evidence that distinguished a bishop's court from a secular court, and because of the charismatic powers of the bishops as holy men capable of discerning the hearts of men, a bishop was not in need of correction by a higher court (*onst. Sirm.* 1 of 333). A similar doctrine of episcopal charism is found in an astonishing document of a Roman synod of 378 which undertook to defend Pope Damasus from the embarrassing charge of responsibility for homicide at the time of his election in 366, when an ugly riot cost the lives of 137 of the plebs who were divided between two candidates.[12] The synod claimed that thanks to this charismatic power of discernment, bishops had no need, as secular judges, to resort to judicial torture to ascertain the truth in cases of conflicting testimony (*PL* 13, 578). That very holy men could discern guilt and innocence was recognised by pagan and Christian alike in late antiquity (e.g. Porphyry's *Life of Plotinus* 11; *Life of Pythagoras* 13, 54; Rufinus, *Historia Monachorum* 16). Augustine, no doubt realistically, declines to claim any special powers of discernment for his decisions. He also remarks (*City of God* 19, 6) that the deplorable use of torture by secular judges leads many innocent men to confess to crimes they have not committed, and censures the use of torture as "abhorrent to Christians" (*Ep.* 104, 16). Whether the same abhorrence was felt by Pope Leo the Great in his inquisition into the crypto-Manichees discovered to be numerous among his congregation in 443 (an inquisition in which the bishop of Rome was assisted not only by other bishops and inferior clergy but also by eminent lay assessors) is unhappily uncertain (Leo, *Ep.* 15, 16); he seems to have been content if the secular arm applied methods stronger than that gentle persuasion which alone was appropriate for the clergy. But a Manichee process was exceptional. The severest punishment of a bishop's court was, at worst, likely to be corporal punishment; and even that was widely held to be ruled out. The sixth-century bishop of the island of Samos who found that he needed a private prison to restrain delinquent clergy (Moschus, *Pratum* 108) may have been unique. (Imperial legislation was against private prisons.) The Arian author of the *Apostolic Constitutions* directs, in the 27th Apostolic Canon, that clergy may not beat sinners. The Canonists Zonaras and Balsamon oppose the view that they might hand the chastisement over to laymen; Balsamon allowing a possible exception for

---

12. On the Roman synod of 378 see Chadwick, *Priscillian of Avila,* 128–29.

schoolmasters in holy orders, but insisting that even they may never cane "in anger and fury" (Rhalli-Potli II 680).

Accusations against the bishop himself could raise complex issues, since internal ecclesiastical faction could give unhappy motives for prosecution against which the bishop needed proper protection. The Council of Constantinople of 382 (in the canon 6 ascribed mistakenly to the council of 381) lays down that a charge on a purely secular matter may be brought against a bishop by anyone under normal procedure; but on any ecclesiastical charge no accusation might be brought by a heretic, a schismatic, an excommunicate person, or anyone himself uncleared of an accusation. Subject to the exclusion of these categories, a charge against a bishop must come first to the provincial synod, from which appeal could be made to a greater synod constituted by the bishops of the civil Diocese whose decision would be final. No appeal could be made to the emperor or to the civil courts or to an ecumenical council as if greater than that of the Diocese under its patriarch. (This canon provided a model for later legislation, e.g., Justinian, *Novel* 183, 21.)

Delicate judicial issues were raised for bishops by the right of asylum, especially when the church's altars were sought by armed bandits on the run.[13] Although the right of asylum was widely criticised (and not, of course, always respected), both Augustine (*S. Guelf.* 25 p. 528) and John Chrysostom (Socrates, *H.E.* VI 5) defended it. In the case of pagan shrines the right of asylum was held to depend on a special privilege granted by the emperor. The Christians raised awkward problems by claiming the right of asylum for any altar. Justinian's final compromise was to allow asylum for oppressed persons, but not for criminals (*Nov.* 17, 7 pr. of 535).

The most frequent duty of bishops was to intercede for members of their flock when they were in trouble with the courts or the fisc. Augustine found these intercessory activities time-consuming and irritating, but recognised that the judicial and fiscal system made them necessary (*Ep.* 151, 2 and 152–153). Otherwise the oppressed would never get justice at all.

The patronage role assumed by fourth-century bishops meant or could mean power. Athanasius of Alexandria (*HA* 78, 1) remarks that the bishop's freedom from *munera* and his role as patron gave a motive leading ambitious men to seek holy orders. The Christian emperors were quickly known to be easily accessible to bishops seeking protection for the oppressed. The Coun-

---

13. Asylum was important for debtors and runaway slaves. Jerome (*in Esai.* xvi, p. 690) picks out high interest rates with the money lenders as the prime cause of sedition in cities, driving many into hopeless debt.

cil of Serdica (343) observed that the name of bishop was being brought into disrepute by bishops going to court to seek favours for their relatives and friends (canons 8 and 13). Moreover, the quasi-judicial role of the bishop's court became a source of revenue to the see,[14] since no doubt to protect themselves against a flood of arbitrations the bishops thought it necessary to charge the standard legal fees. In the 350s Silvanus, bishop of Tarsus, thought it prudent to have a lay adviser to read all the documents submitted by the contestants (Socrates, *H.E.* VII 37, 17). This appears to be the first evidence for the creation of the office of the defensor ecclesiae, a lay lawyer on the bishop's staff who, from early in the fifth century (Pope Zosimus, *Ep.* 9, 3), might take holy orders, and would particularly look after the church's legal interests (e.g. Possidius, *V. Aug.* 12 where the defensor ecclesiae appeals to the civil courts after a Circumcellion attack). At the time of the councils of Ephesus (449) and Chalcedon (451) a prominent role is played by the defensor of the church of Alexandria, who is in presbyteral orders (*Act. Chalc.* i, 222, 235, 305, 311, etc.).

It is hardly surprising that episcopal elections were normally a source of unrest and disorder (Socrates, *H.E.* VII 40, so comments). The Council of Serdica records its outrage at the practice of bribing a claque of laity to shout for a particular candidate (can. 2). It was common for bishops nearing their end to try to avert a riot by nominating their successor, as Augustine himself tried (unsuccessfully) to do. In a surprisingly numerous proportion of cases, the problem of the succession was solved by the dominance of a particular family, round which the church in a town had first been formed and which then expected to supply a suitable candidate. In the second century Polycrates of Ephesus was proud to claim that seven of his relatives had been bishops (Eusebius, *H.E.* V 24, 6). In Mesopotamia and especially in Armenia (see *Trull. can.* 33) it was normal for a see to remain in the family, however widely extended the concept of family might be. Elsewhere the practice was criticised as nepotism. In the 460s Pope Hilarus complains that in Spain bishops treat their see not as a divine gift but as hereditary property that they can dispose of by will (*Ep.* 15 p. 162 Thiel). Origen bitterly complains of hereditary bishoprics (*H. Num.* 22, 4). A similarly negative view appears in the 76th Apostolic Canon. On the other hand Prudentius rhapsodises over the family of the Valerii which had produced a succession of bishops for Sara-

14. Justinian found it necessary to put a ceiling on the legal fees and tips charged in church courts: *CJ* i, 4, 29 (530).

gossa (*Perist.* IV 79–80, supported by the record of the early fourth-century council of Elvira, and probably also that of Saragossa 380).[15]

In 335 the bishop of Constantinople was nearing his end and was asked which of his clergy he wished to see as his successor. He replied that he thought the church should choose between two: if a good teacher of the faith was the prime requirement, they should elect Paul—but if they wanted someone good at public affairs and negotiating with the authorities, then the right man was Macedonius. In the event, Paul was so anxious to be bishop that he got himself ordained by some bishops who happened to be in Constantinople (there was no city in which it was so easy to constitute a quick synod out of casual episcopal visitors); but without the consent of the metropolitan of Heraclea and without the approval of Constantine so that it was easy for his opponents to have him synodically expelled (see Sozomen iii, 3–4). Ascetically minded believers were distressed at the quality of bishops received under the system of popular suffrage. Augustine remarks to Jerome that wealthy candidates with low educational and spiritual qualifications are often preferred to poor men with high qualifications (*Ep.* 167, 18, written, it should be recalled, to a scholarly presbyter who had once much wanted to be bishop of Rome).[16] The standard of education among bishops varied quite widely. Illiterate bishops are a favourite butt for the mockery of the half-educated, observes Augustine (*Cat. rud.* 13). The Council of Chalcedon included at least one illiterate bishop (from Lycia; *Act. Chalc.* i, 1070, Latin version). On the other hand, by the fifth century important sees could be held by ex-senators, men like Nectarius of Constantinople (381–97), or Thalassius who was put into the see of Cappadocian Caesarea just as he was to be gazetted for the office of praetorian prefect (Socrates VII 48). In the West the best known of the great aristocrats to become bishops are Ambrose of Milan and Paulinus of Nola. But in the fifth century a bishopric was occasionally an enforced exile, as for Cyrus of Panopolis (Malalas XIV 362), and for two western emperors who suffered deposition, Avitus and Glycerius. Petronius bishop of Bologna is said by Gennadius to have been praetorian prefect (*Vir. inl.* 42). If we are asking what social role was expected of a fifth-century bishop, the answer can be easily seen in Ennodius's *Life* of Epiphanius of Pavia (Ticinum). Epiphanius's authority is grounded in his

15. Avitus of Vienne succeeded his father Hesychius in the see, and his brother Apollinaris became bishop of Valence: Duchesne, *Fastes* I 184.

16. Jerome's commentary on Ecclesiastes contains some sad observations on the popular preference for unscholarly bishops (ix 11, p. 465; x 5, p. 471). "Whenever you see a much applauded preacher, be sure he is a fool" (ix 17, p. 467).

spirituality as an ascetic and holy man, seen, for example, in his abstinence from baths and his abstinence from an evening meal. At midday he would be hospitable over luncheon. He sought to protect the poor and to make intercession for the oppressed. From Odovacar he won five years' tax exemption for his city. He gathered money to redeem prisoners of war. In the quarrels between the princes, he was trusted by both sides, and was accordingly asked to act as ambassador—for Ricimer to Anthemius, for Nepos to Euric, from Theodoric to Gundobad the Burgundian king.

The redemption of prisoners of war was the one cause for which bishops thought it morally right to sell church plate (Ambrose, *off.* ii.70, 142–43; Possidius, *V. Aug.* 24; Justinian's law of 529, *CJ* I 2, 21, allows its sale for no other purpose). The principle was taken to notable lengths by Acacius bishop of Amida (Diyabakir) on the upper Tigris. He sold his church plate to redeem not Roman citizens captured by the Persians, but Persian prisoners whom the Roman soldiers would not release (Socrates VII 21). It was an extension of the principle that Christian charitable aid to the poor should not discriminate in favour of church members but should have no criterion other than need (see an eloquent statement by Atticus of Constantinople in Socrates, *H.E.* VII 25).

The neutrality of bishops between factions or between warring nations often led to embassies. In their role as ambassadors, bishops shared with philosophers the aura of authority which brought ambassadorial responsibilities to a number of pagan philosophers of the fourth century (Themistius, Iphicles of Epirus, and others listed by J. F. Matthews in *Reallexikon für Antike und Christentum,* art. "Gesandschaft"). The earliest example is Eusebius bishop of Nicomedia sent by Licinius to negotiate terms with Constantine in 324. Ammianus Marcellinus records a number of instances where Christian clergy acted as intermediaries between the Roman army and barbarians, the most interesting of which is the bishop of Bezabde in Mesopotamia whose city was being besieged by the Persians. The bishop went to the Persian camp for parley. Unhappily for him, the next Persian attack was directed at just the weakest part of the wall, and it was suspected that the bishop's neutrality had passed into treachery (Ammian. XX 7, 9; the other instances are XXXI 12, 8–9; 15, 6; XXIX 5, 15). The Christians felt themselves and were felt by others to stand outside the conflicts between Roman and barbarian, and somehow to represent the cause of humanity. On the other hand, some bishops wholly identified themselves with the Roman struggle against the barbarian invasions. Jerome so writes of Exsuperius of Toulouse (*Ep.* 123, 16). According to the *Life of Germanus* bishop of Auxerre, he went to Britain, beset by Pelagianism, with a military force, being himself *dux belli*. He was happily granted the miraculous Alleluia victory in which no bloodshed was necessary.

The more usual Christian view was that the proper role of bishops is to pray for the emperor and his army. Victory in battle is the gift of heaven, and nothing is more likely to make and keep heaven propitious than the devout prayers and holy lives of the people of God. Origen (*c. Cels.* 8, 73) observes that pagan priests are not enlisted in war so that they may offer the customary sacrifices with unsullied hands, and justifies Christian withdrawal from military service on the ground that by their prayers the faithful "destroy all daemons who stir up wars" and "are of more help to the emperors than the soldiers." The ancient Solemn Prayers following the gospel for Good Friday in the Roman Missal probably go back in substance to the fourth century:

> Omnipotens sempiterne deus, in cuius manu sunt omnium temporum potestates et omnia iura regnorum, respice propitius ad Romanum benignus imperium, ut gentes quae in sua feritate confidunt potentiae tuae dextera comprimantur.

The preceding bidding exhorts the faithful to pray that God may "subdue to the emperors all barbarian nations for our perpetual peace."

Wars on earth, explains John Cassian (*Coll.* 8, 13), reflect the internecine wars among the demons.

That the right form of worship is essential if heaven is to be propitious is an axiom of ancient society. The axiom lies at the root of the pagan persecutions of the Christians, as also of the deep unpopularity of the Jews in the Greco-Roman world. The Christians introduced an even greater passion into the matter by their belief that right worship also presupposed right doctrine, and that therefore heresy or schism would, if long tolerated, or regarded as a matter of indifference, provoke the wrath of the Lord. The ferocity of sectarian conflicts in the fourth and later centuries cannot be understood without the centrality of this axiom. In the fifth and sixth centuries the Chalcedonians are sure that the defeats of the imperial armies are the consequence of the prevalence of so many Monophysites; and vice versa. To give illustrations is superfluous, since the assumption is to be met constantly throughout the period in innumerable sources. One vivid example may serve. After the emperor Theodosius I had defeated Magnus Maximus at Aquileia, he came to Milan there to receive a report from the Count of the East that at Callinicum, a fort in Mesopotamia, a synagogue had been burnt down in a riot stirred up by the local bishop; moreover, a conventicle of the Valentinian gnostics in the East had also been burnt by zealous monks, whose procession in honour of the Maccabaean martyrs had been mocked by the imprudent heretics. Theodosius directed that restitution be made, especially to the synagogue which the local bishop must rebuild. Ambrose of Milan thought it grave that the emperor should enable the Jews so to triumph over the church, and recalled the number of churches destroyed by Jewish rioters. His letter of protest made the emperor withdraw his order, though without informing Ambrose. On the next occasion when Ambrose was celebrating mass with the emperor present, he preached a pointed sermon on the prophetic duty to rebuke and on the courage of the prophet Nathan before King David. Descending from the ambo, Ambrose stood within the presbytery, and an irritated dialogue with the emperor ensued: "You have been preaching at me today." "True, I had your edification in view." "My decree that the bishop must restore the synagogue was too harsh; but it is already withdrawn. Yet the monks commit many crimes." . . . After standing for some time Ambrose said to the emperor: "Enable me to offer for you without anxiety, set my mind at rest." Eventually the emperor gave his promise to quash the entire investigation by the Count of the East. "On your promise," said Ambrose, "I will celebrate mass (*ago*)." So he went to the altar at last and, as he reported to his sister, "so great was the grace of the offering that I myself felt that this grace was well pleasing to our God and that the divine presence was not lacking" (Ambrose, *Ep.* 41, 27–28).

The scene is a dramatic enforcement of the point that Ambrose cannot continue with the offering of the mass unless the emperor removes any ground for fear that the church in Mesopotamia may be harassed by the Count. For any such harassment would negative any value that the liturgy might possess in preserving the favour of heaven.

The role of the bishop as protector of the poor made him the natural leader of a large proportion of the urban population, and therefore a figure of political consequence. Particularly intolerant bishops seem to have been markedly unpopular. The terrible lynching of George of Alexandria when the news of Constantius's death reached the city in 361 shows the hatred that could be aroused by a bishop who enraged the pagans by his scorn for their religion.[17] At Arethusa in Syria the Arian bishop Mark died a heroic death at

---

17. George of Alexandria's death followed the fall of the hated *dux Aegypti* Artemius: *Historia Acephala* 8 (Turner, *EOMIA* I 666); Ammianus XXII 11, 8; Libanius, *Or.* 14, 65; *Ep.* 205; Julian, *Ep.* 10.

the hands of a fanatical mob resentful of his anti-pagan measures (Socrates V, 10). A number of other texts could be added concerning the unpopularity of some individual bishops. But in general the bishop was a figure that people wanted to like, and of whom they hoped that their expectations would be realised. The pagan historian Ammianus Marcellinus regarded the Church as a body concerned for justice, mercy, and simplicity (XXII 11, 5; XXVII 3, 15). It is noteworthy that his comments occur in passages criticising bishops conspicuously failing to realise these ideals. Ammianus was also aware that theological disputes within the Christian family could be contentious to the point of almost animal ferocity (XXII 5, 4). (The Church's character as a universalised Judaism has somehow carried over a trait that Jews often remark about their own society, that they quarrel loudly among themselves, but are quickly united by external threats.) But Ammianus much admired the frugality of country bishops. His cordial dislike of anything associated with the city of Rome assigned a prominent place to Damasus (Pope 366–384), whose opulent hospitality was said to surpass the emperor's.

The public insignia assumed by bishops are relevant to their social role.[18] Before the time of Constantine Christian clergy wore no distinctive dress. The *Apostolic Constitutions* (VIII 12) direct that, as the liturgy of the faithful begins, the bishop celebrating is to put on a "shining garment." But otherwise the bishops normally, for everyday wear, dressed themselves in peasant black, no doubt as a sign of identification with the poor. At the end of the fourth century a witty Novatianist bishop of Constantinople wore white; but that was not his only eccentricity (Socrates VI 22). As early as the time of Constantine zealous believers in Phrygia took to wearing sackcloth. An inscription records Severus, bishop of Laodicea Combusta, as "general bishop of several cities and leader of the sackcloth-wearing people" (*MAMA* i 171). But sackcloth came to be regarded as the sign either of exceptional holiness (the emperor Theodosius II acquired for its sanctity a filthy black cassock left by a bishop of Hebron: Socrates VII 22, 14) or of ostentation (Cassian, *Inst.* I 2). To wear sackcloth became the mark of ecclesiastical dissent in Asia Minor (*C.Th.* XVI 5, 7, 9, 11; 381–383).

Marks of public respect were normally paid to a bishop. Socrates the historian observes that he may give offence to ultra-zealots by omitting honorific epithets such as "God-beloved" (*theophilestatos*) which were commonly applied to bishops in formal chancery style (VI pr.). He also tells us in pass-

---

18. T. Klauser, *Der Ursprung der bischöflichen Insignien und Ehrenrechte* (1949), now reprinted in his *Gesammelte Arbeiten* (1974).

ing that it was customary to stand when a bishop came into the room (VI 11, 16). But an acid passage in Jerome's commentary on St. Matthew 21 commenting adversely on the practice of saluting bishops with the acclamation "Blessed is he that comes in the name of the Lord, Hosanna in the highest" has mistakenly been taken as a general observation about a widespread practice of using this acclamation at the advent of the bishop. The travel diary of Etheria gives reason to think it only a snide hit at the bishop of Jerusalem (with whom Jerome's relations were always tense) who reenacted the triumphal entry of Jesus by riding into town on a donkey in Holy Week. One may not generalise from something that happened once a year in one place.

The principal critics of bishops and their developing social role were the monks. "Flee from women and bishops" was an early monastic maxim reported by John Cassian (*Inst.* XI 18), who adds that he never kept away from his sister and had been ordained by a bishop (John Chrysostom, no less). But he understood the point of the saying to be that the monk's prime duty is unremitting concentration in prayer in the solitude of his cell, and to that end neither bishops nor women are conducive. The canons of the Council of Gangra (about 342) show how in Asia Minor the monastic movement had taken on a sharply critical turn in relation to the Church. The Egyptian *Apophthegmata Patrum* do not reflect any such anti-clericalism, and that is one of the more interesting features of these sayings. One monk who left his cell to become bishop of Oxyrhyncus tried, as bishop, to continue his monastic exercises as before, and found he lacked the strength. He asked the Lord if grace had been removed from him because of his accepting the bishopric and was told, No (*PG* 65, 133). But in Egypt Athanasius of Alexandria had fully identified himself with the ascetic movement, had written a *Life* of Antony to show how devoted that holy man had been to orthodoxy, and had gone up the Nile on a solemn visitation of the Pachomian foundations.[19]

---

19. On the political consequences of Athanasius's achievement in winning the solid support of the monks there is direct evidence in Sozomen VI 20. On the tensions between monks and "secular" clergy cf. Jerome, *Ep.* 14, 8–9, and much other fourth-century evidence, especially in the *Apostolic Constitutions,* composed in part to emphasise in the strongest terms the authority of the bishop and his clergy against ascetic indifference. Likewise the pseudo-Ignatian epistles by the same author.

The role of the bishop in the ancient city receives notice in the recent studies of the ancient and medieval city by Mason Hammond. See also F. Prinz, "Die bischöfliche Stadtherrschaft in Frankreich vom 5. bis zum 7. Jht.," *Hist. Zeits.* 217 (1973) 1ff. and the same author's *Klerus und Krieg im frühen Mittelalter* (Stuttgart, 1971). There is also a recent study of late antique Gaul's bishops by M. Heinzelmann.

There is no doubt that independent ascetics were felt by bishops to be disorderly persons (Origen, *in Matt.* 16, 25 says so explicitly). The Origenist tradition, with its anticlerical high churchmanship, adopted a detached, even scornful view of popular worldly clerics, preaching eartickling sermons, favoured by ladies of wealth and refinement, easygoing with sinners in their congregation for fear of unpopularity (Origen, *H. Ezech.* 3, 3; *c. Cels.* III 9; *H. Jos.* 7, 6). Origen felt acutely the scandal caused by clergy of poor quality who were, he felt, a major hindrance to faith (*H. Ezech.* 7, 3). Men blaspheme and say, What a bishop! (*H. Num.* 2, 1). But congregations have the clergy they deserve (*H. Jud.* 4, 3). Augustine likewise remarks that worldly clergy are more popular than unworldly (*Ep.* 21; cf. *S.* 26). The problem arose in part from the fact that so many run to the church for temporal aid rather than for eternal life (Augustine, *en. ps.* 46, 5), and then complain that only widows and old women fill the churches (*S. Denis* 18, 6).

The ascetics went out into the desert because they felt themselves to be suffocated by the worldliness of the church in the towns (so John Chrysostom, *H. Eph.* VI; cf. John Cassian, *Coll.* 18, 5–7). The urban churches seemed so cultured and respectable, no longer identified with the poor and homeless except as the distributor of welfare. The financial resources of the church were increasingly channelled into buildings adorned with noble mosaics and frescoes. Constantine and his mother had lavished benefactions on the churches in the Holy Land and in Rome, had financed the production of exquisite calligraphic codices of the Bible, and had used a substantial part of the estates taken from Licinius to provide permanent endowments for the maintenance of their new buildings. A rich man might build a splendid church and then seem a natural candidate for election to the bishopric. The magnificent mosaic floor of the church at Aquileia records the munificence of the founder, Bishop Theodore (314–320): *Theodore feli(x) (a) diuuante deo omnipotente et poemnio caelitus tibi (cre)ditum omnia (b) aeate fecisti et gloriose dedicasti* (*ILCV* 1863; van der Meer and Mohrmann, *Atlas of the Early Christian World,* pl. 140). At Laodicea Combusta in Phrygia the successor of the sackcloth-wearing Severus, Julius Eugenius, held the see for 25 years during which he "rebuilt the entire church from its foundations [to which it had been razed during the Diocletianic persecution] and all the adornment round it, i.e. with *stoai* and a *tetrastoa* and paintings and mosaics and a fountain and outer gateway and all the stone work and, in a word, with everything" (*MAMA* i 170). A century later at Kyrrhos Bishop Theodoret used the revenues of his church (whose shrine of Cosmas and Damian attracted pilgrims and therefore had extra sources of income) to give dignity to the small and remote town; he built porticos, baths, two large bridges, and an aqueduct (*Epp.* 79, 81, 139, ed. Azema). Yet Theodoret was an ascetic, trained with and in the Syrian monastic milieu, and despite his high literary culture and easy contacts with those in high places, he wrote his "History of God's Friends" (*Philotheos Historia*) to describe the great holy men of Syria such as Symeon Stylites in terms of unreserved admiration.

Theodoret of Kyrrhos could write as cultivated and "literary" a letter as anyone of the fifth century. He combines in himself many of the paradoxes of the church of his time in siding wholly with the illiterate hermits of the desert against the pagan literati. He also illustrates how much a public-spirited bishop could do for his town. There was not much reason to encourage cities of the later Roman Empire to feel a great deal of self-respect unless they had an imperial residence or enjoyed the dignity of being a metropolis. Nicaea and Nicomedia competed with one another in blowing their civic trumpet. But small towns in the provinces can only have been irretrievably dull and undistinguished. The church with its leader could impart a sense of significance to the civic community, especially if its church possessed the relics of a martyr or other holy man.

The relationship between bishops and pagan philosophers was on the whole distant. The church and the pagan philosophers agreed that what is required of man is to practise virtue, to contemplate the divine, and to become like God as far as possible. They disagreed about polytheistic worship, especially the veneration of the Sun-God, and about the authority attaching to the wisdom and culture of classical Hellenism. At the public and social level, bishops and philosophers could sometimes look like rivals for the following of the people, or for the influencing of high officials. Both tended to come forward when the administration was in trouble with the people. But in general the bishops were, like the monks, identified with a community which included many individuals of high culture but was not as such a body intended for the diffusion of high culture and indeed often regarded high culture as aristocratic and elitist. The formidable strength of the church lay in its combination of insistence on the transcendent and supernatural together with the assumption that the church answers to the aspirations of ordinary mortals. The sense of rivalry can be illustrated from the legendary story told by Rufinus about the council of Nicaea in 325. There, he says (*H.E.* X 3 p. 962), the assembled bishops were confronted by clever philosophers skilled in dialectic who engaged the bishops in controversy, an *ingens spectaculum* for everyone to see and hear. One bishop of small education, who had courageously confessed his faith in the Persecution, asked leave to speak to a philosopher scornfully insulting the faith. The cultivated bishops present were embarrassed for their cause to be represented by such *sancta simplicitas.* (One recalls the direction of the *Didascalia* iii 5 that those enrolled as widows should not think themselves entitled to answer questions about the incarnation and atonement, but only about righteousness and simple faith.) But the good bishop stood his ground and stated his faith to the philosopher: that one God created heaven and earth by his Word and Wisdom, which Word and Wisdom was born of a virgin, by his passion freed man from eternal death, and will come as our Judge. Such was the power of the simple bishop's conviction that the philosopher found himself assenting and was carried off by the bishop to baptism. The point of Rufinus's story is that the kingdom of God is not in word but in power; that the authority of the bishop does not reside in internal qualities of mind or natural ability, but in the word of God entrusted to the church; that the bishop's right to be listened to lies in his being the successor of God's fishermen. He was not a gentleman, but "an inspired cad, like the apostles."

The Christianisation of the Roman empire meant, in short, the emergence of a new type of leader within the community, chosen (at least in the early period) by the local church, but through his consecration by bishops from other churches also linked to a world-wide society, and, unless he fell into heresy or resigned to become a monk, enjoying permanent tenure for life. His role was guided by rules formulated within the Christian tradition. He supremely represented the unity and continuity of the Christian society, and by the commission of his ordination combined both an institutional authority and charismatic power. The Roman government had no experience at coping with the phenomenon. The emperors tried to harness the bishops to social purposes by assimilating them to magistrates, by fostering their charitable welfare, and in times of war or political crisis by using their independence and "neutrality" for complex negotiations.

Bishops and Monks

'Alia monachi causa est, alia clericorum'

(Jerome, *Ep.* 14,8 to Heliodorus)

Bishops and monks represent two antithetical aspects of early Christianity. The consequence of Jesus proclaiming the kingdom of God was the arrival of the Church commissioned to realize this on earth. The Christians gathered to worship God in Christ, admitted new believers by baptism after the model of Jesus, and were sustained by the eucharistic memorial of his redemption 'on the first day of the week'. Bishops emerge as heirs of the apostolic responsibility for the unity of local congregations as well as of the whole ecclesia, and for the authenticity of what is taught. They have a commission which is more than a merely human matter of organization, yet which does not make the clergy spiritually superior to laity. (In 400 most names in the calendar of saints were of laity, remarked Augustine).[1] But the bishop is linchpin of his plebs, source of unity and coherence as vehemently urged by Ignatius of Antioch. In controversy over the charismatic prophecy of Montanism it was agreed that the sacred tradition faithfully transmitted by the ministerial succession in word and sacrament was no less Spirit-given than inspired prophecy and was less vulnerable to individual deviations. So, once established, episcopal authority is not challenged except by presbyters, like Aerius in

---

1. Aug., *Tr. in ev. Joh.* 51.13. Cf. Origen, *Hom. in Jerem.* xi.3: 'Many clergy will be lost, many laity blessed'. In general on the theme of this paper see D. König, *Amt und Askese: Priesteramt und Mönchtum bei den lateinischen Kirchenvätern in vorbenediktinischer Zeit* (St. Ottilien, 1985).

fourth-century Asia Minor, disappointed in ambition.[2] A schismatic group led by a Roman deacon dies out because 'without bishops there is no Church' (Jerome).[3] With his people the bishop is based in the city, a public person known to and often respected by unbelievers as early as Ignatius of Antioch.[4]

Early Christians were sharply conscious of standing over against 'the world'. Their citizenship is to be in heaven (Phil. 3:20). Towards the natural order and the struggles of human ambition Jesus taught detachment: value is not in one's possessions. A question ambivalently answered in the New Testament is whether detachment entails actual renunciation if the rich are to penetrate the needle's eye entrance to the kingdom or (what may be even more difficult) an inner attitude.[5] That the created order is a great good is not in doubt. Sexuality being divinely given cannot be evil when used as the Creator intends; but for higher ends it may be restrained (1 Cor. 7—directed against a group for whom the life of the spirit is incompatible with carnal reproduction).[6] That will require *askesis,* much as Epictetus would describe it.[7] 1 Cor. 7 shows the presence in the Corinthian community of an ascetic body, perhaps living in small groups, without identifying clothing, vows, or rule. Matt. 19:12 presupposes ascetics forgoing marriage for the kingdom's sake. Rev. 14:4 even sings of 144,000 saints 'undefiled with women' and so fitted to be a celestial militia.

Accordingly the Church acquires bishops, of necessity much in the world, and ascetics getting away from it as far as possible. Monks were more likely than bishops to be wandering missionaries (resembling Cynic philosophers).[8] An Arabic fragment of Galen shows that their asceticism impressed observers.[9] For philosophers agreed that restraint of bodily appetite is pre-

2. Epiphanius, *Panarion* 75, says that Aerius, who was still living, was a disciple of Eustathius of Sebaste and 'wholly Arian'.

3. *Dial. c. Luciferianos* 21 (*PL* 23.184 B): 'Ecclesia autem non est quae non habet sacerdotes'.

4. *Trall.* 3.2.

5. Hence the classic discussion by Clement of Alexandria, *Quis dives salvetur?*

6. I have argued this point in 'All Things to all Men', *New Testament Studies* 1 (1955), reprinted in the Variorum collection, *Heresy and Orthodoxy in the Early Church* (1991).

7. III 12.

8. On Diogenes (Diog. Laert 6.70–71) cf. Goulet-Cazé, *L'ascese cynique* (Paris, 1986). Lucian, *Toxaris* 27 (III 240 Macleod), speaks of 'the Cynic askesis'. In *De morte Peregrini* 11–15, Peregrinus makes an effortless transition from Christianity to Cynicism. Other well-known texts on the affinity are Aelius Aristides, *orat.* 46 (II 402, Dindorf), Origen, *c. Cels.* 3.50, and Gregory of Nazianzos, *orat.* 25 in praise of Hero alias Maximus (*PG* 35.1197–1225).

9. R. Walzer, *Galen on Jews and Christians* (Oxford, 1949), 25.

requisite for elevating the soul, and that the hubbub of cities is not conducive to thoughtful contemplation.[10]

Episcopate and Monastery became prominent institutions, with a relation to the secular which would oscillate between positive and negative but in the main remained positive. Unpopular bishops occurred[11] but were rare. Monks made their way more slowly; their relation to the laity was seldom acutely problematic. But it is food for thought that the sixteenth-century Reformation felt difficulty with both, and more with monks than with bishops. Monasticism presupposes that devoting one's entire life to religious action and contemplation is to come closer to God. Erasmus and Luther did not think that true.[12] Evidently it is no sufficient condition; for some may it be a necessary condition? (In England Henry VIII's dissolution of the monasteries caused pain to a surprising number of Protestants.) John Cassian thought the ascetic life the way to God for some, not necessarily for all.[13]

10. Porphyrius, *De Abstinentia* I 36, followed by Jerome, *adv. Jovin.* II 9 (*PL* 23.311–12). While Jerome advised ascetic communities to move away from the towns, Augustine protects himself by observing that praise of ascetics in the desert is no disparagement of urban communities such as those he had met in Milan and Rome (*De moribus* I 33, 70), that at Milan being outside the city walls (*Conf.* 8.6.15).

11. After the Council of Ariminum (359) at which most of the western episcopate compromised their orthodoxy, congregations loved their bishops too much to allow them to be treated as penitents (Jerome, *Dial. adv. Lucif.* 19 [*PL* 23.182B]). The *Apophthegmata Patrum* record a bishop who confessed to fornication but was prevented by his devoted flock from resigning his charge (N 31, *Revue de l'Orient Chr.* 12,63). Augustine comments on the fierce lay criticism of bishops responsible for liturgical changes (*Retr.* ii.11). Jerome (*Ep.* 69.9 to Oceanus) speaks of bishops who win the favour of their people by bribery, among whom some are nevertheless cordially hated by everybody. In the sixth century bishop Julian of Bostra was so hated by pagan notables that they tried to poison him; it is not said that he was disliked by his congregation (Moschus, *Pratum* 94 [*PG* 87,3. 2952D]). In 963 the ascetic bishop Aethelwold of Winchester expelled his cathedral canons living unregenerate lives and replaced them by monks from Abingdon; the secular clergy attempted to poison the bishop (see M. Lapidge and M. Winterbottom, *Wulfstan of Winchester, Life of St Aethelwold* [Oxford, 1991]).

12. Erasmus's preface to the 1518 edition of his *Enchiridion,* in the form of a letter to Abbot Paul Volz (*Ep.* 858, Allen), writes of the contemporary corruption of monastic devotion and of the equal authenticity of a lay vocation in which chaste marriage is as virtuous as celibacy. His ironic colloquy 'Virgo Misogamos' warns an aspiring virgin of Lesbians in convents and of unchaste monks whose title 'father' is all too correct. But he concedes that for some monastic life is necessary. Luther's principal statement, *De votis monasticis* of 1521 (WA 8.573–669), makes fewer concessions.

13. *Inst.* 5.4; *Coll.* 18–19.

Bishops and monks did not invariably see eye to eye. Already in the third century the austere Origen could write scathingly about bishops in great cities cultivated by 'ladies of wealth and refinement', regarding independent ascetics as a threat.[14] The fourth-century monastic movement, which Augustine speaks of as a potent social factor taking hundreds to deserts and islands,[15] was not generally welcome. African bishops feared monasteries were Manichee cells fostered by a man who had not wholly shed his Manichee past.[16] In Cappadocia Basil's monks caused alarm,[17] even if not as much as those of his former friend Eustathius of Sebaste.[18] In Spain Priscillian of Avila was deeply suspect, and had to protest that his largely lay movement was not discouraging candidates from ordination.[19] There was pain when clergy under his influence wished to retire to a monastery.[20] An individual place among Latin critics was held by Jovinian, himself a monk, who wore white, denied inherent merit to physical virginity and fasting, and saw no necessity to affirm Mary's virginity *in partu*.[21] Augustine says a humble married woman is superior to a proud virgin, but *caeteris paribus* a virgin's dedication is preferable.[22]

For a period public opinion was uncertain, sometimes hostile and mock-

14. *c. Cels.* 3.9; *In Matt. Comm.* xvi.8 and 25. Jerome knew bishops no less hostile to monks than unbelievers (*in Sophon.* III, 732, Vallarsi [*PL* 25.1452A]), and openly envious towards hospitable laity doing those things which bishops are expected to do (*in Titum* 1 [*PL* 26.603 A]). Some clergy were publicly dissociating themselves from the monks (*Ep.* 54.5).
A valuable linguistic study is Françoise E. Morard, 'Monachos, Moine: histoire du terme grec jusqu'au 4e siècle', *FZThPh* 20 (1973), 332ff.
15. Aug., *De vera religione* 5.
16. Aug., *c. litt. Petiliani* III 41, 43.
17. Basil, *Epp.* 119 and 207.
18. The canons of the Council of Gangra witness to this alarm.
19. Priscillian, *Tract.* II, 35, 3–5; IV, 60, 8–9; VI, 79, 19 (ed. Schepss).
20. Council of Saragossa (Caesaraugusta), canon 6.
21. White: Jerome, *adv. Jovin.* I 40 (*PL* 23.280). White vestments were normal for the celebrant of the eucharist by Jerome's time (*Dial. adv. Pelag.* I 29 [*PL* 23.547 C]). Helvidius argued that there was no necessity to affirm Mary's virginity *post partum,* but that if this was affirmed, it would be natural (and in Helvidius's view absurd) to affirm her virginity *in partu.* Jerome, cautious in polemic against Helvidius on this point, was first moved to affirm virginity *in partu* in the controversy with Jovinian. Augustine (*Cat. rud.* 40; *Tr. in ev. Joh.* 91,3; *S.* 184.1; 186.1) and probably Pelagius (*in Rom.* i.7) have no problem about affirming virginity *post partum* and *in partu*. For a good recent discussion of Jovinian see D. G. Hunter, 'Resistance to the virginal ideal in late fourth-century Rome: the case of Jovinian', *TS* 48 (1987), 45–64
22. *En. in Ps.* 75.16.

ing.[23] Salvian writes of the Carthage mob hissing and jostling monks,[24] Augustine of mockery from the crowd leaving the amphitheatre.

Jerome attacks bishops who openly deplore the demand for clerical celibacy.[25] Celibacy became an expected norm from about 370 onwards, at a time coincident with critical pressure from monks for whom married clergy were too much involved in this world's business. Jerome (not himself one to be merciful to the frailties of unsatisfactory clergy)[26] mentions monks whose principal topic of conversation was 'detractatio clericorum'.[27] Acceptance of celibacy for bishops in the East, for bishops, presbyters, and deacons in the West, allayed criticism and enhanced ministerial authority. Monasteries like Lérins of S. Gaul thereby became recruiting grounds for new bishops where Gallo-Roman aristocrats, like Sidonius Apollinaris, did not come forward. Admittedly the laity were unenthusiastic about a monk-bishop 'more competent to intercede with the heavenly Judge for our souls than with an earthly judge for our bodies', the latter being of some short-term urgency.[28] Nevertheless the ascetic ideal conquered. A married man could still be a bishop but was expected to put his wife into a nunnery or at least to abstain from begetting children.[29] Not all wives liked that. At Clermont the withdrawn wife of Bishop Urbicus, of senatorial class, embarrassed him by hammering and shouting at his door at midnight, gaining admittance to his bed, and nine months later presenting him with a daughter.[30]

Basic to the monk's motivation is the desire not to be hindered in the quest for perfection by the presence of others: 'L'enfer c'est les autres'. He sought a flight of the alone to the Alone — *monachos* (or, if a nun, *monacha*) — a loner, even if a characteristic setting would soon be a *coenobium*. Monks and nuns withdraw from the madding crowd seeking entertainment — sex and violence in theatre or amphitheatre — or transient power, wealth, and honour. Renounced bright lights could still pull even if despised. In uncul-

---

23. *En. in Ps.* 147.8.

24. *De gubernatione Dei* VIII 4.19–22.

25. *Adv. Vigilantium* 2 (*PL* 23.355–56).

26. E.g. *Ep.* 69.8–9.

27. *Ep.* 22.34.

28. Sidonius Apollinaris, *Ep.* VII 9.9.

29. Jerome, *adv. Jovin.* I 34 (*PL* 23.268D): 'Certe confiteris non posse esse episcopum qui in episcopatu filios faciat'. Widowers were commonly elected bishop (*Ep.* 49.21). The canon law of Carthage came to require celibacy of bishops, presbyters, and deacons (*Reg. eccl. Carth. Excerpta* 70, 201 [ed. Munier]). R. Gryson, *Les origines du célibat eccl.* (Gembloux, 1970), 176–79.

30. Greg. Turon., *Hist.* I 34 (44).

tured solitude without the worship and support of the Church, they would envy bishops able to enjoy both culture and fellowship.[31] But the monk was consoled to be avoiding 'witty but mendacious story-tellers, thieves, wanton music and erotic dancers' [commonly provided at dinner-parties],[32] 'the screams of those questioned under torture, the anguish of those condemned', and above all the misery of 'listening to preachers of fine sermons who fail to practise what they preach'.[33]

In Egypt Athanasius's intimacy with the monasteries soon produced some monk bishops, whom he lists in a letter trying to persuade a monk Dracontius to be bishop of Hermopolis Parva.[34] Asia Minor was slower; Basil was glad to discover one in Lycia.[35] At Caesarea he himself was the prime instance, living as bishop a personal life of poverty and austerity racked by appalling health.[36]

The bishop is anything but withdrawn from the community he serves. He is eucharistic president, the normal Sunday preacher (in antiquity presbyters rarely preached in the city),[37] distinct from his presbyters (and deacons) by being the source of orders.[38] During Lent he is teacher of cate-

31. Jerome (*Ep.* 125.17 to Rusticus) says that monks envy urban clergy. Sometimes a lay monk might act out his dream of priestly functions (Cassian, *Inst.* xi.16).

32. Jerome, *adv. Helvidium* 20 (*PL* 23.214B); Augustine, *En. in Ps.* 41.9. During famine at Rome all foreigners were expelled, but an exception was made for 3000 dancing girls (Ammian. Marcellinus 14.6.19).

33. Basil, *Ep.* 42.4 (*PG* 32.353C, 356C). If this letter is not by Basil, as some have thought, it is certainly of his time. Is it presupposed that (sometimes) urban clergy were present in the torture chamber? That was forbidden by the Council of Auxerre (578) canon 33, which shows it could occur.

34. *PG* 25.524–33.

35. *Ep. 218.* The pilgrim Egeria (*Itinerarium* 23) found a holy monk-bishop at Seleucia, Isauria, in 384, probably the bishop Samos of Photius, *cod.* 52.

36. Poverty: *Epp.* 35 and 135 ad fin.

37. Possidius, *Vita Augustini* 5.3, says that Valerius of Hippo allowed presbyter Augustine to preach, though it was contrary to African custom. Jerome, *Ep.* 52.7, thinks it wrong that presbyters are silent in the bishop's presence. Augustine mentions sermons by his presbyters (*S.* 20.4; 137.11 and 13; *Ep.* 41; 63,2–5; 65; 25). From *S.* 20.4 it is clear that the plebs thought little of sermons by these presbyters. Although the bishop was the normal celebrant, *S.* 227 shows that it was also possible for a presbyter to be so, a power also attested in Cyprian's letters (*Epp.* 15.1; 16; 17.2; 31.6; 34.1, 3), evidently if the bishop were absent. In the civil bureaucracy the prefect's deputy had no authority if the prefect were present (Ambrosiaster, *Col.* ii.17, 188, 21 [Vogel]).

38. At Rome a presbyter would be ordained only on the recommendation of one of the seven deacons of the city and was paid less than a deacon (Jerome, *Ep.* 146.2 to Evangelus). Ambrosiaster (*Quaestiones* 101) attacks the Roman deacons for their arrogance.

chumens whom he will baptize on Holy Saturday; he reconciles penitents on Maundy Thursday.[39] His presbyters share in the prayer and imposition of hands at the ordination of other presbyters, but play no part when their bishop joins other bishops to consecrate a new bishop at a neighbouring town. The bishop embodies the universality of the *Catholica*.

But the bishop is more than dispenser of word and sacrament. He has social functions. St. Paul forbade believers to go to law before secular magistrates 'who count for nothing in the Church' (1 Cor. 6:4). Disagreements must therefore go to arbitration. The third-century *Didascalia*[40] describes how early on Monday mornings the bishop sits, flanked by his clergy in the manner of secular magistrates with legal assessors,[41] to seek reconciliation — which in a bishop's court mattered more than 'justice'. Just as in the apse of the basilica his teaching cathedra would be elevated and adorned with fine coverings,[42] so also in the *secretarium* where he normally held his *audientia,* the throne was raised on a dais.[43] Martin of Tours, to whom the dignified aspects of a bishop's role were abhorrent, sat on a rustic tripod in both church and sacristy. This was thought most exceptional.[44]

39. Maundy Thursday was customary at Rome: Innocent I to Decentius, *Ep.* 25.7, 10 (*PL* 20.559); *Sacramentarium Gelasianum* I 28 (p. 63 Wilson = 352f. Mohlberg; A. Chavasse, *Le sacramentaire Gélasien* (1957), 150f.). At Milan Ambrose reconciled penitents on 'the day on which the Lord delivered himself up for us' (*Ep.* 20.(76).26, *CSEL* 82,3, p. 124), i.e. Maundy Thursday. For Africa there is no precise evidence of the day, but Augustine, *S. Guelf.* 9, is a Holy Week sermon on penitence. In general, Augustine has much more to say about the believer's daily contrition than about juridical acts of reconciliation.

40. *Didascalia Apostolorum,* XI (ii 45), p. 111 (Connolly). The Council of Tarraco (canon 4) in 516 forbids bishops to hear cases on Sundays. Some cases of arbitration are recorded in papyri, see e.g. P Oxy 893 s.VI and 903 s.IV, the latter recording a bitter dispute between husband and wife; neither involve ecclesiastical arbiters. But in BGU 103 s.VI–VII an abbot arbitrates. That 'good Christians' would take disputes to arbitration is axiomatic for Augustine, *c. du. epp. Pelag.* III 5,14; *En. in Ps.* 80.21. Scythians in the sixth century B.C. entrusted arbitrations to their shamans (Herodotus, iv 23).

41. For the system see Augustine, *Conf.* 6.10,16; 8,6.13. Providing ignorant judges with expert assessors was a Roman custom thought ludicrous by the Persians (Ammianus Marcellinus 23.6.82).

42. Aug., *Ep.* 23.3. The 'Charta Cornutiana' recording Valila's donation to a country church near Tivoli in 471 (DACL 3 881–884) and many entries in the *Liber Pontificalis* illustrate the point.

43. *En. in Ps.* 126.3; *S.* 23.1; *S. Denis* 17.2, p. 134, 1 (Morin). Augustine's evidence for the audientia episcopalis is gathered by C. Munier, *Augustinus-Lexikon,* s.v. (1990). There is a monograph on the papal throne at Rome by N. Gussone, *Thron und Inthronisation des Papstes* (1978).

44. Sulpicius Severus, *Dial.* II 1.3, p. 181 (Halm).

Once Constantine had given the bishop's decisions legal force — to the astonishment of high bureaucrats[45] — bishops acquired a wider standing. They could be saluted in the street with bowed head,[46] much as in England as late as 1930 a priest was acknowledged with raised hat by a respectful passer-by. Socrates records the custom of standing when a bishop came into a room.[47] Like an emperor or senator, his hand could be kissed.[48] Like an aristocrat he would be addressed as an abstraction ('Your Perfection', 'Your Beatitude')[49] and returned the compliment by addressing his congregation as 'Your Love' (*Caritas Vestra*).

It was no great step from being arbiter in quarrels to being sent as imperial ambassador; the earliest example is Eusebius of Nicomedia sent by Licinius to Constantine in 324.[50] Ammianus records others.[51] A bishop-ambassador might be suspected of neutrality. At Bezabde, besieged by the Persians, the bishop was sent to parley with the enemy; as the next attack hit the weakest part of the wall, he was thought a traitor.[52] To redeem Persian prisoners the Romans would not release, the bishop of Amida amazed by selling his church plate: his cause was humanity. (The redemption of pris-

45. *Constit. Sirmond.*, 1 of 5 May 333, addressed to Ablabius, praetorian prefect (text in Monmsen and Meyer, *Theodosiani Libri XVI* etc. I, 2, p. 907).

46. 'Submisso capite', Aug., *Ep.* 33.5.

47. *HE* vi.11.16.

48. To be admitted to an emperor's kiss was a ceremonial sign of welcome and approval: Ambrose, *Ep.* 24 (30).3 (*CSEL* 82, 1, p. 209); Hilary, *contra Constantium* 10 (*PL* 10.587A). For senators cf. Ammian. Marc. 28.4.10. A bishop's kiss signified a blessing: Aug., *De civ. Dei* 22.8. No kiss could be exchanged with schismatic enemies of peace: *En. in Ps.* 124.10. F. Cabrol in DACL, s.v. 'Baiser' gathers evidence for the liturgical kiss of peace. W. Kroll in Pauly-Wissowa, *Suppl.* V (1931), s.v. 'Kuss' gathers ancient evidence from classical texts.

49. E.g. Basil, *Epp.* 57, 66, 69, 80, 96, 100, 121, 173, 206, 254. Augustine's letters have such formulas as 'tua paternitas' (*Ep.* 12.13, Divjak), 'religio tua' (*c. Gaudentium* 1.3), 'domine venerabilis' (*Ep.* 22.2).

50. This embassy is recorded in the material drawn from Philostorgius in the Life of Constantine in the eleventh-century codex gr. 22 in the Angelica Library, Rome; see Bidez's edition of Philostorgius, p. 180,16. Constantine's letter to the Church of Nicomedia accuses Eusebius of being a dedicated supporter of Licinius (H.G. Opitz, *Urkunden zur Geschichte des Arianischen Streites* = Athanasius, *Werke* III 1, Lief. 2, p. 60, 4ff.).

51. E.g. Valens's negotiations with the Goths before the battle of Adrianople in 378 (Ammian. Marc. 31.12.8) or the African rebel Firmus with the magister militum Theodosius (29.5.15). Other examples are catalogued in the article 'Gesandschaft' in *Reallexikon für Antike und Christentum*, by J. F. Matthews.

52. Ammian. Marc. 20.7.9. Caesarius of Aries suffered a similar accusation of treachery, on a charge of betraying his city to the Burgundians, and was exiled for a time to Bordeaux (*Vita* i.21, ed. Morin II, p. 304).

oners was held to justify the sale of church plate.[53]) In his Life of Epiphanius of Pavia, Ennodius describes his hero as trusted by both sides in quarrels between princes. In the negotiations, however, between Valentinian II at Milan and the 'usurper' Magnus Maximus at Trier, Ambrose found himself in danger and had to represent his audience with Maximus as an abrasive exchange of discourtesies.[54]

The bishop's role as arbiter in disputes and as intercessor with the mighty led ambitious men to seek ordination.[55] Moreover, the *audientia episcopalis* was soon found to need professionally trained lawyers, who also became useful in defending church property when wills were contested.[56] Hence the office of *defensor ecclesiae*. Arbitrations brought the *defensor* fees, but were less costly for the contesting parties than a case in the magistrates' courts where, even if one won the case, the legal costs normally exceeded any gains.[57] Arbitrations brought the bishop anxiety. He was expected to defend the poor, always a substantial proportion of his plebs. It was tough to arbitrate in a family row,[58] or if the controversy were between a rich Christian legally in the right and a pauper for whom a bishop was expected to give protection.[59] Favour to the pauper brought charges of bribery and cordial hatred from those who lost. When an individual and the Church were rival claimants for a property, some bishops conceded rather than fight, but then found they had lost other friends. Ambrose advised bishops to avoid arbitrating in money disputes.[60]

53. Socrates, *HE* 7.21. The fact that the gold and silver vessels had evidently been presented by citizens of Amida made the bishop's action particularly astonishing. For the sale of plate to redeem Roman citizens, see Ambrose, *De officiis* II 28.136–143; Possidius, *Vita Aug.* 24. Justinian forbade clergy to sell church plate for any other purpose: *Cod. Just.* I 2.21. On Caesarius's ransoming of captives at Aries, see W. Klingshirn in *Journal of Roman Studies* 75 (1985), 183–203. He enraged some by selling church treasures to ransom enemies of Aries taken prisoner by the Ostrogoths (*Vita Caesarii* i.32–33, ed. Morin II, 1942, 308–309).

54. *Ep.* 24 (30) (*CSEL* 82,1, 207–215), reporting to Valentinian II and the consistory at Milan towards the end of 384, at a time when Ambrose could well have been suspected of hoping for victory for Magnus Maximus in order to secure Nicene orthodoxy against the Milanese court's pressure to tolerate anti-Nicene worship in the city.

55. Explicit in Athanasius, *Historia Arianorum* 8.1.

56. Good matter on *defensores ecclesiae* is gathered by J. Bingham, *Antiquities of the Christian Church* III xi (Oxford edition, 1855, I, 348–356). Silvanus of Tarsus first used a lay lawyer (Socrates 7,37,17).

57. Basil, *Ep.* 307.

58. Augustine, *Tract. in ev. Joh.* 30.8.

59. *En. in Ps.* 32.ii.12. Cf. 26.ii.13; *Qu. in Hept.* ii.88.

60. *De officiis* II 29.150–151 and II 24.125. A bishop would encounter bitter hostility from

Money matters troubled bishops. They were trustees of the Church chest, expected to raise from the wealthy funds to feed the poor listed on the 'matricula pauperum'.[61] The plebs thought ill of a bishop if he refused a legacy from a father who angrily disinherited his children. Augustine incurred odium for refusing a property entailed with a legal responsibility to provide a ship for the annona; a lucrative thing to have, but if the ship were wrecked, there was a duty to replace it and the value of the lost cargo; moreover, survivors would be tortured at the inquiry, and no bishop could be a party to that.[62]

Protecting the poor was not simple. Many texts attest the oppression of free wage labourers, organized intimidation, and protection rackets. People went in fear of being murdered.[63] Criminals would confidently boast that their patron would protect them,[64] and many judges were open to bribes.[65]

The relation of bishops to civil authority was often uneasy. Bishops offered sanctuary to people in trouble. Augustine would not hand over a truly penitent murderer, though aware this incurred strong criticism,[66] and recalled the courage of Firmus, bishop of Thagaste before Constantine's time,

---

the person against whom his decision was given (Aug., *S.* 125.8). Plotinus (*Vita* 9) succeeded in making no enemies, though arbitrating many disputes in Rome.

61. John Chrysostom, *in 1 Cor. Hom.* 21.7 (*PG* 61.179); Augustine, *c.ep. Parm.* III 2.16; *Ep.* 20.2 (Divjak).

62. Aug., *S.* 355. A law of 390 laid on the heirs of *navicularii* the obligation to pay for ships if wrecked (*Cod. Theod.* XIII 5.19). Discussion by R. Cagnat, 'L'annone d'Afrique', in *CR. Acad. Inscr.* 1916, 247–271, reprinted in *Cahiers de Tunisie* 25 (1977), 205–235.

Hostility to bishops and the Church could be caused when children were virtually disinherited by their parents' benefactions to the Church and to the poor thereby supported; cf. Palladius, *Historia Lausiaca* 66.1.

63. Aug., *En. in Ps.* 96.17.

64. *En. in Ps.* 113.ii.13.

65. Bribery was all-pervasive in the lawcourts. Among many references see, for example, Ammianus 15.13.2; Jerome, *in Sophon.* II p. 720 (*PL* 25.1442B, 'iudices . . . vendentes iustitiam'); Augustine, *Ep.* 153,24; *S.* 133.2; *Tract. in ev. Joh.* 27.10. Pelagius observed that judges were corrupted by 'love, hate, fear and avarice' (*in Rom.* 2.2, p. 19, 16, Souter). Aug., *Conf.* 6.10.16, records the integrity and courage of Alypius withstanding bribery and threats from a powerful senator wanting a privilege to which he was not entitled. Some judges could be either intimidated or bribed into passing sentences of death (Symmachus, *orat.* 4.6.; Palladius, *Historia Lausiaca* 38.5); Pliny, *Ep.* 2.11, shows that this was not a corruption first appearing in the fourth century. John Chrysostom (*in ev. Joh.* 82.4, *PG* 59.446) describes the lawcourts as agencies for judicial murder and theft. The clerk of the court expected a tip from both sides, and sometimes this was a large sum (Aug., *Ep.* 153.24).

66. *S.* 82.11.

who hid a man on the run from arrest; when interrogated, Firmus said that he would neither lie nor betray a man, and thereby won pardon for his refugee.[67] In practice, as both Basil and Augustine candidly confess, bishops had little power to help delinquents.[68] The penitence crucial in a bishop's eyes looked less impressive to magistrates.[69] It was risky to give asylum to a runaway slave whose owner was rich and influential. Basil observed that 'authorities can become deeply irritated by episcopal interventions'.[70] His campaign against the dividing of Cappadocia into two provinces, though he was evidently voicing civic feeling at Caesarea, earned him hostility at a very high level.[71]

Nevertheless the bonds of class and interest could bring officials and bishops together. A bishop was expected to write recommendations — to Augustine's distaste.[72] (He used to quote 'I have too much regard for my own reputation to vouch for that of my friends'.[73])

The custom of having charges against bishops and clergy heard in ecclesiastical courts, first enacted by Constantius II in 355 and, after some fluctuations in policy, accepted by the late fifth century, extended to the western Church the *praescriptio fori* by which different departments of the bureaucracy had jurisdictional privileges with their own courts.[74]

Porphyry remarked that bishops were mainly selected by rich women.[75] His estimate has surprising support in John Chrysostom.[76] Yet once in office the bishop's power base lay mainly in the poor. (Did the rich rely on him to

---

67. *De mendacio* 23.

68. Basil, *Ep.* 317; Aug., *Ep.* 22 (Divjak).

69. Aug., *Ep.* 155.11. Basil, *Ep.* 112, asks for mercy to an admitted criminal now in prison.

70. Basil, *Ep.* 107.

71. *Ep.* 79. Though his campaign was unsuccessful, the irritation caused to the praetorian prefect and the high chamberlain shows that Basil was not uninfluential and knew how to use his aristocratic connections.

72. Aug., *Ep.* 151.2.

73. Possidius, *Vita Augustini* 20.

74. *Cod. Theod.* XVI 2.12. Further references and discussion in A. H. M. Jones, *Later Roman Empire* (1964), 491–492. In the east Basil had more of a struggle than western bishops to establish the authority of his episcopal court; see (e.g.) *Epp.* 73 and 286, asking for transfer to his court of the trial of thieves who stole clothing during a church service; 'The terror of the Lord can achieve what a flogging does not'.

75. Cited by Jerome, *in Esaiam* II.iii.12, p. 57 (*PL* 24.67 C). The lady Lucilla at Carthage early in the fourth century offers a notorious instance.

76. *De Sacerdotio* III 9 (pp. 162–164, Malingrey, 1980). Jerome sadly observed that unedifying motives often played a part in the selection of a bishop (*adv. Iovin.* I 34; cf. *Ep.* 69.10).

keep them passive?) The process of electing a new bishop was complicated by the tension between the electing plebs and the consecrating bishops from other churches of the province.[77] Scandals occurred in which competing candidates hired a claque to shout for them when the plebs met for discussion.[78] Jerome knew of some who 'tried to buy a bishopric with gold'.[79] As in modern democracies, it was thought wicked to bribe the electors with one's own money but acceptable to bribe them with theirs: generous distributions to the poor, financed from loans repaid from the Church chest after successful election, were a means by which ambitious men achieved a bishopric. Basil says the election of 'Arian' bishops favoured by the court was thus manipulated.[80] The most notorious of such elections was that of Pope Symmachus in 498. His repayment of debts was hindered by Theodoric's ruling that he could not have the temporalities of the see until a synod declared him innocent of unedifying friendships with notorious old flames of his unregenerate youth, and by the synod's disavowal of jurisdiction over the Pope, in this or any other matter. Years later, Ennodius reveals, Symmachus had not repaid the bishop of Milan 400 solidi used to bribe persons 'whose names it is not safe to mention in writing'.[81]

The role of the consecrating bishops predominated more and more over the plebs whose veto, however, produced a number of *episcopi vagantes* not accepted by the plebs to whom they had been appointed.[82] Ex-

77. A striking example at Mauretanian Caesarea (Cherchel) in Augustine, *Ep.* 22 (Divjak). Basil, *Ep.* 230, tells the leading laity of Nicopolis to support the election as bishop of the candidate proposed by the bishops responsible for the consecration, the city being the scene of confrontation between pro- and anti-Nicene factions (*Ep.* 240). A good study of the erosion of the power of the plebs in election is R. Gryson, 'Les élections episcopales en Orient au IVe siècle', *RHE* 74 (1979), 301–344; a similar study of the west, *RHE* 75 (1980), 257–283.

78. See canon 2 of the Council of Serdica (342). The method was evidently that employed by candidates for secular office.

79. *Contra Rufinum* I 32 (PL 23.424D; p. 92, Lardet, 1983). At the time when public offices normally went to the highest bidder with cash, it seemed natural to hand out douceurs if one wanted to be a bishop.

80. *Ep.* 92.

81. Ennodius, *Ep.* 10, p. 78 (Hartel). A fuller account in my *Boethius* (1981), 31–41.

82. Not all were as fortunate as Proclus, consecrated in 426 for Cyzicus by patriarch Sisinnius though the plebs had given their vote to the monk Dalmatius. Proclus simply stayed in Constantinople where he acquired such repute as a preacher that, in spite of being twice passed over at the vacancies of 427 and 432, he finally became patriarch in 434 until his death in 446. His career is traced by W. Ensslin in *PWK* 23,1, 183–186. On his sermons see F. J. Leroy, *L'Homilétique de Proclus de Constantinople,* Studi e Testi 247 (1967), and thereon M. Aubineau in *REG* 85 (1972), 572–596. M. Geerard, *Clavis* 5800–5915. Synesius,

cept for Constantinople, imperial nominations were rare in the East. In the West they became common in Merovingian Gaul: any episcopal consecration there required royal assent. For Rome, a Byzantine city, Pelagius I was nominated by Justinian, but could not get the minimum three bishops to consecrate; he had to be content with two laying on of hands and a presbyter representing the bishop of Ostia, normal consecrator of the Pope.[83] (Perhaps the see was vacant.) Despite vehement protestation of orthodoxy he found it hard to get the cooperation and communion of the Italian and Gallic bishops.

A strong bishop could be a thorn in the side of government. Athanasius withstood Constantius when the emperor wished for toleration of Arian bishops, and Basil of Caesarea similarly withstood the praetorian prefect Modestus requiring him to hold communion with Arians (though he did not refuse communion to the emperor Valens).[84] Ambrose opposed Theodosius I over the massacre at Thessalonica and obliged the emperor to accept penance. John Chrysostom's conflict with the empress Eudoxia, when her desire for land in Constantinople dispossessed very poor people, contributed to his fall.

If a governor were an orthodox Christian, the power of a metropolitan could be even greater, since he could excommunicate — which meant not merely exclusion from the eucharist but a social boycott by all Church people. In 371 Athanasius excommunicated a governor of Libya for gross cruelty and licentiousness, and by writing round to other provinces ensured that the delinquent governor would not find things easier if he were transferred elsewhere.[85]

Nevertheless, unless they felt grave moral scandal, bishops were on the

---

Ep. 66 (67), pp. 119–120 (Garzya), complains of the trouble caused by wandering bishops rejected by their plebs or even unwilling to occupy their sees. Canon 16 of the Council of Antioch (ascribed to that of 341) rigidly forbids wandering bishops to take a vacant see, even if wanted by the plebs. The critics of Valens, bishop of Mursa, claimed that in his ambition to achieve translation to Aquileia, he had stirred up a riot in which the bishop of Aquileia lost his life, and then bribed a group to invite him to the see: CSEL 65.128.

83. *Liber Pontificalis* I 303, Duchesne. His protestation of orthodoxy is in *Ep.* 7 (ed. Gasso and Batlle, Montserrat, 1956). For the bishop of Ostia as consecrator of the Pope see Augustine, *Brev. Coll. c. Donat.* iii 16, 29.

84. Vividly described by Gregory of Nazianzos, *or.* 43.48–51 and by Gregory of Nyssa, *contra Eunomium* I 127ff., Jaeger.

85. Basil, *Ep.* 61. When a later governor of Libya, Andronicus, nailed to the church door a proclamation that here was no right of asylum, Synesius threatened excommunication against anyone who ate or spoke with the governor (*Ep.* 42 (58)).

side of law and order.[86] Jerome thought the alliance between bishops and magistrates repressive of the legitimate interests of the poor.[87]

A bishop aspired by means of his sacramental, teaching, and social roles to get his people to heaven, to teach them to pray, to meditate for at least some moments of the day, especially morning and evening. Yet virtually all bishops found themselves so immersed in the active life that there was almost no chance of personal contemplation (a point sharply made in a self-pitying letter of Synesius).[88] Augustine found the 'sarcina episcopi' was heavy: yet 'if all contemplation is abandoned, the burden of office becomes unbearable'.[89] Mary and Martha symbolise contemplation and action; in this life we are all Marthas and must wait for the next to join Mary.[90]

The monk aspired to join Mary in this life. Small monastic communities existed long before monasteries.[91] The fourth century saw the provision of institutions to assist and safeguard communities dedicated to the quest for the vision of God in holiness. Why this movement occurred when it did is a question to which only partial answers can be given. Was it reaction against the consequence of Constantine suddenly making Christianity socially respectable, so that a bishop might be guest at the governor's dinner table, and indeed return senatorial hospitality on a notable scale?[92] ('Make me bishop of Rome', said Praetextatus, 'and I will become a Christian'.[93]) Ammianus thought, as Origen did, that the bishops of great cities had lost the simplicity and frugality of country bishops.[94] Did it seem necessary to create alternative institutional forms to assert otherworldly aspirations? Did the monk wish to recover the heroism of the martyrs, continuing the combat with evil powers through feats of self-sacrifice? The similarity of shrines for

---

86. Ambrose, *Ep.* 40 (74).6 (*CSEL* 82,3, p. 58): 'sacerdotes enim turbarum moderatores sunt, studiosi pacis, nisi cum et ipsi moventur iniuria dei aut ecclesiae contumelia'. Augustine's defence of law and order against Donatist violence is seen in *Ep.* 185 and *c. Cresconium* III 43,47–59,65.

87. *In Michaiam* I 2, 9–10, p. 457 (*PL* 25.1229 A).

88. *Ep.* 41 (57), p. 66, 7ff. (Garzya).

89. *De civ. Dei* 19.19.

90. Aug., *S.* 104.4; 169.17; *S. Guelf.* 4. See A. M. La Bonnardière, 'Marie et Marthe, figures de l'église d'après Augustin', *Vie Spirituelle* 86 (1952), 404–427.

91. Aug., *Tract. in ev. Joh.* 97.4: Monasteries and xenodochia existed long before the words were coined.

92. Jerome, *Ep.* 52.11.

93. Jerome, *adv. Joh. Hieros.* 8 (*PL* 23.377C).

94. Ammianus 27.3.12–15.

martyrs and for holy men, and the intercessions petitioned from both, show that for the people they ranked together.[95]

To say monasteries answered social needs is not to concede that these provided the initial impulse creating them; but quickly they acquired a social and economic function. A starving unemployed labourer was better fed, clothed, and housed in a monastery. Pachomius's houses in the loop of the Nile offered shelter and work on the land for thousands of peasants from derelict villages.[96] North African monasteries drew 'slaves, freedmen, peasants, artisans'. But it was 'unclear whether they come to serve God or are refugees from a life of toil and are in want of food and clothing'. Moreover, 'they may wish to be respected by those who once despised and trampled on them'.[97] Parents dedicated young girls as virgins to solve an economic problem, not because the girls had a vocation.[98] The alternative would be to sell them to slavetraders.[99]

Augustine admitted no clergy to his monastery except from his own diocese, to avert friction with other diocesans.[100] Pachomius refused to admit any clergy regarding them as bossy people productive of envy and faction.[101] Problems in the Pachomian foundations were created first by their economic success,[102] but then by the open ambition of some monks to be higumen or bishop.[103] By contrast Augustine thought monks had a duty to accept a call to the episcopate.[104] Athanasius, Basil, and Augustine did much to bring bishops and monks together. Moreover, both ascetics and bishops exercised *parrhesia,* candour, in addressing dignitaries. To bishops failing in austerity monks were expected to be rude. (Admittedly, Nathanael in the Egyptian desert was accused by the devil of pride when he did not provide the normal courtesy of an escort for seven bishops who visited him. The happy mean

95. Sozomen, *HE* III 14.28; Theodoret, *Philoth. hist.* III 10.13 and 16.

96. *Liber Orsiesii* 47, p. 140,5ff. (Boon).

97. Aug., *Op. Monach.* 25. Some joined monasteries to transfer their debts to the taxman (Basil's Shorter Rule 94, *PG* 31.1148) much as Paul, bishop of Cataquas, Numidia, put his huge debt to the fisc on the Church chest (Aug., *Epp.* 85.2; 96.2; 97.3).

98. Basil, *Ep.* 199.18. Jerome (*Ep.* 130.6 to Demetrias) says 'mothers normally dedicate as virgins deformed or crippled daughters for whom no husband can be found'.

99. E.g. Aug., *Ep.* 10 (Divjak). Basil, *PG* 31.264A, copied by Ambrose, *Nabuthe* 8.40 (*CSEL* 32,2, p. 490, 17ff.).

100. *Ep.* 64.3.

101. *Pachomii Vita Prima* 27.

102. *Vita Prima* 145–146.

103. *Ibid.,* 118 and 126.

104. *Ep.* 48. Deserters from monasteries ought not to be ordained (*Ep.* 60.1; 64.3).

was hard to achieve.[105]) John Chrysostom at Constantinople was a notable practitioner of *parrhesia,* and was author of a defence of monks against their critics.[106] Against some bishops monks became the voice of protest. The anti-Origenist monks of Egypt coerced Theophilus of Alexandria into reversing his policy to disciples of Evagrius.[107] Callinicus's Life of Hypatius describes extreme tension between abbot Hypatius of Rufinianae and the bishop of Chalcedon, Eulalius, when Eulalius failed to support the monks in protesting against a proposal by the city prefect at Constantinople, Leontius, in 435 to revive the Olympic games that used to be held in the theatre at Chalcedon until abolished by Constantine the Great. Hypatius believed there would be idolatrous associations; the bishop was sure no sacrifice would be offered. Hypatius won the day, and thereafter Eulalius could not find a good word to say for him. The abbot had earlier been prominent among the monks opposed to Nestorius patriarch of Constantinople.[108]

The ascetics who caused most trouble to the bishops in fourth- and fifth-century Syria and Asia Minor were the Messalians. (There is reason to think Hypatius of Rufinianae was among those influenced by this movement.) Apart from the evidence of the critics who attacked Messalians for heresy, the great body of testimony from inside the movement is found in the 'Homilies of Macarius' or Symeon of Mesopotamia. The term 'Messalians' derives from the Syriac, and means the people of prayer. They were bands of wandering ascetics, both men and women together (which produced occasional dramas exploited by their critics), indifferent to church institutions. What mattered was inward sensation; the felt experience of the Spirit in intense prayer was alone strong enough to defeat the radical sinfulness at the heart of man, the devil hiding away in the most inner secret chambers of the soul, so well concealed that he was not driven out by baptism or eucharist. A thesis with the Messalians was not peculiar to them, but is mentioned by many of their opponents, namely that manual work is harmful to the soul.[109] Messalians accused unsympathetic bishops of being 'false apostles,

---

105. Palladius, *Historia Lausiaca* 16. A normal courtesy: Basil, *Ep.* 98.

106. *PG* 47.319–386.

107. Socrates, *HE* VI 7.

108. Callinicus, *Vita Hypatii* 32–33 and 39 (ed. SC).

109. Origen once remarks that Jesus is not recorded to have done manual work: his father, not he, was a carpenter (*c. Cels.* 6.36). Augustine met wandering monks who urged that when St. Paul (Phil. 3) confessed that even he had not attained spiritual perfection, that was because as a tentmaker he had engaged in manual labour (*Tract. in ev. Joh.* 122.3). Though Augustine believed that monks should do manual work, meanwhile singing *divina*

modern Pharisees having only outward show, whited sepulchres, men with only second-hand religion'.[110] They scorned rules both of bishops and of monastic leaders like Basil. One leader rejected the common sense practice of prescribing certain psalms for daily offices on the ground that this inhibited the spontaneity of the Spirit.[111]

By 400 some bishops were chosen for their high culture, and especially their rhetorical skills. Ascetics were reserved towards high culture to a degree which Synesius thought embarrassing.[112] But upper class ascetics, Arsenius and Evagrius, recognized in the desert fathers a virtue and wisdom absent in posh society. When Evagrius spoke too didactically at Kellia, the priest rebuked him: 'If you were at home, you would have many calls to be a bishop and would be in charge of many people; here you sit as a foreigner'.[113] The unregenerate Augustine, on learning of the monks at Trier, cried out to Alypius: 'Uneducated people are capturing heaven, while we, with our high culture lacking all heart, roll in the mud'.[114]

John Cassian reports the advice from the desert: 'Flee women and bishops', being equal distractions to hesychast contemplatives.[115] Just as civil governors found bishops an alternative focus of authority to their own, so bishops experienced the same with monks and nuns. The proliferation of monasteries caused disruption, and the Council of Chalcedon ruled that no monastery might be founded without the bishop's consent and jurisdiction.[116] In conflict with heresy and pagan temples, monks acquired a reputation for violence.[117] Bishops used them as a private army, e.g. to rescue condemned

---

cantica (*Op. Monach.* 20), yet he would not criticise those who lived on alms (*Ep.* 157.38). The Messalian view is in Gregory of Nyssa, *De virginitate* 23.

110. Hom. B 34 and 40, p. 62,11 (Berthold); cf. the standard Fifty Homilies (H) edited by H. Dörries: H 43,2; 16.7 and 11.11, etc.

111. Lampetius in Photius, *Bibl. cod.* 52.

112. *Dio* 7 (*Opuscula*, p. 251, Terzaghi, 1944).

113. *PG* 65.176A.

114. *Conf.* VIII 8, 19.

115. *Inst.* xi.18.

116. Canon 4. The tendency to claim that monasteries are somehow beyond the jurisdiction of the diocesan bishop appears in Epiphanius's letter to bishop John of Jerusalem (= Jerome, *Ep.* 51). Pope Hormisdas (*Ep.* 150.2, p. 989 Thiel; Caesarius, ed. Morin II, 1942, p. 126) exempted Caesarius of Arles' nunnery from the jurisdiction of his successors.

117. Ambrose, *Ep.* 41 (extra coll. 1).27 (*CSEL* 82, 3, p. 160), quotes Theodosius as saying 'Monachi multa scelera faciunt', and the magister militum Timasius followed the emperor with a vehement speech against monks. (Timasius had a Christian wife, Pentadia, and there is no reason to think him a pagan; cf. Ensslin in *PWK* VIA, 1240–41).

criminals being escorted to execution.[118] There were always to be wandering monks attached to no house.

Chalcedon's concern that monasteries be under the bishop was at first shared by western councils.[119] But occasional interferences by bishops in the election of abbots or in a monastery's revenues led to papal moves to exempt monasteries from their local diocesan.[120] Thereby popes could hinder individual bishops and regional synods from becoming uncomfortably independent.

The tension between bishops and monks is not to be overstated. In fifth-century Gaul many monasteries were founded by bishops (Arles, Autun, Bourges, Le Mans, Metz, Paris, Poitiers); and royal foundations followed.[121] The Frankish king Chilperic made the famous complaint that in his kingdom bishops had all the money and the power. Already in Ambrose's time it was commonly said that emperors could envy bishops more than bishops envied emperors.[122]

A bishop was largely tied to his city. For the missionary task of evangelising the countryside he depended on landowners providing churches and carrying their coloni with them. Monasteries were also important here.[123] Monks, actively engaged in agriculture themselves, brought peasants and

118. Ambrose, *De officiis* II 21.102, thought this appropriate if it could be done without a major disturbance. Arcadius's law of 27 July 398 (*Cod. Theod.* IX 40.16) forbids this interference with the course of justice.

119. E.g. Agde (506) canon 27; Orleans I (511) canon 19.

120. Gregory the Great, *Reg.* 5.49. A well-known protest against such exemptions is St. Bernard of Clairvaux, *De consideratione* 3.4.14. It remains the case today that a new Roman Catholic abbot promises canonical obedience not to the diocesan bishop, by whom he is blessed, but to the Pope.

121. On monk-bishops in Gaul (Valerius of Cimiez, Faustas of Riez, Exuperius of Toulouse, Hilary of Arles, Lupus of Troyes, Germanus of Auxerre) see R. Nürnberg, *Askese als sozialer Impuls* (Bonn, 1988). Evidence for episcopal foundations is well set out by F. Prinz, *Askese und Kultur* (Munich, 1980), 31f. Even Synesius founded a monastery near Ptolemais (*Ep.* 126 of the year 413, discussed by Denis Roques, *Synesios de Cyrene et la Cyrenaique du Bas-Empire,* 1987, 377f.).

But bishops of monastic background who specially favoured monks in their appointments caused resentment among the secular clergy. The *Liber Pontificalis* (I 319) records how under Pope Deusdedit (615–618) the priests were recalled 'ad loca pristina', lost under Gregory the Great.

The use of monasteries as prisons for delinquent clergy (Cone. Epaonense 517, canon 22) may have contributed to tension.

122. Gregory of Tours, *Hist.* VI 33 (46). Cf. Ambrose, *Ep.* 76 (20).23 (*CSEL* 82, 3, p. 122).

123. Jerome, *Ep.* 58.4–5.

the Church closer together.[124] Benedict's Rule attached high value to manual work; already in Augustine and John Chrysostom it is a common theme that for the Christians there is dignity in manual labour. Monks had a potent work-ethic bringing success in agriculture. Moreover, writing books counted as manual work; so some monasteries became vehicles of high culture in the age when barbarian invasions had destroyed the old schools. Augustine, *De doctrina Christiana,* provided a curriculum. What began as a counter-culture ended by absorbing large parts of what it once opposed. For Cassiodorus and Alcuin the seven liberal arts are the seven pillars of wisdom mentioned in the Proverbs of Solomon (9:1).[125] By the time of Gregory the Great the literate bishops have been educated in monasteries. Thus it came about that bishops, at one time the focal point of dissident communities at odds with society, became major figures in their cities, with their cathedrals as centrally placed and distinguished buildings expressing the Christian conquest of the urban environment. Bishops were on the way to realizing Augustine's prophetic assertion that they are 'principes super omnem terram',[126] the obverse of which is the horrified observation of Gregory the Great: 'There is now almost no secular activity which is not administered by bishops'.[127]

124. Augustine knew farmers who were unenthusiastic about Christianity when they heard St. Paul telling them that God does not care about oxen (*En. in Ps.* 145.13). He assured his people that the one God gives *salus* not only to them but to their beasts, horses, sheep, and hens (*Tr. in Joh.* 34.3). Some bishops became determined evangelists of rural areas, encouraging owners of estates to build churches (*En. in Ps.* 103.iii.12) and especially to destroy pagan shrines (Maximus of Turin, *Sermo* 91.2; cf. 107.1). Cf. Rita Lizzi, *Vescovi e strutture ecclesiastiche nella città tardoantica* (Como, 1989), 193–202.

125. Cassiodorus, *Inst.* II praef. 2; Alcuin, *De grammatica, PL* 101.853. By Jerome's time the primary quality required in a bishop was eloquent preaching (*Dial. adv. Lucif.* 11). Such rhetoric was held in contempt by Jerome in his commentary on Ecclesiastes (ix.17, p. 467, Vallarsi).

126. *En. in Ps.* 44.32. Augustine might have been alarmed by the rite in Toledo cathedral when the Visigothic king and his army were going out to battle (M. Férotin, *Liber Ordinum,* 1904, 149–153).

127. *Hom. in Evangelia* 17.15: 'Ecce iam paene nulla est saeculi actio quam non sacerdotes administrent'.

The Origin of the Title 'Oecumenical Council'

There have been studies of the meaning of the term 'oecumenical' as an epithet of episcopal synods,[1] and this note is not intended to add to their number, but only to ask where the phrase came from. We do not know whether or not the Council of Nicaea described itself as 'oecumenical' in any official or even unofficial document. The extant documents of the council[2] speak of the assembly as 'the great synod', or 'the holy and great synod', or 'the sacred synod'—ἡ μεγάλη καὶ ἁγία σύνοδος, ἡ ἱερὰ σύνοδος—and certainly there was at Nicaea a powerful self-consciousness that this was the largest assembly of Christian bishops hitherto gathered in one place. Constantine's two letters to the Church of Alexandria and to the churches about the date of Easter are not conciliar documents. The emperor is led by his concern to magnify the authority of the council to lay great stress upon the number attending, so much so that he allows himself the exaggeration of saying that there were 300 bishops present, when in fact there seem only to have been about 220. (It is a reflection of the strength of the self-consciousness of the synod about its unique and exceptional character that all those who give a figure for the attendance overstate their case.) Even Constantine, however, does not specifically mention the world-wide nature of the representation of churches at Nicaea. The actual number of Western, Latin-speaking clergy present seems to have been so small that they could be counted on the fin-

1. E.g. A. Tuilier, 'Les sens de l'adjectif œcuménique dans la tradition apostolique et dans la tradition byzantine', *Nouvelle Revue théologique* 86 (1964), pp. 260–71; and the chapters by J. Anastasiou, J. D. Zizioulas, and S. L. Greenslade contributed to the World Council of Churches Study, *Councils and the Ecumenical Movement* (Geneva, 1968).

2. The canons and the beginning of the council's letter to the Church of Alexandria and Egypt (Opitz, Document 23) are especially important.

gers of one hand. Accordingly it might be thought actually unlikely that the epithet 'oecumenical' would have been used in 325 at the time of the council. Yet we are so insufficiently informed about the proceedings of the council that no safe conclusions can be drawn.

The first examples of the epithet 'oecumenical' being applied to the Nicene synod come almost simultaneously from the two opposing camps: first in the letter of the Egyptian synod of 338, which rehabilitated Athanasius after his canonical deposition at Tyre and his *de facto* restoration after Constantine's death. Admittedly the text of this letter is preserved for us by Athanasius in the *Apologia Secunda*,[3] written in the fifties of the century and certainly revised with verbal readjustments in subsequent editions, as Professor A. H. M. Jones proved in *The Journal of Theological Studies*.[4] We therefore cannot exclude the possibility that Athanasius, or a scribe, in the sixties or seventies yielded to the temptation to improve on the original text of 338 by inserting the golden epithet. But this is in no way a necessary hypothesis. The word also occurs in the *Vita Constantini* of Eusebius, whose authorship (to be provocative) I take to be the only plausible hypothesis.[5] Eusebius at first surprises his readers by writing in so fulsome a manner about the splendid nature of Constantine's initiative in calling an oecumenical council. With 'more than 250' bishops coming from many distant provinces, of which Eusebius enumerates twenty-four (the signatory lists would add a further fourteen), the scene recalled for him the Day of Pentecost[6]—not perhaps the impression one would gain from his letter to his church of Caesarea—and the unanimity of the conclusions, especially about Easter and the Melitian schismatics in Egypt, was a sure sign of the Spirit's operation.

When the Egyptian council of 338 and Eusebius of Caesarea give Nicaea the epithet 'world-wide', the historian tends to hear the overtones that this word later came to carry, and begins to be troubled by later theological prob-

---

3. Athanasius, *Apol. c. Arianos* 7.2.

4. *J.T.S.*, N.S.V (1954), pp. 224–27. The mention of Rufus, who took the records of the Mareotic commission in 335, as now holding the post of *speculator* in the *officium* of the Augustal Prefect of the diocese of Egypt, reveals a verbal modification made after 367–70 when the office of Augustalis was created.

5. Cf. F. Vittinghoff, 'Eusebius als Verfasser der Vita Constantini, *Rheinisches Museum*, N.F. 96 (1953), pp. 330–73; F. Winkelmann, 'Zur Echtheitsfrage der V.C. des Eusebius v. Caesarea', *Studii Clasice* 3 (1961), pp. 405–12 (showing that the silence of Jerome's *Vir. illustr.* 81 is irrelevant), and especially 'Zur Geschichte des Authentizitätsproblem der V.C.', *Klio* 40 (1962), pp. 187–243.

6. Eus., *V.C.* iii.6f.

lems: Is there a special category of councils with an authority not enjoyed by others? Whence do they derive this authority? Must they be summoned by an emperor? or by a pope? Do they derive their unique position from their ratification and reception by the faithful? Yet in 325 the grandiloquent word had no theological overtones at all. It is easy to show that it was almost everyday and perfectly natural.

From early in the third century B.C. onwards the actors or artists of Dionysus, the *technitai,* began to form themselves into local guilds or associations which were able to exert pressure to obtain for their members freedom of travel and immunity from hostile attentions.[7] In their early days the local guilds sometimes came into rivalry and conflict with one another. But about Mark Antony's time, they found it wise to constitute a wider professional association. Plutarch tells how all actors of the eastern provinces were required to assemble on Samos to entertain Antony and Cleopatra—circumstances that might well encourage the formation of a single association.[8] From Augustus they succeeded in winning special privileges; and in A.D. 43 Claudius granted them exemptions from taxes and liturgies. Several inscriptions of the times of Trajan, Hadrian, and Antoninus Pius record decisions of the μεγάλη ἱερὰ σύνοδος τῶν ἀπὸ τῆς οἰκουμένης περὶ τὸν Διόνυσον.[9] The association had its headquarters or central office in Rome, and an inscription records 'the great itinerant theatrical synod at Rome, guardian of the shrine' (presumably of the emperor?).

In the third century A.D. the actors joined with the guild of athletes to form a single association enjoying special tax privileges. Three papyri of the second and third centuries, all from Oxyrhynchus, record applications for tax relief by local citizens.[10] They cite imperial grants from Claudius, Severus, Caracalla, and Alexander, and append certificates to prove that the applicant in question is a fully paid-up subscribing member of the ἱερὰ μουσικὴ

7. For good statements of the evidence about the Dionysiac artists see Poland's article 'Technitai' (1934) in Pauly–Wissowa, and A. Pickard-Cambridge, *The Dramatic Festivals of Athens* (2nd ed. by John Gould and D. M. Lewis, Oxford, 1968), pp. 279–321 including the appended documents, and bibliography at p. 336.

8. Plutarch, *Ant.* 56. 7–8.

9. Pickard-Cambridge, op. cit., pp. 297ff. cites the texts in full.

10. *B.G.U.* iv. 1074, with P. Lond. 1176 (A.D. 194), re-edited by P. Viereck in *Klio* 8 (1908), pp. 413–26; P. Oxy. 2475–77 (A.D. 289); P. Oxy. 2610 (late third century). Diocletian and Maximian found it necessary to insist that exemptions be restricted to artists of proved distinction and lifelong career as actors, and should not be sold as honorific positions in the association. See the Latin papyrus text in Mitteis–Wilcken, *Grundzüge und Chrestomathie der Papyruskunde* ii. 2, no. 381; Cavenaile, *Corpus pap. lat.* 241; Pickard-Cambridge, p. 321.

οἰκουμενικὴ περιπολιστικὴ σύνοδος τῶν περὶ τὸν Διόνυσον τεχνιτῶν. Not only actors and athletes found that they derived advantage from this fine title. An undated inscription found in the theatre at Miletus and attesting the tax-exempt status of an athlete records an oecumenical council of linen-workers: τὸ οἰκουμενικὸν καὶ σεμνότατον συνέδριον τῶν λινουργῶν.[11] Games open to athletes from any city were also entitled 'oecumenical' in the third century A.D., as is attested in a remarkable Athenian inscription recording a herald Valerius Eclectus, citizen of many cities and victor in the sacred 'oecumenical games' of several places (Olympian, Pythian, Nemean, Isthmian, etc.), including those celebrating the millennium of Rome in A.D. 248 at which he won the supreme golden trophy.[12]

In short, the Christians borrowed the title 'oecumenical synod' from established usage, especially familiar because of the world-wide professional association of athletes and Dionysiac artists. Certainly when Eusebius of Caesarea, and the Egyptian Council of Alexandria in 338, used the epithet of destiny, they chose a word with a note of authority surrounding it; but at this early date they can hardly have been thinking of an oecumenical council as belonging to a special category of synod quite differentiated in esteem from all other assemblies. That development was a consequence of the Arian controversy, as is clear from Athanasius's use of the term to magnify the status of Nicaea in contrast with the Arian synods of the East.[13] If the epithet 'oecumenical' was actually used at the time in 325 (which on the evidence submitted here appears in no way unlikely), then the inscriptions and papyri about the artists of Dionysus might suggest that perhaps the term had some association in the first instance with the church's plea for exemption from tax.[14]

---

11. *Revue archéol.* 2, 1874, pp. 112f.

12. *I.G.* iii. 129.

13. E.g. Athanasius, *ad episc. Aeg.* 5–7; *de synodis* 14.; 21.1; *ad Afros* 2.1.

14. Cf. the resolution of the huge synod of Ariminum of 359 on precisely this point (*Cod. Theod.* xvi. 2.15). That in 325 the Christians had the highest hopes of tax relief from the emperor is evident from the well-known inscription of Orcistus in Phrygia (Dessau, *I.L.S.* 6091 = *Monumenta Asiae Minoris Antiqua*, vii. 305). That from Constantine's time onwards the treasury paid the church subsidies to support the clergy and the poor is certain (Athan., *Apol. c. Arian.* 18.2; Socr. ii.17; Theodoret, *H.E.* i.11.2; Eus., *V.C.* iv.28). But whether tax advantages for church property were gained by the Council of Nicaea remains obscure unless it was this assembly which won for the church exemption from *extraordinaria munera*, the situation assumed to be in force in 360 by *Cod. Theod.* xvi. 2.15 (cf. A. H. M. Jones, *The Later Roman Empire*, iii, p. 304 n. 65). It may perhaps have been by means of tax relief that Constantius was able so spectacularly to gain the submission of the wretched Western bishops

at Ariminum who signed away their faith. The decisions of ancient church councils were generally taken *en bloc,* as a single 'package', in which it was impossible to accept or reject one item without treating all the council's decisions in the same way. For example, Timothy Salophaciolus, Chalcedonian patriarch of Alexandria, could hope to win Egypt's assent to Chalcedon only if the resolution on the dignity of Constantinople could be annulled (Zachar. Mityl., *Chron.* iv. 10); conversely, patriarchs of Constantinople always had an interest in upholding Chalcedon, however minimal their personal enthusiasm for its Christology (*J.T.S.,* N.S. vi (1955), p. 27). If the suggestion that Nicaea succeeded in obtaining important fiscal relief is a well-founded conjecture, that might explain the astonishing extent of assent which the council's other decisions obtained—just as, *per contra,* its sixth canon subjecting Libya to Alexandrian jurisdiction seems to have reinforced the Arian sympathies of the Libyan metropolitan Secundus of Ptolemais (cf. *Harv. Theol. Rev.* liii (1960), pp. 171–95).

Faith and Order at the Council of Nicaea:
A Note on the Background of the Sixth Canon

I

At the Council of Nicaea all the bishops but two signed the creed and canons. This virtual unanimity must have been very gratifying to Constantine, and it represents no mean achievement in reconciliation on the emperor's part — for it is not what anyone would have expected after the dramatic events leading up to the calling of the council. The creed appears to have been on every ground acceptable to Alexander of Alexandria and to Ossius of Cordova. If it was not, they had only themselves to blame, since they had been chiefly responsible for its form and had previously agreed, at a meeting of the council's steering committee at Nicomedia, on the crucial word *homoousios*.[1] It is not so certain that the creed was equally acceptable to the extreme anti-Arians, Marcellus of Ancyra or Eustathius of Antioch. Eustathius seems to have been ill content that the Nicene fathers had not had the courage of their convictions and had failed to confirm the decisions of the Council of Antioch held shortly before it; in his view they should have roundly condemned the rank Arianism of Eusebius of Caesarea and his two friends, Theodotus of Laodicea and Narcissus of Neronias. We may reasonably doubt whether any document that Eusebius was conscientiously able to sign would have been regarded as satisfactory by Eustathius.[2] But neither Eustathius nor Marcellus would themselves have found difficulty with the content of the creed. And

---

1. Philostorgius, *H.E.* i.7.
2. Theodoret, *H.E.* i.8.1–5. The "Eusebius" of this attack is, I think, more likely to be the Caesarean than the Nicomedian. For the policy of Eustathius and the Council of Antioch in 325 see *J.T.S.,* new series ix (1958), p. 303.

there is no reason to suppose that the nineteenth canon, regulating the terms for the admission of members of the congregation loyal to Paul of Samosata, represented any policy other than that which Eustathius would have been happy to implement. So far as his own position was concerned, he could sign both creed and canons with an untroubled conscience.

On the other side of the house the outstanding feature is the exiguous size of the opposition to the creed. No doubt had any *Acta* been preserved we should know much more of the stern debates that took place. But it is astounding that, after the violent partisanship of the period immediately preceding the council, the creed should have been signed at the end with an apparently negligible pair of recalcitrants. The letter, preserved by Athanasius,[3] in which Eusebius of Caesarea explains to his church how he had come to accept the very extraordinary theology of the Nicene formula is, of course, the indispensable clue which reveals the way in which the creed was understood by many who had previously declared themselves to be for Arius and against Bishop Alexander of Alexandria. Not only Eusebius of Caesarea but Narcissus of Neronias, Theodotus of Laodicea, Macedonius of Mopsuestia, Patrophilus of Scythopolis, Maris of Chalcedon, and Aetius of Lydda, all appear among the signatories.[4] Above all the Bithynian bench, which had formerly been prominent in its outspoken opposition to Alexander of Alexandria, now discloses solid support for the council's decisions, following the powerful lead of Arius's friends, Eusebius of Nicomedia and Theognis of Nicaea. It is very possible that the reasoning of Eusebius of Caesarea's letter to his church is the outcome not of his own purely private thoughts, but represents the party line; it is a statement of a general theological platform, reached after anxious debate and the consumption of much midnight oil. The Eusebian group was without doubt

3. Athanasius, *de Decretis* 33 = Socrates, *H.E.* i.8.3s ff. = Theodoret, *H.E.* i.12. Athanasius (*de Decretis* 3, *de Synodis* 13) observes that Eusebius put his own individual interpretation on the creed, but that at least he accepted the formula (which is more than can be said of his successor Acacius). From *de Synodis* 37.2 it appears that in 359 at the time of the Council of Seleucia Eudoxius, Acacius and the radical group are using Eusebius's letter as evidence that the Nicene formula could not be conscientiously accepted by honest theologians, and urging that the hesitating homoiousian party could not continue to halt between two opinions on the basis which Eusebius's letter seemed to provide.

4. For the lists see *Patrum Nicaenorum Nomina,* edited by Gelzer, Hilgenfeld, and Cuntz (Leipzig: Teubner, 1898). The Latin lists, with which the Syriac closely agree, are best set out in C. H. Turner, *Ecclesiae Occidentalis Monumenta Iuris Antiquíssima,* I, pp. 35-102, where the most reliable tradition is represented in column V, as Turner himself later remarked (op. cit., I, fasc, ii, pars 3, praefatio p. xv). His conclusion has been reinforced by the detailed study of Honigmann in *Byzantion* xiv (1939), pp. 27-44.

a coalition of diverse standpoints, with Eusebius of Caesarea representing the position least approximating to that of Arius. Certainly he stood much nearer to Alexander of Alexandria than to Eusebius of Nicomedia. It appears from a passage of Sozomen, which has no equivalent in Socrates and is probably an extract from Sabinus of Heraclea, that (probably about 328) Eusebius of Nicomedia and Theognis of Nicaea also issued a statement to indicate the sense in which they had declared their assent to the Nicene creed. Sozomen adds that this statement rekindled the whole debate, but unhappily he does not reveal the nature of the glosses which they put upon the formula.[5]

Accordingly, the letter of Eusebius to the church of Caesarea is the sole surviving explanation of an astounding *volte-face*.

Eusebius of Caesarea himself was caught between two fires in 325, since he was being opposed not only by Eustathius of Antioch, but also, nearer home, by Macarius of Jerusalem. Macarius was one of the three bishops who had absolutely dissociated himself from the support given to Arius by several of the Palestinian bishops after Alexander of Alexandria had declared him excommunicate.[6] No doubt the Palestinians, led by Eusebius of Caesarea, supposed that history was repeating itself and that they were again being asked to grant asylum to a learned theologian of Alexandria, who like Origen had been misunderstood by his ecclesiastical superior. Macarius of Jerusalem stood out against his metropolitan's lead and, together with Philogonius of Antioch and Hellanicus of Tripolis, wholeheartedly supported the bishop of Alexandria.[7] He was also present at the Council of Antioch early in 325, led by Ossius of Cordova and by Philogonius's successor, Eustathius, which provisionally excommunicated Eusebius of Caesarea, Theodotus of Laodicea, and Narcissus of Neronias for their Arian sympathies.[8] At Nicaea, therefore, Macarius was in an attacking position; Eusebius of Caesarea was on the defensive, and had to prove his orthodoxy. The dramatic and unqualified support of Constantine

---

5. Sozomen, *H.E.* ii.32.7–8.

6. Sozomen, *H.E.* i.15.11. In his letter to Alexander of Byzantium (Theodoret, *H.E.* i.4.37), Alexander of Alexandria bitterly complains of the action of "three Syrian bishops," Eusebius of Caesarea, Paulinus of Tyre, and Patrophilus of Scythopolis, who have communicated with Arius.

7. Arius's letter to Eusebius of Nicomedia (Theodoret, *H.E.* i.5 = Epiphanius, *Panarion* lxix.6) informs him that he is being supported by Theodotus of Laodicea, Paulinus of Tyre, Athanasius of Anazarbus, Gregory of Berytus, and Aetius of Lydda, while Alexander of Alexandria is supported by Philogonius of Antioch, Macarius of Jerusalem, and Hellanicus of Tripolis.

8. See H. G. Opitz, *Urkunden zur Geschichte des Arianischen Streites* (= *Athanasius Werke,* Band III, 1), document 18.

saved the day for Eusebius, in that the emperor's personal intervention rescued him from condemnation by the extremists lined up against him. But in one fateful respect the emperor's ideas weakened the position of Caesarea: Constantine was mystical about the Holy Places.[9] It looks as if Macarius was able to exploit this mystique if it was he who extracted from the council the seventh canon awarding Aelia special honor. Although the canon concludes with a qualifying clause safeguarding the rights of Caesarea as the metropolis of the civil province, nevertheless the canon obviously marks the beginning of an attempt by the bishops of Jerusalem to create a patriarchate. In any event it is noteworthy that among the Palestinian signatories the first name is that of Macarius, while Eusebius's name stands fifth.

Eusebius had had a narrow escape, and must have counted himself lucky to have won the qualifying safeguard at all. He was no great ecclesiastical politician like his namesake of Nicomedia, and may well have nursed optimistic hopes that the rights still preserved to the metropolis by the seventh canon would continue to be respected by future bishops of Jerusalem.[10] But, with this one exception of Caesarea, there was nothing in the administrative arrangements of the Nicene canons, with their explicit program of concentrating power in the hands of the bishop of the provincial capital, that might cause misgiving to the leading Arian bishops at the council. The Nicene decisions on matters of Order provided no ground for thinking twice about accepting the statement of the Faith.

9. See especially W. Telfer, "Constantine's Holy Land Plan," in *Studia Patristica,* ed. Aland and Cross, i (Texte und Untersuchungen lxiii, Berlin, 1957), pp. 696–700.

10. The dispute between Acacius of Caesarea and Cyril of Jerusalem (Sozomen, *H.E.* iv.25; Theodoret, *H.E.* ii.26) left Caesarea in a position of temporary superiority. About 392 the clergy and people of Gaza went to Caesarea for their new bishop (Marcus Diaconus, *Vita Porphyrii* 11–12). When Theophilus of Alexandria sent round a warning letter against Origenism to the bishops of Palestine and Cyprus, he put first the name of Eulogius of Caesarea, second that of John of Jerusalem; the reply of the synod of Jerusalem follows the same order of precedence (Jerome, *Epp.* 92–93). In passing, it is noteworthy that Theophilus addressed this letter to those provinces of the diocese Oriens which were never effectively under the control of the patriarch of Antioch (see below, pp. 184–85), though at this time, 401, Cyprus and Palestine were understood to belong to Antiochene jurisdiction at least in theory. Add to this observation the Pauline text about "the care of all the churches" quoted in John of Jerusalem's letter to Theophilus (Jerome, *adv. Joh. Hier.* 37), and it looks as if the Origenist controversy was being exploited by Theophilus to attach Cyprus and Palestine to his own jurisdiction or at least to weaken that of Antioch. The final outcome, of course, was the creation of the independent patriarchate of Jerusalem by Juvenal, whose story has been brilliantly told by Honigmann in *Dumbarton Oaks Papers* 5 (1950). Until Juvenal the seventh canon remained effective.

If, therefore, we ask why the opposition was so small, the answer will be that the emperor required assent and was personally at hand to add point to his demand; that the creed, if far from ideal, had at least the merit of being a highly ambiguous formula which both sides could interpret in a way congruous with their standpoint;[11] and that the canons contained nothing that seemed to the leaders on either side to interfere with their existing powers. Accordingly, when at the end of the council the high-ranking bureaucrat Philumenos (either *magister militum* or *magister officiorum*)[12] took the *biblion* round for the bishops to sign with the explicit alternative of deposition and exile, there were found but two out of the two hundred and twenty odd bishops present who were unwilling to stretch their consciences and preferred the severe discomforts of banishment. Admittedly their term of exile was not to prove long. But at the time the two intransigents, Secundus of Ptolemais in the Libyan Pentapolis and Theonas of Marmarica,[13] could have had little feeling of benevolence for their friends and associates who had submitted. As he left the council, Secundus turned on the great leader, Eusebius of Nicomedia, with the angry words "Eusebius, you signed to escape exile!" and prophesied, correctly, that Eusebius would soon follow him on the same road.[14]

The position of Secundus and Theonas at Nicaea is rather odd. They had already been formally excommunicated by Alexander of Alexandria before the Nicene Council was ever called.[15] No doubt Eusebius of Nicomedia and his friends had seen to it that they were nevertheless invited to the council

11. Loofs's judgment that the Nicene creed was "intentionally ambiguous" is, I think, an exaggeration (see his paper, "Das Nicänum," in Festgabef. Karl Müller, Tübingen, 1922, pp. 68–82), but an exaggeration of a truth: it was the ambiguity of the formula which made it possible for almost everyone to accept it, and had it not possessed that virtue Constantine would not have given the formula the support without which it would hardly have become accepted so generally. But I doubt if Ossius and Alexander drafted the creed with the deliberate purpose of providing a comprehensive statement which the Eusebians would be happy to sign. The statement they produced turned out to be capable of an inclusive interpretation, but that was more accident than design.

12. See the Life of Constantine in the codex Angelicus which used Philostorgius (ed. Bidez, p. 10). Philumenos played some part also in the Donatist controversy; in 316 he advised Constantine to keep Caecilian of Carthage a prisoner at Brescia (Optatus i.26).

13. See the letter of the Council of Nicaea "to the Church of Alexandria and to the brethren in Egypt, Libya, and the Pentapolis," cited by Athanasius, *de Decretis* 36; Socrates, *H.E.* i.9; Theodoret, *H.E.* i.9; Gelasius, *H.E.* ii.34. (Opitz, document 23 — as above, n. 8.)

14. Philostorgius, *H.E.* i.10. At i.9 he distinguishes sharply between the Libyan group and "the other block of Arians."

15. See the encyclical of Alexander of Alexandria to all bishops, cited by Athanasius, *de Decretis* 35.6, Socrates, *H.E.* i.6.8; also Athanasius, *Historia Arianorum* 71.4.

specifically called to review the whole controversy, and presumably they were present on much the same basis as Eusebius of Caesarea, Narcissus of Neronias, and Theodotus of Laodicea — provisionally excommunicated at Antioch but given a last opportunity of demonstrating their orthodoxy by submitting to the bishops at Nicaea.

When so many Arianizing bishops signed the creed, it becomes surprising not that the opposition was exiguous but that there were any dissentients at all. Why did Secundus and Theonas alone stand out against submission? If they could not make their own the reasoning of Eusebius of Caesarea, at least they might have followed the example of Eusebius of Nicomedia and Theognis of Nicaea, who signed first and explained later. Moreover, the fact that subsequently they were readmitted to communion and reinstated in their sees suggests that it was not simply a matter of conscience for them. Perhaps, however, their doctrinal dissent was fortified by other, more emotional, considerations. Seeck,[16] for example, threw out the suggestion that Secundus and Theonas were both intimate friends of Arius and were unwilling to break with him for personal reasons — much as the Antiochene bishops at the Council of Ephesus in 431 were tied to Nestorius by close bonds of friendship and intimacy. It is entirely possible that such motives had something to do with it. Nevertheless I suspect that there were deeper reasons than this.

Arianism was remarkably strong in Libya. Philostorgius, according to the *Thesaurus* of Nicetas Choniates,[17] gives a list of the chief bishops on the side of Arius. His catalogue begins thus: "From Libya superior: Sentianos of Boreion, Dachios of Berenice, Secundus of Teuchera, Zopyrus of Barka, another Secundus of Ptolemais, Theonas of Marmarica." Philostorgius continues by enumerating bishops from other provinces; but it is noteworthy that he puts Libya at the head of his list, and that this province not only has more Arian supporters that any other but is also virtually "solid." Almost all the cities of the Pentapolis are included. At Nicaea, admittedly, the united front disintegrated. Dachios of Berenice, Secundus of Teuchera, and Zopyrus of Barka all appear among the signatories. Boreion was a remote spot, the most westerly of the cities of the Pentapolis, where until Justinian applied some pressure the population was predominantly Jewish and the Christians were few.[18] Perhaps Sentianus did not come to Nicaea.

---

16. Otto Seeck, *Geschichte des Untergangs der antiken Welt,* iii² (Stuttgart, 1921), p. 401.

17. Nicetas, *Thesaur.* v. 7 (Migne, *PG* cxxxix. 1368), printed in Bidez's edition of Philostorgius, p. 9.

18. Procopius, *Aedif.* vi.2.14ff.

Philostorgius's statement is independently confirmed by two other pieces of evidence. The first is the fantastic letter from Constantius to Arius, denouncing him in a pompous and theatrical style, in reply to a petition sent by Arius from Libya which asked if, since the bishop of Alexandria (Athanasius) was resolutely refusing to restore him to communion, he might act independently and minister in Libya *where his supporters were numerous.* Constantine seizes the opportunity given by Arius's admission that he is in Libya and quotes a terrible prediction of doom upon Libya from the Sibylline Oracles.[19]

The second piece of evidence is the testimony of Synesius's 67th letter, addressed to Theophilus of Alexandria. Synesius tells Theophilus that two villages of the Pentapolis, Palaebiscus and Hydrax, whither Theophilus had sent him to appoint a bishop, did not constitute a see by any precedent of long standing. For many years past the villages had been subject to the bishop of Erythrum, from whose jurisdiction the inhabitants were now most unwilling to be released, and this was in accordance with the original arrangement. There had been a bishop of Palaebiscus only for a short time during the fourth century when special circumstances called for it. At that time the bishop of Erythrum, one Orion, was weak and senile; the people were dissatisfied, since they expected their bishop to be their *patronus,* the powerful advocate of their secular interests. They therefore chose a young and energetic bishop of their own named Siderius, a local property owner lately retired from Valens's army and influential with secular potentates. Their next problem was to arrange for his consecration. He was eventually consecrated quite uncanonically, without either the assent of the bishop of Alexandria or by three bishops of the province, by Philo of Cyrene, who acted entirely on his own. It is possible that theological motives may have entered in at this point. For later, when Athanasius wanted to find a man who could be relied upon as bishop of the vital metropolitan city of Ptolemais (in all probability this was on the death of Secundus's successor, Stephen),

19. See Constantine's letter in Athanasius, *de Decretis* 40.20 = Gelasius, *H.E.* iii.19.20 (Opitz, document 34). The Arian demand for the toleration of an independent Arian community side by side with the Athanasian churches in Egypt and Libya recurs later. At Antioch on 31 October 363 the Arian bishop of Alexandria, Lucius, one Bernicianus and some others submitted to the emperor Jovian charges against Athanasius ; when it became clear that Jovian was committed to the support of Athanasius, they asked him to "authorise our meeting together for worship," complaining that Athanasius harried them as heretics and deprived their churches of endowments of land. The text of the dialogue survives appended to Athanasius, *Ep. ad Iovianum* (Migne, *PG* xxvi.821 B). The date, 31 October, is given by the Coptic fragment of the Festal Letter for 364 published by M. Pieper in *Z.N.W.* xxxvii (1938), p. 75.

he discovered the virtues of Siderius and translated him to Ptolemais, suppressing the dubiously established see of Palaebiscus. The cavalier treatment of Church Order disclosed by the story is, however, justified by the special circumstances of the Libyan churches. For, Synesius remarks, "at that time the mass of the people in the Pentapolis were on the side of heresy": τότε δὲ καὶ ἐκράτει τὰ τῶν αἱρέσεων· πλήθει γὰρ περιῆσαν.[20]

It is therefore certain that Arianism had a deep hold in Libya during the first half of the fourth century and perhaps even later. The question arises why this should have been so. A possible answer might be that Dionysius of Alexandria had conducted so successful a campaign of suppression against Sabellianism in the Pentapolis that the churches there had taken the lesson only too well to heart.[21] Dionysius's theological position made him reckoned the father of Arianism by many in the fourth century, both Arian and orthodox, and Athanasius's attempt to vindicate his good name has the character of a rearguard action.[22] Perhaps the theologians of the Pentapolis had remained Dionysian and had failed to keep up with the more recent developments in dogmatic theology now represented by Alexander of Alexandria. They were heretics because they were behind the times. On such questions one can only speculate with analogies in mind. One contrast between the two controversies is noteworthy. In 259–60 the prevailing theology in the Pentapolis is inclined to be modalistic, and the local temper is critical of the bishop of Alexandria. They look across the sea for a superior authority who can be invoked against him. In 325 the theological situation is exactly reversed. But the controversies are parallel rather than contrasting in this respect, that the Pentapolitans show an independent spirit and welcome a view opposed to that of the bishop of Alexandria.

Perhaps this independence of mind is an important clue. The Pentapolis,

---

20. Synesius, *Ep.* 67 (Migne, *PG* lxvi.1413 C). It also appears (1417 A) that at the end of his life Siderius returned home to Palaebiscus and Hydrax. It is unlikely that he retired. More probably he was extruded under Arian pressure in the period after Athanasius's death when Peter of Alexandria was a refugee at Rome.

21. For the story of the controversy see H. G. Opitz, "Dionys von Alexandria und die Libyer," in *Quantulacumque: Studies Presented to Kirsopp Lake* (London, 1937), pp. 41–54.

22. A fragment of Athanasius of Anazarbus (Migne, *PL* xiii.621) illustrates the Arian appeal to his authority. See the discussion of the fragment by D. de Bruyne in *Z.N.W.* xxvii (1928), p. 110, and by G. Bardy, *Recherches sur S. Lucien d'Antioche et son école* (Paris, 1936), p. 208. Athanasius not only has to write a special tract to vindicate his revered predecessor from the smear of Arianism (*de Sententiis Dionysii*), but also has to deal with the matter in later works, *de Decretis* 26 and *de Synodis* 43–44. Basil, *Ep.* 9, is openly critical of much of Dionysius's work.

after all, was a considerable way from Alexandria. For an ordinary traveller without encumbrances the four hundred miles would require nearly three weeks.[23] Distance encourages the desire for self-determination. Against this background it is necessary to reconsider the sixth canon of Nicaea.

II

Of the twenty canons of Nicaea the most famous and controversial is the sixth. Unfortunately the text is not well set out in any convenient collection of the canons. I print the text of the first sentence as I think it ought to be printed:

> τὰ ἀρχαῖα ἔθη κρατείτω τὰ ἐν Αἰγύπτῳ καὶ Λιβύῃ καὶ Πενταπόλει ὥστε τὸν Ἀλεξανδρείας ἐπίσκοπον πάντων τούτων ἔχειν τὴν ἐξουσίαν, ἐπειδὴ καὶ τῷ ἐν τῇ Ῥώμῃ ἐπισκόπῳ τὸ τοιοῦτον σύνηθές ἐστιν· ὁμοίως δὲ καὶ κατὰ τὴν Ἀντιόχειαν καὶ ἐν ταῖς ἄλλαις ἐπαρχίαις τὰ πρεσβεῖα σῴζεσθαι ταῖς «τῶν μητροπόλεων» ἐκκλησίαις.

The variants in the Greek manuscripts make no difference to the sense and are not important, viz., ἐν Ἀλεξανδρείᾳ, the omission of πάντων, and τοῦτο instead of τὸ τοιοῦτον.[24]

The supplementary words "of the metropoleis" at the end are attested in no known Greek manuscript, and are equally unattested in the Syriac translations.[25] They are presupposed by the oldest Latin translations, printed by C. H. Turner in his *Monumenta*.[26] It will be convenient to have them set out.

First, the version read at the Council of Carthage in 419, as that made from the copy of the canons brought home by Caecilian in 325:

> De primatibus qui ad quasdam pertinent ciuitates. Antiqua per Egyptum atque Pentapolim consuetudo seruetur ut Alexandrinus episcopus horum

---

23. Procopius, *Aedif.* vi.2.3.

24. For the variants see the critical text of V. Beneševič, *Ioannis Scholastici Synagoga L Titulorum* (Abhandlungen der Bayerischen Akademie der Wissenschaften, Phil. hist. Abt., N. F. 14, 1937), p. 32.

25. See F. Schulthess, *Die syrischen Kanones der Synoden von Nicaea bis Chalcedon* (Abhandlungen der königl. Gesellschaft der Wissenschaften zu Göttingen, Phil. hist. Kl., N. F. X, 2, 1908), p. 18.

26. *Eccl. Occid. Mon. Iur. Ant. I,* pp. 120–121. Schwartz was the first to draw attention to the importance of these translations (cf. below, n. 45).

habeat sollicitudinem, quoniam et urbis Rome episcopo similis mos est ut in suburbicaria loca sollicitudinem gerat; necnon et apud Antiochiam itaque et in aliis prouinciis propria iura seruentur metropolitanis ecclesiis.

Secondly, the version made from the text sent to Carthage by Atticus of Constantinople at the invitation of the same council:

> De primatibus qui ad quasdam pertinent ciuitates. Antiqui mores obtineant qui apud Aegyptum sunt et Libiam et Penthapolim ut Alexandriae episcopus omnium habeat sollicitudinem, quia et urbis Romae episcopo similis mos est. similiter autem et circa Anthiociam et ceteris prouinciis priuilegia propria reseruentur metropolitanis aecclesiis.

Thirdly, the version of the Chieti manuscript (= Vatic. regin. 1997), written in the first half of the ninth century for an otherwise unknown bishop of Chieti, at that time in the Lombard duchy of Benevento, named Ingilram. This manuscript, with its characteristic combination of the Nicene and Serdican canons under a single heading, gives the oldest Roman translation of the Nicene canons in the form current at Rome early in the fifth century.[27] The first sentence of the sixth canon as given in the Chieti manuscript is quoted in exactly this form by Paschasinus of Lilybaeum, the Roman legate at the Council of Chalcedon:[28]

> Ecclesia Romana semper habuit primatus. teneat autem et Aegyptus ut episcopus Alexandriae omnium habeat potestatem, quoniam et Romano episcopo haec est consuetudo. similiter autem et qui in Anthiocia constitutus est: et in ceteris prouinciis primatus habeant ecclesiae ciuitatum ampliorum.

The same Greek text is likewise presupposed in the fifth-century Italian version called Prisca, but as it is dependent upon the tradition lying behind the Chieti manuscript it is of no independent value.

The problem of the text in this instance is bound up with the interpretation of the sentence as a whole. Some of the labor expended upon the exege-

---

27. See C. H. Turner in *J.T.S.* xxxi (1930), pp. 9ff.

28. The text cited by Paschasinus is preserved by the Latin version, printed by Schwartz, *Acta Conciliorum Oecumenicorum* II.iii.548. The second half of the sixth canon follows not the Chieti manuscript's form but that of the "Isidorian" version.

sis of the sixth canon has treated it as if it were anticipating Damasus and his successors and attempting to determine the hierarchical order of the great sees, Rome, Alexandria, and Antioch. This is the exposition followed, for example, by the great Byzantine canonist of the twelfth century, Theodoros Balsamon.[29] It was an exegesis much favored at Rome between Damasus and Leo, where the question of precedence was a major preoccupation. The original context is quite different.

The Nicene canons, as is well known, lay down the general rule that the bishop of the provincial capital shall have the right of assent or of veto upon any consecration to the episcopate within the secular province (canon 4).[30] Canon 6 grants that there are precedents for making exceptions to this rule which, in the cases of Rome, Alexandria, and Antioch, are confirmed as proper and correct. The seventh canon treats the position of Jerusalem as also being in some sense exceptional, but not sufficiently so to upset the normal metropolitical privileges of Caesarea. With regard, however, to the continuance of "the ancient customs" by which the jurisdiction of Rome, Alexandria, and Antioch extends beyond the narrow limits of the civil province, the sixth canon is decisive.

Later preoccupations in both East and West obscured the meaning of the canon in its original setting. The wording of the canon left deplorably uncertain the status of Antioch in the diocese Oriens. In fact, the sixth canon does not make any attempt whatever to define Antiochene jurisdiction; the Nicene fathers are reaffirming generally known precedents from Syria, parallel to those from Italy which justify Alexandria's privileges in Libya, but they do not specify what the Syrian precedents are. It is sufficient for their point that these precedents are known to exist. In the course of time this ambiguity needed clearing up. In 381 at the Council of Constantinople the opportunity came with the ending of the Arian controversy. For a long time Antioch had been racked by the Arian disputes, and since 362 the orthodox had been divided into the congregation loyal to the memory of Eustathius, led by Paulinus, and the larger group under Meletius. The long controversy had greatly weakened the standing of the see, and it was important that the position of the bishop of Antioch should be reinforced.

---

29. Rhalles-Potles, *Syntagma Canonum* ii (Athens, 1852), p. 129: "This sixth canon and the seventh lay down that the four patriarchs, viz., Rome, Alexandria, Antioch, and Jerusalem (for Constantinople will be treated in other canons) must be honoured according to the ancient customs."

30. The best study remains that of Konrad Lübeck, *Reichseinteilung und kirchliche Hierarchie des Orients bis zum Ausgange des vierten Jahrhunderts* (Münster, 1901).

The bishops at the Council of Constantinople tried to extend the principles of the Nicene canons by which the ecclesiastical and civil provinces are (in the East) coterminous, and to organize the Church in larger units coterminous with the civil dioceses.[31] They declared that Flavian, the newly appointed bishop of Antioch, should be "exarch" of the diocese Oriens, i.e., he should possess patriarchal status throughout all the provinces of which the civil administration was in the hands of the *comes Orientis* whose residence was at Antioch.[32] This was understood to be the intention of the sixth canon of Nicaea.[33]

The first and probably immediate breach in this Antiochene exarchate was the defection of Cyprus. Early in the fifth century Alexander of Antioch successfully invoked the support of Pope Innocent I in his contention that on

31. The recognition by the Council of Constantinople that the bishop of the capital of the civil diocese is exarch for the provinces belonging to that diocese is nominally reaffirmed at Chalcedon. But the great patriarchates were already making the Constantinopolitan arrangement superseded, and this is virtually admitted in the ninth and seventeenth canons of Chalcedon which allow any dispute with the metropolitan to be taken *either* to the exarch of the diocese *or* to the patriarch of Constantinople. The system of organization by dioceses never took root.

32. Domnus of Antioch's letter to Dioscorus of Alexandria, extant in the Syriac version of the Acts of the second Council of Ephesus, 449, attests the fact that "Flavian accepted the exarchate." See the edition of the Syriac text, with Hofmann's German translation, by J. Flemming, *Akten der Ephesinischen Synode vom Jahre 449* (Abhandlungen der königl. Gesellschaft der Wissenschaften zu Göttingen, Phil. hist. Kl., N. F. XV, 1, 1917), pp. 146–147. In the English translation by Perry (The Second Synod of Ephesus, 1881), the letter is on pp. 352–356.

At one point in the proceedings of the synod of Antioch of 444, the acts of which are transcribed in the *Acts of Chalcedon,* Domnus of Antioch is entitled "exarch of the Oriental diocese" (*Act. Chalc.* xv. 135; Schwartz, *A.C.O.* II.i.438). Jerome assumes that the Nicene canons make Jerusalem subject to Caesarea as metropolis of the province and the whole of the diocese Oriens subject to Antioch; see his *adv. Ioh. Hier.* 37: "Tu qui regulas quaeris ecclesiasticas et Nicaeni concilii canonibus uteris . . . responde mihi, ad Alexandrinum episcopum Palaestina pertinet? ni fallor hoc ibi decernitur, ut Palaestinae metropolis Caesaria sit et totius orientis Antiochia" (Vallarsi², ii. 447). It is noteworthy that the Latin version of the Nicene canons called Gallo-Hispana interprets the limits of Antiochene jurisdiction as being "the whole of Coele-Syria": "Et ut antiquos mos maneat, Aegyptum Liben Pentapolin Alexandriae episcopus habeat potestatem; sicut urbis Rome episcopus habit uicinas sibi prouincias et Anthiocie totam Coelem" (Turner, *Monumenta* I, p. 196).

33. According to the canon of Constantinople (381) "the bishops of the Orient are to control only the Orient, the privileges accorded to the church of Antioch by the canons of Nicaea being preserved." Domnus of Antioch appeals to this canon in his letter to Flavian of Constantinople (= Theodoret, *Ep.* 86) protesting against Alexandrian interference in 448.

the ground of the sixth Nicene canon he had patriarchal authority over the entire Oriental diocese, including Cyprus.[34] The Cypriots were absolutely refusing to recognize the patriarchal privileges of Antioch. A good reason may be conjectured for this refusal. The leading Cypriot bishop during the period in question was Epiphanius of Constantia, bishop from 367 until his death in 403. Epiphanius enjoyed particularly friendly relations with Paulinus of Antioch.[35] Neither he nor Paulinus attended the Council of Constantinople in 381. They appeared, however, at Damasus's Council of Rome in 382 which issued a formal counterblast to the decisions of Constantinople and protested vigorously against the appointment of Flavian at Antioch.[36] Relations between Flavian of Antioch and the bishops of Cyprus must have been extremely strained, and in all probability Flavian could not even begin to exercise effective control of the island. The correspondence between Alexander of Antioch and Pope Innocent shows that the bishops of Antioch had not forgotten about their claims to Cyprus; probably Innocent's support strengthened Alexander's hand enough for him to enlist the help of the *comes Orientis.* But the Nestorian controversy gave the Cypriots their long-awaited chance to denounce enosis and to become autocephalous. They exploited the split between Cyril of Alexandria and John of Antioch, giving their whole-hearted support to Cyril. A special session of the Council of Ephesus held on 31 August 431, during the agonizing period of waiting when both sides had sent delegations to the court and the other bishops had to stay in Ephesus with nothing to do but pray for a decision from the emperor favorable to their own side, filled in a spare day by considering the Cyprus question. On receiving the assurance that no Cypriot bishop had yet been consecrated under mandate from Antioch, a statement which may well have been true, the synod agreed to affirm Cypriot independence.[37]

The next breach came with the creation of a patriarchate of Jerusalem by the ambitious and successful adventurer, Juvenal. Already by the time

---

34. Innocent, *Ep.* xxiv (Migne, *PL* xx. 547–551).

35. Epiphanius, *Panarion* lxxvii. 20ff. (concerning his negotiations at Antioch about the Apollinarian group).

36. Jerome, *Ep.* 108.6; 127.7 (Paulinus and Epiphanius at Rome in 382). For the general situation see a brief account in Hans Lietzmann, *Geschichte der alten Kirche* iv (1944), pp. 34, 56 = *The Era of the Church Fathers,* translated by Bertram Lee Woolf (1951), pp. 45, 65f.; more detail in Schwartz, *Z.N.W.* xxxiv (1935), pp. 196–213, or in Cavallera, *Le Schisme d'Antioche* (Paris, 1905), pp. 245–262.

37. *Collectio Atheniensis* 81, *A.C.O.* I.i.7, pp. 118–122. See a summary of the debate in B. J. Kidd, *A History of the Church to A.D. 461,* iii (Oxford, 1922), pp. 248–249.

of the first Council of Ephesus in 431 Juvenal appears to have gained control of the three Palestinian provinces, an achievement which he must have owed to the direct support of the Emperor Theodosius II,[38] and was already laying claim to the two Phoenician provinces and to Arabia.[39] Under the terms of the reunion with John of Antioch in 433 Cyril denounced Juvenal as a usurper,[40] and his claims perhaps even in Palestine had to wait. His chance came in 449 when Antioch under Domnus was again at odds with Alexandria under Dioscorus.[41] For support given to Dioscorus at the second Council of Ephesus, Juvenal was rewarded with jurisdiction over his coveted provinces of Phoenice I and II and Arabia. At Chalcedon, however, he had to yield them up under the terms of a formal agreement with poor Domnus's successor, Maximus, which allowed him to keep the three Palestines.[42] A few years later Maximus of Antioch regretted this loss of three provinces and tried to recover them by making a formal appeal to the sixth canon of Nicaea and invoking the aid of Pope Leo. Leo himself was using the sixth canon as the basis of his great attack upon Anatolius of Constantinople and upon the Chalcedonian resolution confirming the canon of Constantinople (381) by which New Rome was declared the second see of Christendom. Leo's argument ran that by the terms of the canon the hierarchical order — Rome, Alexandria, Antioch — had been immutably laid down by the 318 holy fathers. When, however, Maximus asked Leo if he would please protest with equal vehemence against Juvenal of Jerusalem's infringement of the Nicene

---

38. Cf. *Act. Chalc.* viii.17, *A.C.O.* II.i.366.

39. *Collectio Atheniensis* 62.4, *A.C.O.* I.i.7, p. 73.

40. Cyril, *Ep.* 56 (Migne, *PG* lxxvii.320); critical edition in Schwartz, Codex Vaticanus gr. 1431 (Abh. Bayer. Akad. d. Wiss. XXXII, 6, 1927), p. 17. Leo, *Ep.* 119, shows that Cyril wrote in the same sense to Rome. But about four or five years later John of Antioch writes to Proclus of Constantinople enumerating provinces subject to his obedience: he does not include either Cyprus or the Palestines (*A.C.O.* I.iv.210).

41. At the second Council of Ephesus, 449, it was among the charges against Domnus of Antioch that he had invaded Juvenal's rights in Palestine. He was also accused on the ground that, when appointing a bishop for Antaradus in Phoenice I, he merely sent the mandate by post instead of going in person to enthrone the bishop, a complaint which may reveal something of Juvenal's methods in stealing the hearts of the men of Phoenicia and Arabia. See the Syriac Acts of Ephesus, ed. Flemming, pp. 126f., tr. Perry, pp. 313ff.

42. At Chalcedon on 23 October 451 a private agreement between Maximus and Juvenal was made, which was given official sanction by the synod and the emperor on 26 October. The official proceedings of 26 October survive in Greek in *Act. Chalc.* viii (*A.C.O.* II.i.362–66); the whole story is only known from the Latin version, *A.C.O.* II.ii.109ff., and is subjected to a masterly discussion by Schwartz in Abh. Bayer. Akad. d. Wiss. XXXII, 2 (1925).

canon, which was indeed even more spectacular, the papal trumpet blew with a less certain sound.[43]

The decisions of the two ecumenical councils of Ephesus and Chalcedon greatly modified the interpretation put upon the Nicene canon by the fathers of Constantinople in 381. The patriarchs of Jerusalem remained in a strong enough position to hold their own against Antioch for the future. The metropolitan of Cyprus was not so secure. In the fifth century the patriarch of Antioch once more reaffirmed his privileges in Cyprus. This time the Cypriots left nothing to chance. If in 488 Peter the Fuller could invoke St. Peter as his predecessor, the Cypriots could produce St. Barnabas. The Son of Consolation himself appeared and disclosed the whereabouts of his body, which was duly found, together with a copy of St. Matthew's Gospel written in the hand of St. Barnabas himself. This priceless relic was presented to the Emperor Zeno who placed it in the church of St. Stephen in Daphne at Constantinople. Thereafter there was no question about the autocephalous rights of Cyprus.[44]

From all this evidence it is clear that the patriarchs of Antioch had a strong interest in the precise wording of the sixth canon of Nicaea. Schwartz[45] acutely suggested that this interest may have been responsible for the omission of the words τῶν μητροπόλεων, a conjecture which receives additional support from the likelihood that the first Greek *corpus canonum* originated at Antioch.[46]

The conventional punctuation (reproduced above, p. 71) takes the phrase ὁμοίως δὲ καὶ κατὰ τὴν Ἀντιόχειαν closely with the words that follow. Linguistic analogy supports this (e.g., Neocaes. can. 10, Nic. can. 19,

---

43. Leo, *Ep.* 119. It is only fair to add that the Roman legates at Chalcedon had fatally compromised him by formally assenting to the agreement between Maximus and Juvenal on 26 October 451. To Maximus Leo protests that he disowns any action of his legates which exceeded their brief, but it was awkward for him in the circumstances.

44. This story, solemnly recorded in the Roman Martyrology (11 June), is attested by Theodoras Lector, *H.E.* ii.2 (*PG* lxxxvi.1, 184); Victor Tunnensis, Chron. (*PL* lxviii.947); and among other late writers by Cedrenus (I pp. 618–19, ed. Bonn). See G. Downey, "The Claim of Antioch to Ecclesiastical Jurisdiction over Cyprus," *Proc. Amer. Philos. Soc.* 102 (1958), pp. 224–28.

45. "Der sechste nicaenische Kanon auf der Synode von Chalkedon," *Sitzungsberichte der preussischen Akademie der Wissenschaften,* 1930, Phil. hist. Kl., pp. 611–40, especially at pp. 633ff.

46. This is argued with great ingenuity by Schwartz, "Die Kanonessammlungen der alten Reichskirche," in *Zeitschrift der Savigny-Stiftung für Rechtsgeschichte,* lvi, Kan. Abt. xxv (1936), pp. 1–114.

Laodic. can. 20). Nevertheless the observation concerning the jurisdiction of Antioch is probably not simply parallel to the affirmation of privileges attaching to churches in other provinces. There is also an implied contrast. It is noteworthy that the Latin version in the Chieti manuscript (above, p. 72) does not understand the phrase concerning Antioch as integrally linked with what follows but marks a distinction.

The blurring of the original force of the sixth canon is probably to be ascribed to the needs of the Antiochene patriarchate during the period after 381. The phrase required some interpretation to make it apply to the situation then prevailing. A similar but even more spectacular attempt to bring the sixth canon up to date with contemporary circumstances appears in the Latin versions. Here, naturally enough, it is the reference to Rome which is altered.

At least from the time of Siricius onwards, and perhaps earlier, the Popes are regularly invoking the authority of the Nicene canons. Roman reverence for them comes perilously near to superstition. In his protest against the proceedings taken against John Chrysostom, when Theophilus of Alexandria had accused John of infringing the twelfth canon of Antioch forbidding appeals to the civil power, Pope Innocent I affirms that the canons of Nicaea are the only canons recognized by the Catholic Church, and that any which dissent from them or which have been composed by heretics are *ipso facto* rejected; he adds that heretical canons must not be appended to orthodox.[47] In the East the canons of Antioch had simply been added to those of Nicaea to form part of a single code of canon law with consecutive numeration,[48] in much the same way as in the West the canons of Serdica were added to those of Nicaea (as they are in the Chieti manuscript where the Serdican canons run on after the Nicene without any break or scribal comment) so that in controversy with the Africans over the case of Apiarius Pope Zosimus could quote the Serdican canons as Nicene.[49] Pope Boniface probably has

---

47. Palladius, Dial, *de Vita Joh. Chrys.* ix (ed. Coleman-Norton, p. 52), mentions Theophilus's appeal to the Antiochene canons. For Innocent's protest see ibid. iii (p. 17) ; the full text of Innocent's letter to the clergy and people of Constantinople in Sozomen, *H.E.* viii.26.7–18.

48. *Act. Chalc.* xii.24–5 cites the 16th and 17th canons of Antioch as "canons 95 and 96" (*A.C.O.* II.i.407); xviii.9–10 cites the 4th and 5th canons of Antioch as "canons 83 and 84" (*A.C.O.* II.i.459–60). These and other examples are collected by Schwartz, *Zeitschrift der Savigny Stiftung,* art. cit. (above, n. 46), p. 1.

49. For Apiarius and the consequences of his moral obliquities see B. J. Kidd, *History of the Church to A.D. 461,* iii, pp. 162ff.

in mind the sixth canon of Nicaea when he affirms that Peter's church is supreme over all and that no one can be a Christian who is not in communion with Rome.[50] It was especially important for the Roman Church to exploit the sixth canon in its war against the pretensions of Constantinople.[51] To be really effective for this purpose, however, the wording of the canon needed minor alterations at the start.

The notion that the sixth canon was interested in Rome as such first appears in Rufinus's summary: "Et ut apud Alexandriam vel in urbe Roma vetusta consuetudo seruetur, quia uel ille Aegypti uel hic suburbicariarum ecclesiarum sollicitudinem gerat."[52] Rufinus assumes that the Nicene fathers were somehow concerned to specify the scope of Rome's patriarchal authority, and therefore defined the area as the ten "suburbicarian" provinces of central and southern Italy with Sicily and Sardinia. He drops any reference to Libya and the Pentapolis. There is not a word about Antioch. The original context of the canon has been forgotten.

A much more dramatic modernization of the canon appears in the form quoted by Leo's legate, Paschasinus of Lilybaeum, in his protest at the last session of the Council of Chalcedon.[53] The wording of the first sentence of the sixth canon is identical with that of the Chieti manuscript (above, p. 72). Here again the original reference to Libya and the Pentapolis has wholly disappeared, and any real interest in the scope of Alexandrian jurisdiction has fallen by the wayside. The canon has been redrafted to meet Rome's urgent needs in the different circumstances of a later time, when the Petrine primacy over the whole Church has become integral to the program, and the sacred Council of the 318 fathers must give its sanction. Damasus had observed that the primacy of Rome was not dependent upon any conciliar decisions, but upon (a) the TV ES PETRVS, and (b) the martyrdom in

---

50. Boniface, *Ep.* xiv.1 (*PL* xx.777 B): "Institutio uniuersalis nascentis ecclesiae de beati Petri sumpsit honore principium, in quo regimen eius et summa consistit. Ex eius enim ecclesiastica disciplina per omnes ecclesias, religionis iam crescente cultura, fonte manauit. Nicaenae synodi non aliud praecepta testantur, adeo ut non aliquid super eum ausa sit constituere, cum uideret nihil supra meritum suum posse conferri; omnia denique huic nouerat domini sermone concessa. Hunc ergo ecclesiis toto orbe diffusis uelut caput suorum certum est esse membrorum; a quo se quisquis abscidit, fit christianae religionis extorris, cum in eadem non coeperit esse compage."

51. See especially Leo's letters of 22 May 452 addressed to Marcian, Pulcheria, and Anatolius (*Epp.* 104–106).

52. Rufinus, *H.E.* x.6 (ed. Mommsen, pp. 966f.).

53. Above, n. 28.

Rome of St. Peter and St. Paul.[54] The revision of the Nicene canon in the Roman interest does not make the Nicene fathers *award* authority to Rome. Rather do they recognize that Rome "has always had the first place" (Ecclesia Romana semper habuit primatus).

At Nicaea in 325 the Roman primacy was not an issue, and it would be anachronistic to expect any reference thereto. Nor were the bishops interested in defining Rome's patriarchate in Italy. The Western representation at the council was in any event so absurdly small that it is inconceivable that the council should have attempted to regulate the affairs of the Western churches.[55] The existence of Rome's supra-provincial standing in Italy is simply taken for granted because it justifies the continuance of comparable powers in the see of Alexandria. The vagueness of the clause concerning Antioch shows that in Syria no serious controversy had as yet arisen. The canon is only explicit and decisive in its ruling about Alexandrian jurisdiction extending over Libya and the Pentapolis. These powers were evidently being disputed by somebody, and it is conventional to assume that it was the Melitian schism which constituted a challenge to the authority of Alexander of Alexandria and so called forth the reassertion of his traditional powers.[56] But the Melitian schism was confined to Egypt and the Thebais; there is no evidence that the Pentapolis was involved.[57] It seems altogether more probable that the canon was directed against a move on the part of the Libyan metropolis to be free of Alexandrian control.

Little is known of the date of Diocletian's reform of the provincial orga-

---

54. The text of Damasus's statement is printed in Turner's *Monumenta,* I, p. 157, in *J.T.S.* i (1900), p. 560, and in E. von Dobschütz, *Das Decretum Gelasianum* (Texte und Untersuchungen xxxviii.4, 1912), p. 7.

55. The only certainties are Ossius the Spaniard, the two Roman presbyters representing Silvester, a couple of bishops from Dacia and one from Moesia. A rather improbable Calabrian and Caecilian of Carthage appear in some less trustworthy lists. Caecilian, of course, may well have been there — at least the Council of Carthage in 419 thought he was present and Donatism would not keep him at home. His successor Gratus was able to go to Serdica. Caecilian's troubles at home would have given him good reason to make (at imperial expense) a journey that would again bring him into direct touch with Constantine to whose support he owed so much.

56. William Bright, *The Canons of the First Four General Councils with Notes*[2] (Oxford, 1892), p. 22; Kidd, op. cit., ii, p. 46; A. H. M. Jones, *Constantine and the Conversion of Europe* (London, 1948), p. 170.

57. See the list of Melitian clergy given to Alexander of Alexandria, preserved by Athanasius, *Apol. c. Arianos* 71. There are nine from Thebais, twenty-five from Aegyptus, and a few presbyters and deacons actually at Alexandria.

nization of the Empire; it seems likely that the splitting up of the provinces was not carried out all at once, like the establishment of the four prefectures and the twelve dioceses, but went forward gradually. Egypt he divided into three provinces, while Libya, at first left undivided, was later split into two. The Verona list which, at least in its catalogue for the diocese Oriens, seems to reflect the situation of about 320, begins with the 18 provinces constituting Oriens. The first five are: "Libia superior, Libia inferior, Thebais, Aegyptus Iulia, Aegyptus Herculia."[58] According to Ammianus,[59] the splitting of Libya into two was not original, but followed later. Until Diocletian Libya had been separately administered; but the creation of the diocese Oriens under the *comes Orientis* at Antioch linked the Pentapolis more closely with Egypt. At the same time the rise, in the last years of the third century, of the idea that the bishop of the provincial metropolis was *primus inter pares,* would have encouraged the spirit of ecclesiastical autonomy. We have other examples in the fourth and fifth centuries where the splitting of a secular province carried ecclesiastical consequences, with a corresponding multiplication of metropolitans. The best-known example is the division of Cappadocia under Valens in 372 which resulted in the successful assertion of metropolitical rights by Anthimus of Tyana against the claims of Basil of Caesarea to continue his jurisdiction over the entire region as hitherto.[60] It is not therefore unreasonable to conjecture that at Ptolemais there may have been some attempt to assert ecclesiastical independence. There is no actual evidence for this during the period of the Nicene Council. But there is the testimony of Synesius a century later that in the Pentapolis in his time the churches were still anxious to affirm their privileges. Synesius, pressed by the people of Ptolemais to become their bishop, was determined not to fall foul of Theophilus of Alexandria, and became virtually Theophilus's agent in Cyrenaica,[61] acting throughout as a loyal and devoted servant and so little prepared to

---

58. The Laterculus Veronensis is printed by Seeck in his edition of the Notitia Dignitatum, and its evidence discussed by A. H. M. Jones, "The Date and Value of the Verona List," *Journal of Roman Studies* xliv (1954), pp. 21–29.

59. Amm. Marc. xxii.16.4.

60. Cf. Basil, *Ep.* 98. That the first sentence of the sixth canon is directed against a division consequent upon Diocletian's splitting of Egypt into provinces is already seen by Schwartz, *Zur Geschichte des Athanasius* VIII, in *Gesammelte Schriften* iii (1959), pp. 213f.; J. Gaudemet, *L'église dans l'empire romain* (Paris, 1958), p. 91.

61. Synesius, *Ep.* 67 init. (*PG* lxvi.1412 A) addressing Theophilus: "It is my personal wish, and a divine necessity is upon me, that I should deem as law any instruction from your throne."

challenge any decision that at Ptolemais they reproached him for failing to uphold "the metropolitical rights of the city."[62] He admits himself to be an innocent in all matters of canon law, being only a recent convert.[63] Probably the citizens of the Pentapolis were disappointed in him for his reluctance to affirm the prestige of his metropolitan city. Synesius's open letter to his brother, declaring the terms on which he is accepting the bishopric, indicates that he will on no account become the target for Theophilus's attack.[64] His 76th letter shows that he feels unable to proceed to the consecration of a village bishop without the written mandate of Theophilus.

But in Synesius's time Ptolemais was already in decline under the stress of barbarian raids, and its economic condition became disastrous with a failure in the water supply. During the fifth century much of the population moved out, and also, it appears, the secular administration, since in the sixth century the metropolis is now Sozusa.[65] Justinian did much to restore the Pentapolis and rebuilt the aqueduct at Ptolemais.[66] It is, of course, very possible that Justinian's activities in Cyrenaica were accompanied by efforts on the part of the patriarch of Constantinople to rekindle the spirit of autonomy and to wean the Pentapolis from any dependence on Alexandria. But I know of no evidence to this effect, and the silence of the sources precludes any continuation of the story. The one and only scrap of evidence which might conceivably bear on the point is an inscription of the sixth century from the cathedral at Cyrene, recently found by R. G. Goodchild in the course of excavation for the Libyan government's Department of Antiquities, which I am allowed to use through the kindness of Miss Joyce Reynolds, Fellow of Newnham College, Cambridge. She reads the inscription as

ΝΕΑΡΩΜΗΚΥΡΗΝΗ

(MHK being in ligature). Does this mean that the patriarch of Constantinople sent some substantial benefaction for the cathedral fabric at Cyrene? If so, were there strings attached?

---

62. *Ep.* 66 (1409 B).

63. *Ep.* 66 (1409 A).

64. *Ep.* 105.

65. Sozusa is mentioned first of the cities of the Pentapolis by Hierocles, *Synecdemus* (ed. Honigmann, pp. 47–48), copied by Georgius Cyprius, *Descriptio Orbis Romani,* ed. Gelzer (Leipzig: Teubner, 1890), p. 41.

66. Procopius, *Aedif.* vi.2.9–11.

III

The question remains: how immediately effective was the sixth canon in bringing the Libyans to heel? Secundus and Theonas may have gone into exile for a time. But Constantine did not (it seems) allow Athanasius to replace them — just as he did not allow any successor to be appointed at Alexandria when Athanasius himself was exiled to Trier at the end of 335.[67] Constantine always hoped for submission, and he was usually right. There was therefore no difficulty about reinstating Secundus and Theonas in their sees after their submission. The date of their restoration is wholly unknown;[68] but probability favors the view that their return was quite soon, perhaps about 327–328. It was certainly earlier than the Jerusalem dedication of September 335 when the inferior clergy of Alexandria, once associated with Arius, were reconciled.[69]

It is conceivable that until the Council of Tyre in 335 Athanasius may have accepted Secundus at Ptolemais, but if so coexistence must have been very uneasy. The breach must have become absolute in the summer of 337 when, while Athanasius was still at Trier, Secundus consecrated the (ex-) Arian presbyter Pistus as bishop of Alexandria in place of Athanasius.[70] The very act of consecrating a bishop for Alexandria in itself marks the ambitions of the metropolitan of Ptolemais. But Pistus was not equal to the situation, and Athanasius's return from exile made his position impossible. In 339 the Eusebians sent another candidate for the see of Alexandria, Gregory, who was consecrated at Antioch and enthroned at Alexandria by force in the spring of 339 when Athanasius fled to Rome. Of Secundus's relations with Gregory we know nothing. Presumably his position was secure, and Gregory had enough to worry about at home without trying to control distant Libya. Gregory's death after a long illness on 26 June 345 and the eventual return of Athanasius in October 346[71] must have led to extreme tension for

67. See the letter from Constantine II to Alexandria in Athanasius, *Apol. c. Arianos* 87. For the date cf. W. Telfer, *H.T.R.* xliii (1950), pp. 59–60.

68. Philostorgius, *H.E.* ii.1, records the fact that Constantine ordered the recall of τοὺς περὶ Σεκοῦνδον but gives no hint of the date. Athanasius, *Ep. ad episc. Aeg. et Lib.* 7 and 19, likewise records Secundus's reconciliation, but not its occasion.

69. The Jerusalem encyclical in Athanasius, *Apol. c. Arianos* 84 and *de Synodis* 21, addressed to the churches of Alexandria, Egypt, Libya, and Pentapolis, mentions the restoration of the Arian "presbyters," but there is no word about any bishops.

70. Julius of Rome in Athanasius, *Apol. c. Arianos* 24.

71. The dates are recorded in the Festal Index for Athanasius's Festal Letters.

Secundus. Since Secundus appears to have survived, we must suppose either that he withdrew for a time or that Constantius did not allow Athanasius to interfere with Libyan affairs. Athanasius, of course, never grants that the Pentapolis falls outside his jurisdiction. The encyclical of the Council of Alexandria of 338 is not only written in the name of "Egypt, Thebais, Libya and Pentapolis," but also subjoins a document signed by some from Libya and the Pentapolis as well as from Egypt which proves the falsity of charges against Athanasius accepted by the Council of Tyre.[72] In his transcript of the encyclical letter of the Western Council of Serdica, the address bears the title to the "bishops of Egypt and Libya."[73] On his return in 346 Athanasius held a synod of 94 bishops at Alexandria which signed the Serdican encyclical. Of these at least one came from Marmarica, and others are possible holders of Libyan sees.[74] Elsewhere Athanasius remarks that the number of sees in Egypt and Libya totals "nearly a hundred";[75] the phrase is unhappily too vague to be the basis of any calculation about the number of absentees, but it allows us to suppose that some bishops from the Pentapolis stayed away. It is noteworthy that the Festal Index records a visitation in the Pentapolis in 331–332. But we do not read of any episcopal appointments made by Athanasius for the Pentapolis; his letter to Serapion of Thmuis written from Rome in 340 nominates one bishop for the see of Garyathis in Marmarica.[76] But we have too little of Athanasius's correspondence for any real conclusions to be drawn from the phenomena. Some Marmaricans attended the Council of Alexandria in 362.[77]

In 356 the flight of Athanasius into the desert and the advent of the advanced Arian, George of Cappadocia, as bishop of Alexandria, would again have meant power for Secundus. Athanasius paints a horrific picture of the violent persecution of the orthodox in Egypt and in Libya while the soldiers were hunting for him.[78] He relates that Secundus, abetted by one Stephen, not merely kicked to death a recalcitrant presbyter of Barka, but even committed this outrage during the holy season of Lent.[79] He also mentions a certain Sisinnius as the leader of a group of young Arians who have obtained

72. Athanasius, *Apol. c. Arianos* 3 and 19.

73. Ibid., 41.

74. Ibid., 49 (with the commentary thereon in Opitz's edition).

75. Ibid., 1 and 71. Cf. *Ep. ad Afros* 10 ("about 90").

76. Migne, *PG* xxvi.1414 A.

77. Athanasius, *Tomus ad Antioch.* 1 and 10.

78. *Historia Arianorum* 51ff.

79. Ibid., 65; cf. *de Synodis* 12.

possession of the Libyan churches.[80] The last we hear of Secundus is that he and Serras, the bishop of Paraetonium in Marmarica, tried to consecrate the radical Arian Aetius to the episcopate (presumably as part of their program of filling Libyan sees with sound men), but Aetius refused on the ground that Secundus's hands were defiled: his allegiance to the true faith had been fatally compromised by his submission to the Nicene formula under Constantine.[81] It is an ironic conclusion to a strange career.

The date of Secundus's death is not known exactly, but must have been approximately 357. He had certainly died before 359. At Seleucia in 359 the bishop of Ptolemais was Stephen, perhaps to be identified with the Stephen who assisted him in the violent coercion of the poor presbyter of Barka. The bishops of Libya at Seleucia seem to have been determinedly Arianizing. The group led by George of Alexandria and Acacius of Caesarea included not only Stephen of Ptolemais, but also Heliodorus of Sozusa, two bishops from Marmarica, Serapion of Antipyrgos and Polydeuces of an unnamed see, and also Serras of Paraetonium on the Marmarican frontier.[82] Almost all these names recur in the list of those who attended the enthronement of Eudoxius as bishop of Constantinople in 360.[83] Heliodorus of Sozusa, Stephen of Ptolemais, and Serras of Paraetonium soon became involved in the split within the radical Arian party caused by the emperor's demand for the condemnation of Aetius. The three Libyans refused to assent to this abandonment of their friend, and joined with the Eunomian group in attempting to establish a distinct Arian Church.[84]

The return of Athanasius to Alexandria during the sixties meant that he could at long last set about the restoration of orthodoxy in the Pentapolis. Evidently it was about this time that he translated the orthodox Siderius to the metropolitan see of Ptolemais. Thereafter the Libyan churches must gradually have been recaptured for the Nicene faith and for Alexandrian jurisdiction.[85] The rigorous control exercised by Theophilus is clear from the

---

80. *Historia Arianorum* 71.

81. Philostorgius, *H.E.* iii.19 (cf. Sozomen, *H.E.* iv.12.2, for independent attestation of this puritan attitude of Aetius). Philostorgius (iii.20) goes on to say that it was Secundus who had introduced Eunomius to Aetius. He also remarks (ii.3) that Secundus's theology was more purely Eunomian than that of Arius himself.

82. Epiphanius, *Panarion* 73.26 (ed. Holl, iii.300f.). Stephen and Heliodorus also turn up in the *Historia Acephala* 13–14 (Turner, *Monumenta* I, pp. 667f.).

83. *Chronicon Paschale, PG* xcii.736 (in Bidez's edition of Philostorgius, pp. 244f.).

84. Synodical letter to George of Alexandria in Theodoret, *H.E.* ii.28.3.

85. Cf. Epiphanius, *Panarion* lxviii.1 (ed. Holl, iii.141): "It is customary that the arch-

letters of Synesius. In the time of Cyril the bishop of Ptolemais, Euoptios, was his devoted adherent and gave the patriarch faithful support at Ephesus in 431. It was to him that Cyril dedicated his answer to Theodoret's attack upon his Twelve Chapters.[86] Ptolemais ended in sad economic decline, but at least it was now orthodox.[87]

---

bishop in Alexandria has ecclesiastical control over all Egypt and Thebais, Mareotis, Libya, Ammoniake, Mareotis (*read* Marmarica), and Pentapolis."

86. Migne, *PG* lxxvi.385 ; *A.C.O.* I.i.6, p. 110.

87. The only evidence of later tension between Libya and the Alexandrian patriarch is the charge against Dioscorus at Chalcedon in 451 that he had not allowed the Libyan churches their share of the government grant of corn (*A.C.O.* II.i.213). It is likely that this was also a source of trouble in the time of Athanasius (cf. *Apol. c. Arianos* 18).

Ossius of Cordova and the Presidency
of the Council of Antioch, 325

A little over fifty years ago Eduard Schwartz[1] startled historians of the ancient church by his acute discovery of a Syriac translation of a synodal letter, purporting to have been sent to Alexander, bishop of Byzantium, by a council of Antioch attended by fifty-nine bishops from the provinces of Palestine, Arabia, Phoenicia, Coele-Syria, Cilicia, and 'some from Cappadocia'. Nothing about the existence of this council is to be found in any other ancient evidence, and the discussion of its date and significance turns entirely on the internal content of the document itself. It begins by mentioning the critical state of church affairs at Antioch which has led the president of the council to summon bishops from the surrounding provinces to take synodical action, a course not hitherto open to them on account of a ban precluding episcopal assemblies in the east. Although, the letter continues, many matters need setting to rights and the canons have been sadly disregarded, yet there is one problem of pre-eminent importance, namely, the theological question of orthodox faith; it is therefore upon this that the council has concentrated its attention. It appears indeed that the council did not succeed in passing beyond this first item on its agenda. Faith and Order are issues inextricably bound up. For the chaos in the order of the eastern churches has been primarily caused by the action of certain bishops in receiving to communion presbyters who had been expelled by Bishop Alexander of Alexandria as associates of Arius. These dissident bishops are represented in the synod, and cross-examination has disclosed that three of them, Theodotus of Laodicea, Narcissus of Neronias, and Eusebius of Palestinian Caesarea, have

---

1. E. Schwartz, 'Zur Geschichte des Athanasius, VI', *Nachrichten d. Gött. Ges. d. Wiss.*, 1905, pp. 271–88.

been found to be tainted with the Arian heresy. They have therefore been solemnly excommunicated, with the proviso, however, that they shall have an opportunity of repentance at the 'great and hieratic synod of Ancyra'. The letter concludes with a request that Alexander of Byzantium will spread the news round to 'all the like-minded brethren'.

Schwartz perceived that the document exactly fitted the situation at the beginning of 325, and that the council of Antioch was the curtain-raiser for the council of Nicaea. Forty-nine of the names recur in the Nicene lists. There is an evident allusion to Licinius's prohibition of synods during the time of tension between himself and Constantine, and to the support found by Arius among his friends on the Palestinian episcopal bench. Schwartz likewise saw that his new document vindicated the much-doubted authenticity of the letter, also known only in a Syriac version first published by B. H. Cowper in his *Analecta Nicaena* (1857), by which Constantine summoned the bishops assembling at Ancyra to transfer themselves to Nicaea;[2] and he noted that it illuminated the action of Eusebius of Caesarea when he submitted his creed to the Nicene fathers. The great church historian was clearing himself of heresy and pleading for restoration to church communion.

The newly found document at once became the centre of heated controversy. Harnack, following the lead of Duchesne,[3] published a paper denying the authenticity of the Antiochene letter;[4] and when Schwartz replied with a peppery rejoinder,[5] Harnack declared himself as unconvinced as ever.[6] In 1913 the entire question was subjected to a careful overhaul in an elaborate monograph by Erich Seeberg,[7] who decided in favour of the authenticity of the text and persuaded some others to follow him. But many eminent historians of that generation appear to have remained sceptical to the end of their days.

Schwartz never saw reason to argue the point afresh. He had said his say, and thereafter quietly stood his ground. The correctness of his view was

---

2. The translation of Cowper (*Syriac Miscellanies,* London, 1861, pp. 5–6) is conveniently reproduced by J. Stevenson, *A New Eusebius* (London, 1957), p. 358.

3. *Histoire ancienne de l'église,* ii (1907), p. 137 n. (= E.T. ii, p. 108 n.).

4. 'Die angebliche Synode von Antiochia im Jahr 324–5', *Sitzungsberichte der preuß. Akad. d. Wiss.,* 1908, pp. 477–91.

5. 'Zur Geschichte des Athanasius, VII', *Nachr. d. Gött. Akad. d. Wiss.,* 1908, pp. 305–74.

6. 'Die angebliche Synode von Antiochia im Jahr 324–5', *Sitzungsberichte der preuß. Akad. d. Wiss.,* 1909, pp. 401–25.

7. *Die Synode von Antiochien im Jahre 324–5* (Neue Studien zur Geschichte der Theologie und der Kirche, hrsg. von N. Bonwetsch und R. Seeberg, Heft 16, Berlin, 1913).

taken for granted by Otto Seeck.[8] Gradually more and more historians rallied to his side, and in 1930 Dr. Norman Baynes could shortly say that 'most scholars agree that the document is genuine'.[9] Today the general consensus of opinion is almost unanimous. At least if any sceptics still survive, they are keeping their doubts to themselves. By 1950 it might even be thought an understatement when Dr. J. N. D. Kelly wrote of 'a growing body of responsible opinion' as being prepared to accept the genuineness of the letter.[10]

Nevertheless, one question has never been put quite beyond all probable, possible shadow of doubt, namely, the identity of the presiding bishop whose name appears in the position of honour, heading the list of bishops in the address.

It will be recalled that Schwartz found the document in a ninth-century manuscript in the Bibliothèque Nationale, codex Parisinus syr. 62, containing an important collection of canon material. He provided his *editio princeps* with a retroversion into Greek. The original text was re-edited from the Paris manuscript by Schulthess in 1908 in his standard edition of the Syriac canons of the councils from Nicaea to Chalcedon;[11] and from Schulthess the Syriac text was reprinted, together with Schwartz's conjectural Greek version, by H.-G. Opitz in his *Urkunden zur Geschichte des arianischen Streites* (1934).[12] Opitz's edition is likely to be that most generally accessible today. It omits, however, the important historical notice appended at the end of the letter, containing the interesting information that the council wrote in similar terms to 'the bishops of Italy subject to the see of Rome'; and it does not take any account of a reprint of the Syriac text, with a French translation, published in 1909 by Nau,[13] the importance of which is that Nau had before

8. *Geschichte des Untergangs der antiken Welt,* iii² (Stuttgart, 1921), pp. 409ff. Schwartz's view is also accepted by G. Bardy, 'L'Église d'Antioche au temps de la crise arienne', *Bull. Anc. Litt. Arch. Chr.* iv (1914), pp. 243–61, at p. 254, n. 2; cp. his note in Fliche-Martin, *Histoire de l'église,* iii (1936), p. 79.

9. N. H. Baynes, *Constantine the Great and the Christian Church* (from *Proc. Brit. Acad.* xv, 1929), p. 85.

10. *Early Christian Creeds* (London, 1950), p. 209.

11. Friedrich Schulthess, *Die syrischen Kanones der Synoden von Nicaea bis Chalcedon nebst einigen zugehörigen Dokumenten* (Abhandl. d. Gött. Ges. d. Wiss., Phil.-hist. Klasse, N.F. X, 2, Berlin, 1908), pp. 160–63.

12. The only complete English translation was made by Dr. F. L. Cross, 'The Council of Antioch in 325 A.D.', in *Church Quarterly Review* cxxviii (1939), pp. 49–76, where it is introduced by a full critical survey of the historical problems.

13. 'Littérature canonique syriaque inédite', in *Revue de l'Orient chrétien* xiv (1909), pp. 1–31. Not much attention has been paid to Nau's article, perhaps because he not merely

him collations of a second manuscript authority, namely, codex Vaticanus syr. 148, fols. 129–31.

The list of bishops in the opening paragraph of the letter is headed by the two names: Eusebius, Eustathius. On this, it seems from Nau's edition, both the Paris and the Vatican manuscripts are in agreement. The second name is manifestly that of the well-known bishop of Antioch, whose theological opinions and unhappy career have been the subject of some controversy in modern as also in ancient times. But who is the bishop named first? 'Eusebius' remained inexplicable, and it was the weakest point in Schwartz's position before the onslaught of Harnack that he was driven to identify the president of this obviously important synod with a very undistinguished itinerant bishop of this name from the city of Isaura, who figures in the lists of the Nicene signatories but is otherwise totally unknown. The presiding bishop of a gathering of such consequence. that it could take upon itself to excommunicate three leading bishops for heresy (to say nothing of their breach of church order in communicating with persons excommunicate from Alexandria), a man to whom Eustathius could yield first place at an assembly held in his own church of Antioch,[14] must surely have been no mean personage. To identify him with a small-town Isaurian bishop of no personal eminence is to strain credulity to breaking-point. Moreover, though the main part of the synodal letter is written in the name of all the bishops as a corporate statement in the first person plural, the opening introduction, explaining the genesis of the synod, is written in the first person singular:

> When I came to the church of the Antiochenes and saw the church greatly disturbed by tares through the teaching and dissension of some,

---

denies the existence of a council of Antioch before Nicaea but because he asserts that the newly found document is a genuine letter of the Dedication council of Antioch, presided over by Eusebius of Nicomedia! Nau burnt his fingers very badly here, and the pages that he devotes to the historical criticism of the letter are utterly worthless. But his reprint of the text and his French version remain of permanent value.

14. Schwartz's explanation was that the see of Antioch was still vacant after Philogonius's death and that it was due to the intervention of Eusebius of Isaura that the council was called in order to quash an Arian attempt to get one of their own folk made bishop; he was responsible for the translation of Eustathius, and it was therefore 'only natural' that Eusebius should have presided at the synod. In Schwartz's view, the replacing of Philogonius was the immediate occasion of the synod, and the discussion of the Arian question only came up suddenly at the synod itself at the instigation of the anti-Arian majority; the dogmatic question had not been announced on the agenda. Cp. *Nachr. d. Gött. Ges. d. Wiss.*, 1905, p. 282. For criticism of the not dissimilar interpretation of Dr. Kelly see below, p. 97.

I decided that this should not be cast out and removed by my authority alone, but that I ought to call in our friends and colleagues from the neighbourhood. . . .

The presiding bishop had wondered whether or not to deal with the crisis on his own initiative and personal authority, but had decided that a synod, under his control, would be a more effective weapon for rooting out the dissent. A man who could speak so self-consciously must certainly have been a distinguished ecclesiastical dignitary, one set under authority whose commands could be sure of being respected throughout the diocese Oriens.

In 1911 the solution to the difficulty was seen by the Russian scholar A. I. Brilliantov. He proposed to emend the text, omitting a single letter in the Syriac word so as to read ܘܐܘܣܝܘܣ instead of ܘܐܘܣܒܝܘܣ, thus making the president of the council Ossius (or Hosius) of Cordova, Constantine's ecclesiastical adviser and imperial commissioner for dealing with the eastern church controversy. Brilliantov supported his case by producing three other texts in which Ossius's name has become corrupted into 'Eusebius'—two in the *Chronicle* of Michael the Syrian and one in the *Liber Chalifarum*.[15]

The probability of Brilliantov's suggestion seems obvious now. Yet it took a long time to make its way. Seeberg, while acknowledging the emendation's attractions, declined to be seduced by it;[16] and his reviewer, G. Krüger, whose opinion concerning the authenticity was changed by reading his monograph, altogether ignored the notion, holding with Lebedev that the name Eusebius must simply be deleted as an interpolation,[17] so that Eustathius, newly translated from Beroea to Antioch and full of anti-Arian reforming zeal, becomes the natural president and moving spirit of the council. Harnack's own solution, the impossible emendation εὐσεβεῖ, would in effect produce the same story.[18]

15. Michael the Syrian, *Chronicle,* vii. 2, ed. Chabot (Syriac text, p. 124); *Liber Chalif.,* p. 119, ed. Land (Syriac text, p. 20). Brilliantov's emendation was first reported by D. Lebedev in *Khristianskoe Chtenie* (1911), p. 1017. His arguments are conveniently accessible in Seeberg's summary, op. cit., pp. 69ff. Another example of the confusion between Eusebius and Hosius may be found in B. H. Cowper's *Syriac Miscellanies,* p. 89.

16. Op. cit., p. 71: 'There is much to be said in favour of it. . . . Its possibility must be admitted; yet it would be methodologically wrong to base the entire investigation upon so hesitant a possibility.'

17. *Theologische Literaturzeitung,* xxxix (1914), col. 14. So also F. Haase, *Altchristliche Kirchengeschichte nach orientalischen Quellen* (Leipzig, 1925), pp. 238–39, and Seeck (below, p. 97).

18. Harnack, *Sitzungsber. d. preuß. Akad.,* 1908, p. 487.

Since 1934, however, Brilliantov's emendation has achieved widespread recognition, thanks in the main to Opitz, Schwartz, and Lietzmann. Opitz even ventured boldly to print Ossius's name in place of 'Eusebius' in his reprint of Schwartz's retroversion into Greek. Although this has the unfortunate consequence that the actual reading of the manuscript cannot be discovered from his book by any readers without knowledge of Syriac, Opitz's confidence is not unjustified. For Opitz first noticed that there is indirect, independent testimony to Ossius's visit to Antioch in a fragment of Marcellus of Ancyra, quoted by Eusebius of Caesarea. Marcellus reports that Ossius asked Narcissus of Neronias whether, like Eusebius of Caesarea, he believed in two *ousiai*—to which Narcissus replied that he believed in three![19] In all probability this is a fragment of the cross-examination conducted by Ossius at the council of Antioch, and therefore Brilliantov's conjecture receives strong confirmation. Schwartz himself was entirely convinced, and abandoned his original hypothesis of Eusebius of Isaura.[20] Lietzmann likewise took it for granted that the council was under the presidency of Ossius. But he felt bound to acknowledge in a footnote that the text was not beyond doubt: 'The name of Ossius is corrupt in the decisive document and is only restored by conjecture—admittedly extremely probable.'[21] Lietzmann did not regard the matter as incontrovertible. And in the minds of others this element of critical doubt may yet persist. At any rate, in 1948 Professor A. H. M. Jones[22]

19. Marcellus, quoting Narcissus's letter to Chrestus, Euphronius, and Eusebius, ap. Eus., *Contra Marcellum* i. 4. 38 (p. 25 Klostermann). Discussion in Opitz, 'Die Zeitfolge des arianischen Streites von den Anfängen bis zum Jahre 328', in *Zeits. f. d. Neutest. Wiss.* xxxiii (1934), p. 152.

20. So far as I can discover, Schwartz first announced his conversion in *Deutsche Literaturzeitung,* 1935, col. 718: 'No doubt is now possible that Ossius presided over the Antiochene synod in 324–5.' This is repeated in the 1936 edition of *Kaiser Konstantin und die christliche Kirche,* p. 124, and in his article 'Die Kanonessammlungen der alten Reichskirche', in *Zeits. d. Savigny-Stiftung f. Rechtsgeschichte,* lvi, Kan. Abt. xxv (1936), p. 21 n. 1.

21. *Geschichte der alten Kirche,* iii (1938), p. 102 n. 1 = *From Constantine to Julian,* translated by Bertram Lee Woolf (1950), p. 114 n. 1.

22. *Constantine and the Conversion of Europe* (London, 1948), p. 149. That Ossius is the most probable reading is affirmed by F. L. Cross, *Church Quarterly Review* cxxviii (1939), p. 59. It was regarded as a possibility by N. H. Baynes, *Journal of Roman Studies* xviii (1928), p. 219 ('Hosius may have been present . . .'). No consideration even to the possibility of Ossius's presidency is given by Mgr. R. Devreesse, *Le Patriarcat d' Antioche depuis la paix de l'église jusqu' à la conquête arabe* (Paris, 1945), pp. 124, 127, who holds that the see of 'Eusebius' must remain unknown, and who dates the council *after* Nicaea but before the synod that deposed Eustathius of Antioch. Devreesse thinks the occasion of the council was 'the reticent attitude adopted towards Arius' by Theodotus, Narcissus, and Eusebius.

unhesitatingly reverted to the original position of Schwartz, that we may accept Eusebius as the leader of the synod.

A little over a year ago I had the opportunity of visiting the Mingana Collection at Selly Oak and, led on by an entry in the catalogue, turned over the leaves of Mingana syr. 8, a manuscript very similar to the canon law collection of Parisinus syr. 62 in all its essential contents, but very much later in date. According to the colophon on fol. 74a, the manuscript was written at Mosul in A.D. 1911 by the deacon Matthew, son of Paul, and was copied from a vellum manuscript, believed by the copyist to be of the tenth century.[23] If the copyist's judgement of the date of his model is roughly correct, then the text has not had a long and complex history in transmission, and we need not be too disturbed at the thought of a twentieth-century copy. At fols. 38a–41b the manuscript contains the text of the synodal letter of the Antiochene council in a form virtually identical with the Paris text edited by Schwartz and Schulthess.[24] But there is no corruption in the name of the presiding bishop: his name is Ossius, ܐܘܣܝܘܣ.

Some minor details may be noticed in conclusion. Dr. Kelly has remarked concerning the Antiochene letter that 'many obscurities remain to be cleared up'.[25] I suspect that some of these obscurities are the consequence not so much of the inherent unintelligibility of the document itself as of the super-imposition of modern theories (by scholars other than Dr. Kelly) to try and make it fit with risky hypotheses that are neither necessary nor demonstrable.

To the question of the address, i.e. whether the letter was sent (as the manuscripts affirm) to Alexander of Byzantium or (as Lebedev, Bolotov, Schwartz, and Opitz have maintained)[26] to Alexander of Thessalonica, I hope to return upon some other occasion in a different context.

A speculative hypothesis that has had a surprising following is that of Loofs concerning the connexion of Ossius with one Paulinus, supposed by Loofs to have been bishop of the schismatic congregation at Antioch faithful

---

23. A. Mingana, *Catalogue of the Mingana Collection of Manuscripts,* i (Cambridge: Heffer, 1933), p. 28. I have to thank the Librarian, Mrs. Leonard, for help at the Library and subsequently in providing microfilms.

24. The manuscript has some corruptions in common with the Paris text, e.g. in the list of bishops 'Agamanes' for Salamanes; and for Sopatros, where the Paris text has Opatros, Ming. has Petros, which presumes the same corruption. In section 10 (Opitz, p. 10, line 3) Ming. omits 'the scriptures'. Otherwise the variants are negligible.

25. *Early Christian Creeds,* p. 209.

26. Cp. Seeberg, op. cit., p. 60 n. 1; Opitz, art. cit. (above p. 92, n. 19), pp. 150, 153.

to the memory of Paul of Samosata since his removal in 270.[27] Since Loofs's theory has been accepted and restated not only in a widely noticed article[28] by Opitz but also by V. C. de Clercq in his recent dissertation on Ossius's life,[29] it seems right here to express some sharply sceptical dissent. Loofs started from a sentence in the abusive encyclical of the Oriental Council of Serdica preserved in a Latin version in Hilary of Poitiers.[30] The sentence occurs almost at the end of the letter where the eastern bishops are busy justifying their excommunication of Ossius as the leader of the western half of that unhappy council. They explain that they have excommunicated Ossius on three grounds: first, because he entered into communion with Athanasius of Alexandria and Marcellus of Ancyra, the one a man of violence and the other a Sabellian heretic; secondly, 'because he persistently inflicted grievous wrongs upon Mark of blessed memory';[31] and thirdly, because

> when he was in the east he lived with scoundrels and blackguards—for he disgracefully became the inseparable friend of Paulinus, formerly bishop of Dacia, a man who was originally condemned for witchcraft and was driven out of the church, and who is still living in apostasy to

27. F. Loofs, *Paulus von Samosata* (Texte und Untersuchungen, xliv, Heft 5, Leipzig, 1924), pp. 186–95. It is noteworthy that Loofs followed Harnack in denying the authenticity of the Antiochene letter (as also the letter from Constantine transferring the council of Ancyra to Nicaea—cp. *Theol. Lit.-Zeit.*, 1884, col. 574), and that he remained unable to convince himself of its genuineness, even though that would have added greatly to the plausibility of his argument.

28. *Zeits. f. d. Neutest. Wiss.* xxxiii (1934), pp. 131–59.

29. Victor C. de Clercq, *Ossius of Cordova: a Contribution to the History of the Constantinian Period* (The Catholic University of America Studies in Christian Antiquity, No. 13, Washington, D.C., 1954), pp. 206–17.

30. *CSEL* lxv, p. 66, ed. Feder: 'Sed Ossium [sc. damnavimus] propter supradictam causam et propter beatissimae memoriae Marcum, cui graves semper iniurias irrogavit, sed et quod malos omnes pro criminibus suis digne damnatos totis viribus defendebat et quod convixerit in Oriente cum sceleratis ac perditis. turpiter namque Paulino quondam episcopo Daciae individuus amicus fuit, homini qui primo maleficus fuerit accusatus et de ecclesia pulsus usque in hodiernum diem in apostasia permanens cum concubinis publice et meretricibus fomicetur, cuius maleficiorum libros Machedonius episcopus atque confessor a Mobso combussit.'

31. Who was this Mark? P. B. Gams, *Kirchengeschichte von Spanien*, II. i (1864), pp. 362–63, suggested that he was the heretic Mark, said to have been the teacher of Priscillian by Sulpicius Severus (*Chron.* ii. 46). Gams's guess has been persuasively restated by V. C. de Clercq, 'Ossius of Cordova and the Origins of Priscillianism', in *Studia Patristica,* i (Texte und Untersuchungen, lxiii, Berlin, 1957), pp. 601–6.

this day openly committing fornication with concubines and harlots; his magical books were burnt by Macedonius, the bishop and confessor of Mopsuestia.

Who was this *Paulinus quondam episcopus Daciae* with whom Ossius entered into so compromising a relation on his visit to the east? Sozomen, reproducing what is without doubt Sabinus's précis of the oriental encyclical, says that the eastern bishops excommunicated Ossius 'because he had been friendly with Paulinus and Eustathius who were bishops of the church of Antioch' (ὅτι φίλος ἐγένετο Παυλίνῳ καὶ Εὐσταθίῳ τοῖς ἡγησαμένοις τῆς Ἀντιοχέων ἐκκλησίς).[32] Valois suggested in his note on this passage that Hilary's *Daciae* might be explained as a misreading of an abbreviated form of *Antiochiae.*[33] Loofs went one better. He conjectured that the Paulist community at Antioch had placed itself under the charge of an excommunicate western bishop from Dacia; that on the occasion of Ossius's visit to Antioch early in 325 he entered into an understanding with this Paulinus; and that this understanding provides the background for the nineteenth canon of Nicaea, laying down the terms for the reconciliation of the Paulist community.[34]

This theory was described as 'precarious' by Dr. Telfer long ago in *The Journal of Theological Studies* when reviewing Loofs's book.[35] The most probable solution is surely that proposed by Schwartz,[36] namely, that *daciae* in the text of Hilary is a corruption of *adanae,* and that τοῖς ἡγησαμένοις τῆς Ἀντιοχέων ἐκκλησίς is a mistaken explanatory addition made by Sozomen

32. Sozomen, *H.E.* iii. 11. 7.

33. Valois's note is reprinted in the editions of Sozomen (Hussey, iii, pp. 89f.; Migne, *PG* lxvii. 1061).

34. Loofs (*Paulus v. Samosata,* p. 192) conjectures a lacuna in the text of Hilary; the lost matter described the objectionable 'deal' between Ossius, Eustathius, and Paulinus. Opitz, in his note on the Antiochene synod's letter (*Athanasius Werke,* iii, p. 37 n.), thinks the disorder at Antioch there described was caused by the schismatic Paulist congregation, and appeals to Loofs's discussion for support. But the synodal letter gives the impression that the troubles at Antioch were a very recent crisis, in that they could have been sorted out but for Licinius's prohibition of synods, and that the disregard of the canons, of which the letter complains, was the consequence of the friends of Arius taking advantage of the situation to give him their help in the fight against his bishop. The Paulist congregation was the least of the synod's worries, if indeed they discussed the matter at all. If they did, why was Nic. can. 19 necessary?

35. *J.T.S.* xxvi (1925), p. 195. Cp. Bardy, *Paul de Samosate*[2] (Louvain, 1929), p. 389: 'La construction de Loofs a certaines apparences de séduction; mais à l'épreuve elle se révèle terriblement fragile.'

36. *Deutsche Literaturzeitung,* 1935, col. 719.

(or noted in his margin by some early scribe, whence it found its way into the text). Paulinus of Adana figures in the Nicene lists, and he is also no doubt the Paulinus who appears in the list of Antiochene bishops at the head of their letter to Alexander of Byzantium. At the council of Antioch Ossius found in the bishop of Adana an invaluable ally. Perhaps in the reaction after Nicaea the Eusebian party took their revenge, and Paulinus was ousted from his see; but we need not suppose that the charges of witchcraft and immorality were necessarily invented. In any event, the fact that his magical treatises were burnt by Macedonius of Mopsuestia strongly suggests that a Cilician see must be found for Paulinus.

It has been suggested by Professor Jones that the council of Antioch was 'packed'.[37] There can be no doubt that its anti-Arian conclusion was predetermined. Ossius controlled it from start to finish, and called it (I think) with the intention of carrying through a purge of the episcopate in the diocese Oriens where Arius was finding friendly support. But the term 'packed' may imply that only those known to be unfriendly to Arius were summoned to the council, and that the rest were virtually excluded. The list of bishops in the address gives no support to this view. There were Arian sympathizers present whose courage was not equal to that of the three who stood their ground against the big battalions of Ossius and Eustathius of Antioch and were provisionally excommunicated. Macedonius of Mopsuestia is a case in point; he signed the Antiochene letter, as also the Nicene creed later in the same year, but he was subsequently to play a prominent role in the Eusebian party as a member of the Mareotic commission of inquiry sent to collect evidence against Athanasius in 335. Other examples of bishops who bent their consciences to Ossius's will are Aetius of Lydda and Gregory of Berytus. If there are notable absentees like Paulinus of Tyre and Patrophilus of Scythopolis, that is probably because they had the good sense to stay away from Ossius's council rather than because they were not invited. The extant letter of Eusebius of Nicomedia to Paulinus of Tyre, exhorting him to break his reticence and to come out on the 'Lucianist' side,[38] suggests that Paulinus of Tyre thought this was to be reckoned a time to keep silence. It must have been clear to him and to everyone else what Ossius intended to do.

It may very well be the case that it was Ossius's authority which carried through the translation of Eustathius from Beroea to Antioch after the death of Philogonius on 20 December 324. The establishment of an avowed

---

37. *Constantine and the Conversion of Europe*, p. 149.
38. Ap. Theodoret, *H.E.* i. 6. 1 (= Opitz, *Urkunden* 8).

anti-Origenist in the great see of Antioch would have afforded much satisfaction to Macarius of Jerusalem, Hellanicus of Tripolis, and Alexander of Alexandria. The presence of Ossius at Antioch immediately after Philogonius's death would ensure the appointment of a sound successor.

Whether or not the council of Antioch was called with the 'ostensible purpose', as Dr. Kelly claims,[39] of electing Philogonius's successor appears less than certain. If Ossius gave this as the reason for his summons, he discloses nothing of it in the synodal letter. It seems at least equally possible that Ossius's arrival at Antioch coincided with the time when the church there was about to elect a new bishop, and that he threw in his weight decisively on the side of the anti-Arian faction ('the city contains many righteous inhabitants', remarks the synodal letter). Having secured the position at Antioch by translating the reliable controversialist Eustathius, Ossius may then have decided to call together the bishops of the oriental diocese in order to stifle critics of Alexander of Alexandria like Eusebius of Caesarea and his two friends.

The synodal letter directs that the three excommunicated bishops shall have the opportunity of repentance at the forthcoming synod of Ancyra. What is the relation between the councils of Antioch and Ancyra? The Antiochene description of the synod of Ancyra as 'great and hieratic' at least implies that the forthcoming council was expected to be attended by many more bishops and to be quite a noteworthy event with grave matters on its agenda.[40] But how far did the fathers of Antioch forestall the decisions of Ancyra? Some acute speculation has been devoted to this question by Otto Seeck and Dr. Norman Baynes. According to Seeck[41] Constantine himself called the council of Ancyra, sending out the summons soon after the battle of Chrysopolis; the council of Antioch he believes to have been an emergency assembly, 'probably under the presidency of Eustathius', intended to forestall any possibility of toleration for Arian sympathizers being imposed at Ancyra, whether by the faction of Eusebius of Nicomedia or by the emperor's authority. Constantine's answer to Antioch was simply to take no notice whatever, and to place the bishops of Ancyra firmly under his personal surveillance by transferring them to Nicaea. The exclusivism of Eustathius and of Marcellus of Ancyra was not to be allowed to control events there. Seeck's general theory has been partly taken over and partly modified

---

39. Op. cit., p. 208.

40. Cp. the self-conscious term 'the great synod', Nic. can. 2, 3, 6, 14, 15, 20.

41. *Geschichte des Untergangs der antiken Welt,* iii², pp. 405ff.; cp. Seeck's *Regesten der Kaiser und Päpste* (Stuttgart, 1919), p. 152.

by Baynes. Baynes thinks it more likely that the notion of holding a larger council at Ancyra was the brainchild of the bishops assembled in Antioch, and that therefore the invitations to Ancyra were sent out after, not before, the Antiochene synod.

> Why did Constantine choose Ancyra for the meeting place of *his* council? As modem travellers to Angora know, it was a curiously remote place for bishops from the west of Europe. If with Seeck we place Constantine's summons to the bishops *before* the council at Antioch, I see no answer to this question. But suppose we reverse the order: Constantine is parrying the decision of Antioch: he will make the Council of Ancyra his own by promising to constitute it as an ecumenical assembly. In the winter of 324 he issues his invitations to the Christian world, and then, those invitations issued and his point secured, he transfers the gathering to Nicaea where he can influence its deliberations.[42]

The force of Baynes's criticism of Seeck turns on his question concerning the unaccountable choice of Ancyra, if the selection of the place for the council lay in the emperor's will. But is his question so unanswerable as he assumes? A city in Bithynia might not seem at all the right location, since it would inevitably lie under the influence of Eusebius of Nicomedia; and he, having acted as ambassador for Licinius after the battle of Chrysopolis, was not at all in favour with Constantine.[43] The Bithynian bishops had indeed already declared themselves to be general supporters of Arius against Alexander.[44] The very remoteness of Ancyra might have seemed, in November 324, an asset in the emperor's eyes. Moreover, as the see of Marcellus it would be warmly welcomed by Ossius and Alexander of Alexandria. The point cannot, of course, be proved; it is enough for the purposes of the present argument to suggest that such considerations might have weighed with the emperor and with Ossius, and that this reconstruction is not impossible.

---

42. Baynes, *Journ. Rom. Stud.* xviii (1928), p. 219. This interpretation is restated in his British Academy lecture of 1930, *Constantine the Great and the Christian Church*, where he also notes (p. 85) that Brilliantov had independently suggested that the council of Ancyra was originally called by the bishops assembled at Antioch. Baynes is followed by J. Vogt, *Constantin der Große und sein Jahrhundert* (Munich, 1949), p. 198.

43. Constantine, *Ep. ad Eccl. Nicomedensium,* ap. Athan. *de Decretis* xli. 9 (= Opitz, *Urkunden* 27), calls him ὁ τῆς τυραννικῆς ὠμότητος συμμύστης.

44. Sozomen, *H.E.* i. 15. 10.

It is, however, the text of the Antiochene letter itself which makes Baynes's reconstruction seem doubtful. Seeck's general conception of the pattern of events makes an unhappy and unedifying story. But I cannot escape the conviction that the language of the synodal letter supports him. The Antiochene document surely presupposes that the council of Ancyra has already been called to meet soon after Easter 325, and that Alexander of Byzantium is expected to have information about it. Above all, it is because a 'great and hieratic synod' with a very wide representation has already been called to deal *inter alia* with the doctrinal dispute that the council of Antioch feels itself compelled to allow the three excommunicate bishops an opportunity of recovering their position. The condition attached to the condemnation may well have been granted only with deep reluctance by Ossius and Eustathius; but the proviso was all-important, since it saved the council from the appearance of grossly prejudging the question which was explicitly set down for discussion by a greater and more 'ecumenical' synod at Ancyra, only two or three months distant. No doubt Constantine was not deceived and, in the event, Ossius and Eustathius may have made a fatal tactical mistake by overreaching themselves at Antioch, if it was their precipitate action there which moved Constantine to intervene by transferring the council of Ancyra into Bithynia where he could more easily prevent the exponents of a rigid orthodoxy from dominating the scene. Left to themselves at Ancyra they would have enjoyed more freedom and more power. At Nicaea, in Constantine's presence, Eusebius of Caesarea submitted his creed. As he tells his church with impassioned fervour, 'our beloved emperor himself was the very first to declare that it was most orthodox, and indeed that he held exactly the same opinions. . . .'[45] The council of Antioch had received its answer.

No one had good reason to look back on the council of Antioch as a happy occasion. If it is asked why no ancient historian mentions it, the answer is surely plain, that its attempt to prejudge the issue proved abortive, and it was submerged by the vast and sacrosanct assembly of Nicaea. The Nicene decisions made those of Antioch irrelevant; and in so far as they were not irrelevant they were embarrassing.

The controversy concerning the date of Easter was certainly on the agenda for Ancyra/Nicaea. Dr. de Clercq has numbered it among the 'several obscure points which have not been satisfactorily answered' that the synodal letter of Antioch makes no reference to the Easter dispute, 'which is difficult

---

45. Eusebius, *Ep. ad Eccl. Caesar.,* ap. Athan. *de Decretis* xxxiii. 7 (= Opitz, *Urkunden* 22).

to explain on the supposition of Ossius' presence'.[46] This difficulty disappears if we suppose that the summons to meet at Ancyra had already gone out when the synod gathered under Ossius at Antioch earlier in the same year. The meeting at Antioch was a sudden decision on Ossius's part, an urgent attempt to close the ranks before the wider and therefore less controllable assembly met at Ancyra. Easter could wait; orthodoxy could not.

46. *Ossius of Cordova*, pp. 216–17.

The Chalcedonian Definition

1. The Religious Framework

A detailed survey of all the decisions of the ecumenical councils of the Church quickly shows that a very substantial number now belong to the forgotten past. At the time the decisions were no doubt right and important. But in the later and present memory of the Christian community they are recalled only by a handful of historians and canonists; and that is virtually to say that they are perished as though they had never been. But Chalcedon is different. It has remained like Nicaea a great name—a mass of rock irreversibly diverting the course of the river. If in 1982 we ask what the Church of the great tradition believes about the person of Christ, at least in formal terms, we shall be pointed to this Council of 451 with its carefully articulated, lapidary definition which retains classical status and authority not only for Roman Catholic, Orthodox, and Anglican, but also for the main traditions of Reformation theology.

The Chalcedonian Definition holds together two contrasting ways of answering the questions, Who is Christ? and What does he mean to those who trust in him as the way, the truth, and the life? It gives its answer to these questions in the technical terms of the fifth century—*physis, prosopon, hypostasis*. One phrase above all others in the Definition, 'in two natures', became a cause of bitter controversy and eventual division, splitting the Greek churches of the East so deeply that the wound remains incompletely healed to this day. The Definition therefore raises vast questions fundamental to the life of Christian theology within the Church. We have to ask whether the Definition's intended synthesis is a statement of real consensus and substantial agreement or only an ingenious juxtaposition of disparate bits and pieces, intriguing mainly because of its verbal dexterity—perhaps with something of the pleasure given by an artist's abstract collage. Secondly, it is legitimate to ask an ecumenical council from which schism has stemmed whether or not its divisive language was strictly necessary. Is there any element of insisting on a formula for its own sake? Or is it right to penetrate behind the external words to the inward meaning (a principle dear to Athanasius in the fourth century and far from being merely a convenient invention of modern ecumenists)? Thirdly, the resort to a technical vocabulary of non-biblical and abstract terms raises the question whether talk of 'one person and one hypostasis known in two natures' is altogether adequate to so grand and delicate a subject. Do the static abstractions of the Definition protect the reality of the humanity of Christ at the price of almost concealing his dynamic life from our view?

Chalcedon offers a statement of consensus between the rival Christologies which in broad terms (taking no account of many subtle nuances) we label those of Antioch and Alexandria. The long history of Christian thought shows how easy it is for a lasting and deep polarity to develop between two patterns of affirmation, each of which has behind it the force of a powerful sense of religious commitment and of a fear of its rival. On the one hand, Christians intuitively want to affirm that our redemption is made possible by the perfect and free self-offering of Jesus the Christ, model to all humanity in faith, obedience, and holiness; the very head of the church which is his body and which is called to enter by faith into the movement of his offering to the Father, therefore making its supreme act of intercession—as in the eucharistic memorial. It continues this line of thinking to say that, on the ground of this priest and victim, the Church sacramentally makes an offering which is so one with Christ's self-offering in propitiation for the sins of the whole world that what the Church there offers is said to be Christ. For we cannot stand before God except as we stand with him and in him, and except as he stands with us and in us. Only one who is as we are can be our Redeemer. Because none less than he can fully represent our humanity before the Father, we must affirm that the humanity of the Redeemer is no mere cipher, no mere temporary tool of the divinity, but fully free and self-moved, acting for our salvation.

On the other hand, Christians also know and need to affirm that we fallen creatures are too far gone to find redemption from within the creaturely order even at its highest and best. We want a redemption such as only our Creator can achieve, one which enters the innermost depths of our corrupt being to purge away guilt and sinful habit and to conquer alienation by incorporating us within the community of the Church. Therefore we need a Redeemer who is not as we are, or is at least more than we. Hence the drive to affirm that, just as God does not change in himself when he created the world, so also the Word of God is not changed into something else when he is made flesh. He who is incarnate and who once for all suffered in the flesh remains immutably 'one of the Trinity', and his mother is Theotokos. The eternal fully enters time and history in order to bring to his own eternal love us time-conditioned creatures, finite and yet retaining that freedom and rationality and individual uniqueness which is to be 'made in the image and likeness of God'.

Of these two approaches to the person of Christ, the first is the way adopted by the ancient school of Antioch. It is a way which goes naturally with a high estimate of the nature and value of man as the very image and agent of God, damaged indeed by sin, but repaired through the perfect humanity of Jesus of Nazareth. This type of Christology therefore implies an anthropology in which human freedom is crucial and central, and where the fallen state of man, though grave, is not understood to be utterly irremediable other than by an act of grace indistinguishable from a sovereign and creative omnipotence creating out of nothing. Redemption is a restoration of the high dignity and value of man. Therefore this Christology deeply fears the submergence, or the reduction to hardly more than a nominal symbol, of the Redeemer's moral being as man and second Adam. The fear is not without foundation, since the concept of God incarnate has indeed become legitimately labelled myth if the Redeemer's humanity has become merely an accidental tool to the substantial work achieved by the divine presence within the veil.

Beginning from the axioms that Christ is not from below but 'from above' (John 8:23) and that one who is himself part of the world, though free of sin, is nevertheless not mighty enough to bring redemption in the sense of remission of sins and eternal life, the Alexandrian Christology affirms the complete, concrete, and real presence of God in the incarnate Lord. This fullness of divine presence imparts redemptive value to his life, death, and resurrection. Contrast the Antiochene school which grounds this value in the moral perfection of the Lord's humanity as a model for faith and freedom, filled with, inspired through, and indwelt uniquely by divine grace and Holy Spirit. To Alexandrian ears the Antiochene Christology arouses deep fear. It sounds reductionist. Its merits—a greater accessibility and intelligibility to human minds—make it suspected of making Christianity altogether too easy, and it can be represented as rationalist or humanist. In modern dress such a Christology 'from below' hardly needs the miraculous element in the gospel: Virgin Birth and Resurrection are not merely an unnecessary decoration but a positive obstacle on the path to a rational faith. To ancient men (as to Islam) the crucifixion was the apparently insuperable obstacle to faith, and certainly the element in the gospel hardest to reconcile with the Alexandrian Christology. To modern man the Resurrection is the prime difficulty; hence the greater power today of an Antiochene understanding of the person of Christ in which the Resurrection is more the crowning glory of humanity than a divine intervention. No ancient critic of Antiochene Christology observed its implicit individualism and virtual indifference to the corporate dimension of salvation.

The anthropology implied in Alexandrian Christology is substantially less optimistic. Is the Nestorian Christ the natural saviour of Pelagian man? Admittedly this formula of accusation has cogent force only (a) if redemption by grace in Christ, which makes human freedom to stand erect, becomes an assertion that this grace is limited to the provision of a striking ethical example, and (b) if redemption is attached to the person of Christ not because of the discernment of a distinct or substantial divine presence in him, but merely as an accidental historical consequence of the fact that this human life happens to be the event from which, in the stream of time and chance, there springs up the community of Christians who take him as their moral leader and exemplar. The latter Christology touches the point of disintegration, since it is in effect a Christology minus a doctrine of God. (Theodore of Mopsuestia and Nestorius would not have warmed to that; Theodore was no Liberal Protestant, and Theodoret no Pelagian.)

Because of the mutual fears mentioned above, the tendency of both Christologies is to seek to oust the other from citizenship rights within the Church. But the price of such exclusion is the loss, or the threat of loss, of elements essential to the viability of each. The high Christology of Alexandria finds its religious strength in the deep need of man for a Redeemer able to give remission of sins and eternal life and who is therefore coming from the divine side of the gulf between the immutable Creator and the unstable, transient creature. It betrays its weakness when it slides towards losing the reality, fullness, and freedom of the human life of Jesus Christ.

The Antiochene Christology finds its strength in its evident roots not only in the Synoptic Gospels but also in St. Paul and in the epistle to the Hebrews. It answers to the human longing for moral freedom, the will to love and to obey. It obviously takes with the utmost seriousness the human achievement of Jesus Christ without which there is no salvation. Its weakness is betrayed when (in a modern humanist dress) it slides into making the Redeemer so human, so merely human, that he ceases to be seen to be able to redeem. It seems almost to offer religion without God—and man, if faced by the choice, would prefer God without religion!

Both Christologies are in acute difficulty in finding words in which to give a coherent statement of the unity of divine and human elements in Christ. The Alexandrian theologians want to assert the maximum degree of unity compatible with the preservation of completeness in the Redeemer's humanity. But will a full and distinct presence of God wholly absorb the human creature 'like a drop of honey in the ocean'? Or is the union more like that of iron in the fire where the iron remains distinct, even though it acquires all the properties of fire? The Antiochene theologians assert the maximum freedom of Christ's moral being as man, to the limit of compatibility with genuine assertion of the full and distinct presence of God in Christ. They therefore tended to affirm a unity of role and function, of external form and appearance; the inner reality is a duality, the elements of which are to stand in as intimate relation to one another as is possible without any actual loss of duality. Nestorius expressed this unity in terms of *prosopon*. The Alexandrians, by contrast, wanted a unity which passed far beyond role or function or external appearance. For them the union must be expressed in terms of the constituting, from the two elements, of a single nature (*physis*) and a single concrete entity (*hypostasis*). Against Nestorius, Cyril of Alexandria affirms a union in hypostasis, a union in which the incarnate Lord is made a single 'nature', even though by logical abstraction the reflective mind is aware that he is constituted out of two.

2. The Historical Framework

With these observations we have already passed from broad generalisations about the two constant patterns of Christology to more detailed consideration of the ancient background of the Council of Chalcedon. Both 'Antioch' and 'Alexandria' were in origin rival reactions to the dilemma put by the Arians: If the Logos is truly incarnate, how can he remain free of suffering, free (that is) from necessity, conflict, the ills that flesh is heir to, the limitations of a human body in time and space? But if, as the Arians held, he is truly taking flesh, is ignorant, weeps, cries out at dereliction, then he is not on the same level as the highest, transcendent God. The Arians argue, therefore, that if God is impassible, a suffering Christ must be less than God.

The Antiochenes answer this contention by separating the distinct natures: for them the Logos is truly incarnate, but remains what he is in himself, impassible, and therefore untouched by the sufferings of the humanity that he has assumed. The human nature of the incarnate Lord must be complete, with body, living soul or life-principle, and Nous or powers of intellection. The insistence on this completeness averts the Arian presupposition that in Christ the Logos has replaced the elements of his human nature through which he is capable of suffering.

The Alexandrians (with Gregory of Nazianzus in support) concede that the humanity and the Logos are conceptually separable, but express fear of an interpretation of the union which makes the two natures so independent of each other as to leave the man only the supreme instance of inspired prophecy. To the Alexandrians Jesus Christ is not a person with an identifiable life without the very Word of God who is incarnate in him. The Arian question about divine impassibility is therefore answered by a bold assertion of paradox: 'The Word suffered impassibly'. Plotinus and the Neoplatonic school had already used the same paradox to safeguard the higher soul's immutability while united to the inferior body. But whereas the Neoplatonists concede the soul's awareness of its body's experiences, the Alexandrian theologians want to glory in a directly theopaschite affirmation: in Christ God has become passible. And that affirmation must sound to the school of Antioch like a doctrine of the conversion of immutable divinity into mutable flesh. To the ears of Theodore and Nestorius and Theodoret, Alexandrian Christology failed to exorcise the spectre of Arianism.

The terms in which the Chalcedonian Definition is cast appear formal and remote to a modern reader, but are in fact the current coin of the fifth-century debate. The context of the council did much to decide the precise shape of its dogmatic decision. The bitter division between Cyril of Alexandria and the friend of Nestorius, John of Antioch, at the first Council of Ephesus (431) was resolved by the terms of reunion in 433. Under these terms John of Antioch agreed to drop Nestorius, while Cyril of Alexandria accepted the Formulary of Union drafted by Theodoret. The Formulary affirmed Mary to be Theotokos and Christ to be (of) 'two natures' (without any preposition in Greek). In his covering letter to John of Antioch accepting the Formulary, Cyril accepts 'of (*ek*) two natures'. It was a tacit convention of the restoration of ecclesiastical communion in 433 that Cyril's third letter to Nestorius, with his militant and extremist twelve anathemas, was not a requirement of orthodoxy binding upon the faithful. In the eyes of the school of Antioch Cyril's twelve anathemas offered dangerous cover for Apollinarianism; Cyril's most zealous supporters regarded them as the one certain defence against Nestorianism. In 447 the tacit convention not to impose the twelve anathemas as a requirement was deliberately challenged by Cyril's successor at Alexandria, Dioscorus (444–51) in collaboration with Eutyches, archimandrite at Constantinople, an ultra-monophysite dissatisfied with Cyril's political compromise of 433. Eutyches was accused of heresy by Eusebius, bishop of Dorylaeum in Phrygia (the same zealot who had brought the crucial accusations against Nestorius in 429) and was brought for examination before the patriarch Flavian and his 'home synod'. Before Flavian Eutyches affirmed 'two natures before the union, one after' (which Flavian allowed to pass without critical comment), and then caused consternation by rejecting the double *homoousios* of the Formulary of Union of 433, 'of one substance with the Father in respect of his divinity, of one substance with us in respect of his humanity.' Eutyches granted that Mary is one substance with us, and that from her the divine Word took his body; he denied that there was any good precedent for saying Christ to be of one substance with us.

When Pope Leo the Great received the transcript of Eutyches' examination before Flavian, he was astonished that Flavian had not commented on the formula 'two natures before the union, one after'. Both parts of Eutyches's formula alarmed him: the first half because (if 'nature' is taken in a concrete sense, as it obviously must be in the second half) it easily suggested a time, however brief, when the humanity of Christ existed apart from the divine Word; the second half because it suggested the virtual obliteration and absorption of the humanity and its enjoyment of a total, immediate, and unqualified deification.

At the examination of Eutyches before Flavian, some important interventions were made by individual bishops. Basil of Seleucia declared that Christ is 'known in two natures', a formula which in effect echoes Cyril's proviso that the dual nature of Christ is discerned only in the abstract by the reflective mind, not in the concrete by the worshipping soul. Basil also adds his full acceptance of Cyril's formula 'hypostatic union'. At the same examination Eusebius of Dorylaeum affirmed 'the union of two natures in one prosopon and one hypostasis', which he took to be a summary of Cyril's formulas. Flavian himself also stands in the Cyrilline tradition, confessing 'one Christ of (*ek*) two natures in one prosopon and one hypostasis,' and also accepting the pseudo-Athanasian (Apollinarian) formula 'one nature of the incarnate word'. So Flavian stands a long way from Nestorianism; much further than Leo from it.

Leo's Tome, sent to Flavian on 13 June 449 with the intention that it be read before the imminent second Council of Ephesus, insists on the completeness of both divinity and humanity. 'Each nature retains its own property' (a phrase which was a philosophical axiom), but 'they come together into a single persona', so that 'one and the same' is both God and man—the humanity being elevated, the divinity undiminished. The Word performs the miracles, the flesh suffers the bodily weaknesses (an echo of Augustine, *Tr. in Joh.* 8, 12). Because Christ is one person, Scripture and Tradition speak of the Son of man descending from heaven, and of the Son of God being crucified and buried (a borrowing from Augustine, *c. serm. Arianorum* 8).

Leo speaks of the 'unitatem personae in utraque natura intellegendam'—a phrase which may echo Basil of Seleucia's intervention in the examination of Eutyches. Augustine is the authority for his formula 'one person in two natures' (*Enchiridion* II, 36; *Tr. in Joh.* 78, 3, etc.).

Before Chalcedon the pro-western policy of the empress Pulcheria and of her consort Marcian had long been clear. The new patriarch of Constantinople, Anatolius, had already held a council at which Leo's Tome was formally accepted, interpreted as teaching that after the union there remain 'two natures without confusion, change or separation'. Dioscorus of Alexandria had already censured Leo as a Nestorianising heretic thereby forfeiting his Petrine authority to lead the churches. Leo had already approved of the orthodoxy of Theodoret, the leading theologian of the school of Antioch. From the start, therefore, the council's goal was declared with the reinstatement of Theodoret and the arraigning of Dioscorus. Precisely what status Theodoret occupied was a matter of dispute: was he present as a bishop taking his seat among the judges or as the complainant against Dioscorus? Ambiguity also surrounded the process of Dioscorus: was he accused of holding Eutyches' heretical doctrines? or was the charge merely contumacy (as Anatolius was to urge upon the synod, v. 14)?

There was no doubt a political element at the back of the imperial anxiety to please the West. The influence of Byzantine power over the West would be drastically diminished if Rome were to remain dissatisfied with the orthodoxy of the Greek churches. Moreover, Marcian's elevation by Pulcheria to the rank of Augustus had not yet led to his recognition by the western emperor Valentinian III. Marcian's need for recognition would provide additional incentive for an ecclesiastical policy which submitted the Greek churches to Leo's will. Accordingly, the overwhelming desire of the Greek bishops at Chalcedon to avert any new formula, and to rest content with the creed of Nicaea as interpreted by Cyril of Alexandria and Leo's Tome, was forced to give way, under threat that the emperor might even transfer the entire council to the West if the Greek bishops refused to assent.

The formula first proposed, though initially acceptable, was deemed inadequate. Its precise content is uncertain except that it included Theotokos and declared Christ to be 'of (*ek*) two natures'. The *ek* attracted attention, because it had already been the subject of subtle undercurrents in the examination of Eutyches. At one point Eutyches rejected it, but later came to accept (*Acta* i. 451, 489). At Chalcedon Dioscorus of Alexandria, at all times courageous to the point of gross political imprudence, avowed himself happy to accept *ek*: 'I accept "*Of* two"; I do not accept "Two"' (*Acta* i. 332).

The disclosure that the *ek* formula was acceptable to Dioscorus and even to Eutyches was fatal. The Roman legates could forgive the leaders among the Greek bishops who had followed Dioscorus's lead at the Council of Ephesus in 449; but towards Dioscorus who had dared to censure the Tome of Leo their hostility was implacable. They wanted a formula that he would find it hard to accept without grave loss of face.

After reference to the emperor himself, a new drafting commission was appointed with explicit instructions from the presiding officers of state that the new formula must include Leo's doctrine, which is summarised as 'two natures united without confusion, change, or separation' (*Acta* v. 26). The adverbs here translated 'without confusion, change, or separation' are not in Leo, and evidently reflect the concern of men like Basil of Seleucia that, without these qualifiers, Leo's diphysite doctrine would be catastrophically vulnerable to the charge of Nestorianism. It cannot be insignificant that they first occur in the record of the minor synod at Constantinople when Anatolius had formally accepted the Tome (*Acta* iv. 9). This will have been the source from which the officers of state learnt what Leo's doctrine was. The direct influence of the text of the Tome on the wording of the final form of the Definition is extremely small. But the drafting commission carried out their task with the utmost refinement and skill by reexpressing Leo's diphysite doctrine in a series of quotations from Cyril of Alexandria in whose original context they mainly have the force of parenthetic concessions.

This way of proceeding had good justification. The main task of the drafting commission was to produce an agreed statement of consensus in which everyone present, except the obstinate Dioscorus, could find his faith. It inhered in the method that the Definition could not achieve this if it included too many negatives on subordinate and peripheral issues, as was no doubt the case with Cyril's twelve anathemas attached to his third letter to Nestorius. The Illyrian and Palestinian bishops, for whom Cyril ranked as an authoritative and indeed inspired teacher, needed to be reassured that Leo was not leading the Church into heresy and that his Tome could be interpreted in a way that conformed to Cyrilline orthodoxy. The commission exercised high skill in discovering phrases from Cyril which could be used with a diphysite intention. They interpreted *hypostasis* as the equivalent of *prosopon* rather than of nature, *physis*. This equivalence had already been made before Chalcedon, e.g. by Eusebius of Dorylaeum (*Acta* i. 487). From Cyril's second letter to Nestorius they took the crucial phrase 'the difference between the natures being not destroyed by the union'. They constructed most of the first half of the revised Definition out of the Formulary of Union of 433 as contained in Cyril's letter to John of Antioch. There was in effect only one minuscule detail in which the language of the definition could not claim some precedent in the text of Cyril, and that was in the abandonment of 'of (*ek*) two natures' and its replacement by the phrase, already found on the lips of Basil of Seleucia in 448 and certainly intended as an interpretation of Cyril, 'known in (*en*) two natures'. Cyril never said 'in'. But it was in the Tome of Leo, 'in utraque natura'.

The Definition brilliantly executes the intention stated in the preamble declaring that its object is to bring peace and to end dissension in the Church, that being the reason why the emperor has called the bishops together in synod. The many bishops hostile to any new formula at all had been able to appeal to the ruling of the Council of Ephesus of 431 that no addition might be made to the Nicene creed. The preamble therefore replies with its assertion of concurrence with the Council of Ephesus on the sufficiency and binding force of the Nicene creed, but then adds that the creed of Constantinople of 381 is also valid. At the first session of the Council of Chalcedon (i. 158ff.) the status of the Council of Constantinople was the subject of dispute. Diogenes of Cyzicus, who appears throughout the *Acta* as a zealous and ingenious supporter of the dignity of New Rome, declares that Eutyches insisted on the Nicene creed alone, without addition, because the Council of 381 had censured Apollinarianism. His intervention provoked protest from the Egyptian bishops. It is impossible to escape the deep impression that at Chalcedon the creed of Constantinople (381) was insisted on not only to justify a new formula or because this council had censured Apollinarius (though without actually writing any clauses into its creed which an Apollinarian could not accept) but also because it had enacted the famous canon according special dignity to Constantinople as New Rome. Anatolius had an interest in stressing the high dignity of this assembly.

The insertion of the full text of both Nicene and Constantinopolitan creeds is followed by the formal acceptance of Cyril's letters to Nestorius (unspecified) and to John of Antioch as well as Leo's Tome. The council disowns any innovation. It is following the fathers when it lays down the following propositions:

1. Jesus Christ is no duality but a single identity.
2. Within this identity and unity, however, he is both fully God and fully Man.
3. As fully divine, he is of the same *ousia* as the Father.
4. As fully human (of rational soul and body) he is of the same *ousia* as his mother.
5. Nevertheless, his humanity has no share in our sinfulness.
6. He has a double birth: before the ages of the Father and 'in these last days' of Mary Theotokos.
7. 'Known in two natures' (the formula of Basil of Seleucia).
8. Without confusion, change, separation, or division (the four negative adverbs, going back to the qualifiers to 'two natures' in the summary of Leo's doctrine; see above).
9. The difference of natures is not destroyed by the union (cited from Cyril's second letter to Nestorius where it is a parenthetic concession).
10. Each nature therefore preserves its individual property (a phrase corresponding to a sentence in Leo's Tome, but not adding to the substance of no. 9).
11. They (i.e. the two natures) 'run together into a single *prosopon* and a single *hypostasis*'. ('Run together' comes from Gregory of Nazianzus, *Orat.* 37, 2.).
12. They are not divided into two *prosopa*.

The supremely sensitive clause is no. 7, 'known in two natures'. The preposition 'in' when combined with the participle 'known', was very far from being irreconcilable with Cyril. But the fact that it was evidently chosen both to leave legitimate room within the Church for Theodoret with the school of Antioch and to displease Dioscorus had the consequence that this two-letter word became the grand *skandalon* on which the emperor's hope for the peace of the churches was to make shipwreck, bringing a split in communion with vast social and political consequence.

Yet it cannot be claimed that the precise force of the preposition 'in' is utterly clear. Divisive formulas in the long history of theological controversy are seldom free of all ambiguity. Schism and muddle are much more often linked than schism and lucidity. Moreover, it gives food for thought that the crucial obstacle to unity was located in a preposition. The preposition 'in' seems to exercise a magnetic force upon theological controversy, as a consideration of post-Reformation eucharistic doctrine would show. At Chalcedon the motives for using this word appear mixed. Certainly 'in' possessed obvious merits. In the historical context of the fifth-century debates the word did not incisively exclude any particular Christology. It was fully compatible with the simultaneous assertion 'of two natures', though the antithesis between *ek* and *en* created a temporary illusion that this was not the case. The so-called 'Neo-Chalcedonianism' of the early sixth century made the double affirmation 'in and of two natures' one of its central theses, as part of its very legitimate programme of demonstrating the harmony of Chalcedon with Cyril against the Monophysite conviction of their total incompatibility. Successive generations of Chalcedonian theologians were baffled by the Monophysite rejection of 'in' as a sufficient ground for breach of communion.

Nevertheless the Christian historian who cares, as he must, for the unity of the people of God, may question whether it was in all respects wise and prudent when the drafting committee adopted this way of carrying out their instruction from civil authority that the Definition be so framed as to conform to Leo's Latin Tome (with its very different tradition behind it) and to use a preposition which was sure to exclude Dioscorus and his Egyptian suffragans of the Nile valley. Pressure from civil authority is not in the interest of free affirmation of consensus at the level of faith.

The Chalcedonian Definition is a landmark in the history of Christian thought by reason of its distinction between nature and person. The development of discussion about the Holy Trinity had already encouraged exactly such a distinction to be made; but now this was to be applied to Christology. The Monophysites argued that if Christ is one person, he must also be one nature: since unity of *prosopon* might mean, as for Nestorius, a unity merely of function or public role, they felt that the unity must be expressed in terms of *hypostasis* and *physis*. At Chalcedon a sharp disjunction is presupposed between *physis* on the one hand and *prosopon* and *hypostasis* on the other. Christ is declared to be one person and one concrete existent entity resulting from the concurrence of two natures which, like two streams, have their confluence in him. Here again the Definition is remarkable for its imprecision. It does not prescribe or even hint that the one hypostasis is that of the divine Word.

Like Cyril before it, the Council of Chalcedon makes use of neoplatonic philosophical terms, but that was no innovation in 451. The contemporary pagan Proclus is found, in his commentary on the *Timaeus,* distinguishing the highest degree of union, possible to Nous with another Nous, from the conjunction (*synapheia*) possible to a bond between Nous and Psyche, and from the 'participation' (*methexis*) which is the level of material bodies (*In Tim.* II 102, 24 Diehl). In his commentary on *Parmenides* 129a Proclus discusses the familiar Neoplatonic problem of identity and difference, making use of the same negative adverbs that we find in the Chalcedonian Definition. Such parallels in no way imply disparagement of the Christological Definition, as if it were an invasion of the holy of holies by a profane logic inappropriate to the matter under discussion. The neoplatonists were fascinated by the discussion of identity and difference (after Plato's *Parmenides*), and Christian theologians had quickly seen that the logical problems unravelled in this discussion had a bearing on elucidations of the doctrines of the Trinity and of the Person of Christ. What does it mean to say that x and y, being distinct, are nevertheless 'the same'? or vice versa?

It is, however, a fair criticism to observe that the technical philosophical terms and the negative adverbs of the Definition convey a sense of abstraction inadequate to express the richness of a biblical Christology. Univocal use of 'nature' (*physis*) applied to both God and Man arouses misgivings. Eutyches perhaps spoke wisely when he confessed his repugnance to treating of God under the category of *physis* (*Acta* i. 451, 456, 524), though it is very unclear why this repugnance should then favour monophysite rather than diphysite language. Abstract terms do not do justice to the vivid figure of the four Gospels, and by their abstraction may seem to take him out of the particularity of the historical process.

On the other side of the balance, however, there is a substantial defence of the Definition's achievement. The Council of Chalcedon protected the *droit de cite* of Antiochene Christology. It is a misplaced criticism which accuses Chalcedon of obliterating the fullness and reality of Christ's humanity. The fourth ecumenical council offers a classic example of the function of authority in defending a legitime position from a formidable attack, and therefore preserving a freedom under dangerous threat. The function of authority must often be to keep options open rather than to close them. The monophysite Christology presupposed that in Christ the natural order of creation has no autonomy but is virtually extinguished. The relationship of grace to nature is one of overmastering absorption; not of completion, not of a restoration of freedom and dignity. In short a monophysite Christology is open to criticism comparable to that levelled against Transubstantiation if and when that term is interpreted not so much as an affirmation of the Real Presence as an annihilation of a fundamental physical constituent of nature, or to that brought against the more extreme forms of an Augustinian doctrine of Grace in which redemption seems to bring creation to nought.

In contending for the affirmation that Christ is both God and man the Council of Chalcedon was contending for that without which the shape of Christian faith would be utterly changed. The Definition's merit is to mark a sign of impasse against pathways which either so devalue nature and creation as to disparage man's capacity for God and aspiration for perfection, or so stress the human perfection of Christ as to discover in an individual man, and not in God, the crown towards which all creation moves. This is not to deny that the Chalcedonian Definition has weaknesses. It is conditioned by the controversy which provoked it and is cast in the terms of its time. It therefore speaks of Christ's person in strange isolation from his work of redemption. To say what Christ does for us is crucial to attempts to answer the question who Christ is. Nevertheless, analysis soon shows that the motive force of the Definition is soteriological: for our redemption we need a mediator who is fully God and fully man. The Definition is therefore more than a mere juxtaposition of bits and pieces from incompatible schools in the hope that everyone will find something he likes somewhere. It is rooted in a conviction that behind the warring formulas of the schools there is an underlying agreement at the level of faith, and that the Church has to hold together, without either separation or 'confusion' (i.e. a blend producing some third entity), the two main patterns of Christology inherited from the New Testament itself.

The Circle and the Ellipse:
Rival Concepts of Authority in the Early Church

It is not given to many to be as intimately associated with the study and teaching of their subject over nearly half a century as Leonard Hodgson has been. Apart from an interlude as professor at the General Theological Seminary, New York, where he is still remembered with affection, gratitude, and profound respect by those who had the good fortune to come under his influence, and then as canon of Winchester, he has continuously taught in Oxford since 1914, and possesses the sure touch and insight born of long experience in university affairs and of a lifetime of study in theology and philosophy. Theology today is so vast a field of inquiry that there is constant danger of its disintegration into several autonomous disciplines which have lost sight of the uniting principles which give them meaning and coherence. For my predecessor theology is emphatically a unity, rooted in the experience of which the Bible is the record, a record through which he moved surely, with the confidence of one who is not afraid to follow the evidence where it leads. It would be an impertinence for one far his junior to attempt an evaluation of his achievement in Oxford. By his writings and by his manifold labours for the ecumenical movement he has become *doctor gentium.* We wish him a happy retirement, and hope that he will give us many more books.

The origins of the papacy have long remained an area of controversial debate for theologians and historians. Yet it ought to be possible for historical theology to cut across the confessional differences and to examine the question on the one hand *sine ira et studio,* on the other hand without the sceptical detachment which says in effect, A plague on both your houses! How was it that the see of Rome came to occupy so important a position in the ancient Catholic Church?

Primitive Christianity is a circle with Jerusalem at its centre. The first

Christians were Jews divided from their fellow countrymen only by the fact that they believed the long expectations of God's people had indeed been fulfilled: Jesus of Nazareth was God's Anointed. A prophet had risen up among them, God had visited his people. But this event did not abrogate the past. It was a fulfilment of God's plan. The earliest Christians were not conscious of any discontinuity between the new and the old covenant. The word was still to Israel, and they understood their task as a mission to their own nation, none of whom were likely to be persuaded by an announcement that the Mosaic law had now been abrogated.

Very early within the primitive church at Jerusalem there appeared disturbing men who despaired of the conversion of their own people and believed that the failure of Jerusalem to recognize the things belonging to its peace was theologically significant. According to St. Stephen the failure of Israel to recognize the Messiah is but one more example of that agelong resistance to the prophetic message that may be discerned throughout the Old Testament: the history of the Jews is a long catalogue of apostasy from the Golden Calf to the building of the Temple and the offering of sacrifices. It is not odd that St. Stephen was stoned to death if St. Luke's account of his speech is anything like correct. In any event, some of those who first launched the mission to the Gentiles felt that they should shake the dust of Jerusalem from their feet and take the light of the gospel to lighten the Gentiles.

The Gentile mission was launched gradually on the initiative of private individuals moving ahead of any official authorization by central authority. It was regarded with anxiety at Jerusalem, where conservative Christians thought the Gentile converts ought to be treated like Jewish proselytes and accept the Mosaic law of circumcision and sabbath-observance. For us only one point in this well-worn story is significant: St. Paul's account of his private meeting with the 'pillar' apostles presupposes that it was vital to the success of his labours in the Gentile mission, with which he was now identified, that the Jerusalem church should recognize his converts as true and full members, albeit extra-mural members, of the one Church of God. Otherwise he would be running and would have run in vain. To the apostle's gratification and also perhaps his astonishment James, Peter, and John made no demand that Gentile Christians must keep the Mosaic law but gave him the right hand of fellowship, laying down only the one condition, that the Gentile communities should show their solidarity with the Jerusalem church by sending money, just as the synagogues of the Jewish dispersion sent annual contributions for the Temple. The epistles offer abundant testimony to show the importance of the collection for the saints in symbolizing the solidarity between Gentile Christians and the Jerusalem community. Even when relations with a church like that at Corinth had become severely strained, St. Paul felt he had to persist in calling on them for contributions, however tortuous and embarrassing his request (witness the syntax of 2 Cor. 8–9), and however doubtful that the Jerusalem church would be pleased to accept the money at his hands (Rom. 15:31).

The entire story has a single theological presupposition at its foundation: Christendom has a geographical centre and this is Jerusalem. Gentile Christians might be free from Judaism; they remained debtors to Zion.

The predominant position of the Jerusalem community was deeply affected by the two Jewish revolts, with the consequent destruction of much of the city and Hadrian's exclusion of all Jews from the new foundation of Aelia Capitolina. Even so there were parts of the old city that remained unharmed. One of its seven synagogues was quite untouched. The temple area itself was damaged rather than razed to the ground. Admittedly Eusebius of Caesarea grieves over the sad sight of stones from the Temple used for the construction of Hadrian's pagan temples and theatres. But much still remained; and more could be exploited for credulous tourists. The Bordeaux pilgrim of 333 was shown four notable items: the room in which Solomon had written the book of Wisdom, gruesome traces of Zachariah's murder before the altar, the pinnacle from which the Lord had been tempted to cast himself down, and the very stone which the builders had rejected. More reliable evidence is supplied by Cyril of Jerusalem and John Chrysostom: commenting on Christ's prophecy that one stone shall not be left upon another, they explain that this is yet to be fulfilled since substantial parts of the old Temple are still identifiable. In a word, there was much left to give a sense of continuity with what had gone before. Likewise the church of Jerusalem continued, though now an exclusively Gentile community. All the evidence goes to show that this Gentile church of Jerusalem rapidly became deeply conscious of itself as the inheritor of the most primitive traditions of Christendom. Here was holy ground where the sacred feet of Christ and his apostles had walked not long before. In the third century they claimed to have salvaged the very throne on which James had sat to preach the word to his people. The claim may have been true, since their little church was located in an undevastated part of the old city—on the site, they believed, of that upper room where the gift of the Spirit had been poured out at Pentecost.

The sense of a numinous aura attaching to the church of Zion was not confined to Christians who lived there. It was shared by many throughout the Near East. The first pilgrim to the holy places of whom we have record is Bishop Melito of Sardis, about 170. Forty years later we hear of Alexander, a Cappadocian bishop who having received the attractive but uncanonical proposal of a transfer to the see of Jerusalem was granted a revelation directing him to accept it. In the mid-third century Origen and Firmilian, bishop of Cappadocian Caesarea, had a strong interest in the holy places. We know of these four names by chance: the fact of their pilgrimage is recorded by writers primarily interested in telling us something else about them. It is safe to conclude that the volume of devout tourism must have been much greater than these isolated examples might suggest; no one saw anything noteworthy in the mere fact of pilgrimage as such.

We may take it as certain that the visitors would have been specially interested in the continuity of the Church with the original community of apostolic times. Melito went to discover the true limits of the Old Testament Canon; Firmilian was interested in the ancient liturgy of the Jerusalem church. The lavish benefactions of Constantine and his mother laid great emphasis on the places of Christ's birth and death, and did much to publicize the sacred sites. Constantine's personal sense of the holiness of Palestine comes out in the explanation he gave for the postponement of his baptism until his deathbed: it had been his desire to be baptized in Jordan. But all this only illustrates the mystique. Constantine does not create the Jerusalem idea; he is dependent upon an existing way of thinking, a way of thinking illustrated by the widely held belief that Golgotha (rather than the Temple, as the Jews thought) was the site of Adam's grave and the very centre of the earth.

In a word, the original predominance of Jerusalem in the thought of the Church did not die with the surrender to Titus's legions or with the Hadrianic war. The city remained at the very heart of things. All this, of course, is in one sense poetry rather than truth, literature rather than dogma, symbol rather than cold reality. But the myth is what matters, and can dominate the minds of those who do not actually believe it. The most extreme mythological account of the central role of Jerusalem in the divine plan is the idea unhappily known as Chiliasm or Millenarianism; that is, the belief that the Lord will return to reign with his saints for a thousand years in a renewed Jerusalem, a notion fostered by the Apocalypse, regarded as orthodoxy by Justin Martyr, Irenaeus, Tertullian, and even the young Augustine. Even Cyril of Jerusalem in the middle of the fourth century, who did not regard the Apocalypse as canonical scripture and was no Millenarian, thinks of his city as the scene of an imminent eschatological conflict, when there will be fighting between the saints of the Jerusalem church and Antichrist with his Jewish supporters. It was widely believed that the Lord's second coming would take place at Jerusalem. Tertullian tells us that during Severas's campaigns the new Jerusalem appeared hovering in the sky over Judaea every morning for forty days, visible even to heathen observers. As day advanced the vision slowly faded, though, he adds, on some days it vanished instantly. The Lord was expected to come from the East with the cross preceding him—a belief, first attested in the *Didache,* which explains why Christian places of worship have normally been built so that the worshippers pray eastwards and have a cross at the east end. The cross, so Cyril of Jerusalem told his flock, was the sign of the Son of Man (Matt. 24:30), and they believed him. At 9 a.m. on Tuesday, 7 May 351, a parhelion appeared in Palestine and seemed like a cross of light in the east. The terrified citizens of Jerusalem stampeded into church thinking it the sign of the End. In the sobriety of the morning after, Cyril assured them that the Lord's return was deferred, but the sign was an assurance that he was indeed on the way.

These examples, selected from much other evidence, illustrate the continuity of the Jerusalem idea. 'We make offering for Zion,' says the Liturgy of St. James, 'the mother of all churches.' The fact that the administration and effective power in the East was organized round the great sees of Alexandria, Antioch, and Constantinople did not diminish the magnetism of this mystique.

And yet there was one qualification to this claim to be the mother of all churches. The church of Aelia was an exclusively Gentile community, and Aelia was not the secular capital of the Gentile world. That lay in the West; and Rome too was the centre of a mystique, potentially a rival mystique.

The story of the Rome idea runs parallel to that of the Jerusalem idea, except that perhaps its controversial potentialities begin to be exploited earlier. From the first epistle of Clement to the Corinthians, it appears that already at the end of the first century the Christians in Rome are taking their leading position for granted, and looking back with proud local patriotism on the fact that the two most eminent apostles, St. Peter and St. Paul, had been martyred within their city. A century or so later, memorial monuments were erected to the apostles' honour, St. Peter's on the Vatican hill and St. Paul's by the road to Ostia. These monuments are mentioned about A.D. 200 by the Roman presbyter Gaius, and the recent excavations under St. Peter's have unearthed the actual remains of the Petrine monument. The construction of these memorials reflects a growing self-consciousness that the Roman church has a distinguished past.

For the Western churches it always seemed natural to look to Rome as the *prima cathedra*. The church there was the headquarters from which the Christian mission spread through the Western provinces, and no other city could make any plausible claim to apostolic origin. The Roman church was the only Western community to whom St. Paul had addressed an epistle, and it was proud of the fact. Christians elsewhere instinctively share this sense of respect for the church which preserved the memory of the teaching and practice of St. Peter and St. Paul. Bishop Polycarp of Smyrna travels to Rome to discuss differences in observing Easter; he and Bishop Anicetus agree to differ, since both must follow the traditions of their own apostles. A generation later such divergence seems intolerable; Bishop Victor of Rome excommunicates all who do not follow the Roman Easter. We are not told the reasons he gave, if any, for taking this short way with dissenters; but the fact that the bishop of Ephesus answers his 'threats' by appealing to the tombs of Philip and John in Asia suggests that Victor appealed to St. Peter and St. Paul; he must have believed he was observing Easter in the way the apostles had done. A few years later we have the fragments of the Dialogue between the Roman presbyter Gaius and a Montanist from Asia Minor named Proclus, where the disputants make rival claims to apostolic foundations. Proclus vindicates the apostolic tradition of the Asian churches and the proper place of prophecy within church life by appealing to the tombs of Philip and his daughters in Phrygia. The Roman is one up there; he can point proudly to the memorials of the martyred apostles, St. Peter and St. Paul—those, he says, with pardonable exaggeration, who 'founded this church'—and adds, for good measure, that the superiority of the Roman church to the Eastern churches is also proved by the mistake of the benighted Orientals who imagine St. Paul to be the author of the Epistle to the Hebrews. Rome knows better than that.

Victor's actions disclose to the Greek East that Rome is thinking of Christendom as a circle now centred upon itself. The Eastern churches think rather of an ellipse with two foci. The legacy of this controversy is disastrously apparent in the centuries that follow. In the middle years of the third century there was sharp controversy concerning the rebaptism of those baptized by schismatics, and against the claims of Rome to settle the controversy over the heads of the dissenting Africans, Cyprian appeals for support to Eastern bishops. We possess the letter written to him by Firmilian of Cappadocian Caesarea, mentioned earlier as a pilgrim to the holy land. He tells Cyprian that the Roman bishop's claim to observe the liturgical customs of the apostles is proved false by this significant fact: 'They do not do everything exactly as it is done at Jerusalem' ('nec observari illic omnia aequaliter quae Hierosolymis observantur'). The latent resentment flares into open war in the Arian controversy. In 340 Pope Julius admitted to communion some bishops who for various reasons, not all discreditable, had been excommunicated by Eastern councils, and justified his action by the dignity attaching to the church of St. Peter and St. Paul. The Eastern bishops were horrified. For Rome, they say, we have profound regard as a centre of orthodoxy from apostolic times; but the bishop of Rome will remember that the apostles went to Rome from the East. The Eastern bishops take it for granted that the bishop of Rome is patriarch of the West and bishop of the world's greatest city, of a church that can justly take pride in its apostolic origin and noble fight for the faith. The bishop of Rome takes it for granted that he is at the centre of the circle, successor of the prince of the apostles. And if it is asked wherein lies the superiority of Rome to Antioch, of which Peter had also been bishop, the answer comes that Rome's unique distinction lies in the possession of the remains of the martyred apostles. Rome has got the bones.

The tension concerning Easter was decided in favour of Rome. In the fourth century further disagreement arose over the observance of the Nativity. Western custom was now to keep 25 December as Christ's birthday; but about the same time the Eastern churches had come to observe this feast on 6 January. Gradually the feast of the Epiphany made its way into Western churches, either as a commemoration of Christ's baptism or as a celebration of the visit of the Magi. But there was some resistance to the Epiphany festival in the West, notably among sects that had separated from the church before the feast came in. St. Augustine attacks the African Donatists on the interesting ground that their refusal to keep Epiphany proves their schismatic character; they cannot be members of the universal church if they are out of step with the church of Jerusalem where the star of the Nativity appeared. (The point incidentally illustrates the perennial truth that sects remain conservative, while the church moves with the times.) Likewise in the East the Western festival of 25 December made its way slowly. The strongest resistance came from Jerusalem, which only introduced the festival in the middle of the fifth century, probably after the Council of Chalcedon, and from Armenia, which to this day does not keep the Nativity on the Western date.

Western writers long remain sensitive on the score of the original primacy of Jerusalem. It is noticeable with what pleasure Jerome and Leo draw attention to any defections from the strict path of orthodoxy on the part of Eastern bishops in general and bishops of Jerusalem in particular. The

Eastern bishops on their side resent what they regard as high-handed interference from the Western patriarch. At the second ecumenical Council
at Constantinople in 381 a proposal to reach a settlement acceptable to the
West was met with the cry: 'Christ came in the East!' It was one thing for this
argument to be used by Eastern bishops. It was another when the same argument was used by bishops in Gaul or England in order to deflate the claims
of Rome in Europe. Saint Columban writes angrily to the pope early in the
seventh century, reminding him that though Rome is a famous church, justly
proud of its secular dignity and its relics of St. Peter and St. Paul, nevertheless it yields the primacy to Jerusalem. The same argument recurs in the York
Tracts of about 1100, perhaps the work of the then Archbishop of Rouen.
When we hear this sort of thing from the West, we may fairly conclude that
something like Gallicanism or even Anglicanism has already been born.

It would be tempting to continue by observing how in the modem world
the ideological tension between East and West has become secularized in the
form of competition between Russia and America. But I beg leave to resist
these temptations, and rather to invite you to go back in time and to examine the roots of this cleavage, the development of which I have attempted
to trace. I submit that the seeds of the subsequent development are in the
New Testament.

St. Paul, as we have seen, had to gain the recognition of the Jerusalem
authorities if his Gentile converts were to be admitted as full members of
the Church. He is continually stressing the need for unity in the Church,
and the solidarity of the Gentile Christians with the church of Jerusalem
expressed through the collection for the saints. St. Paul himself has a deep
instinctive respect for Jerusalem and for the church leaders there which
may be discerned behind his ironical references to 'those who seemed to
be pillars'. Nevertheless, he also affirms, in Galatians stridently asserts, his
own independent and equal standing as an apostle on a par with the others.
According to Gal. 2, James, Cephas, and John gave Paul the right hand of
fellowship, recognizing that he had been entrusted with the apostleship of
the Gentiles just as St. Peter had been entrusted with that of the Jews. In
the mind of St. Paul this was certainly more than an allocation of different
spheres of activity; it implied a parallel status between Jewish and Gentile
Christendom. The circle is already on the way to becoming an ellipse.

A second piece of evidence is provided by Romans 9–11. There St. Paul
wrestles with the problem of the failure of God's elect people to believe in
the Christ of expectation. Why have the Jews failed to believe? The answer is
that they have been temporarily blinded, and the light has passed to the Gen-

tiles to provoke the Jews to jealousy, to wake them up to their responsibilities that they should be a light to lighten the Gentiles. At the same time the Gentile Christians must remember the rock whence they have been hewn, must not become conceited or proud of their privilege in receiving the gospel when the elect nation has rejected it, and must realize that God's promise to his chosen will finally be fulfilled. In the end all Israel will be saved, together with 'the fullness of the Gentiles'. The position of Gentiles within the people of God is compared to that of a branch grafted into a vine, which may be cut off if it proves unfruitful. Gentile Christianity is a parenthetic, Protestant movement to recall Catholic Judaism to its true vocation.

In St. Paul's mind there is a duality in the idea of the Church. On the one hand there is his assertion of the need for recognition by the church of Jerusalem; on the other hand he is deeply aware of the equal status of the Gentiles within the one commonwealth of God. The idea of two distinct entities within the one Church is widely current in the second and third centuries. For example, the Alexandrian exegetes significantly expound St. Matthew's account of the Triumphal Entry into Jerusalem to the effect that the colt and the foal symbolize two churches, Jewish and Gentile, who in double harness draw the chariot of the Lord's triumph. But this kind of exegesis was not to last long. Soon the Gentile Christians came to constitute an overwhelming majority. 'Christian Jews', Origen sadly observes, 'are very rare.' They never had any great success in their mission to their fellow countrymen; they were suspect for lack of patriotism, in that the Jerusalem church had left the city when the war began in 66 and retired to Pella in Transjordan, and were again killed off as fifth-columnists during the second revolt of Bar-Cochba, as we know from Justin Martyr and (if correctly interpreted) from the autograph letter of Bar-Cochba himself recently discovered in the Judaean desert. They were even more suspect for their attitude to the Gentile mission, to the approval of which they were committed by the Apostolic Council. We know that in the fourth century the Jewish Christian communities were proud of the missionary achievements of St. Paul, even if they must at times have regarded him as a gift horse whose mouth needed close inspection. Unfortunately the Gentile Christians were less tolerant. Justin Martyr has to admit that, while he himself does not object to Jewish Christians who continue in the observance of the Mosaic law, some Gentile Christians deny them all hope of salvation. It was the latter view, not Justin's, which became predominant. It is the complete reversal of the situation that had confronted St. Paul when he went up to confer with James, Cephas, and John a century earlier. It is now for the Jewish Christians to seek recognition from the Gentiles, and they seek it largely in vain.

It is a short step from this position to the identification of Christianity with Gentile Christendom *tout court*. This identification is made easier by the widely-held conviction that in the providence of God the destinies of the Church and the Empire were bound up together. At least by the middle of the second century and perhaps much earlier Christians were already looking forward to the day when the Roman emperor himself would be converted to the faith. Is it not providential, asks Melito of Sardis, that Augustus established the Pax Romana at the same time as the birth of Christ's religion of peace? Nearer and nearer draws the time when the earth shall be full of the knowledge of the Lord as the waters cover the sea. With the conversion of Constantine the dream comes true. To Ambrose, *Romanus* and *Christianus* are interchangeable terms. To Leo, St. Peter and St. Paul are the new Romulus and Remus, founders of Christian Rome. The African Optatus instinctively treats the barbarians outside the empire as being beyond the scope of the gospel. Christianity belongs to the Roman world. We are assisting at the birth of 'Western values'.

The apostle Paul is the creator of the idea of a quasi-independent Gentile Christendom within the one Church of Jewish and Gentile believers, and for him this stands or falls with recognition of his own apostolate. What, then, is his own attitude to the capital city of the Gentile world? Among the motives that led him to write the epistle to the Romans a large place must be given to the assertion of his authority in relation to the Roman church. In Rom. 15:14ff. he tells the Roman Christians that, although they are indeed so mature as scarcely to require his instruction, 'yet on certain points I have written to you very boldly, by way of reminder, because of the grace given to me by God to be a minister of Christ Jesus to the Gentiles. . .'. Now he has finished his labours in the East and 'having longed for many years to come to you' will make the journey as soon as he has delivered the collection for the saints at Jerusalem, if the church there will accept it, and if he is not lynched by the unbelieving Jews on arrival. (Evidently St. Paul knows that the welcome barometer is near zero.) In case the Romans feel a little apprehensive they are assured that he will soon be off again on a missionary tour of Spain—an assurance in which, as John Chrysostom pointed out, there is probably more than meets the eye. We may be sure that the central goal in the apostle's mind was Rome rather than the Costa Brava.

The epistles tell us nothing of the way in which Paul reached Rome. But in the last eight chapters of the Acts we have a very remarkable account

of his journey. As he had himself feared, he was attacked by the unbelievers and only rescued by the Roman military authorities putting him under
arrest. From then on, St. Luke's story is the account of a journey overruled
and guided through a series of dramatic crises by the intervention of providence. Humanly speaking the apostle stood not the remotest chance of
reaching Rome at all. A succession of divinely inspired situations enabled
him to circumvent all the obstacles, ultimately to arrive at the capital, there
to preach boldly, no man forbidding him. The key to the story is the account
of the storm and shipwreck in Acts 27. It is unfortunate that this chapter
has been misunderstood by commentators. The story occupies a quite dis-
proportionate amount of space, and one asks why St. Luke thought it so
important. The commentaries either tell us that the story is there because it
is an eyewitness account—it happened—or that it was invented by a fertile
imagination, constructed out of the literary conventions of contemporary
adventure stories. The answer is surely that the story is there to underline
the extreme improbability that the apostle would ever reach Rome. The very
stars in their courses were fighting against him. When land had nearly been
reached, only the centurion's intervention prevented the soldiers killing the
prisoners. When they landed on Malta, there was a serpent to bite him. For
the author of Acts the preaching of the apostle of the Gentiles in the capital
of the Gentile world is a supernatural fact.

Dean Inge once remarked that the apostle Paul has never been a very
popular saint in the Roman Catholic Church. 'St. Peter', he continued
characteristically, 'the Blessed Virgin, and a host of lesser lights have been
wheedled and cajoled. St. Paul has been spared this crowning humiliation.'
The point could be more eirenically put. Let it simply be that the visitor to
Rome who passes from the great church of St. Peter's to that of St. Paul's-
without-the-Walls is struck by the isolation and neglect of the latter. There
is perhaps irony here. For if there is one man who more than any other one
man may be regarded by the historian as founder of the papacy, that man is
surely St. Paul.

St. Peter and St. Paul in Rome:
The Problem of the Memoria Apostolorum
Ad Catacumbas

If the warm welcome that has been properly given to the magistral accounts of the Vatican excavations, both in the original Italian report of 1951[1] and in the subsequent, independent reviews of the story in German by Oscar Cullmann,[2] in French by Jérôme Carcopino[3] and by H. I. Marrou,[4] and now in English by Miss Jocelyn Toynbee and Mr. John Ward Perkins,[5] is tempered with respectful moderation, that is perhaps a consequence of an intelligible regret that almost all the crucial historical questions remain to baffle and tantalize us as much as they ever did. The following observations are intended to invite attention to a tiny scrap of literary evidence which appears to be in some danger of being overlooked, and, perhaps more rashly, to cut across the current discussions with the suggestion that some of the questions put to the ancient evidence are unconsciously loaded. They are not intended to offer any lengthy survey of the course of the innumerable past contributions to the debate,[6] but rather to present the essence of the matter in terse and summary form.

1. B. M. Apollonj-Ghetti, A. Ferrua, E. Josi, E. Kirschbaum, *Esplorazioni sotto la confessione di San Pietro in Vaticano eseguite negli anni 1940–9* (Vatican City, 1951).

2. *Petrus: Jünger—Apostel—Märtyrer* (Zürich, 1952); English translation by F. V. Filson (London, 1953).

3. *Études d'histoire chrétienne* (Paris, 1953).

4. *Dict. d'arch. chr.* xv.2 (1953), s.v. 'Vaticanum'.

5. *The Shrine of St. Peter and the Vatican Excavations* (London, 1956); cp. J. M. C. Toynbee, 'The Shrine of St. Peter and its setting', in *Journal of Roman Studies* xliii (1953), pp. 1–26; E. R. Smothers in *Theol. Studies* xvii (1956), pp. 293–321.

6. For an excellent survey of French literature prior to the recent finds, cp. H. Leclercq in *Dict. d'arch. chr.* xiv. 1 (1939), s.v. 'Pierre (Saint)'.

All but an exiguous and diminishing minority are likely to agree that the spade has disclosed the very 'trophy' of St. Peter on the Vatican hill to which the Roman presbyter Gaius made his famous reference at the beginning of the third century, and that this monument was erected not many years after A.D. 160. That the memorial existed there was already known from Gaius. It has now been found. While the excavations have vastly filled out and confirmed in detail the already existing picture, broadly speaking it remains true that for many of the fundamental questions the historian is in much about the same general position as he was on the publication of the second edition of Lietzmann's *Petrus und Paulus in Rom* in 1927. If the matter is now going to be taken farther, the evidence must come from either one or both of the other two ancient apostolic shrines in Rome: that is, either by rigorous interpretation of the so-called 'Memoria Apostolorum ad Catacumbas' at the third milestone of the Via Appia beneath the church of St. Sebastian, excavated in 1915 with spectacular results by de Waal and Styger and recently discussed at length by Francesco Tolotti,[7] or from future excavation under the noble fourth-century church of St. Paul on the Via Ostiensis, hitherto undug by the archaeologists. In any event, no account of the memorials of the martyred apostles in Rome is adequate if it fails to offer a satisfactory theory to account for the existence of the double shrine on the Via Appia and to explain its relation to the other two individual memorials on the Vatican and the Via Ostiensis. This remains the *crux interpretum* that it has now been for sixty years and more; and it is hard to suppress a feeling bordering on disappointment at the extreme caution concerning its significance, amounting to virtual agnosticism, expressed by Miss Toynbee and Mr. Ward Perkins. Its origin, they observe, 'remains an unsolved problem'.[8] They are of course right to be candid. Nevertheless, the problem contains within itself the burning question at issue. Must we capitulate with them to the hard fact that no current hypothesis, however ingenious, actually derives any concrete support from the ancient evidence, literary or archaeological, and therefore cannot be more than an intelligent conjecture? For so long as this problem remains unsolved, the entire problem of the interpretation of the Vatican excavations is also unsolved. The issues are inextricably interrelated. It is perhaps significant that the only hypotheses concerning the Via

7. *Memorie degli Apostoli in Catacumbas* (Vatican City, 1953), resuming his earlier articles 'Ricerche intorno alla Memoria Apostolorum', in *Rivista di archeologia cristiana* xxii (1946), pp. 7–62; xxiii– xxiv (1947–48), pp. 14–116.

8. Op. cit., p. 181.

Appia which they discuss are those which are compatible with the view that the Vatican possesses the authentic tomb of St. Peter.

Gaius mentions only the two individual memorials, not the double memorial on the Via Appia.[9] It is, however, certain that in his time under Zephyrinus the Memoria ad Catacumbas did not yet exist. The archaeological evidence is decisive not only that the construction of the Memoria itself falls between 238 and 260 with a very strong probability in favour of the last years of this period, but that this particular part of the existing mausoleum on the site did not fall into Christian hands before that period.[10] The simplest hypothesis is without doubt to link the origin of the Memoria with the baffling consular date in the entry for 29 June given by the *Depositio Martyrum* in the Calendar of Philocalus of A.D. 354: 'III Kal. Iul. Petri in Catacumbas et Pauli Ostense Tusco et Basso consulibus' (= 258).[11] It is a reasonable probability that this consular date represents an event of significance in the history of the Memoria, whether its original establishment (much the most probable view) or its subsequent recognition by ecclesiastical authority (which would

9. Eusebius, *H.E.* ii. 25. 7: ἐγὼ δὲ τὰ τρόπαια τῶν ἀποστόλων ἔχω δεῖξαι. ἐὰν γὰρ θελήσῃς ἀπελθεῖν ἐπὶ τὸν Βασικανὸν ἢ ἐπὶ τὴν ὁδὸν τὴν Ὠστίαν, εὑρήσεις τὰ τρόπαια τῶν ταύτην ἱδρυσαμένων τὴν ἐκκλησίαν.

10. 238 is the earliest possible date for the tomb, of the years preceding the Memoria, with its inscriptions in Greek lettering ('Pupenio, Balbeino, Innocentiorum; Gordiano, Innocentiorum; duobus Gordianis, Innocentiorum') recording members of the imperial household who had taken as *cognomina* the names of their imperial masters Pupienus and Balbinus. 9 August 260 is the date of one of the *graffiti* in the triclia, recently deciphered by R. Marichal as *Celeri[nus] V Idus Aug[ustas] Saccul[ari II] et Donat[o II cos]* (*Comptes rendus de l'Acad. des Inscr.* (1953), pp. 60–68). For criticism of the view of Tolotti that the site was a centre of Christian veneration from apostolic times, see A. M. Schneider, 'Die Memoria Apostolorum an der Via Appia', *Nachr. d. Gött. Akad. d. Wiss.* (1951), 3, pp. 8–9. His book is reviewed to the same effect by Ward Perkins in *Journ. Rom. Stud.* xlv (1955), pp. 205–7; by Miss Toynbee in *Antiquarie; Journal* xxxv (1955), pp. 104–6; and by both in *The Shrine of St. Peter*, pp. 176–77. Cp. P. Testini, 'Noterelle sulla Memoria Apostolorum', in *Rivista di arch. crist.* xxx (1954), pp. 210–31. The pre-history of the mausoleum before the making of the Memoria has recently been discussed by Carcopino, *De Pythagore aux Apôtres* (Paris, 1956), who argues that the decoration and inscriptions in the tombs (especially of the Innocentii) show them to have belonged to a sect with affinities with Judaistic Christianity and using Pythagorean symbols. He thinks the construction of the Memoria marked not only the translation thither of the apostolic relics (see below, p. 137) but also the reconciliation of these dissidents to the church. In so far as he is concerned with the pre-history of the Memoria his views do not affect the argument of this paper.

11. Conveniently in Lietzmann, *Die drei ältesten Martyrologien* (Kleine Texte 2), p. 3; also ed. Mommsen, *Chronica Minora,* i (1891), p. 71; ed. Duchesne, *Liber Pontificalis,* i (1886), p. 11.

presuppose that the place had been made a few years previously under private enterprise, about the time of Pope Cornelius) with the consequential inclusion of the third shrine in the official celebration of the martyrdom of the two apostles on 29 June.

But the meaning of the consular date is really less important than the discovery of the impulse which led to the establishment of the place at all. And here the ancient evidence is concrete and unambiguous in pointing to the existence in the latter part of the third century of strong belief, held at any rate in some quarters even if it is not safe to assume that it was universal, that this place at the third milestone of the Via Appia was the actual site of the remains of both apostles. No other view will satisfactorily explain the *graffiti* attesting the semi-pagan practice of *refrigerium* in honour of the dead apostles (e.g. 'Petro et Paulo Tomius Coelius refrigerium feci, ad Paulum et Petrum refrigeravi', &c.). And those which consist merely of simple, moving invocations ('Petre et Paule in mente nos habeatis, Paule et Petre petite pro Victore', &c.) are thus made readily intelligible.[12] These naïve scratchings covering the walls of the triclia and the courtyard make a strange contrast with the astonishing absence of invocations of St. Peter, with a single exception, among the less numerous pre-Constantinian *graffiti* found by the Vatican Aedicula. There they consist of simple prayers, in Latin, for the friends and relatives of the visitors, such as *Pauline vivas, Prima vivas, Simplici vivate in ☧*, and many more of this type.[13] The one exception, in Greek, consists of the lettering ΠΕΤΡ ΕΝΙ scratched on the Red Wall.[14] This contrast is so striking that it inevitably invites the questions whether, whatever the official view of the Roman clergy may have been, it was not the firm belief of popular piety that here at the Via Appia was the true site of both apostolic graves, and whether on any showing the double shrine at the Via Appia was not far more popular among Christians of mean education and culture in the latter half of the third century than the two earlier, individual memorials on the Vatican and the Via Ostiensis.[15] The *graffiti* attesting *refrigerium* and the convenient

12. Cp. Toynbee and Ward Perkins, *Shrine,* pp. 171–72.

13. Ibid., p. 165.

14. Deciphered by A. Ferrua, and first published in *Civiltà Cattolica,* ciii. i (Jan. 1952), pp. 15–29.

15. Carcopino, *Études d'hist. chr.,* p. 282 (with whom H. Last concurs, *Journ. Rom. Stud.* xliv [1954], p. 114) observes that the *graffiti* on the wall by the Vatican Aedicula 'porteraient témoignage contre la présence de ses reliques au Vatican'. This question is hardly answered by the desperate rearguard action of Toynbee and Ward Perkins, *Shrine,* p. 166. But Carcopino exaggerates; if the Greek *graffito* is certain, only special pleading could interpret it

kitchen built for the purpose certainly suggest that the cultshrine at the Via Appia was a distinctly 'down-town' affair.

A belief that the shrine on the Via Appia had *in time past* possessed the actual remains of the apostles is presupposed by the only really probable interpretation of the famous metrical inscription of Pope Damasus in the Basilica Apostolorum built above the Memoria in the fourth century. It must be quoted:[16]

> Hic habitasse prius sanctos cognoscere debes,
> nomina quisque Petri pariter Paulique requiris.
> Discipulos Oriens misit, quod sponte fatemur;
> sanguinis ob meritum, Christum per astra secuti
> aetherios petiere sinus regnaque piorum:
> Roma suos potius meruit defendere cives.
> Haec Damasus vestras referat nova sidera laudes.

That is: 'Whoever you may be that seek the names[17] of Peter and Paul should know that here the saints once dwelt. The East sent the disciples—that we readily admit. But on account of the merit of their blood (they have followed Christ through the stars and attained to the ethereal bosom and the realms of the holy ones) Rome has gained a superior right to claim them as her citizens. Damasus would thus tell of your praises, you new stars.'

The meaning of lines 3–6, with the contrast *Oriens misit, Roma meruit,* cannot be seriously doubted by anyone familiar with the history of the Arian controversy.[18] Here, as also elsewhere (below, p. 145), Damasus reflects the

---

as a cry of disappointment, 'Peter is not here' (*de Pythagore,* p. 284). The Vatican *graffiti* are only negative by comparison with San Sebastiano.

16. Damasus, *Epigr.* 26, ed. Ihm; 20, ed. Ferrua.

17. Carcopino (*Études d'hist. chr.,* pp. 261ff.; *de Pythagore,* pp. 246ff.) draws attention to several N. African inscriptions (but none from Italy) in which *nomina* is the equivalent of *reliquiae.* This interpretation seems clearly preferable to the suggestion of Last (*Journ. Rom. Stud.* xliv, p. 115) that *nomina* may be explicable from the liturgical practice of reading the names of the departed at the eucharist. Remembering, however, the level of Damasus's skill as a poet, we may accept the simpler view that the whole phrase is a periphrasis, *metri causa,* meaning 'Petrum Paulumque' (cp. Toynbee and Ward Perkins, *Shrine,* p. 267).

18. The truth was first seen by G. Ficker, 'Bemerkungen zu einer Inschrift des Papstes Damasus', in *Zeitschrift f. Kirchengeschichte* xxii (1901), pp. 333–43, an article of restraint and good sense. It is odd that his view is peremptorily rejected by Ferrua, *Epigrammata Damasiana* (1942), p. 143. The rivalry between East and West in claiming apostles goes back to the second-century controversies over Easter (Polycrates of Ephesus, ap. Eus., *H.E.*

answer given by Rome to the Eastern denial that the Roman see had the right to sit in judgement upon the synodical decisions of the Eastern churches. There is no need whatever to regard the inscription as specifically directed against the Council of Constantinople of 381,[19] though the issue in a slightly different dress is of course prominent there. The Orientals' question is raised at a much earlier time, namely, during the tense negotiations between East and West of 340–341, which were the consequence of Rome's insistence on receiving to communion Athanasius of Alexandria and Marcellus of Ancyra in flat opposition to the canonical sentences of deposition passed against them at Tyre in 335 and at Constantinople in 336 respectively. The ninety-seven bishops who assembled on 6 January 341 for the dedication of the great church at Antioch, in the presence of the emperor Constantius, made the point quite clear in their letter to Julius of Rome, as that is preserved in the précis of Sabinus of Heraclea.[20] For the see of Rome, they declared, they had indeed profound respect as a centre of apostolic teaching and of

---

iii. 31.3; v. 24), the effect of which in creating a sense of tension between Greek and Latin Christians probably goes far to explain the fourth-century situation. In the Dialogue of Gaius with Proclus (Eus., *H.E.* ii. 25.7; vi. 20.3) we hear the Roman side of the story with the appeal to the apostolic 'trophies' and to the Roman community's superior knowledge as compared with their Oriental brethren who mistakenly suppose St. Paul to be the author of the Epistle to the Hebrews. And the main idea of Damasus's verses is of course earlier than the Arian controversy; Tertullian, *Scorpiace* 15: 'tunc Paulus civitatis Romanae consequitur nativitatem cum illic martyrii renascitur generositate'. Cp. the letter of the Council of Arles (1 Aug. 314) to Pope Sylvester, doubtless quoting back to him the reason he had himself given for not attending the council, namely, that he could not leave Rome at the time of the celebrations of 29 June: 'sed quoniam recedere a partibus illis minime potuisti, in quibus et apostoli cotidie sedent [*Turner:* apostolorum corpora usque hodie sedent] et cruor ipsorum sine intermissione dei gloriam testatur . . .' (text in Ziwsa's edition of Optatus, *CSEL* xxvi. 207; better in C. H. Turner, *Eccl. Occid. Monumenta Iuris Antiq.* i. 382).

19. This opinion, rightly denied by Ficker, is adopted by G. la Piana, 'The Tombs of Peter and Paul ad Catacumbas', in *Harv. Theol. Rev.* xiv (1921), at pp. 63–65, and by E. Caspar, *Geschichte des Papsttums,* i (1930), pp. 251–52.

20. Ap. Sozomen, *H.E.* iii. 8. 5: φέρειν μὲν γὰρ πᾶσι φιλοτιμίαν τὴν Ῥωμαίων ἐκκλησίσν ἐν τοῖς γράμμασιν ὡμολόγουν, ὡς ἀποστόλων φροντιστήριον καὶ εὐσεβείσς μητρόπολιν ἐξ ἀρχῆς γεγενημένην· εἰ καὶ ἐκ τῆς ἔω ἐνεδήμησαν αὐτῇ οἱ τοῦ δόγματος εἰσηγηταί. (Cp. Chrysost., *in Rom.* ii. 1: ἄνδρες Σύροι Ῥωμαίων ἐγένοντο διδάσκαλοι.) On the reconstruction of the document in detail see E. Schwartz, 'Zur Geschichte des Athanasius, IX', *Nachr. d. Gött. Ges. d. Wiss.* (1911), pp. 494–95. It is a straight line from this Antiochene letter to the third canon of Constantinople (381) and the decree of Chalcedon in 451 concerning the privileges of New Rome (thereon *J.T.S.,* N.S., vi (1955), pp. 26–27). Julius could not regard such language as other than ironical and replied (ap. Athan., *Apol. c. Ar.* 21): καὶ ἐν οἷς ἐδόξατε ῥήμασιν ἡμᾶς τιμᾶν, ταῦτα μετασχηματιζόμενοι μετὰ εἰρωνείας τινὸς εἰρήκατε.

orthodoxy from the beginning; but the bishop of Rome should remember that St. Peter and St. Paul had gone to Rome from Antioch whence they were now writing. The implication was evident: Had not the East a senior *cathedra apostolorum*? Was St. Peter's authority any more transmissible to Rome than to Antioch? Or did Julius really think that the dignity of his see was determined by the secular importance of his city? The Roman answer to these formidable questions was evidently to base the claim to primacy not upon the fact of the apostles' residence in Rome and alleged foundation of the church there, but upon the fact of their martyrdom in the city. The unique authority of the Roman see was sealed by the apostles' blood; it depended upon their death rather than upon their life.

More attention has been directed towards the first two lines of Damasus's inscription. Some discussions of their interpretation have curiously tended to treat the text in splendid isolation. Admittedly, if the verses were taken quite alone, their meaning could be a matter of the gravest doubt. The possibility that *habitasse* might mean that the apostles had lived here during their lifetime[21] would need to be taken seriously. But is it necessary (or, for that matter, in accord with sound historical method) to take the inscription by itself in this way? The opening words, *hic habitasse prius sanctos,* give an intelligible and entirely satisfactory sense if they are understood to refer to the same belief as appears in later documents, namely, that the shrine on the Via Appia was the original resting-place of the apostles, but that at a later time their relics were transferred elsewhere. Whether or not this belief is true is a wholly different matter. No progress towards a solution of the problem is likely to be made unless a rigid line of demarcation is drawn between what happened and what was believed to have happened; too much debate on this issue has been bedevilled from the start by a failure to hold the two questions (admittedly not absolutely unrelated) far enough apart. The point is rather that the belief was held, that it is presupposed by Damasus, and that the evidence of his metrical inscription thus interpreted is entirely congruous with the story told by the *graffiti* at the Via Appia.

Moreover, the existence of some such belief in and prior to the time of Damasus is required to account for the threefold nature of the festival on

---

21. This is argued, for example, by H. Delehaye, *Les Origines du culte des martyrs*[2] (1933), pp. 265-68, and la Piana, loc. cit., against the translation-theory of Duchesne, despite the evidence that Damasus elsewhere uses *habitare* of the tomb of a martyr (Lietzmann, *Petrus und Paulus*[2], pp. 147-48). Cp. Toynbee and Ward Perkins, *Shrine*, p. 168: 'Whether it was in life or in death that the Apostles "dwelt" there is not made clear.' Miss Toynbee is less merciful to Delehaye's view in *Journ. Rom. Stud.* xliii (1953), p. 14.

29 June, current in the middle of the fourth century. That during this period the celebration of the apostles' martyrdom took place at all three shrines is certainly attested by the early hymn, *Apostolorum Passio,* attributed probably rightly to Ambrose and in any event of fourth-century date:[22]

> Trinis celebratur viis
> Festum sacrorum martyrum.

With this coheres the entry for 29 June in the *Martyrologium Hieronymianum* according to the reading of the eighth-century Berne manuscript: 'III kal. Iul. Romae via Aurelia natale sanctorum Petri et Pauli apostolorum, Petri in Vaticano, Pauli vero in via Ostensi, utrumque [*sic*] in Catacumbas, passi sub Nerone, Basso et Tusco consulibus.'[23] Although less than certain, it is not unreasonable to suppose that this threefold celebration was intended by the entry in the *Depositio Martyrum* in the Calendar of Philocalus (above, p. 128), and that the text of that document is here to be amended in accordance with the *Martyrologium Hieronymianum.*[24] But the interpretation of Damasus's inscription does not stand or fall by the correctness of the emendation.[25] All that is urged here is that the metrical inscription is not to be treated as an epigraphic Melchizedek, without father, mother, or descent, but is in substantial agreement with the story which, with admitted variations in matters of detail, is current during the fifth and sixth centuries, and that Damasus is simply our earliest extant witness to it.

This story is that the Via Appia was the place at which the apostles were buried at the actual time of their martyrdom, but that at a subsequent date their relics were transferred to the individual tombs on the Vatican and the Via Ostiensis. The best-known form is that which appears in the letter writ-

---

22. Migne, *PL* xvii. 1215. For its authenticity see G. M. Dreves, *Aurelius Ambrosius, der Vater des Kirchengesanges* (1893), pp. 74ff.

23. *Mart. Hieron.,* ed. de Rossi and Duchesne (*Acta Sanctorum,* 11 Nov. i [1894]), p. 84. The Codex Epternacensis reads 'natale apostolorum Petri et Pauli . . . '; the Codex Wissemburgensis has 'natale sanctorum Petri Pauli apostolorum, Petri in Vaticano, Pauli vero Via Ostensi . . . '. The reading of Codex Bernensis looks more like a conflation of sources than an original text, but that does not diminish its evidential value, and a fourth-century calendar entry must lie behind it.

24. Cp. Toynbee and Ward Perkins, *Shrine,* pp. 169–70.

25. It is still not absolutely impossible that Erbes was right (*Zeits. f. Kirchengesch.* vii [1885], p. 28) in emending the *Depositio Martyrum* entry to read 'III kal. Iul. Petri et Pauli ad Catacumbas Tusco et Basso cons.' Cp. J. B. Lightfoot, *The Apostolic Fathers,* Part I, *St. Clement of Rome,* ii (1890), p. 500.

ten in June 594 by Pope Gregory the Great to the Byzantine empress Constantina. According to Gregory, at the time of the martyrdom Christians from the East arrived to claim the bodies and to take them back home; but they only got as far as the second milestone from the city and buried the bodies together at the place called Catacumbas. When the entire multitude of the Greeks (later?) attempted to take them farther on the way, frightful portents effectively deterred them, and in due course the Romans, being counted worthy, went out to collect the relics and put them in the places where they are now buried.[26] A very similar version appears in the *Martyrium Petri et Pauli* of Pseudo-Marcellus, who differs in attributing to Roman initiative the temporary burial at the third milestone of the Via Appia, and in adding that the relics remained buried there for one year and seven months.[27] For the detail of this form of the story there is clearly no need to look for any further source than misunderstanding of the metrical inscription of Damasus.

Another variant appears in the Salzburg itinerary of the seventh century, according to which the bodies of the apostles lay at the Via Appia for forty years before being transferred.[28]

The most amusing variant, perhaps, is that of the Syriac *Acts of Sharbil*,[29] or rather of an appendix to the *Acts* added by someone with a considerable interest in Rome, since it is no doubt he also who added the appended note to the *Martyrdom of Barsamya* which traces the apostolic succession of the church of Edessa through Palut to Serapion of Antioch 'who was consecrated by Zephyrinus' (there follows the Roman succession-list traced back

26. *Epist.* iv. 30 (*M.G.H.*, ed. Ewald-Hartmann, i (1891), pp. 265–66): 'De corporibus vero beatorum apostolorum quid ego dicturus sum, dum constet quia eo tempore quo passi sunt ex Oriente fideles venerunt, qui eorum corpora sicut civium suorum repeterent? Quae ducta usque ad secundum urbis milliarium, in loco qui dicitur Catacumbas conlocata sunt. sed dum ea exinde levare omnis eorum multitudo conveniens niteretur, ita eos vis tonitrui atque fulguris nimio metu terruit ac dispersit, ut talia denuo nullatenus temptare praesumerent. tunc autem exeuntes Romani eorum corpora, qui hoc ex Domino pietate meruerunt, levaverunt et in locis quibus nunc sunt condita posuerunt.'

27. *Martyrium Petri et Pauli*, 66 (ed. Lipsius-Bonnet, *Acta Apostolorum Apocrypha*, i (1891), pp. 174–75).

28. Text in G. B. de Rossi, *Roma sotterranea cristiana*, i (1864), p. 139: 'postea pervenies via Appia ad sanctum Sebastianum martyrem cuius corpus iacet in inferiore loco, et ibi sunt sepulcra apostolorum Petri et Pauli in quibus XL annorum requiescebant, et in occidentali parte ecclesiae per gradus descendis ubi sanctus Cyrinus papa et martyr pausat'. The *Passio S. Sebastiani* (*Acta Sanctorum*, 20 Jan., p. 278) also gives good evidence that the translation-story was current in the middle of the fifth century (cp. below, p. 144).

29. Edited with English translation from two British Museum MSS. (Add. 14644, saec. vi, and 14645, saec. ix) by W. Cureton, *Ancient Syriac Documents* (1864), pp. 61–62.

to St. Peter).[30] This appended note to the *Acts of Sharbil* cannot be later than the sixth century, since the earlier of the two manuscripts containing the work is of sixth-century date. According to this version Barsamya, bishop of Edessa, converted the pagan high-priest Sharbil (stated in the main body of the *Acts* to be of Trajanic date: as *Martyrologium Romanum* for 29 Jan.). 'But he lived in the time of bishop Fabian of Rome', in whose time the Roman citizens complained to the praetor of the city that the foreigners were causing famine (not, it seems, because as Christians they offended the daemons, but by eating too much). Accordingly all foreigners were expelled. But they obtained leave to take their martyrs' bones with them, and assembled together to remove Peter and Paul, whereupon the Roman citizens protested. To the foreigners' assertion that Peter was of Galilee and Paul of Cilicia the Romans had to agree. But when the attempt was made to remove the relics, an earthquake and portents dissuaded the foreigners from their purpose.

It is remarkable that the *Liber Pontificalis* of the sixth century wholly ignores the form of the story given by Pope Gregory. Instead we are given an astonishing variant, diverging very widely, in the Life of Cornelius. Here it is said that Cornelius acceded to the request of a certain lady Lucina and had the bodies of Peter and Paul removed by night from the Via Appia; Lucina buried Paul on her own property on the Via Ostiensis near to the place of his execution, whereas Cornelius took possession of the body of Peter and buried it near the place where he was crucified among the bodies of the holy bishops in the temple of Apollo on the Vatican on 29 June.[31]

These statements of the *Liber Pontificalis* are so unexpected that it is not altogether surprising that a few scholars have been inclined to regard the Life of Cornelius as containing some substratum of truth. There is naturally the widest possible disagreement as to what that substratum might be.[32] It is

---

30. Ibid., pp. 71–72. The *Martyrdom of Barsamya* is only contained in Add. 14645.

31. Duchesne, *Liber Pont.* i, p. 150: 'hic temporibus suis, rogatus a quodam matrona Lucina, corpora apostolorum beati Petri et Pauli de Catacumbas levavit noctu: primum quidem corpus beati Pauli accepto beata Lucina posuit in praedio suo, via Ostense, iuxta locum ubi decollatus est; beati Petri accepit corpus beatus Cornelius episcopus et posuit iuxta locum ubi crucifixus est, inter corpora sanctorum episcoporum, in templum Apollinis, in monte Aureum, in Vaticanum palatii Neroniani, III Kal. Iul.'.

32. E.g. K. Erbes, 'Die geschichtlichen Verhältnisse der Apostelgräber in Rom', *Zeits. f. Kirchengesch.* xliii (1924), at pp. 52–57; G. Belvederi, 'Le Cripte di Lucina', *Rivista di arch. crist.* xxi (1945), pp. 121–64, and his book *Le Tombe apostoliche nell' età paleocristiana* (Vatican City, 1953). It is a pity that Toynbee and Ward Perkins (*Shrine*, p. 188) seem to approve the wild and irresponsible assertions of A. S. Barnes, *The Martyrdom of St. Peter and St. Paul* (1933), p. 89: 'It is one of the few points on which all critics are unanimous that this statement

tempting to see here possibly some traces of fanatical competition between Cornelius's supporters and the party of Novatian to obtain possession of the relics of the apostles, and especially of St. Peter, a conjecture which might claim support in the explicit statement of the *Depositio Martyrum* that the Novatianists actually did succeed in making off with the remains of one martyr of this period, Silanus.[33] But where speculation has already run to excess of riot, these temptations are best resisted. Lucina is a conventional figure who appears in numerous *Acta martyrum;* if all were historical she must have lived a long life of about 300 years spent in devotion to the care of the departed.[34] We must regretfully conclude that the Life of Cornelius cannot be used as a historical source, and may be content to note that it agrees with the testimony of Gregory, Pseudo-Marcellus, the Salzburg itinerary, the *Acts of Sharbil,* and Damasus's inscription on the single essential point that the Via Appia was the original site of the burial of both the apostles, and that the relics were translated thence to the two individual shrines. In face of all the variations in detail the legends are impressively unanimous on that single theme.

I venture to submit that insufficient attention has been paid to this story of an original burial at the Via Appia in consequence of the fact that the wrong question has been put to it. The question has been implicitly formulated: Is it true? Did it happen? The majority who have answered in the negative (in full accord with the archaeological evidence from San Sebastiano that there was no cult at the Via Appia before the middle of the third century and no evidence of any primitive apostolic tombs there) have thereupon proceeded to conclude that these late stories of a translation from the Via Appia can be discarded by hard-headed modern historians who search for the truth, or that at best they preserve the memory of a translation which was not in fact what they say it was.[35] But this is to underestimate the value of

---

does not belong to the time of Cornelius at all, but that it has been misplaced and should be put elsewhere. Oddly enough, while they have differed widely as to what its proper place may be, it does not seem to have occurred to anyone that it really belongs to the time of the martyrdom and not to any later date.'

33. Entry for 10 July: '. . . et in Maximi Silani. hunc Silanum martirem Novati furati sunt.' Delehaye (*Culte des Martyrs*[2], p. 65) remarks that this is the earliest known example of the theft of relics.

34. Delehaye, *Étude sur le légendier romain* (1936), p. 36; Lietzmann, *Petrus und Paulus*[2], pp. 179–89.

35. 'Possibly the sole historical kernel in these late traditions is just the memory of a transfer': Cullmann, *Petrus,* p. 140 (E.T., p. 128).

vital evidence not indeed of any events which happened in the first century but of beliefs concerning 'events' which probably never happened at all. And to account for the origins of the Memoria it is necessary to look more for beliefs than for events. The question is: What does it mean?

That the origins of the Memoria are to be sought in an event is the basic presupposition of the hypothesis associated in recent times with Duchesne and Lietzmann (it is too often forgotten that it goes back to John Pearson, bishop of Chester, in the seventeenth century), that in the time of the persecution of Valerian, *Tusco et Basso consulibus,* the remains of the two apostles were translated for safety's sake to the Via Appia from their original tombs on the Vatican and the Via Ostiensis, to remain there until the time of Constantine (note the forty-year stay at the Via Appia mentioned in the Salzburg itinerary).[36] At bottom Duchesne's theory (as we may label it for convenience) is simply the ancient legend with trappings discarded and with the crucial difference that the direction of the translation is reversed. There is no need to repeat here the arguments that have been urged for and against this hypothesis.[37] It can claim the dubious merit of being irrefutable only because it is unverifiable. The recent excavations have done nothing to support it. Certainly it has gained and still holds the allegiance of many eminent and learned students, and where perhaps the fashion of scholarly opinion has turned against it, that has often only led to despair of discovering any reasonable alternative. The case in favour of it has recently been argued with eloquence and lucidity by M. Carcopino.[38] But all his charm and persuasive arts cannot surmount the twofold difficulty that no ancient evidence, whether literary or archaeological, either attests a translation to the Via Appia in the middle of the third century or, perhaps even more surprisingly, ascribes any translation from the Via

---

36. Pearson, *Annales Cyprianici,* p. 62, *ad ann.* 258 (printed in John Fell's edition of Cyprian, Oxford, 1682) followed by Bingham, *Antiquities,* XXIII. ii. 3, and criticized by Le Nain de Tillemont, *Mémoires pour servir à l'histoire ecclésiastique des six premiers siècles,* i² (Paris, 1701), pp. 534ff.; Duchesne, *Liber Pontificalis,* i (1886), pp. civ ff., and his posthumously printed paper 'La Memoria Apostolorum de la Via Appia', in *Atti della Pontificia Accademia Romana di Archeologia,* serie iii, *Memorie,* i (1923), pp. 1–22. (Duchesne does not refer to Pearson.) For the necessity of an event cp. Lietzmann, 'The Tomb of the Apostles ad Catacumbas', in *Harv. Theol. Rev.* xvi (1923), p. 148: 'In antiquity church festivals were not instituted by an arbitrary decree but arose out of some tangible liturgical act.'

37. See Toynbee and Ward Perkins, *Shrine,* pp. 179–81.

38. *De Pythagore aux Apôtres,* pp. 262ff. He regards the theory as 'inattaquable' and even argues that the very date of the translation in 258 is preserved by the festival of the *Cathedra Petri* on 22 Feb., attested in the *Depositio Martyrum* and several fifth-century sources.

Appia back to the original graves on the Vatican and the Via Ostiensis to the time of Constantine.

In face of this double difficulty Duchesne's hypothesis is not and cannot be more than a piece of highly acute guesswork. He sacrifices so much of the ancient evidence that almost the sole secure points are the evidence of the *graffiti* and the consular date in the *Depositio Martyrum.* Seldom has so much history been constructed out of so little actual testimony. It is unquestionably true that if we are in search of evidence of events, there is little enough to go on. But is it necessary to look for witness to any event? What we have is plentiful evidence of passionately held belief, and not all beliefs are the consequence of the historical events which they presuppose, as ecclesiastical historians have, of all people, most reason to know. The causal relation, in short, should be reversed. May we not go far towards breaking the impasse if, instead of looking in vain for an event (translation to the Via Appia) to account for a belief, we see rather in the belief the primary *datum* which produced the Memoria and subsequently the legendary story of an event (translation from the Via Appia)? This means that the ancient story of a translation from the original burial at the Via Appia is to be classified as aetiological myth, and that it is accordingly to be explained as an attempt to comprehend two originally rival and antithetical traditions.[39]

Much here turns, first, on the very difficult question whether the Aedicula constructed on the Vatican was really believed, at the time when it was built, to mark the grave of St. Peter. Unfortunately the archaeologists appear far from unanimous about the interpretation of the evidence disclosed by the spade. To Miss Toynbee and Mr. Ward Perkins it has seemed likely that the pagan builders of the Red Wall into which the monument was built were surprised by a grave which they took emergency steps to avoid disturbing, a hypothesis which would account for the curious rise and fall of the foundations of the wall below the Aedicula.[40] The pagan builders are presumed to have been persuaded to allow the Petrine monument to be built into their

---

39. Cp. A. von Gerkan, ap. Lietzmann, *Petrus und Paulus*², p. 297.

40. *Shrine,* pp. 157–58. On the other hand (p. 155) 'the excavation has revealed no certain traces of a grave beneath the Aedicula'. For the argument that this is indeed the authentic grave of St. Peter see the careful statement of J. Ruysschaert, 'Réflexions sur les fouilles vaticanes', in *Revue d'histoire eccl.* xlviii (1953), pp. 608ff., xlix (1954), pp. 5ff.; his argument would be clearer if he distinguished even more rigidly between (*a*) the establishment of the fact of the apostolic martyrdoms in Rome—not disputed except by either the irresponsible or the ignorant, (*b*) the discovery of the authentic graves. Considerations applicable to (*a*) are not relevant to (*b*).

wall at this point. If this hypothesis is right, it at least suggests that in the discovery of the grave there was some element of chance, which suggests in turn that even on this view it is not more than possible that this is the authentic grave. But the much more important question is rather whether at the time when it was built the memorial was generally believed to mark St. Peter's grave. That this was believed by the time of Constantine is certain. Did the Christians in Rome believe it in 160? The archaeological evidence is compatible with the view that they did. But unhappily it seems compatible with the view that they did not. To Marrou, Schneider, and von Gerkan[41] it has seemed unlikely that at the time of its construction the Aedicula was believed to mark the apostle's tomb. Even from the urgent presentation of the alternative view by Miss Toynbee and Mr. Ward Perkins one thing is clear, namely, that the archaeological evidence from the actual memorial is insufficient, *taken by itself,* to place it beyond doubt that this was at that time universally[42] thought to mark the grave.

Secondly, there arises the thorny question of the meaning of τρόπαια in Gaius. Carcopino has urged that the word means neither tombs nor memorial cenotaphs, but the actual physical remains of the martyrs' bodies. His examples suggest that in the latter half of the fourth century such a meaning was possible and current.[43] They do not prove that this was the meaning of Gaius. And when he goes on to argue that Eusebius equates τρόπαια with σκηνώματα in glossing Gaius,[44] alternative opinion remains open. In fact Eusebius equates τρόπαια with οἱ τόποι ἔνθα τῶν εἰρημένων ἀποστόλων τὰ ἱερὰ σκηνώματα κατατεθεῖται. To Eusebius Gaius's τρόπαια is parallel to Proclus's τάφος. Originally, however, these terms may have been par-

---

41. Marrou in *Dict. d'arch. chr.* xv. 2 (1953), 3344; Schneider in *Theol. Lit. Zeit.* (1952), pp. 322–26; A. von Gerkan in *Zeits. f. d. Neutest. Wiss.* xliv (1952–53), pp. 196–205. Von Gerkan's paper, 'Kritische Studien zu den Ausgrabungen unter der Peterskirche', in *Zeitschrift f. Geschichte u. Kunst des Trierer Landes* xxii (1953), pp. 26–55, summarized in *Riv. arch. crist.* xxxi (1955), p. 129, has been wholly inaccessible.

Toynbee and Ward Perkins (p. 184) rightly criticize the Italian report for failing to give a detailed report on some bones found in a recess under the foundations of the Red Wall. Of course all the evidence ought to have been made available; but it would be over-optimistic to expect a report on the bones to be in any sense decisive (except perhaps negatively).

42. Cullmann, *Journ. Eccl. Hist.* vii (1956), p. 240, remarks that in the *Acta Petri* (*c.* 200) Peter is buried in Marcellus's tomb, not on the Vatican.

43. *Études d'hist. chr.,* pp. 99ff., 251ff.; *de Pythagore aux Apôtres,* pp. 251ff. Cp. C. Mohrmann, 'A propos de deux mots controversés de la latinité chrétienne: tropaeum—nomen', in *Vigiliae Christianae* viii (1954), pp. 154–73.

44. Eus., *H.E.* ii. 25. 6.

tially antithetical. In any event it remains true that τρόπαιον is not a natural word to describe a martyr's tomb. It is, however, used in Christian language with a primary reference to the Cross of Christ (cp. Justin, *Apol.* i. 55; Tert., *adv. Marc.* iv. 20). It would surely be a very easy transition to use the same word of the triumphal memorial to the leader of the apostles on the very mount of his crucifixion.[45] The tradition that Peter was crucified is extremely well attested by John 21:18; by Tertullian's phrase *Petrus passioni dominicae adaequatur* (*Praescr.* 36, cp. *Scorp.* 15); and by Origen's commentary on Genesis, cited by Eusebius, *H.E.* iii. 1. Origen had visited Rome, and may be assumed to reflect good Roman tradition here. In short, the evidence of Gaius is not incompatible with the view that he believed the Vatican Aedicula to be the grave, and his language does not tell against that opinion; but it does nothing whatever to support it positively.

The impulse behind the cultus of the saints and martyrs was in large part dominated from the third century on by belief in the supreme value of veneration in proximity to the dead body. No body, no cult. Sooner or later, no doubt, any such memorial monument would tend to be taken for a tomb. The devout folk who sought the aid of the saints in obtaining supernatural blessings might be glad to pray beside an Aedicula close by the very spot where the apostle had been crucified, but they wanted much more to be near his mortal remains. The *propinquitas Petri* is the leitmotiv of this popular devotion.[46] Whether or not Gaius believed the Vatican Aedicula to mark the tomb is another matter; Gaius is first-class testimony to Roman tradition, but not to the whereabouts of tombs and bodies. But it is not unlikely that in response to popular demand the answer of the Roman clergy about the middle of the third century would be that the tombs were located at the Vatican and the Via Ostiensis. The evidence, however, of the *graffiti* from the shrine on the Via Appia point in the direction of a popular piety standing under little direct control by the clergy. The Petrine Aedicula on the Vatican is set in the middle of a pagan necropolis. To enthusiasts of the third century would it really have seemed conceivable that the very apostles themselves could be buried among pagan tombs? 'Licet convivere cum ethnicis, commori non licet', remarks Tertullian (*de Idol.* xiv). To Cyprian it was not the least conspicuous of the failings of the Spanish bishop Martialis, of Legio

---

45. Clement of Rome (*Ep. ad Cor.* 5) describes the place of his martyrdom as ὁ ὀφειλόμενος τόπος τῆς δόξης. Rome remembered the site of its Golgotha.

46. Cp. Tertullian, *de Pudicitia* 21, 'omnis ecclesia Petri propinqua', and thereon W. Köhler, *Sitzungsber. d. Heidelberger Akad. d. Wiss.* (1938).

and Asturica, that he was a member of a pagan burial club and allowed his kinsfolk to be 'apud profana sepulcra depositos et alienigenis consepultos' (*Ep.* lxvii. 6).[47] But if such feeling told against the popularity of the Vatican, the same objection would hold for the Via Appia.

One possibility to account for the origins of the Memoria on the Via Appia is a submerged tradition with a considerable following among the less instructed and perhaps also the less orthodox which, when during the first half of the third century the impulse towards the cult of the martyrs began to be felt in Rome, was prepared to claim that the true graves were 'ad Catacumbas' on the Via Appia and believed that the 'trophies' erected in the latter part of the second century were either cenotaphs or not the genuine graves. The existence of such a tradition is not impossible. Granted that the archaeological evidence is decisive against the view that the Memoria was a centre of Christian veneration prior to the middle years of the third century, it may none the less be possible that simple believers suspected that the true apostolic graves were located there, even as far back as the late second century. The analogy of the holy places at Jerusalem may suggest that the Christians did not always find it easy to obtain possession of the sites they wanted. During the second and early third centuries they found themselves strenuously competing with powerful rivals for possession of the sacred grotto at Bethlehem where, in the Christian view, Jesus was born.[48] And they remained unable to obtain authority to take over the site of the holy sepulchre before the time of Constantine. (Since there was a shrine of Aphrodite on the site dating from the time of Hadrian and excavation would involve its demolition, it is intelligible that they had to wait for a Christian emperor to give them authority to start digging.)[49] Accordingly the possibility cannot be excluded (though it cannot be claimed a probability) that one reason why the Memoria was not established earlier was simply that the place was in pagan or heretical hands, and the Christians were unable to obtain possession of the property.

47. A few isolated Christian graves at Rome are noted in pagan company by Schneider, 'Die ältesten Denkmäler der römischen Kirche', in *Festschrift zur Feier des zweihundertjährigen Bestehens der Akademie der Wissenschaften in Göttingen,* ii (1951), p. 192. The Vatican necropolis contains some.

48. Justin, *Dial.* 70 and 78; Jerome, *Ep.* 58. 3; Origen, *c. Cels.* i. 51.

49. Jerome, *Ep.* 58. 3; Eus., *V.C.* iii. 26. Cp. also Constantine's letter to Macarius of Jerusalem (*V.C.* iii. 30) with the comment of W. Telfer, *Cyril of Jerusalem and Nemesius of Emesa* (1955), p. 195, that 'it would seem to show that they [i.e. the Christians] had sought excavation under Licinius and been refused.'

Another hypothesis that has recently been canvassed is that the Memoria started life as a rallying-point for a dissident group, either heretical or schismatic, and that at some time in the fourth century it passed into the hands of the great church. (This view needs to be carefully distinguished from the argument of M. Carcopino that the site was in dissident and sectarian hands prior to the establishment of the Memoria in 258 but not thereafter.) Commenting on Dom L. C. Mohlberg's ingenious argument[50] that the Memoria was a Novatianist centre, Miss Toynbee and Mr. Ward Perkins object: 'In order to account for the continuation in Catholic hands of what had begun as a schismatical cult-centre (whether Novatianist or other), we should have to postulate the existence, by the middle of the fourth century, of some tradition, common to Catholics and schismatics alike, but almost certainly not founded on fact, that the Apostles had either lived on this site in their lifetime or been temporarily buried there at the time of their martyrdom' (op. cit., p. 179). In view of the evidence of Damasus it is hard to see the force of this objection. The difficulty is rather to discern any evidence of the probable or even possible circumstances under which the place could have passed from schismatic to Catholic hands in the fourth century. Mohlberg has indeed an answer to this question—unlike the comparable view of Schneider,[51] who is content to regard the Memoria as heretical or schismatic without specifying any particular sect or any precise date when the place passed into the hands of the Catholic clergy, except that this was probably before the Basilica Apostolorum was built in Constantinian times (it is certainly prior to 345; cp. P. Styger, *Die römische Katakomben* (1933), pp. 345f.). For Mohlberg, on the other hand, the cult-centre remained Novatianist until the end of the fourth century, and the extrusion of the Novatianists at that time under state suppression explains why at the beginning of the fifth century a schismatic cult of the apostles is superseded by a Catholic cult of St. Sebastian. How all this can be reconciled with Damasus's inscription *Hic habitasse* is obscure. But in any event Mohlberg's question is wrongly formulated. Once the story of the translation from the Via Appia was established (and Damasus shows that this was long before his time), the Memoria was bound to lose ground before the other two individual cult-centres, furnished by Constantine with far more impressive basilicas. Tourists might go out of

---

50. 'Historisch-kritische Bemerkungen zum Ursprung der sogenannten "Memoria Apostolorum" an der Appischen Straße', in *Colligere Fragmenta: Festschrift Alban Dold* (= Texte und Arbeiten hrsg. durch die Erzabtei Beuron, Abt. i, Beiheft 2, 1952), pp. 52–74.
    51. *Nachr. d. Gött. Akad. d. Wiss.* (1951), 3, p. 14.

interest to see where the apostles had once lain; here also there would come the young bloods of the city on Sunday afternoon walks.[52] But the devout who sought for miraculous aid would not visit it often; they would prefer the sites where the bodies were now believed to be. No further explanation of the superseding of the apostles by St. Sebastian seems necessary. Moreover, the cult of St. Sebastian at the Via Appia is earlier than 336. It is attested in the *Depositio Martyrum* (entry for 20 Jan.), and his feast was observed at Milan in the time of Ambrose.[53] Are we seriously to suppose that St. Sebastian was a Novatianist? His cult was established long before the time of Innocent I, and the supersession of the apostles must have been a less abrupt business.[54]

There is, therefore, room for an alternative hypothesis. I venture to submit that the most reasonable interpretation of the available evidence is that the year 258 marked an 'invention' on 29 June in consequence of a special revelation. The researches of Tolotti have shown that the Memoria was not conceived as an independent construction, but was set within the precinct of a newly laid out family mausoleum.[55] We are therefore dealing with something which in its early stages is a matter of private enterprise, and probably remained so for a considerable period of time before it finally passed into the hands of the community. The *graffiti* attesting the practice of *refrigerium* strongly suggest that the place was the property of some layman exceedingly ill-instructed in the faith—perhaps a visionary and somewhat superstitious lady (Lucina?). There is good evidence that the devotional excesses of people of this type were a matter of some anxiety to the clergy. At the end of the century there is the well-known figure of Lucilla of Carthage, whose quarrel with archdeacon Caecilian seems chiefly to have originated with the refusal of authority to grant recognition to the relics of a martyr in her private possession (Optatus, i. 16). We have plenty of evidence for the frequency of 'invention' by private revelation.[56] For example, in the fifth-century *Passio*

52. Jerome, *Comm. in Ezech.* xii. 40 (Vallarsi, v. 468).

53. *Expos. Ps. CXVIII*, xx. 44 (*CSEL* lxii. 466).

54. For a more sympathetic review of Mohlberg's argument see Miss Toynbee's remarks in *Journ. Rom. Stud.* xliii, p. 15; she there regarded it as a difficulty for Schneider's view that 'in that case the question as to why St. Sebastian ousted the Apostles would still remain unanswered'. See also J. Lowe, *St. Peter,* p. 40.

55. Ward Perkins in *Journ. Rom. Stud.* xlv (1955), pp. 206–7.

56. Much material illustrative of this phenomenon is collected by E. Lucius, *Die Anfänge des Heiligenkults* (1904), pp. 143ff. Cp. H. Grégoire, *Les Persécutions dans l'empire romain* (1951), p. 102: 'L'événement de 258 pourrait n'avoir été qu'une *inventio,* et non une *translatio.*'

S. Sebastiani the saint's body would not have been recovered had he not appeared in a dream to Lucina, told her where to find it, and instructed her to bury him 'ad Catacumbas . . . in initio cryptae iuxta vestigia apostolorum'.[57] To ecclesiastical authority visions and revelations of this nature were neither invariably welcome nor very easily controllable. An interesting canon of the third council of Carthage directs that all martyr-shrines without demonstrably genuine relics or traditions are to be destroyed: '. . . et omnino nulla memoria martyrum probabiliter accepteteur nisi ubi corpus aut aliquae reliquiae sunt aut origo alicuius habitationis vel possessionis vel passionis fidelissima origine traditur. nam quae *per somnia et per inanes quasi revelationes* quorumlibet hominum ubicumque constituuntur altaria, omnimodo improbentur'.[58] To implement this decision must have been a task calling for either extreme delicacy or extreme ruthlessness.

If something of this sort accounts for the origins of the shrine at the Via Appia, there is no need for surprise that the evidence has suggested (as to Schneider and Mohlberg) tension between this place and the official Roman community. Here was a zeal for God untempered by knowledge, with which it would ultimately become necessary for authority to come to terms. The happy thought of reconciling the divergence by concocting a story of a translation from an original burial at the Via Appia, which was assigned either to the remote past in the apostolic age or at least to a period only just within living memory (in which case it was essential to emphasize that it had been carried out at dead of night under conditions of secrecy),[59] would have made possible a policy of comprehensiveness. It would also have made it certain that the rather embarrassing cult-centre at the Via Appia would lose ground before the 'trophies' at the Vatican and the Via Ostiensis. The supersession of the apostles by St. Sebastian was hardly an accident; the entire translation story could have been deliberately intended to have exactly that effect by its original inventors. How early the story was put into circulation it is impos-

---

57. *Acta Sanctorum,* 20 Jan., p. 278.

58. Canon 83 in the *Codex Canonum Ecclesiae Africanae* (ed. Bruns, p. 176). Even Jerome conceded to Vigilantius that the cult of the martyrs led to excesses 'per imperitiam et simplicitatem saecularium hominum vel certe religiosarum feminarum de quibus vere possumus dicere: Confiteor zelum dei habent sed non secundum scientiam', but consoled him with the reflection that it did no one much harm: 'quid inde perdis?' (*Adv. Vigil.* 7; Vallarsi, ii. 393). Jerome clearly saw that by this time the movement had gathered far too much impetus for the clergy to put any brake on it; any serious attempt to do so could only be too little and too late.

59. Cp. above, p. 40, n. 1 (*noctu*).

sible to say, but as a tentative guess (the *graffiti* at the Via Appia do not, it seems, continue far into the fourth century) its origins may be assigned to the time of Pope Marcellinus or thereabouts.

A hypothesis along these lines can claim to be built upon the rock of attested belief as opposed to entirely unattested event, and to have the merit of taking much more seriously than Pearson and Duchesne the legend of a translation from the original graves at the Via Appia, well established before the time of Damasus. In a word, we have to do with a spectacular example of what Jules Lebreton in a famous article described as 'le désaccord de la foi populaire et de la théologie savante dans l'Église chrétienne du IIIe siècle'.[60]

Finally, attention may be drawn to a neglected scrap of evidence which may have some bearing upon the liturgical commemoration of the apostles in the fourth century. In the third chapter of the *Decretum Gelasianum* there survives part of the reply produced by Damasus and his Roman council of 382 as a counterblast to the recent claims of Constantinople to be, as New Rome, the second see of Christendom and thus to rank before Alexandria and Antioch.[61] Damasus begins by claiming, partly as in the metrical inscription in the Basilica Apostolorum, that the unique authority of the Roman see resides not in any synodical decisions of other churches, but in a primacy based on (*a*) *Tu es Petrus,* and (*b*) the martyrdom in the city of St. Peter and St. Paul, who were crowned 'non diverso, sicut heresei garriunt, sed uno tempore uno eodemque die'. The occurrence of this phrase in so highly charged a polemical document points towards the conclusion that in the time of Damasus there was active dissension concerning the date of the deaths of the apostles. It is not a calm and detached statement. The official view was that both had died on one and the same day. But there were also others (were they adherents of Damasus's rival Ursinus?) who believed that they had died on different days and presumably expressed their belief by two distinct celebrations, commemorating St. Peter on one day and St. Paul on another. If so, there was not merely a twofold tradition concerning the place of burial but a rivalry concerning the dates. This inevitably raises the question whether these two rivalries were not in fact associated and bound up with one another. We should then suppose that the single commemoration of both apostles on the same day, 29 June, was originally connected

60. *Revue d'hist. eccl.* xix (1923), pp. 481–505; xx (1924), pp. 5–37.

61. Text in C. H. Turner, *Eccl. Occid. Monum. Iuris Antiq.* i. 157, and in *J.T.S.* i (1900), p. 560; also E. von Dobschütz, *Das Decretum Gelasianum* (Texte und Unters. 38, Heft 4, 1912), p. 7.

with the shrine on the Via Appia at which both bodies were believed to have been buried together; while the separate commemorations on different days (was perhaps 25 January one of them?)[62] would clearly be attached to the two individual shrines at the Vatican and the Via Ostiensis.

If at the last the ultimate question is to be raised concerning historical events, probability is no doubt overwhelming in favour of the view that the apostles died on different days.[63] The notion that they died on one and the same day would naturally catch the imagination as far more dramatic,[64] though it is interesting to observe that there was also current a compromise that the apostles had died not on the same day but on the same date a year apart[65]—a view which would have the advantage of involving no liturgical complications. In the second-century *Acta Petri* and *Acta Pauli* it is simply taken for granted that the apostles died at different times. It is, however, futile to seek for any record of the actual dates in the late calendars; the problem is put outside the realm of discussion by the absence of public liturgical cult of the martyrs at Rome before the middle years of the third century, though no doubt veneration officially recognized by authority was long preceded by private devotion.[66] The consequences of this private devotion cannot have been a simple matter for the Roman clergy to control. There does not appear anything unreasonable in the supposition that for a time during the third century private devotion to the memory of the apostles was not unanimous about the annual commemoration; that when ecclesiastical authority took the cult-centre at the Via Appia under its wing it was decided to eliminate these divergences in so far as they affected the

---

62. *Mart. Hieron.* VIII Kal. Feb.: '. . . Romae translatio Pauli apostli.'

63. The martyrdom of the apostles is mentioned by several ante-Nicene authors: Clement of Rome, *Ep. ad Cor.* 5; Irenaeus, *adv. Haer.* iii. 3.2–3; Tertullian, *Praescr.* 36; *Scorp.* 15; Origen, *Comm. in Gen.* iii, ap. Eus., *H.E.* iii. 1; Eusebius, *Chron.,* p. 185, ed. Helm, and *H.E.* ii. 25.6f. The only one to give any indication of the time is Dionysius of Corinth, *Epist. ad Rom.* ap. Eus., *H.E.* ii. 25. 8, with the vague statement that they died κατὰ τὸν αὐτὸν καιρόν. It is possible, of course, that this letter from Corinth to Rome was narrowly interpreted, and thus originated the tradition that they died on the same day.

64. Besides Damasus this tradition also appears in the Liberian Catalogue (Duchesne, *Liber Pontif.* i, p. 2), Rufinus's translation of Eus., *H.E.* ii. 25. 8 (*uno eodemque tempore*), and Jerome (*Vir. Inl.* 5 and in Morin, *Anecd. Maredsolana,* III. iii. 93).

65. Prudentius, *Peristeph.* xii. 5 ('unus utrumque dies, pleno tamen innovatus anno'); *Sacramentarium Leonianum,* p. 49, ed. Feltoe; Gregory of Tours, *de Gloria Martyrum* 28; Arator, *de Act. Apost.* ii. 1248 (*CSEL* lxxii. 149). Cp. also Turner's references in *Eccl. Occid. Monum. Iuris Antiq.* i. 245f.

66. Delehaye, *Culte des Martyrs*[2], pp. 260ff.; Lietzmann, *Petrus und Paulus*[2], p. 235, n. 1.

calendar by celebrating both martyrdoms on one and the same day, but to compromise on the question of place by observing the feast on 29 June at all three shrines; and that the old view which celebrated them on different days was an unconscionable time a-dying (it is just the sort of thing about which people would be conservative). Damasus shows himself anxious to eradicate its last traces. He was the kind of person who liked tidying things up; and perhaps his final success in this direction was the simplification of the proceedings on 29 June (which must have been extremely exhausting) by quietly dropping the visit to the shrine at the Via Appia, leaving only two places to be included, and by erecting the metrical inscription *Hic habitasse* in commemoration of what was henceforth to be regarded only as an interesting chapter of past history. Any who might still come thither seeking for the apostles were firmly advised to look elsewhere. The fact that the legend of a primitive translation from the Via Appia was by now generally accepted would make this a comparatively simple operation.[67]

If the argument so far is sound, one conclusion about the primitive martyrdoms and burials seems to follow, namely, that the Christians of Rome during the second and early third centuries had no reason to be much more certain about the true sites of the apostolic graves than we are today, and in fact that most of our modern confusions and doubts are little more than a consequence of theirs. We cannot attribute to the Roman church of the first century an anachronistic interest in the cult of the martyrs. And it is not *a priori* likely that in the circumstances of the Neronian persecution the Christians obtained possession of the bodies or necessarily knew exactly where they were buried if someone had been able to achieve this. But it would be idle to argue from doubt as to the circumstances to doubt as to the fact of the martyrdoms in the capital.[68] The problem is basically an acute variant of

67. Cp. Dreves, *Aurelius Ambrosius*, p. 76: 'Vielleicht bezeichnet diese Inschrift gerade den Moment, in welchem die jährliche Feier am 29. Juli [*sic*] in der Katakombe aufgelassen wurde?' The main ground for ascribing this to Damasus is that Prudentius (*Peristeph.* xii) describes the great procession of 29 June, conducting the Pope, as visiting first St. Peter's and then hurrying to St. Paul's to repeat the liturgy there; nothing is said of any visit to the Via Appia. On the other hand, at the Basilica Apostolorum there must surely have been still some celebration, conducted by a presbyter, since the Gelasian Sacramentary (ii. 30–32, p. 181 Wilson) provides for three masses on 29 June *(a) in Natali S. Petri proprie, (b) in Natali Apostolorum Petri et Pauli, (c) in Natali S. Pauli proprie.* Thus the church at the Via Appia retained its celebration, but was not visited by the papal procession. By the time of the Gregorian Sacramentary it was felt that even the two visits to St. Peter's and St. Paul's were an excessive physical strain, and the celebration at St. Paul's was held on 30 June.

68. On this point again modern scholarship has had little to add to Bishop Pearson,

one with which New Testament scholars have long been familiar; nothing is harder than the discovery of the martyred apostles of history when almost all the extant evidence concerns only the saints of faith.[69]

'Dissertationes duae de serie et successione primorum Romae episcoporum', in his *Opera Posthuma Chronologica,* edited by H. Dodwell (London, 1688). Pearson may fairly be described as the first writer to transfer St. Peter's martyrdom in Rome from the realm of δόξα to that of ἐπιστήμη.

69. I have to thank Professor Toynbee, Mr. Woodhead, and Professor Ratcliff for the opportunity of discussing with them some of the questions raised in this article, and Dr. Telfer for kind help in criticizing an early draft. It was delivered as a lecture at Bonn on 29 June 1956, at the invitation of the Faculty of Protestant Theology.

Unhappily the acute study of Theodor Klauser, *Die römische Petrustradition im Lichte der neuen Ausgrabungen unter der Peterskirche* (Köln and Opladen, 1956), appeared too late to be used or discussed.

The Power of Music

The title of these lectures prescribed by the learned president of our ceremonies, Professor Margaret Bent of All Souls, brings together two elements of human achievement and greatness, or at least of human experience, which we do not necessarily or immediately associate. Indeed music and power may seem to have only the most accidental and peripheral connection with each other rather than a substantial and integrated link. But whether this is more true of music than of the other arts may be matter for reflection during the long winter evenings. In this modest discourse my intention is to offer first an analysis of the role of music as a vehicle and support for the assertion of power, and then to change gear, so to speak, and to inquire about the inherent power of music as an art with the ability to put some constraint upon us. What is it that music in particular does for us, or rather does to us, when we give it concentrated attention and allow these ordered sounds to claim the full right of entry which they demand?

Music is a mysterious and very ancient art and activity of two basic ingredients, rhythm and pitch, the latter is determined by the physics of sound. Musicians look to the physicist to explain differences in loudness, or in musical quality, whether between different instruments or between differing uses of the same instrument. The physicist can also analyse for us harmonics—the partial tones present in any note which have decisive influence on the shape of the scale between a note and the octave above it. If the keyboard player wants the intonation modified sufficiently to allow the possibility of modulation, then the physicist will have advice and probably

Lecture given on 30 October 1995 in the Examination Schools, University of Oxford, in the series *Music and Power*.

some frowns at this necessary but uncomfortable tampering with the true sound.

So music is not so much a human creation as a discovery, and its progress during the first two or three millennia of recorded history was gradual. But from primitive times early kings found song and dance a source of enrichment and ennoblement for ceremonial solemnities. Down to our own time music remains the first symbol of political allegiance, and that is prominent at Olympic Games when national anthems celebrate victories. 'God Save the Queen', 'Land of Our Fathers', the 'Marseillaise', 'Stars and Stripes', the Red Flag, and the emperor quartet of Haydn (taken to provide a song to unite the German federation). On Remembrance Sunday at the Cenotaph in Whitehall there is deep emotional power in the collocation of 'O God Our Help in Ages Past' with the buglers sounding the Last Post in commemoration of the fallen. Though in more aggressively cheerful mood, comparable feelings may attach to the Last Night of the Proms.

These are moments when group loyalty, gratitude for the relative freedom this society enjoys, even a touch of self-dedication, need music to find their voice. Words alone would seem weak. The oldest beginnings of musical celebration in dance and cult, or in both together, give music strong associations with the feeling of community.

These are situations where the music is a vehicle for the expression of community power, and is bound up with an emotion that is about power.

But to be an instrument for the articulation of power music needs a context provided by some external source. Verdi could write operas like Nabucco where the libretto is allegorically related to contemporary liberation politics in Italy at the time. One asks: Did Wagner design Die Meistersinger to carry a symbol of the reconciliation between the higher bourgeoisie, represented by Hans Sachs, and the old aristocracy represented by Walther von Stolzing? Beckmesser then becomes the representative of embarrassingly gauche and unpolished bourgeois behavior. I recall a dreadful performance of the Meistersinger at the New York Met when Beckmesser's part was sung so much better than Walther's, that the prize was obviously wrongly allocated.)

Music has never been more obviously elevated by a conscious background in political power than when Beethoven wrote a symphony in honour of, and with an original dedication to, Napoleon. As we all know, he originally inscribed Bonaparte on the score, but then deleted it in anger when his hero arrogantly assumed the imperial title. After eight of his symphonies had been performed. Beethoven was asked which of them he himself felt to be the one that best realized what he wanted to say, and his answer was the

Eroica. There have been many listeners since that time who have shared the composer's personal assessment. And in the first movement the sublimity is achieved by means of extraordinary, indeed elemental simplicity. The first subject announces at the start an innocuous arpeggio on the chord of E flat, but this acorn becomes the mightiest of oaks, ending the movement with a massively powerful relentless crescendo during a statement of this theme in intense exaltation repeatedly answered by different sections of the orchestra. Naturally Beethoven makes the statement a concord. When he wanted us to know a movement was ending, he liked a lot of emphatic concords.

The simplicity is as great in the Missa Solennis with its combination of lyrical devotion and galvanic energy in the Vitam Venturi fugue, or in the electrifying anti-war protest of the Dona nobis with its trumpets and guns. And perhaps no movement of the Missa Solennis is invested with more emotional power than the quarter of an hour of the Benedictus, certainly the longest setting of one line of Latin in all the repertory, so exquisite in feeling that he could hardly bring himself to end it.

It is rather rare for concord to be used in this way to express emotional power. At least since the sixteenth century the means most frequently used by composers to express deep or even passionate feeling has been the discord. There are exceptions like the famous second Agnus Dei in Palestrina's Missa Brevis where the double choir proceed in canon, and put the participant listener through a mangle of feeling. But if we take another famous example, William Byrd's mass for four voices, there in the Agnus the resolution of each successive suspension leaves you with another one at a different pitch, so that the sense of pathos becomes overwhelming. Naturally you will think of cases where a composer who has used much dissonance will give a huge sense of triumph at the conclusion by harmony which if not violently dissonant is a near miss for being a concord. One thinks of Stravinsky's Firebird or of the numinous ending to his Symphony of Psalms. The one ending is forte, the other pianissimo.

One of the questions one could ask about music and power is sociological. You will recall that in 1921 Max Weber published a study of the sociology of music, and a generation later Adorno wrote an often obscure little book on the same theme.

Beethoven's music has a volcanic effect on his contemporaries. In the family house at Bonn you will be shown a contemporary print portraying the processing and attendance at his funeral. A crowd of between fifteen and twenty thousand turned out to witness the scene, and that turn-out is surely eloquent of what he had meant to people of his own time. Why did they feel him to express their aspirations? The French Revolutions had brought irreversible social changes, with reverberations all over Europe. Did Beethoven express something deep in the aspirations of the bourgeois finding their place in a world previously dominated by the landed aristocracy? Like all composers of his age, Beethoven remained dependent on the patronage of powerful and wealthy aristocrats, of course. Very good music costs money. In the Tempest Stefano yearned to live in a kingdom where he would have his music for nothing. It is a dream not confined to drunken butlers.

Those dedications of Beethoven's works to major patrons such as Prince Lobkowitz or Karl von Lichnowsky or Count Waldstein or the Archduke Rudolf acknowledge a crucial debt, though perhaps there is no more eloquent acknowledgement of debt than his dedications of the early piano sonatas to Joseph Haydn who had provided a role model and shown how a piano sonata could work for him. Beethoven may have expressed the emancipation of people who were not aristocrats but were still glad to have their support and patronage in an age when their wealth and resources were far from extinct. Today such patronage has to be less romantically exercised by high street banks or United Biscuits or ICI.

Does it illustrate something of the link between music and contemporary power that Berlioz's transformation of the orchestra, by a huge increase in the number of a string players, has analogies to the style of contemporary industry and its technology? He may easily be taken to reflect his age's admiration for large-scale power in the physical sense producing steam, ironclad ships, and soon the ability to drive tunnels through the Alps—the kind of wonder expressed in Turner's Steam and Speed. In my youth Arthur Honegger in Paris would write Pacific 231 in praise of a huge locomotive.

In our time the advent of computer technology has deeply affected the kind of music some composers want to write.

Twentieth-century music has had a problem in its exploration of new worlds. Abandon tonality, write a polyphonic structure where the various parts manifest sublime indifference to each other and seem positively to enjoy a quarrel. Initially the logic of dissonance requires the presupposition of some concord from which the harmony can be heard to be dissonant. But that soon moves on to a music which is simply indifferent to the resolution of dissonance. The ear knows what, if there were to be harmony or some ultimate resolutions, it might all sound like. In radical composers the love of dissonance and the horror of concord have expressed an attitude to the tradition of the past.

The radicals regarded concords as sickly bourgeois illusions, covering with decent obscurity the dreadfulness and misery of the twentieth century. Concords pretend that our human life and our experiences are not a series of battering traumas, either because of what other people do to us or, worse, because of what we do ourselves and endure remorse at the memory. Alban Berg's Wozzeck takes the story of a wretched solider for whom the bread has consistently fallen butter side down. His Lulu is not exactly cheerful stuff. Schönberg's Erwartung tells of a lovesick woman searching at night for her lover, ending by finding his murdered corpse.

The preference for dissonance is an expression of horror and shock. Only of course one would be quite wrong to deduce from this that if their chosen librettii had been telling of a man equally successful both in love and in his career, then Berg and Schönberg would have provided us with a soothing flower garden of dominant sevenths.

Something of the power in music of this family group consists in the moral fervor of its wish to reject deceptive fantasies of peace and serenity engendered when the music is smooth on the ear and like Benjamin Britten broadly keeps a relationship to the conventional rules of the classical past. In this music you know that if you suddenly happen to hear a concord, it will certainly not be on a stressed beat and will at best be a merely transitory passing note set in a more serious musical discourse.

The social foundation of support for music can be diminished by compositions which are felt to be too taxing for the ear to be comprehensible. Audiences can vote with their feet, and since audiences are actually needed for economic reasons some compromises may be necessary. There is difficulty in the task of educating a modern democratic society to sit back and enjoy the uncompromising sounds written by, say, Ligeti—the enchanting charismatic Hungarian composer now living in Hamburg, who would directly tell you that he has not intended his music to be 'beautiful' in any traditional sense. But the sound does not lack power. What he makes little or no pretence to touch is the aesthetic sense of proportion and order which music can bring into lives otherwise deficient in these qualities.

There is always a problem for the ordinary listener with a reasonably good ear if the music makes a powerful statement requiring an apparently exclusive cerebral attention, but making little or no effort to touch aesthetic feeling. But if one is to compromise, how far can one go?

On the other extreme, one has only to recall most of the music that came out of Stalin's Soviet Union to recognize that it was merely vulgar kitsch. There has perhaps never been a time when the music liked by cultured and sophisticated ears has not been resented by people whose ears prefer something different. In the sixth century in an Italy ruled by barbarian Goths, the Roman aristocrat Boethius experienced pain at the Goths' liking for hairgrease, for lederhosen, and for noisy vulgar music.

In the urbane cultivated modern West, music's freedom can be threatened by other forces. There is a narrow power exercised by those who control the programmes in our concert halls, by record companies, and by those who select the small circle of performers we are commonly allowed to hear—agencies that can make opera unreasonably costly to the extent that shamingly the National Lottery has to step in to rescue our principal metropolitan opera house. Because costs are high, prices have to be high, and it is then mistakenly supposed that opera is intended only for the rich—a reaction which reminds of de Tocqueville's warning that a characteristic of democracy is a fairly high degree of intolerance.

In practice great wealth lies with the purveyors of pop. Harold Wilson was absolutely right to confer an honour on the Beatles in the sixties. Right, not merely because their kind of music was liked by Eastenders and had many touches of freshness and originality, but perhaps above all because their exported recordings earned far more than the British motor car industry for the national balance of payments.

Noel Coward famously remarked: 'Extraordinary how potent cheap music is.' The elemental simplicity of its underlying structure is no doubt one cause responsible for that potency. It has a basic rhythmic vitality and utilises a severely limited range of harmonies. Anything as grand as a modulation therefore has to be achieved by jerking all the players up a semitone to prevent boredom and heighten the excitement. In jazz of the highest New Orleans school the restriction on the number of chords used is a practical necessity in order to make possible individual improvisations as the successive variations on the theme follow. These variations will or may have new melodies but must not vary the harmonies.

Among the merits of pop is the fact that it can provide good audible wallpaper as background to some other activity such as writing an essay for a tutorial or driving a bus or erecting a new building. Thirty years ago at the time of the erection of the new Robbins-era universities, I recall the Vice-Chancellor of one university drily remarking that the only way he could tell the difference between his students and the construction workers was that at least the students turned off their transistor radios on entering the university library.

Pop is a kind of music that touches the solar plexus rather than the head or the heart. Does it coerce the ear into listening to what it has to say? There is classical music which does just that. If by way of dulling the pain of writing your essay you play a CD or tape of, say, Schubert's string quintet in C, you will find yourself in the gravest trouble. The sense of almost unendurable sadness and tragedy pervading the first two movements will have an imperious effect, hardly allowing you to give thought to anything else. This is music that could be described as contemplation of the mystery of death and its apparent negation of value in human achievement. My violinist brother once played in a performance of it where at the end of the second movement the viola player was so overwhelmed by its emotional power that there had to be an interval to enable him to recover and play on for the last two movements. 'Such sweet compulsion doth in music lie', wrote Milton.

There is another line of Milton where he immediately justaposes 'most musical and most melancholy' as equipollent. Some of the lutenist songs by John Bowl and his contemporaries may have been in his mind, and now long after his time Henry Purcell would explore and exploit chromatic harmonies to produce music of deep sadness. Perhaps music with a touch of melancholy is found particularly beautiful. If you ever have any close contact with cathedral choirs, you will notice that whereas the austerities of Lent are tough to the rest of us, to the singers there is no time of the church year when they are able to sing more exquisite stuff and they look forward to these weeks with special delight.

Milton's Thoughtful Man, Il Penseroso, spoke of music possessing the power to dissolve him into ecstasies and bring all heaven before his eyes. Shakespeare's 'Venus and Adonis' has the express link between 'Ear's sweet music and heart's deep sore wounding' (VA 432). Jaques in *As You Like It* could suck melancholy out of a song as a weasel sucks eggs. And in *The Merchant of Venice* Jessica is never merry when she hears sweet music (V 1, 69).

Die Winterreise or many a composition by Debussy or Ravel would have done for her. It is no accident that in British music, Vaughan Williams's Tallis variations have been valued as an eloquent statement of the glory and misery of humankind. They are the apotheosis of melancholy, and at the same time an expression of celestial yearning and aspiration.

The power of music to compel us to listen is an obvious reason why in the religious community music has been simultaneously accorded intense value and some degree of fear and misgiving. Both the council of Trent and the English Puritans and Swiss Protestants wanted to restrict the part of music in worship, the Puritans to a degree that caused vexation. Shakespeare regretted the Puritan stance.

'The man that hath no music in himself
Nor is not moved with concord of sweet sounds
Is fit for treasons, stratagems and spoils . . .
Let no such man be trusted.' (*Merchant* V 1 83–88).

In *The Merchant of Venice* Lorenzo wanted the sounds of music to creep into Jessica's ear; so he expounded to her the ancient Pythagorean and Platonic belief in the music of the spheres, now modelled, however, on the singing of angels even higher in the hierarchy of being. The music of the spheres rested on a Pythagorean belief that the distance between the planets was determined by the mathematics of musical intervals. The Pythagoreans knew that the ratio of an octave is 2:1, of a fifth 3:2, of a fourth 4:3. The whole tone is the difference between fourth and fifth, or in mathematical terms a proportion of 9:8.

There was a problem succinctly stated by Aristotle, namely that the most remarkable thing about the planets' movement through the skies is that they do not make a sound. As a good Platonist, Lorenzo explains away this embarrassing inaudibility by referring to the weakness of our mortal body: 'this muddy vesture of decay doth grossly close it in, we cannot hear it.'

His affectionate courting of Jessica continues with another theme of immense antiquity, namely the power of music to tame wildness and excess. It is a particularly prominent theme in ancient references to music that it has almost magical power of emotional therapy. We get the oldest of all mentions of this power in the Hebrew scriptures of the Old Testament when David and his harp are brought to King Saul's court to play and calm the king's disturbed and troubled mind. Pythagoras in Sicily was reported to have tranquillised a riotous and over-excited young man by a wisely judged performance in a restful mode.

Therapy of the emotions was a much-discussed topic in the classical philosophical schools of the Greek world.

Caliban in *The Tempest* found his wretchedness allayed and made bearable by music.

'The isle is full of noises,
Sounds and sweet airs that give delight and hurt not.
Sometimes a thousand twangling instruments
Will hum about mine ears . . .
. . . and then in dreaming
The clouds methought would open and show riches

Ready to drop upon me, that when I waked
I cried to dream again.' (III 2 138-46)

For Caliban, Shakespeare's portrait of the human condition, music offered an anaesthetic to dull the pain of living with himself.

The therapeutic effect of music is felt by a sensitive audience in the
Judgement music at the end of Mozart's *Don Giovanni*. Terror in the Com-
mendatore's utterly justified condemnation of the murderous rapist who
has been made endurable only by the delicious wit of his servant Lepcrello,
is expressed in a formidable passage not only rising in semitones in tonality
but deploying three sonorous trombones not previously heard in the opera.
For the Don the last trump is sounding, and it cannot be claimed that he has
not deserved those terrifying trombones.

In modern society music of all the arts enjoys a huge following, and
there appears to be an ever-increasing level of technical competence in performance. It is a plausible hypothesis that this increasing social importance
of music is a legacy of its old association with religion, and for many it has
come to fulfil at least some of the functions of religion. In the 1570s a couple of
Frenchmen, a poet and a composer, aspired to transform French society into a
Platonic ideal republic by founding, with royal support, a special musical academy, much as Wagner dreamt of using Bayreuth as an engine for recreating an
ideal Germany. Adorno once observed that in Wagner's operas in one way or
another all the characters need redemption. Wagner could even declare that
in Beethoven's pastoral symphony he could hear the word of the redeemer.

In our own century the Russian Scriabin nursed an ambition to con-
struct a temple in honour of the new gospel of music. He thought it would
need to be built in India. The outbreak of the first world war he at first
thought to be the inauguration of his new age of ecstasy. In 1915 he died.

Individual musicians have granted divine status to particular composers.
What Wagner would feel about Beethoven was much the same as Richard
Strauss would feel about Mozart. The old oratorio, of which Handel's *Messiah* is justly deemed the supreme masterpiece in the class, is now succeeded
by a bizarre invention, the secular oratorio.

Rameau once wrote, 'To enjoy music fully we must completely lose
ourselves in it.' Certainly it is true that to perform anything, even a simple
hymn tune well, requires total concentration. To lose oneself in something
is akin to the language of mysticism.

When John Henry Newman was made a cardinal, he took as the motto
for his escutcheon, *Cor ad cor loquitur*. Heart speaks to heart. Was it an echo,

probably an unconscious echo, of words which Beethoven had written at the head of the Kyrie of the Missa Solennis: 'Von Herzen—möge es zu Herzen gehen—From the heart may it go to the heart.'

Somewhere in this mysterious and profound region of the psyche lies the reason for the power of music.

For therapy of our souls music can evidently do much. At two points at least it must yield to the greater power of religion. It cannot easily cope with death. And it is not equipped to bring healing to the conscience haunted by shame or guilt.

New Letters of St. Augustine

The discovery by Johannes Divjak of a substantial group of unknown and unprinted letters, twenty-seven by Augustine himself, two from Consentius his prickly correspondent in the Balearic Islands (*Ep.* 120), and a letter from Jerome to Aurelius of Carthage, whose presence in the collection is not easy to explain, is an achievement for which high credit is due to the finder and first editor.[1] In the course of the Vienna Academy's great survey of manuscripts of Augustine, the letters were found in two manuscripts: Marseille 209 s. xv (A) from the Jesuit house at Aix-en-Provence, adorned with illuminated initials identified by Otto Pächt as the work of 'Maître Jouvenel des Ursins' active 1455–65, and Paris BN 16861 s. xii (C) from the monastery of S. Cyran. A is no direct copy of C, but ultimately derived from a model akin to it. The two manuscripts share a number of misreadings, mistaken division of words, lacunae, and other common corruptions. The transmitted text is in poor health, and offers much scope for a critical editor to apply conjectural remedies. A quantity of good suggestions is contributed by Adolf Primmer. It is no slight to say that there is much more to be done on this difficult text. The present notice will principally report on the content. Of the authenticity of the new texts there will be no argument. Their interest to the student of Augustinian theology is modest, except perhaps for *Ep.* 2* to Firmus, and that does not tell us something we do not already know about Augustin-

---

1. A paper read to the Cambridge Patristic Seminar on 17 May 1982 and revised in the light of discussion. The text considered is in *Corpus Scriptorum Ecclesiasticorum Latinorum,* lxxxviii (Vienna, 1981). I have not been able to take account of the papers by French scholars imminent from *Études Augustiniennes* (1983).

ianism. The main harvest falls to the historian of church and society and to the biographer of Augustine himself.

On Pelagianism, Donatism, and Priscillianism there is major evidence; also on the Roman law of slavery, on rights of asylum, and a political riot at Carthage in 422 otherwise unattested. Some will regret that the new letters have not been given numbers consecutive on Goldbacher, but begin a new series distinguished by an asterisk.

A reasoned inventory will quickly show how much the new documents offer. *Ep.* 1* to Count Classicianus gives the full text of the letter of which *Ep.* 250A in Goldbacher is a fragment. The essentials of the story are already known from *Ep.* 250 to Bishop Auxilius (see unnamed, but perhaps he is the Auxilius of Nurcona, in the Catholic list at the Carthage colloquy of 411: *Gesta coll.* i. 135, 103 Lancel, *PL* xi. 1314). Augustine is there critical of Auxilius's act in pronouncing excommunication not only on the count personally but also on all his household after he had come with soldiers to Auxilius's church asking the bishop not to grant asylum to criminals. They had sworn a false oath on the Gospels. Moreover, they had left the sanctuary of their own choice, not by force. Nevertheless angry words had been exchanged. Classicianus appealed to Augustine against Auxilius's ban, asking whether or not canon law allowed excommunication of an entire household rather than of an erring individual. Augustine's reply is that he knows of no conciliar decrees, only of instances where individual bishops have excommunicated entire households without incurring censure from their colleagues. An infant born in an excommunicate house would be refused baptism 'and would have more than original sin to contend with'. Augustine tells the count that he himself would never do such a thing. Moreover, in the case of criminals who had broken solemn oaths Augustine would not defend inviolable asylum (to which, as in *Ep.* 28* below, he can be much more sympathetic—e.g. *Sermo Guelf.* xxv, p. 538 Morin; in *S. Denis,* 19. 2, p. 99 M. he says that the apparitor sent to arrest a man respects sacred asylum).[2] Nevertheless the count would lose nothing and indeed would gain in standing if he felt able to apologize for his altercation with the bishop. Meanwhile Augustine will request a discussion of houschold excommunications in full synod, including a subsequent reference to the apostolic see 'to ensure common policy and

---

2. The council of Carthage on 27 April 399 sent Bishops Epigonius of Bulla Regia and Vincentius (see unknown, possibly Culusis) to the court to negotiate the granting of rights of asylum in churches: C. Munier, *Concilia Africae a.345–a.525,* Corpus Christianorum Series Latina 149 (1974), p. 194.

to obtain confirmatory support'.[3] (The new letters contain several indications of Augustine's warm view of Roman authority. The episcopate lacks a clinching authority in disputed cases if their consensus is not confirmed by the apostolic see; but Rome does not issue decrees in solitary sovereignty or apart from the college of bishops.) The letter to Classicianus cannot be assigned a precise date, but Augustine's manner is that of an old man.

Ep. 1A* is a re-edition of the letter to Firmus accompanying a special copy of *De civitate Dei;* therefore it was written soon after 426. The document was first edited by C. Lambot, *Rev. Bénéd.* li (1939), p. 109 = *P.L.S.* ii. 1373, and is discussed by B. V. E. Jones, *J.T.S.*, n.s., xvi (1965), pp. 142–45. The copy was made at the expense of Firmus's brother Cyprianus. Augustine advises that the work be divided either in two codices with 1–10 and 11–22, or into five split thus: 1–5, 6–10, 11–14, 15–18, 19–22. Firmus is asked to allow other copies to be made from this one.

The same Firmus is also the recipient of *Ep.* 2*, a text which proves he is no cleric but an unbaptized layman with a Christian wife. Firmus is exhorted to follow his wife's example. Why should upper-class women be allowed to surpass men in conversion? Firmus, however, wishes to remain a catechumen and excuses himself from enrolling as a candidate for baptism by two arguments. The first is that his *tarditas* is only a sign of greater reverence and shows how seriously he is taking the vows—an argument to which Augustine replies by reminding him of the precariousness of human life. To meditate on the possibility of sudden death is not morbid—no 'vana atque damnabilis curiositas'. With a happy quotation from *Aeneid* ix. 13 (which needs adding to the apparatus and index of the edition), Augustine exhorts Firmus 'Rumpe moras omnes et munita arripe castra'.[4] Firmus's second argument appeals to Augustine's characteristic doctrine that the will is God's gift. Firmus is awaiting the gift. This touches Augustine at an embarrassing spot, and leads him into a lengthy exposition of a doctrine of grace which still leaves responsibility intact. The theme evokes extended treatment of the Fall and a justification of the ways of God in having allowed such a catastrophe to occur. The Church sings of both the mercy and the judgement of God in the Jubilate. All that is just is good. If it is just to punish sins, it is also good. Because of the damnation of Adam's posterity, our life is full of hard and

3. Augustine's conciliar assumptions about papal authority clearly emerge from the documents of the Pelagian crisis and from *Ep.* 22* (below, p. 180) where the Pope normally upholds conciliar canons but retains discretion where rigorous enforcement would produce scandal or riot.

4. For *munita* manuscripts of Virgil read *turbata*.

bitter misery 'quam ferre omnes volunt nec omnes sciunt'.[5] Human goodness contributes nothing to God but our evil acts provide occasions for him to turn all to good ends. Above all, let not Firmus idly wait for God to grant the will when he has given precepts to be obeyed. 'Be confident you could not obey unless it were God who gave you the will. The *caritas* by which you will is of God; the *concupiscentia* by which you are held back is not of God.'

The letter concludes by a short reply to a second letter received from Firmus concerning a clever 'Greek' whom he commends to Augustine. He is admirable for his good liberal education, skill in rhetoric, and training by teachers in both Greek and Latin. Augustine approves, but hopes the young man may give himself not merely to clever eloquence, which Cicero declares useless without wisdom (*Inv.* l. 1; cf. *Doctr.* iv. 5, 7), but also to a good moral life.

Ep. 3*, undated, is to Felix a deacon about a widow who vowed the perpetual virginity of her daughter when she was sick. Now she has recovered, she wishes her daughter to be released from obligation and asks if, as a substitute, she may please vow her own widowhood. Augustine urges (as *En. Ps.* 75.16 or *S.* 148.2) that if possible the promise should be kept: the mother's duty is to encourage her daughter to become a nun. If she fails to keep her mother's vow, she will not lose the kingdom of heaven, but will forfeit greater reward therein. Finally, Augustine asks if the child of the lately deceased Innocentia received baptism before the mother's death.

Ep. 4* is to Cyril of Alexandria, written perhaps about 417, after he had sent a copy of the Acts of the synod of Diospolis which Augustine had tried without success to extract from John of Jerusalem (*Ep.* 179.7). Augustine tells Cyril he has written an account of the synod in *De gestis Pelagii.* Cyril's messenger Justus has returned to Hippo to check a passage in *De gestis Pelagii* which he (Justus) is accused of having falsified, since in iii. 9 Augustine spoke of 'some' sinners, not all, going to hell. A group of Latin-speaking Pelagians in the East, whom Augustine regards as tricksters exploiting Greek ignorance, have made the text a ground of complaint against Justus. Augustine defends Justus as the victim of slander at the hands of these Latins 'de occidentali ecclesia' (a significant phrase, like 'orientalis ecclesia' in *S.* 202. 2, revelatory of the way in which Augustine

---

5. This has the ring of a quotation. The sense and language are akin to the excerpts from Cicero's *Hortensius* in *De Trinitate* xiii. 7. 10, and I suspect that the *Hortensius* is the source at least of the idea and probably of the language. *Hortensius* is also cited in *De Civ. Dei* xxii. 22 in a similar context.

has come to think of the world-church) who have migrated to the East 'ut inter Graecos impune latitent'.

The text of this important letter is evidently linked with the letter in *Avellana* 49 (*C.S.E.L.* xxxv. 113) disclosing Cyril's hesitations on the proper course with Pelagian refugees arriving at Alexandria and of the anger at Rome when Cyril received them to communion even after they had been excommunicated by Innocent of blessed memory. Julian of Eclanum (in Augustine, *Op. impf.* iv. 88) refers to a letter which Augustine had written to Alexandria, declaring that Jerome had crushed Pelagius with the authority of the Scriptures.

Ep. 5* to Bishop Valentinianus (see not given) is undatable and answers two questions: Why do the baptized, whose sins have been forgiven once for all, pray 'Dimitte nobis debita nostra'? The theme is recurrent so often elsewhere in Augustine's writings that he simply gives his usual answer. The Council of Carthage of 418 attacks those who say that the 'saints' pray the petition for forgiveness in the paternoster not for themselves but either in humility or as an act of intercession for others.[6] The exegetical question was therefore a hot current debate. Secondly, in Bishop Valentinian's codex of Gen. vi. 3, the Latin version read: 'Non permanebit spiritus meus in istis hominibus in saeculo.' Augustine explains that 'in saeculo' for *eis aiona* is a mistranslation; he should read 'in aeternum'. Valentinian's variant is not among those recorded by Sabatier.

Ep. 6*, like *Ep.* 4* to Cyril of Alexandria, illustrates the way in which the Pelagian controversy was bringing Augustine into direct touch with the great sees of the Greek churches. Addressed to Atticus of Constantinople, it is dated by Divjak in 416–17, but is certainly later, probably of 420–21, as is already argued by M. F. Berrouard in *Revue des études augustiniennes* xxvii (1981), pp. 264–77. Augustine observes that although Atticus recently sent a reply to his 'brother' (presumably Aurelius of Carthage) to report suitable action to discourage a group of Pelagians at Constantinople, the bearer of the letter, the presbyter Innocentius, brought no reply for Augustine. Innocentius excused his master by saying that rumour had reported Augustine dead. Augustine was not serene. It seems that Atticus's letter to Aurelius

---

6. *Concilia Africae*, ed. Munier, p. 223. *De Nuptiis et Concupiscentiae* i. 33. 38 explains that in baptism there is forgiveness not only of the past but also proleptically of future sins; yet the Christian's daily cleansing is through the petition of the Pater. Cf. *c. Ep. Parm.* ii. 10. 20; *Sermo* 58. 5. 6 and many passages. The best discussion of Augustine's understanding of penitence and reconciliation is by A.-M. La Bonnardière in *Revue des etudes aug.* xiii–xiv (1967–68).

must have made some fairly sympathetic allusion to the complaints of the Pelagians that their adversary Augustine was adopting a Manichee estimate of sexuality. Augustine is moved to offer a rebuttal of the slander that he slights and scorns marriage as a necessary evil, and seeks to draw a distinction (cf. *De nupt. et concupisc.* ii. 12.25) between *concupiscentia nuptiarum* and *concupiscentia carnis* (p. 34.5ff.). Cf. G. I. Bonner, 'Libido and Concupiscentia in St. Augustine', *Studia Patristica*, vi = TU 81 (1962), pp. 303–14. Romans 7 is interpreted, as regularly by the mature Augustine, to describe Paul's experience as a Christian.

Ep. 7* discloses a tangled story of church finance. Augustine asks the deacon Faustinus, though about to leave for Gaul on the business of the presbyter Heraclius, to press Novatus bishop of Sitifis (Sétif in Algeria)[7] to investigate the tangle. Long previously, at the time 'when the domesticus Florentinus was still alive', money was set aside for the Church by count Boniface and entrusted to the tribune Bassus. He, however, meanwhile used it to satisfy two men, one being a banker, to whom he was in debt. Both gave him receipts. When one of the two wished to transfer the money to the Church, he asked Bassus for his receipt, but Bassus refused to surrender it and asked 80 solidi for his own needs. Meanwhile Bassus died and then the banker died, leaving Boniface's money in the hands of heirs. Bassus's widow accordingly came to Hippo to take control of the money, the larger sum from the banker's heirs; and for the solidi she gave her receipt. She declared her readiness to pay these solidi to the Church and to hand over the receipt of the man who had the other portion of the money, provided that her husband's IOU, originally given to the count, was returned to her or, if this could not now be found, legally cancelled. Leave for the cancellation was given before the count Sebastian, on condition that she handed the money over to the Church. In fact, she was unwilling to pay it over to the Church, but deposited the funds with a *sequester,* or trustee to hold the disputed money in escrow, and asked for a stay of execution until 1 July. She then travelled from Hippo to Sitifis, perhaps intending to go on to Tipasa, and a few days thereafter the tribune Felicianus instructed the depositary trustee not to pay the solidi to the Church. Augustine therefore asks Faustinus to move Novatus of Sitifis to mount an inquiry 'lest we seem to oppress the widow'. If she is not at Sitifis,

---

7. The biography of Novatus of Sitifis is best set out by S. Lancel, *Actes de la conférence de Carthage en 411* = Sources Chrétiennes 194, i, pp. 194–95. He was bishop from 403 and died on 23 August 440 (*C.I.L.* viii. 8634 = Diehl, *I.L.C.V.* 1101), exiled by Geiseric. Florentinus: Aug. *Epp.* 114–15.

Novatus may put the issue before the tribune Felicianus, on whose report the count Sebastian will decide where justice lies.

Ep. 8* to Bishop Victor (see unnamed) concerns another case of church property. A Jew named Licinius is reclaiming family land which his mother sold to Bishop Victor. Augustine advises the return of the land to Licinius and the recovery of the money from the mother.

Ep. 9* to Alypius of Thagaste, probably written at the time (*c.* 422–23) when Alypius was in Italy, replies to a commonitorium he has received on 26 August and to which an answer is immediately sent off on 27 August. The reply deals with a Thagaste layman (name not given) who, for fornication with a nun (*professa sanctimonialis*), suffered a drastic flogging from the irate clergy. In anger at the humiliation the delinquent has appealed to Pope Celestine (Pope 422–32), and has also been to see Augustine himself. Augustine's letter reflects on the insoluble problems attaching to ecclesiastical discipline for which little or no respect is felt by either those who are not Christians and Catholics or those who so live that they are almost not so (cf. *Ep.* 22* below). In the episcopal court one cannot order a flogging of people who hold positions of honour in the world. (*Ep.* 133, 2 to Marcellinus mentions that flogging is a frequent penalty for delinquents brought before the episcopal court.) The offender has protested that he holds a civil rank (*honorem vel curiae vel fori*), and should therefore not have been subjected to the indignity of corporal punishment. Augustine has evidently seen a copy of his libellus to Celestine, since he remarks that the appeal is culpably silent about the fault for which he was beaten. The laws of the state forbid anyone to gain an imperial rescript in his favour without total disclosure of the facts (similarly *Tr. in Joh.* vii. 11): what then of a man who fails to disclose all to so holy a see? His sole legitimate ground for complaint would have been that his flogging by the clergy exceeded the bounds of Christian moderation.

Ep. 10* is again to Alypius in Italy. Alypius has sent Augustine books by Julian of Eclanum and Celestius by the hand of the deacon Commilito. Augustine expresses surprise that Alypius's letter says nothing of the recantation of Pelagianism by Turbantius, to whom Julian dedicated four books (cf. Clavis 774). A reliable informant had told Augustine that Turbantius condemned the heresy with a humble confession and was received 'in pacem catholicam' by papa Coelestinus. Perhaps Alypius simply forgot. Since the matter had received mention in an earlier letter from Augustine to Alypius, Augustine tactfully suggests that this earlier letter cannot as yet have reached Alypius and may arrive after the present one. Among his papers at Hippo Augustine has found a copy of Alypius's commonitorium written when he was sent to the imperial court from the council, and from reading this Augustine has noticed how many necessary things Alypius has not yet been able to achieve. Alypius's commonitorium is again mentioned in *Ep.* 23A* and is cited in *Ep.* 15*. From these references the following story can be conjecturally reconstructed.

At Carthage, for reasons unspecified, there had been a considerable disturbance of public order, probably an anti-imperial riot, after which a considerable number had sought asylum in the churches of the city. A council of bishops had decided to commission Alypius (perhaps in view of his considerable legal experience early in life) to go to the court at Ravenna and to Rome, and intercede on behalf of the delinquents. In a memorandum to his church at Thagaste sent by the hand of Severianus Longus, who passed through the harbour at Hippo, Alypius reported that he had enjoyed considerable success in his mission. Augustine clearly did not think his achievements so notable. However, the emperor and the court decided to send a high official, *maior comes* (*Ep.* 23A*) or *sublimis vir* (*Ep.* 15*), who was seconded from duties in Gaul to carry out a judicial inquiry—a fact from which it is reasonable to deduce that perhaps even some of the higher officials at Carthage were compromised. North Africa was agog with rumours. It was said that the sublime officer of state was known to have left Gaul and could be expected by the Ides of October, a possibility that might enable Alypius to be home at Thagaste by winter. Alypius also reported that a silentiary had left to travel to Carthage with an indulgence for the people, addressed to the proconsul Largus (*P.L.R.E.* ii. 657). Alypius's special mandate from the council is to intercede for those who are still claiming asylum in the churches. In *Ep.* 23A* Augustine reports that Josia, presbyter of Rusicade, met the legation from Carthage on the day he left (where? the court?), and learnt that the patrician was now getting near his destination. The outcome is not recorded, but the Carthaginian affair certainly caused Augustine considerable anxiety: 'de quorum facto solliciti maxime fueramus' (*Ep.* 23A* 1, p. 121, 12).

Ep. 10* concludes by telling Alypius of another problem, evidently in the hope that during his stay in Italy he may be able to get influential people to do something about it. Africa was being ravaged by slave-traders who, through the harbour at Hippo, were shipping off Roman provincials across the seas. Some of these slaves had been sold by their parents, not for a fixed term of twenty-five years as allowed by Roman law,[8] but absolutely. At Hippo

---

8. To the best of my knowledge, the figure of twenty-five years is not found elsewhere. *C. Theod.* iii. 3.1 [March 391] presupposes that, if free parents sold their children as slaves,

one colonus of the church, whose work on the estate was perfectly satisfactory, sold his wife saying he would prefer the money. But most of the slaves had been simply kidnapped. Report had it that in one village the men were all killed and the women and children carried off; the rumour was unconfirmed, but Augustine's inquiries did discover that one young girl, redeemed at Hippo by using the church chest, had been snatched in a night raid which the villagers thought an attack by barbarians. One woman of Hippo was found to have been operating a lucrative traffic in girls from Giddaba, the wooded hill-country south-west of Constantine, today Chettabah. Augustine also mentions these highlands in *Sermo* 45.7 and *in Ep. Joh. ad Parthos* 1.13. A young man of about twenty years working as a financial clerk, *calculator notarius,* was actually seduced from the Hippo monastery and sold. About four months previously Galatian slave-traders (such as we also hear of in Ammianus xxii. 7. 8 and Claudian, *In Eutropium* i. 59–60) gathered at Hippo a consignment of slaves for transportation overseas. A layman who knew about Augustine's habit of trying to use church funds to liberate such captives reported the matter to the church at a time when Augustine was absent, and he returned to find that his congregation had taken direct action. They recovered the captives partly from the ship, partly from the place where they were hidden, and it emerged that only five or six had been sold by their destitute parents. The rest were kidnapped children of free citizens. Worst of all, the rich profits of the trade meant that powerful patrons in Africa had an interest in the continuance of the traffic.

Augustine discovered from a legal friend (probably Eustochius of *Ep.* 24*) that a too little advertised constitution of the emperor Honorius (not in the *Theodosian Code*) addressed to the prefect Hadrian imposed fierce penalties on slave-traders who kidnapped free people and sold them into slavery. Augustine is therefore wishing to plead 'pro Romana libertate'. One of Augustine's sermons mentions surprised distaste at seeing slave-traders in his congregation on one occasion (*En. Ps.* 127. 11). The sermons contain other references to barbarian raids for the acquisition of slaves and to the use of church money to redeem them (*S.* 134.3; 344.11). The presupposition of the letter is that in North Africa there is a large population of poor but free

---

it could be only for a limited period of time, after which the progeny recovered their indefectible liberty. Gothofredus's commentary in his edition conjectured a limit of five years. Novel 33 of Valentinian III discloses that, because of famine in Italy, free parents have been selling children into slavery, and penalizes those who sell to the barbarians. For a convenient short summary of the texts see W. W. Buckland, *The Roman Law of Slavery* (Cambridge, 1908, repr. 1970), pp. 420–22.

labourers, vulnerable to being made captive and sold into slavery in overseas markets. Only a small minority of the labour force in Africa consists of slaves; for the cost to the master of slave labour exceeds that of employing free labour, as Adam Smith would observe many centuries later (*Wealth of Nations*, I. viii. 41). Augustine himself expressly informs us of a fact which one could have guessed, namely that the economic condition and standard of living enjoyed by many slaves much surpassed that of free labourers (*S.* 159.5).

Closely related to Augustine's letter to Alypius is the letter 24* to Eustochius, a lawyer who at one time in the past had lived at Hippo and was friendly with Augustine. Augustine consults him because in the episcopal court he finds cases being brought before him which are not mere matters of arbitration and judgment; they require knowledge of the secular law. What, he asks, is the legal position when parents sell their children for a term of years? He knows that the child of a freeman and a slave-girl is a slave. But are children sold by their parents for a fixed period required to serve out the full term if their parental vendors die? Does the parents' death set them free? And can a free father sell his children into perpetual slavery? If a colonus sells his son, has the buyer rights in law which take precedence over those of the landowner on the estate where the colonus is attached? Eustochius's reply would have been even more interesting than the questions.

Ep. 11* is a commonitorium to Augustine from Consentius, to whom he addressed *Ep.* 120 endeavouring to correct some idiosyncratic and highly autodidact notions about the doctrine of the Trinity, and also the *Contra Mendacium* in which he deplores Consentius's opinion that one is not obliged to deal honestly and truthfully with heretics.[9] Consentius's memorandum to Augustine is of 420, twenty years after the extant acts of the Council of Toledo (400), and it fills a large gap in our information about the position of the Spanish churches and of the Priscillianist movement, at a time when the Germanic raiders are already making it impossible for the Roman imperial government to exercise effective control. Although Spain is the prime theatre for Priscillianist activity, the new letter shows that its old hold in southern Gaul is as tenacious as ever. The movement continues to be an object of grave anxiety to Bishop Patroclus of Arles, whose role appears as both suppressing Priscillianism in Gaul and stiffening the resolve of the Spanish episcopate to do the same. But his attempt to organize a council of Spanish bishops, at which pressure can be put on the numerous bishops sympathizing with the Priscillianist cause, comes to nothing because he

---

9. Chadwick, *Priscillian of Avila* (Oxford, 1976), pp. 11, 154f.

lacks authority to enforce their attendance. The main motive of Consentius's memorandum emerges at the end: among the Catholics in Spain there are 'friends' of the Priscillianists who urge that, on condition of condemning the heresy, ex-Priscillianist bishops should be allowed to continue in office, and who justify this by appealing to Augustine's policy of advocating the recognition of Donatist orders and the admission of Donatist bishops as possessing valid orders on their reconciliation to the Catholic Church. The main body of Consentius's letter is therefore designed to justify Consentius's opposing and critical standpoint by painting a lurid picture of what has been going on. Consentius achieves this by transcribing a report he has received from Fronto, 'a servant of Christ', i.e. an ascetic, whom he encouraged to visit Spain and to use 'the most innocent cunning' in unmasking the heresy. Consentius also says that he has already composed a work against the Priscillianists at the suggestion of Patroclus of Arles, who supplied a commendatory foreword. The third book was written 'ex persona haeretici'; that is, Consentius has pretended to be offering a Priscillianist's reply to his first two books. In that reply no doubt highly damaging admissions were made by Consentius's man of straw. (Is much of Fronto's story fiction too?)

Fronto agreed to undertake his dangerous and disingenuous mission. He proceeded to Tarraco where he built a *monasterium* (perhaps a hermit's cell rather than a house containing several brothers in a common life?). Using the crafty techniques recommended by Consentius, he won the confidence of a lady named Severa. Through her he obtained names of the heretics, prominent among whom was a presbyter of Huesca named Severus—rich, well educated, and alarmingly well connected. Severus turned out to be father-in-law to the count Asterius, whose responsibilities included battle against the barbarian invaders.

The presbyter Severus of Huesca had inherited three Priscillianist codices from his lately deceased mother. On his way to the castellum where she used to live, he met with a raiding party of barbarians, who seized his baggage and eventually sold the codices to Bishop Sagittius of Ilerda (Lérida). Sagittius read the texts and found them congenial, for he was touched by the Priscillianist movement. But he realized that there was dangerous matter in them, and cut out some sorcerer's spells; the expurgated remainder, as if the worst of all, he sent on to the metropolitan Titianus of Tarraco. The other two codices he thought sufficiently innocuous to be deposited in the church library at Ilerda. Titianus of Tarraco passed the expurgated codex on to Severus's bishop at Huesca, Syagrius, whom Fronto calls catholic, but too credulous and kind.

Meanwhile, Fronto persuaded the naïve lady Severa to reveal all. He then laid a formal charge against both her and the presbyter Severus. Severa, however, took refuge with Asterius's daughter, *potentissima femina*—the daughter of the presbyter Severus—and disavowed all her indiscreet disclosures. Fronto became unpopular. The people of Tarraco became excited against him, and he had to defend himself with the claim that the codices would prove Severus's heretical sympathies. So Titianus made arrangements to have the codices examined.

At Tarraco a council of bishops was assembled to hear the case in the secretarium of the church, where Fronto had sought asylum from the angry populace. There at an early hour the count Asterius also came. He was surprisingly sympathetic to Fronto. He even asked Fronto's prayers for his victory in the coming battle with the barbarians. However, Fronto received rough treatment from a bishop named Agapius (see unspecified) who had earlier had some contact with Fronto by conveying to him from Consentius a sealed package and letter advising him how to discover the Priscillianists. A slave serving as major domo at the household of Asterius's daughter also adopted unpleasantly hostile attitudes to Fronto; but soon afterwards he died in consequence of overeating at a feast, and thereafter Fronto began to be treated with respect by the crowd. By Asterius's household he was accused of homicide, presumably through sorcery or poisoning.

After further encounters of a painful kind with Bishops Agapius, Sagittius, and even Syagrius who had begun to discern the threat to his own position in the attack upon his old presbyter Severus, Fronto succeeded in escaping and in making his way to Patroclus of Arles. Patroclus invited the Spanish bishops to meet with him in council at Biterrae (Béziers), but he had no power to compel and the council never met. Accordingly Fronto journeyed on to Consentius's island, after a hazardous time, and submitted the report which Consentius now thinks it well to send to Augustine.

This summary has much abbreviated and simplified a long and complex story. It will be evident that the new letter gives rich evidence for the pervasive and tenacious continuance of Priscillianist ideas in the Spanish and Gallic churches, and of the far-reaching extent to which many of the Spanish bishops, even outside Galicia where Priscillianism had its citadel, were touched by the movement. It is instructive that, to lend a plausible face to endeavours to make easy contact with secret Priscillianists, at Tarraco Fronto had to act as a monk. The anti-Priscillianists of Spain still regarded the movement as associated with asceticism, as also with a liking for the occult (witness the allegations of magic spells cut out of the codex by

Bishop Sagittius). Moreover, Priscillianism seems to have retained its firm hold upon well-connected ladies. But by 420 it is a wholly underground and esoteric faith, the unmasking of which requires a man to pretend to be a sympathizer.

Ep. 12* is also from Consentius to Augustine. It is a faintly ostentatious piece, apparently written with the motive 'se faire valoir', with quotations from Cicero, Horace, Ovid, and Terence, lest Augustine should suppose that in the Balearic Islands, where Consentius avows that there are very few educated people, there is no culture whatever. On the other hand, several turns of phrase in the letter almost go out of the way to disparage advanced theological speculations. Consentius perhaps thought Augustine needed to be taught a lesson. An awful warning he sees in Origen, a man of learning, yet an evader of martydom and the victim of vain curiosity.[10] Though not censured in his lifetime, he was without question condemned 200 or more years later. And how, wonders Consentius discourteously, will posterity judge Augustine? Twelve years previously he had himself obtained a copy of the *Confessions;* but he had read only a few pages of the work. Once he had put it down, he could not bring himself to pick it up again. Consentius is a Bible Christian whose determination is to reduce the compass of theology to a manageable size by restricting it to the study of the canonical scriptures. Outside them Lactantius alone has given him pleasure by his plain style; but once read he too was discarded with the other non-biblical writers.

In the Balearic Islands Consentius is self-consciously a man who has had to work on his own. Not only educated people other than himself are rare; there are very few Christians. Nevertheless he has already written two books, feeling it 'more profitable to write than to read'. The quest for leisure had brought him to the Islands. But he has been touched to receive a letter from Augustine, apparently instigated by two deacons, Maximianus and Caprarius, who are avowed admirers of Augustine's writings. So it is a source of self-congratulation to Consentius that in Augustine he feels he has a 'convalis' (p. 75.12; p. 77.22). In addition, Consentius reports that lately there has been sharp local tension between the bishop Severus and the Jewish community. The new letter therefore adds a touch of amplification to what we already know from the famous, hair-raising letter in which Bishop Severus of Minorca describes the riots between Jews and Christians at Mago on the eastern side of the island when relics of St. Stephen arrived there in

---

10. See now N. Brox, 'Consentius über Origenes', *Vigiliae Christianae,* xxxvi (1982), pp. 141–44.

417 or 418.[11] Consentius had been moved to compose twelve *capitula adversus Judaeos* and also a letter to Patroclus of Arles. He has even ventured to enlarge his *œuvre* by sketching out some criticisms of the *quaestiones Pelagii*. In the previous year he had received a letter from Pope Zosimus of blessed memory against Pelagius and Calestius. Having read this, even though much encumbered with worldly responsibilities, Consentius felt impelled by his customary passion for composition to work away at what has nearly become a fourth book. However, he has not felt sufficiently confident of its content to bring it all to completion and publication.

The letter is a bizarre revelation of its author's character, longing to be admired by the famous Augustine but at the same time discharging his olive-branch with a catapult; courageously tackling grand theological problems of the day but hardly possessing the finesse and the broad sense of the coherence of Christian theology which marks Augustine's enterprises. The *contra Mendacium* can only have been painful reading to him.

Epp. 13* and 18* both deal with alleged moral lapses in clergymen. The substance of the story told in the two letters is strikingly parallel, yet the policies which Augustine proposes in the two letters are wholly and diametrically opposed. I venture to submit that we should apply Ockham's razor and understand both letters as dealing, at different stages of development, with the same priest. *Ep.* 18* is addressed to the church of 'Membliba'. I do not know that such a place is attested, but the form is good African, e.g. Membressa and the smaller town Memblona, near Utica in Proconsularis, where Theasius was Catholic bishop in 411—he suffered a Donatist mugging later. Membliba may be miswritten for Memblona, but it is perhaps a little unlikely that a church so much nearer to Carthage than to Hippo should look to Augustine to sort out its problems. It seems best to accept Membliba, and to assume this is the name of some rural village in Numidia consularis. Augustine's letter tells the church that they ought not to be considering the promotion to the presbyterate of a deacon Gitta, who served the church at Unapompei (is this a corruption of Uzippara in Proconsularis?) and had there been degraded after a woman claimed that he had slept with her. Gitta admitted to having embraced and kissed her, but denied more. The woman's view apparently prevailed. Augustine felt that even the admission to a hug and a kiss was too damaging to allow of the promotion. His letter is sent by the hand of the presbyter Restitutus, who was plunged into deep sadness

---

11. *PL* xx. 731–46 or xli. 821–34, discussed by E. D. Hunt, 'St. Stephen in Minorca', *J.T.S.* n.s. xxxiii (1982), pp. 106–23.

by the affair. From *Ep.* 18* it is not clear whether his sadness was caused by Gitta's imprudent compassion or by Augustine's hard line in a doubtful case on contested evidence of a probably not very culpable act done on a passing impulse. There was no question of charging Gitta with making a habit of it.

Ep. 13* is a commonitorium addressed to the presbyter Restitutus, and concerns a man who has been promoted to be presbyter. By whom he received ordination to the priesthood is not stated. At the time when he was. still a deacon, however, he was guest at a house and slept in the solarium, where he was tempted by a woman. Rain providentially intervened and he fled. Moreover, according to the account which he had submitted to Augustine, the woman had at first made no amorous proposition to him, but had unbosomed no more than her troubles and necessities, which had led the deacon to offer a consoling hug. The woman claimed that things had gone much further than that. The hurried flight suggested that more than consolation was threatened. Now Augustine declares that he accepts the man's story, not the woman's. The congregation at his church appears to be divided, but if it is willing to accept the man as presbyter, Augustine has no objection. And if there are censorious persons who take exception to him, then let Restitutus show them Augustine's commonitorium. It leaps to the eye that in both letters the decision rests on the depth of the physical relationship. On the hypothesis that we are dealing with the same Restitutus in both letters, then it is likely that Restitutus's sadness in *Ep.* 18* is distress at Augustine's initial rigorism; that is, Restitutus came to represent the majority in the congregation who knew that they needed another presbyter, liked Gitta, and wanted to persuade Augustine to give the man both the benefit of the doubt and moral support. In that case, *Ep.* 18* is the earlier of the two letters, and *Ep.* 13* is in effect declaring a change of mind. Augustine frankly confesses in *Ep.* 22* how hard it is to find suitable and willing clergy in the towns, and the difficulty may have increased his feeling that it would be right to relax the hard line with which he had started. The Catholics were experiencing a crisis of vocations, the *indigentia clericorum* lamented by Aurelius of Carthage at the council of 16 June 401.[12]

Ep. 16* sends Aurelius of Carthage a couple of sermons for Christmas and Epiphany. From *Ep.* 23A* it emerges that Augustine was in the habit of supplying a hungry primate with sermons; he there says he is glad to send them as long as Aurelius does not delay publication. It therefore looks as if

---

12. *Concilia Africae,* ed. Munier, p. 194, l. 421. R. Crespin, *Ministère et Sainteté* (1965), pp. 55–60, has suggested that this is connected with the generous line towards Donatist orders.

there was a market for Augustine's sermons at Carthage. Augustine adds in *Ep.* 16* that he knows about Alypius's commonitorium sent to Thagaste (above) because the silentiary carrying the indulgence for the Carthaginians passed through Hippo. Moreover, since Alypius's memorandum was sent by a ship landed at Hippo he knows that a silentiary with an indulgence has already been sent, and that Alypius claimed to have won this concession by submitting a letter. Furthermore, at Hippo there are some even better informed persons (CA offer *inrecentiores;* Divjak emends to *indecentiores,* i.e. impertinent gossips; I suggest *in re certiores*) who have reported to Augustine that, through a Numidian bishop named Renatus,[13] Alypius also sent a copy of the 'beneficium' which they claimed had been granted to the proconsul Largus. But 'whether this is the document sent by the silentiary mentioned in the commonitorium to Thagaste or some order made by him concerning those who have fled for asylum to the church, I do not know unless (as I suppose) the aforesaid bishop could have arrived at Carthage'. Meanwhile, the primate of the province of Mauretania Caesariensis, Priscianus, reports new action by papa Bonifatius against the Pelagians. Augustine concludes by asking Aurelius, please to see that his *tractatoria* is sent to Valentinus primate of Numidia, so that through him it may also reach 'our part of Numidia, that is Consularis'.[14]

Ep. 17* briefly encourages the count Boniface with the thought that even in his operations on the battlefield he is seeking eternal peace.

Ep. 19* is a major addition to the archive on the consequences of Pelagius's acquittal at the Council of Diospolis. It is addressed to Jerome and shows what a frenzy of correspondence in 416 the Diospolis decision generated. It is evidently written soon after Jerome's 'Dialogue against the Pelagians', which Augustine knows to have reached the imperial court. In high aristocratic circles and at the court Pelagius has had young friends and admirers. But support for his cause has begun to wane since it became clear that Pelagius was defending himself rather than the propositions associated with him by denying that he held them. Augustine reports the receipt of a

---

13. An inscription of this period records a Renatus, bishop of Tipasa: *Année epigr.* 1929, no. 91; J.-L. Maier, *L'episcopat de l'Afrique romaine, vandale et byzantine* (Rome: Swiss Institute, 1973), p. 398. This is clearly another Renatus.

14. I do not know that Renatus and Priscianus are otherwise attested (assuming the latter is not the Mauretanian bishop Priscus debarred from the primacy according to Aug., *Ep.* 209.8, by decision of the apostolic see). But Valentine is otherwise known at the council of Mileu of 402; at Ravenna in 406 (Aug., *Ep.* 88.10); and see the index to Munier's *Concilia Africae.*

letter from Jerome brought by the deacon Palatinus (lost), and the prior receipt of a letter by the presbyter Orosius, which will be identical with *Ep.* 172; also one through the presbyter Innocent (*Ep.* 202.1) 'by whom I sent reply not only to you but also to other letters which he brought from some who wished for copies of my letters'. Augustine also reports receiving a short defence written by Pelagius against the accusations of the Gallic bishops, Hero and Lazarus (cf. *gest. Pel.* 2). He is giving the bearer Lucas (cf. *Ep.* 179.1) recommended by Palatinus a copy of Pelagius's work, *De natura,* which came into his hands from Timasius and Jacobus (*Ep.* 179). He is attaching a copy of his own *De natura et gratia,* by the reading of which Timasius and Jacobus were converted from following Pelagius. He is also writing about Pelagius to Eulogius of Caesarea and John of Jerusalem (*Ep.* 179) and briefly to Bishop Passerion (cf. Orosius, *lib. apol.* 6–7).

Ep. 20* to Fabiola is an even longer document than Consentius's letter about the Priscillianists, and runs to twenty-five pages of Latin. It enormously increases our knowledge of the traumatic affair of Antoninus of Fussala, the Punic-speaking ex-Donatist congregation at a castellum forty miles from Hippo[15] and in Augustine's diocese, where he decided to create a bishopric and the man of his choice proved a disaster. The essentials of the story are in *Ep.* 209 to Pope Celestine of the year 422, but the account to Fabiola is much fuller and throws new light on the canonical procedure in appeals. Antoninus was the son of a poor mother whose husband was still alive, but she was living with another man. On condition of her leaving the second man Augustine supported her and the boy from church funds, the mother on the *matricula pauperum,* the boy in the monastery at Hippo, where he was educated and grew to be a Reader. He was a promising young man, and at a time when Augustine was absent the provost of the monastery Urbanus (to become bishop of Sicca) proposed his name to be presbyter on a large estate near Hippo, but the neighbouring bishop refused to ordain. Urbanus's confidence, however, led Augustine to overestimate

---

15. The conjecture that the anti-Donatist sermon of about 411–12 on the duties of a bishop, preached at the consecration and installation of a new man, *S. Guelf.* xxxii, p. 563 Morin, may have been preached at Fussala has received support from Peter Brown, *Augustine of Hippo* (1967), p. 412. I am not persuaded. The warnings that a criminous clerk can be no true bishop and that none may hide behind a bad bishop's example to excuse theft, suggests to me a Catholic congregation tempted by Donatism because a previous bishop had been delinquent, especially with the church chest. That would exclude Fussala, Antoninus being its first bishop. A fine sort of sermon for his successor; or after a catastrophic incumbency like that of Paul of Cataquas (*Epp.* 85 and 96).

his capacities. After the conference of 411 and the subsequent edict, the influx of ex-Donatists to the Catholic Church 'not only in the towns but even in the countryside' so increased Augustine's work-load that he decided to appoint a bishop at Fussala. Under coercion the plebs had lately switched allegiance from Donatism to Catholicism. Moreover, there were Catholic congregations at nearby estates served by country presbyters. The primate of Numidia consularis (Silvanus of Summa, *Gesta coll.* i. 57, if the date is 411–12) agreed to make the long journey to Hippo for the consecration. But at the last moment the presbyter designated for the appointment fled. Augustine could not bear to send the old primate away with a fruitless journey; what a laugh the enemies of the Church would enjoy too! So he asked the primate to consecrate the youthful reader Antoninus who spoke Punic.

The first indication of an amber light came when Antoninus recruited as his presbyter a monk and notarius from the Hippo monastery, who had a poor track record: he had once been beaten for being found talking with nuns at an unfitting hour. A deacon was also supplied to him from the Hippo monastery, but had given no cause for alarm before arriving at Fussala. With his presbyter and deacon, an army deserter, the *defensor ecclesiae,* and the strong arm of the night watch, Antoninus determined to cow the resentful Fussalans into submission to his brief authority. When some of his people were harassed by the vicarius Celer, whose sympathies were Donatist (*Epp.* 56–57 and 139.2),[16] Antoninus seems to have felt he had cause for biting back. Soon the Fussalans were sending a stream of complaints to Augustine at Hippo. Unskilled at presenting their case, as one might expect of Punic peasants, they made the mistake of accusing him of four grave sexual crimes which he was easily able to prove to be false charges. But other charges Augustine came to believe very true: he oppressed the people, especially the poor and widows who had a right to look to their bishop for protection. They lost money, furniture, clothing, beasts, fruit, timber, and even the stones of their houses which were taken and sold to developers brought in to build new houses. With church money Antoninus bought a villa in his own name. Augustine had provided him, for the support of himself and his staff, with an estate belonging to the church of Hippo in the territory of Fussala. Antoninus leased it out, and by obtaining five years' rent in a lump sum, he found the cash for his villa. Not that it was a high price. On a charge of some kind the owner of the villa was being held in custody at Fussala; on Antoninus's orders, the *defensor ecclesiae* got the man's release from the cells on condition

---

16. *P.L.R.E.* ii, s.v. Celer 1. He rose to be proconsul of Africa in 429.

of selling his villa to Antoninus at a knock-down price. After the release the cheated seller appealed to the emperor, and at the subsequent inquiry the *defensor* was saved from condemnation only through the intercessions of Augustine on his behalf. Moreover, the proceedings in Antoninus's episcopal court seemed to those brought before it to be highly prejudiced. Despite the regular custom by which a bishop was supported by his clergy as assessors, his presbyter and deacon on whose support he had relied came in time to withdraw themselves from the *episcopalis audientia*. All who protested at their treatment were placed under excommunication.

The volume of complaint was so great that Augustine gathered a small council at Hippo to examine the charges. The sexual charges were disproved, and the council agreed that Antoninus had not behaved so badly that he should be stripped of office. He could remain a bishop, but on condition of making restitution to the Fussalans of what he had appropriated. Until he had repaid them, he should be excommunicate. Antoninus was quickly able to gain the cancellation of the ban by borrowing from moneylenders, and all seemed set for his return to Fussala. Meanwhile, however, the Fussalans were asking the primate for a new bishop, and declaring their total unwillingness to have Antoninus to reign over them. Antoninus persuaded the primate to refer the request to a council, to which the primate agreed. The council, however, entirely supported Augustine's earlier decisions, and Antoninus made no appeal. The primate went ahead with plans for a new consecration, but on the very morning of the day appointed Antoninus formally entered an appeal. Tough bargaining took place, ending in Antoninus's consent to the consecration of a bishop replacing him at Fussala on condition, however, that he was given eight neighbouring (evidently not ex-Donatist) congregations plus the rich plum of a neighbouring estate, Thogonoetum, owned by a *clarissima femina*. There he would establish his principal chair. The lady was deeply unenthusiastic at the prospect of having Antoninus to care for her and the coloni on her land. Moreover, the coloni were telling her that they would simply leave if he were to be their bishop. At an interview between the lady and Antoninus words of anger were exchanged. The allocation of the *beneficium* of her estate to his new diocese became a crucial point of contention.[17]

Antoninus decided to appeal to Pope Boniface in a letter which claimed that his troubles were caused by the hostility of the Donatist sympathizer Celer. He was able to send a copy of a softheaded letter he had received

17. Is not this the earliest use of *beneficium* in a sense closely anticipating our 'benefice'? (The scheme was to comply with canons against translation: p. 98.28.)

from the old primate at an early stage of his troubles, declaring him to have 'nullas omnino culpas' (p. 100.19). Boniface appointed judges to examine the case, and the bishops met at Tegulata in Numidia. (The little place was represented at the Conference of 411.) Alypius and Augustine both attended, but Augustine did not sit with the bishops, seeing that they were reviewing the justice of decisions he himself had made. To the episcopal court the Fussalans sent a presbyter with their complaints. Antoninus asked for a commission of inquiry to investigate on the spot at Fussala. So the primate, with his customary entourage of three bishops when on circuit (*Ep.* 20*. 16 includes this interesting and, I think, unparalleled scrap of information), went together with two of the bishops appointed to the episcopal court. At Fussala the six bishops listened to vehement protests from the natives, but individuals absolutely refused to allow their names to be recorded in the *gesta* for fear of the reprisals which Antoninus would take when he looked up the record. They also refused to appear if the manager of the estate (*conductor*) were there to take their names, a fact which suggests that Antoninus had some friends at Fussala. The primate addressed them in Punic (20*. 21). But when it appeared that he was trying to persuade them to accept Antoninus after all, there were loud protests; anger and fear led them all to leave, including even the nuns.[18]

Augustine himself had prudently been keeping out of Fussala, where the people 'deservedly' held him directly responsible for the calamity. But his concern both for Antoninus and for the Fussalans led him to come to Fussala to meet Antoninus, pleading with him to act as a bishop should. He should immediately lift the ban on those he had excommunicated, lest they should lapse into sad depression 'per tristitiam rusticanam' (p. 105.17). Some were beginning to apostatize (*apostatare*). Moreover, the impartial primate had come to put a distance between himself and Augustine, who was kept out of town together with Antoninus at a *castellum Giluense* (p. 107.13), where Augustine again besought him to mend his ways and to give solemn undertakings for the future, to be formally recorded in the *gesta*. 'Nihil ego gestis loquor' replied Antoninus, rightly scenting a trap, and declared that he would again put his appeal to the apostolic see. Augustine with all speed prepared a letter for Rome (clearly *Ep.* 209) and a copy of the episcopal acts.

18. The Donatists had their own *sanctimoniales* (*En. Ps.* 44.31; *c. Ep. Parm.* ii. 9.19); so these religious were probably converts with the Fussala community rather than Catholic sisters imported by Augustine to teach the ex-Donatists milder manners. The primate Aurelius (p. 101.18) is of Macomades, not Carthage.

Augustine saw that in Fabiola Antoninus had found a sympathetic feminine ear, and warned her to tread cautiously. No doubt she did so after receiving so passionate a reply. Augustine did not tell her, as he told the pope, that he would resign his see if Rome vindicated Antoninus and ordered his reinstatement at Fussala. It was surely no empty threat. The threat would have been unnecessary if Augustine's case against Antoninus had been cast iron. The letter to Fabiola shows that it was not: Antoninus had at least some supporters who thought he had a reasonable defence and who may well have thought Augustine too ready to listen to alienated and resentful rustics, to whom the bishop of Hippo seemed keen to make any concessions to win their hearts for Catholic unity. The letter to Fabiola, like several other letters in the new collection, illustrates how dependent Augustine and the African churches were on metropolitan Italy, on the great aristocratic ladies now adhering to Christianity and beginning to carry their menfolk with them, on the support and ultimate judgment of the apostolic see, and on good connections at court. That was where the real decisions were being made.

Ep. 21* replies to the landowning members of the church at Suppa. The Suppenses were to the south-east of Thagaste in the direction of Thagora, located by an inscription marking the boundary between Suppenses and Vofricenses published by L. Leschi, *Études d'épigraphie, d'archéologie et d'histoire africaines* (1957), pp. 111–12. They wanted a particular person to be made deacon despite the opposition of their bishop Honoratus (who appears in *Ep.* 26* as Honorius). Augustine tells them that it is improper for them to appeal to him over the head of their bishop, but that he will discuss the question with him. In *Ep.* 26* he does so.

Ep. 22* is addressed to Alypius and Peregrinus, both being on a mission in Italy on behalf of the African churches. Peregrinus is probably to be identified with the bishop of Curubis in Proconsularis. Augustine writes to tell them about a council of Numidian bishops 'apud Mazacos' (cf. Ammian xxix. 5). Apronianus Mazacensis appears among the Catholics present at Carthage in 411 (*Gesta coll.* i. 215.11–12 Lancel); and the same place-name appears in the Numidian list of the Carthaginian *Notitia* of the late fifth century (*C.S.E.L.* vii. 122.81). The Numidian synod met on 6 March and passed a resolution deploring the poverty of the clergy resulting from the laws about *munera*. They have sent Bishop Peter (see unnamed) to the court, and, as he passed through Hippo, he asked Augustine to write a letter to the two African bishops already at court. Accordingly Augustine has done so, 'that if it finds you in a position where you can help along the cause, then the Lord will have greatly supported their labour'. (At p. 113.15 read *quia si* for *qui si.*) The root of the trouble is that in pagan times many enjoyed immunity from these burdens. 'But now we are in such difficulties that especially in cities it is hard to find people to be ordained.' As things stand, the wicked are scornful of ecclesiastical discipline (cf. *Ep.* 9* above). If ecclesiastical sanctions are used against them, they complain to the civil authority that the bishop is obstructing public necessities. To those who flee to the Church for refuge, Augustine finds that he is of little help because he and his people lack a *defensor.*[19]

The same letter 22 also deals with a second matter, namely the succession to Deuterius at Mauretanian Caesarea (Cherchel). For many years the Catholic Deuterius and the Donatist Emeritus had been rivals in the town, while being blood-relations to each other. Augustine had lately had much to do with Caesarea. In the late summer of 418, together with Alypius of Thagaste and Possidius of Calama, he had gone to Caesarea to meet with the Mauretanian bishops at the request and commission of Pope Zosimus to sort out an awkward but unspecified problem in the province (*Ep.* 190.1, 193.1; Possidius, *Vita* 14.3). There is obvious plausibility in the widely held opinion that the disciplinary measures taken with Roman authority against three bishops of the province listed in *Ep.* 290.8 were taken at this synodical court of inquiry. While at Caesarea Augustine also engaged in the formal debate with the sullenly silent Donatist bishop Emeritus, recorded in the *Gesta cum Emerito*. He also met the monk Renatus agitated about creationism, traducianism, and the origin of the soul; a subject on which he addressed Renatus's correspondent, Bishop Optatus of Spain (*Ep.* 23A*.3) in *Ep.* 190. A dangerous game of stone-throwing he successfully discouraged (*Doctr.* iv. 23.53). In 419 Deuterius died, and there was hot contention (as the newly printed letter discloses) about the succession, which would be very intelligible if Emeritus were still active and in effect making a bid to be bishop of the compulsorily united church. The Catholic plebs said loud and clear that the man they wanted was Honorius, Catholic bishop of Cartenna. The bishops of the province assembled at Caesarea and were exposed to vigorous lay demands, *cum magno scandalo* since they had become very conscious of the prohibition against episcopal translations in the canons of Nicaea and other councils. They could do nothing to persuade the noisily demonstrating plebs to support another candidate of their choice. The turbulent crowd coerced the bishops into installing Honorius as a deputy bishop, on a provisional and

---

19. African conciliar records show that the appointment of a *defensor* had to be cleared with the emperor: pp. 202 and 215 Munier.

temporary basis, until the apostolic see and the bishop of Carthage had been consulted. From *Ep.* 23* it is clear that the bishops also nominated Augustine as an arbiter. The consensus of religious men was that a translation would be a dangerous precedent. It was felt that only the authority of Rome and Carthage could justify the transfer, and that these two bishops would never wish to go against conciliar canons. The Apiarius case had clearly made the Africans very conscious of this point.

The feeling among the bishops against the translation was so great that Honorius agreed to go to Augustine at Hippo, his people allowing him to leave Caesarea only on his swearing a solemn oath that he would return. He assured Augustine that he would wish to act entirely on Augustine's advice. It is clear that although this advice was persistently negative, Honorius deeply hoped to persuade Augustine to change his mind and to lend his moral authority to the proposed translation. Augustine expressly says that while he was satisfied with all that Honorius said, only deeds would prove the truth.

Nevertheless, Honorius's personal qualities were impressive. Despite the suspicions of his critics, Augustine saw no evidence of hunger for power, and Alypius was asked to mention this point to Pope Boniface before whom the matter would inevitably come for decision. But he was surely committed to Cartenna. *Defensores* of Honorius were busily, to Augustine embarrassingly, collecting instances and precedents to justify translation, and Augustine regretted the impression that the practice should be encouraged rather than suppressed. Honorius's friends did not have to look far in either space or time. At Cartenna itself very recently the see had been held by Honorius's father, who was invited to move to Caesarea. Before leaving he installed his son as bishop at Cartenna. Honorius's father is presumably none other than Deuterius. Perhaps he also divided the diocese of Cartenna, since Rusticus in 419–20 emerges as Catholic bishop of some congregations in the territory of Cartenna. Perhaps he had been put there, like Antoninus of Fussala, in a frontier outpost adjacent to strongly Donatist enclaves. Rusticus might reasonably hope that, if Honorius could be promoted to Caesarea, he might gain control over the *matrix* at Cartenna as well as his little group of village congregations.[20]

Judgment was made more difficult for Augustine because rival factions at Caesarea started circulating spurious letters. One letter in the name of

20. For 'Matrix' (p. 117.19) compare examples in *Concilia Africae,* p. 225, l. 1462; p. 226, l. 1509. Bishop Rusticus was at the public disputation between Augustine and Emeritus at Caesarea in 418 (*Gesta c. Emer.* 1). His position may perhaps be connected with the policy encouraged by the council of 1 May 418 in favour of splitting dioceses between Catholic and ex-Donatist bishops, no doubt to be reunited on the death of one of them.

Rusticus, taking it for granted that Honorius's translation was settled and that therefore he could now have the whole diocese, had to be disowned by Rusticus in a letter to Augustine. The anti-Honorius faction circulated a letter headed by the names of fifteen bishops, including the Mauretanian primate (Priscianus, *Ep.* 16*. 3), telling Honorius that they would not hold communion with him if he accepted the uncanonical translation. Augustine remarked that the document bore only one signature (unreadable), not fifteen, and his doubts were reinforced by Honorius's friends at Caesarea to whom it appeared a blatant forgery. A third letter written in the name of the people of Caesarea to the primate of Mauretania claimed that they wished to send Bishop Honorius to court *in causa publica,* and would the primate please provide a passport letter of recommendation (*formata*)?[21] Augustine doubted its genuineness. The primate provided no such letter. Moreover, Honorius did not wish to go to court *in causa publica sed in causa propria:* he wanted to recover legal costs from a certain Felix or an old man called Quietus who had submitted to Augustine a libellus of complaint against Honorius. Augustine assured Alypius and Peregrinus that he had been doing all in his power to settle the dispute he had been asked to arbitrate. But the information that the matter was being referred to him had precipitated shouts at Caesarea not, it seems (but the text is corrupt at the critical point), in favour of Honorius. Augustine's hope was to persuade Honorius himself to write telling the Caesareans to elect someone else.

Augustine had special reasons for being anxious to settle the dispute at home on African soil. Those who appealed to the emperor's court for judgment might get more than they bargained for and put their own position at risk. Augustine feared that the crowd demonstrating in favour of Honorius at Caesarea, though Catholic in sympathy, might be roughly handled by the government as if they were Donatist schismatics. But he conceded that only the apostolic see really possessed the standing to put an end to the matter. The fear which Augustine expresses may provoke one to speculate that among Honorius's supporters some were ex-Donatists who thought they would get a better deal from him than from some rigorist installed by the bishops to impose discipline.

Ep. 23* is addressed to Renatus, the monk of Caesarea, and begins as a covering letter for the first book *De anima et eius origine* written to answer

---

21. For the need of an *epistola formata* from the primate if a bishop was going to Rome and the court, see *Concilia Africae,* p. 106, l. 235; p. 193, l. 385, from Carthage, 26 June 397; esp. p. 218, l. 1255, from Carthage, 13 June 407.

the ex-Donatist (Rogatist) Vincentius Victor of Caesarea who complained of Augustine's agnostic indecisiveness on the origin of the soul. As the text transmitted by the manuscripts later tells the recipient that he has suddenly received a letter from Renatus, Divjak is evidently correct in assuming that *Ep.* 23 must consist of the beginning of one letter and the last part of another, so that it should be divided into 23 and 23A. He gives only the first two paragraphs to the letter for Renatus, the remainder being addressed to some intimate friend other than Alypius and Aurelius of Carthage, who are both mentioned. The content of the second letter suggests to me that it was addressed to Possidius of Calama, but I should not wish to press the conjecture. Letter 23A reports that the only news he has had from Alypius (in Italy) is through his commonitorium to Thagaste. The correspondent is then given a list of all Augustine's writings between 11 September and 1 December, the latter being evidently the date of the letter. During this period Augustine has written almost 6,000 lines, and the tale of his writings is long: (1) a treatise to the Spanish bishop Optatus, i.e. *Ep.* 202A, which is thereby dated September 419 (a little earlier than the Maurists suggested), and whose recipient is now known to be in Spain, not Tingitana; (2) the second book in reply to Gaudentius of Timgad; (3) *contra Arrianos,* in reply to a piece sent by Dionysius of Vicus Iuliani, with three sermons destined for sending to Carthage; (4) the first book *De anima et eius origine* for Renatus in reply to Vincentius Victor—which prevented returning to the *City of God;* (5) an attempt to complete the series of homilies on St. John by writing short sermons to be sent to Carthage (perhaps *Tr. in Joh.* 55–60).

Augustine's correspondent has written to him in terms he approves about Donatianus (presumably the bishop of Thelepte, primate of Byzacena, mentioned in *Ep.* 196.1). 'May the Lord grant that your plan comes about.' 'I do not know what the brothers have added to the same question which they had not said already, to which I have a duty to reply. I would have inserted a reply in that work unless it had already been published by the Spanish bishops, our dearest brothers, and so I will have to put it into another work.' (The reference is unhappily unclarified; perhaps *De animae et eius origine* i, the subject of which was certainly getting lively discussion in Spain.)

Augustine is arranging for his correspondent to be sent a copy of the *gesta* in the acquittal of Maurentius, bishop of Thubursicu in Numidia, whose case came before the Council of Carthage on 13 June 407.[22]

---

22. Ibid., p. 217 Munier. Augustine was one of the panel of judges for whom Maurentius asked.

Meanwhile Pope Boniface has sent a reply to Augustine's report on the affair of Honorius at Caesarea, which he believes was also sent on to his correspondent; he proposes a joint letter to the church at Caesarea. The community there remains riven by factions, and the outcome is still indeterminate. A bishop Priscillian has arrived at Hippo coming from Rome via Carthage, where he first communicated on African soil (a phrase that suggests some past controversy about him? Perhaps a successful appellant to the apostolic see?). He intends to come on from Hippo to see Augustine's correspondent, but has decided to wait at Hippo until definite news comes from Caesarea that a new bishop has been ordained.

Ep. 24* to the lawyer Eustochius consults him about the law on children sold into slavery by their parents, and is discussed above. *Ep.* 25* to the presbyters (of Carthage) Deogratias and Theodore with the deacons Titianus (cf. *Ep.* 173A), Quintianus (in Possidius's *Indiculus*), and Quodvultdeus, and the brother Comes, reports Augustine's safe return to Hippo in time to celebrate the feast of the most blessed martyr (presumably Cyprian on 14 September) with his people who were complaining of his absence. He commends the bearer, the presbyter Mascelio, for whom Comes is asked to provide lodging.

Ep. 26* to Bishop Honorius (evidently bishop of Suppa, not the bishop of Cartenna who has loomed large in the Caesarean affair) is about Donantius, a native of Suppa who came to Hippo with his father, the family being supported by the alms of the church. The church at Suppa now wants Donantius as deacon (*Ep.* 21* above). But the man was unable to endure the monastic life in the Hippo monastery. The late primate Antiphon made him a deacon, contrary to the canons of episcopal councils (i.e. Augustine was not consulted in the matter?), but found him unsatisfactory and returned him to Augustine. To find a means of support for him Augustine made him ostiarius at the shrine of St. Theogenes (mentioned in *Sermo* 273.7; *S. Mai* 158.2, p. 381 Morin), but he could not do even that job properly, and 'when I was absent the presbyters ejected him'. Augustine does not forbid Suppa to invite him, but suggests that he is not given greater responsibility than the rank of Reader 'which we have normally granted to laity in case of necessity'. The letter illustrates Augustine's honest refusal to solve a problem at home by wishing it on to someone else with a less than candid testimonial.

Ep. 27* is an oddity in the collection, a reply from Jerome to Aurelius when Aurelius wrote to inform him of his ordination as bishop of Carthage (392). Jerome recalls having met Aurelius in Rome with his predecessor Bishop Cyrus when as archdeacon he was sent as legate from Carthage to Pope Damasus. Aurelius had mentioned that he possessed some of Jerome's writings: a few homilies on Jeremiah and two on the Song of Songs (works written 381–83), and a commentary on Matthew whose authenticity Jerome denies. Jerome had not yet written on the first Gospel. Now by the hand of Felicissimus, travelling to Africa on domestic necessities of which he will speak, Jerome sends a piece on the tenth psalm and his 'Hebrew Questions on Genesis'. In comparison with the great African rivers Tertullian, Cyprian, and Lactantius, Jerome feels himself to be a ridiculous stream. Nevertheless he suggests that Aurelius might wish to follow the example of bishops in Gaul and Italy by sending a reliable copyist to the Holy Land to make copies of all Jerome's works. At Jerusalem scribes capable of Latin are few; the two notaries that Jerome has can hardly keep pace with all that he writes. The monks Paulianus and Eusebius (are they the two notaries?) send a special greeting to Aurelius. Jerome would welcome copies of Aurelius's writings by the hand of Felicissimus on his return.

Ep. 28* takes us back to the joys and agonies attending the conversion to Catholicism of Donatists in the aftermath of the Conference of 411. About 418 Bishop Novatus (here spelt Novatius) of Sitifis wrote to inform Augustine at length of the sudden change of allegiance on the part of the nearby Donatist community at Abessa. All basilicas are now in Catholic hands, he reports. Of the recalcitrant who feared neither hell nor the secular arm, only a handful of councillors in the *ordo* remained alienated who had obtained an *interlocutio* from a judge, namely the *vicarius* (p. 135.6ff.), assuring them of protection. The judge had written a subsequent letter encouraging them to yield. In an earlier letter to Sitifis Augustine had suggested the public reading each Lent of the Acts of the Carthage colloquy before the Sunday liturgy, a practice already established at Carthage and Hippo and recommended for general use in Africa. Moreover, Augustine mentions his own short summary of the proceedings. At Hippo, he adds, the Readers do not read the Acts from the ambo as a formal part of the liturgy, wearing fine *casulae,* but sit as they please where they can be heard by the people sitting (not standing as at the liturgy) as if in their own houses. Both sexes are encouraged to listen. He recommends that Novatus introduces something of the kind. He also complains that Novatus has not sent him copies of the correspondence with the *vicarius,* and suggests that a joint letter from himself and Alypius may in due course be effective.

A further matter is a case where asylum has not been respected (cf. *Ep.* 1* above). A man named Victorinus has an affair *de annonis* which Novatus is trying to settle. He is engaged in a dispute with his mother and stepfather, as a result of which he has sought asylum at the church. Augustine mentioned the case in a letter to the count. But the tribune Peregrinus claimed that he had received an instruction from the count to remove Victorinus from the church by force. Augustine went to see Peregrinus who would not give him a copy of the instruction, but read him the text. Augustine refused to believe in its authenticity, the count being 'vir christianus et religiosus', but did not wish to put the tribune in an impossible position.

Augustine concludes by commending Victorinus's man as deserving help; by thanking Novatus for a notarius whom he had sent to Hippo; finally, by mentioning two men who have suffered atrocious attacks from Donatists, namely, Olympius and Bishop Rogatus, whose hand and tongue were cut off by Circumcellions (*Gesta cum Emerito* 9); after being Donatist bishop of Assuras in succession to Praetextatus, he then became Catholic and paid the price.

The final letter in the new collection, *Ep.* 29*, is to Paulinus, deacon of Milan and biographer of Ambrose. Augustine replies to the gift of a group of *Acta martyrum.* The letter is of exceptional interest for the reason that Augustine declares the highest respect for those Acts which consist of transcripts of the trial, but is much less confident of those which are free literary composition. Yet he is aware that Ambrose wrote about the martyrs including information not found in the official records. And an anonymous life of Cyprian includes a story not found in the legal *gesta* to the effect that when he was taken to his *passio* and was being held at the Vicus Saturni, a great multitude of the brothers slept out all night, and he ordered the girls to be guarded. (The story is also mentioned in *Sermo* 309.4.) Augustine tells Paulinus that he has no reliable information beyond the *gesta publica,* unless it be what he had read in the writings of predecessors. Perhaps there is a case for re-expressing the story taken from *gesta* in one's own words?

That the problem was one of which Augustine was conscious is evident from *Sermo* 315.1: of other martyrs we are hardly able to find *gesta,* but St. Stephen's *passio* has a special standing because it is in canonical scripture.

Johannes Divjak has been granted great good fortune to discover this rich collection. Fortune is kind only to those equipped to make good use of it. That he has also done.

New Sermons of St. Augustine

In 1990 there was published a catalogue of manuscripts in the city library at Mainz, and one codex (I. 9) particularly caught the eye of the distinguished French scholar François Dolbeau. It contained homilies ascribed to Augustine of Hippo. M. Dolbeau went to investigate and found a late fifteenth-century manuscript containing a homiliary written for the Carthusian house at Mainz about 1470–75. The collection included in total sixty-two sermons, sixteen of them being *inedita* known, if at all, through fragmentary citations in Caesarius of Arles and Bede. Eight turned out to be fuller versions of homilies hitherto known only in truncated forms, abbreviated by medieval scribes who needed something shorter for a lection. M. Dolbeau has published 'provisional' texts of all twenty-six sermons containing new matter, underpinned by highly erudite commentaries. He has shown that half of these came from a collection known to have existed at one time in the library of the Carolingian monastery at Lorsch, not far from Mainz. The catalogue of the Lorsch collection was printed in 1976 by the late Père Patrick Verbraken in his indispensable instrument to guide the reader in the use of Augustine's sermons.[1] The other half of the Mainz collection came from a Carthusian manuscript. The purpose of the present paper is to underline the importance of M. Dolbeau's discovery.[2] Sermons are not likely to offer the scandal-interest associated with the letters discovered by Johannes Divjak, printed in *CSEL* 88 (1981) and discussed in a descriptive paper in *JTS*,

---

1. P. P. Verbraken, *Etudes critiques sur les sermons authentiques de S. Augustin* (Steenbrugge, 1976), 232–33.
2. There are studies in progress by Prof. R. Klein, 'Die neugefundenen Augustin-Predigten aus der Mainzer Bibliothek', *Gymnasium* 100 (1993), 370ff.; 102 (1995), 242ff.

NS, 34 (1983), 425–52. Nevertheless, they contain at least a few dramas on a domestic scale and shed new light on Augustine's endeavours to convert educated pagans mainly in Africa Proconsularis. In his own Numidia the majority of Christians were Donatists, and the level of education cannot have been high. There, the principal missionary problem was either to detach the peasants (few of whom had any Latin)[3] from the Donatist community, to which the intimidation of the circumcellions would securely cement them, or to emancipate them from dependence on astrologers and other forms of divination by which they guided their lives. These alternatives were not mutually exclusive.

It may be convenient immediately to set out a list of the Mainz sermons with their number in the Mainz codex, and a note of the location in which the provisional publication of the text is to be found. Pending the full un-provisional edition of the texts, it is convenient to prefix M to the number of the new sermons in the Mainz codex.

> M 5 on Obedience. REAug 28, 1992, 63–79. At Carthage after minor disruption.
>
> M 7 Nativity of John the Baptist. REAug 29, 1993, 384–95. 24 June.
>
> M 9 SS. Peter and Paul. REAug 29, 1993, 411–20. 29 June.
>
> M 12 The Last Things. REAug 29, 1993, 73–87.
>
> M 13 Ps. 81 Deus stetit in synagoga deorum. REAug 29, 1993, 97–106.
>
> M 15 on burial of a catechumen. REAug 27, 1991, 294–95.
>
> M 21 on Ps. 117:1 Confitemini domino. Vigil of Pentecost. RBen 101, 1991, 280–89.
>
> M 24 on Ps. 115:10f. (Eucharistic matter) RBen 101, 1991, 251–56.
>
> M 27 on Gal. 2:11f. RBen 102, 1992, 52–63.
>
> M 40 de dilectione dei et proximi. RBen 102, 1992, 66–74.
>
> M 41 de bono nuptiarum. RBen 102, 1992, 275–82.
>
> M 42 de honorandis vel contemnendis parentibus. RBen 102, 1992, 288–97.
>
> M 44 The kingdom is near. RBen 103, 1993, 313–20.
>
> M 45 Martyrs of Maxula. AnBoll 110, 1992, 282–89. 22 July.
>
> M 46/47 Good tree, good fruit. RBen 103, 1993, 327–38. (Much on Ps. 4.)
>
> M 48 on Luke 13:11–13 (woman bent 18 years). RBen 104, 1994, 41–48.
>
> M 50 St. Quadratus of Utica. AnBoll 110, 1992, 296–304. 21 August.

---

3. Augustine, *Ep.* 84.2. In the towns the Donatists possessed adherents of high ability; *Tract. in Joh.* 13.15: *Diserti sunt multi inter illos, magnae linguae, flumina linguarum.*

M 51 John 6:41 Ego sum panis . . . RBen 104, 1994, 56–66. (Crede deum, credere deo, credere in deum . . .)

M 52 on Ps. 17:36 Disciplina tua direxit me in finem. RBen 104, 1994, 69–76.

M 54 on Rom. 11:33 o altitudo. REAug 27, 1991, 271–88. Preached at Tignica.

M 55 on Ps. 21 'et quomodo tribus modis dicatur Christus . . .' REAug 40, 1994, 171–96.

M 59 Epiphany. *Philologia Sacra, Studien für H. J. Frede und W. Thiele* (Freiburg, 1993), 537–59.

M 60 de testimoniis scripturarum. REAug 37, 1991, 42–52.

M 61 'habitus Boseth cum pagani ingrederentur' (Lorsch catal.). REAug 27, 1991, 58–77.

M 62 de calendis contra paganos. Recherches, Aug. 26, 1992, 63–79.

M 63 de his qui se ad unitatem cogi conquerentur, contra partem Donati. REAug 27, 1991, 303–306.

The account of the sermons which follows does not discuss the questions of dating, on which the introductions of M. Dolbeau offer masterly considerations. The intention of this paper is rather to survey in fairly general terms the content of the new sermons, and especially to bring out any matters which are in some degree distinctive in relation to Augustine's other works.

The sermons vary considerably in length and weight. Some are quite short, others of substantial length. The sermon for the Kalends of January (M 62) is surprisingly long. From *Tract. in ev. Joh.* 7.24 we know that Augustine liked to prolong a sermon on the day of a big pagan festival to deter his flock from being drawn into the festivities and their accompanying sideshows. In that sermon he expressed regret (7.2) that many women had not come to church. The festival was evidently a celebration of Cybele and Attis, since there is mention of a scourge (7.8) and of a lamb (7.6), and the well-known quotation from a priest of Cybele who claimed that Attis tenderly nursing his lamb was no different from the Christian good shepherd—*ipse pilleatus Christianus est,* the fellow with a Phrygian cap is Christian.[4] On the Kalends of January the pagan custom was to exchange presents, to gamble,

---

4. For a representation of Attis holding his lamb see *JTS*, NS, 3 (1952), 90. There is a good discussion of *Tract. in Joh.* 7 by J. Pépin in *De la philosophie anc. à la théol. patristique* (Variorum, 1976), XIII, 263ff.

to drink a great deal, and to sing obscene songs. Since Tertullian's admonitions in *De idololatria* 14, puritan preachers had difficulty in discouraging believers from participating in the junketings.

Not all the sermons have been perfectly transcribed by scribes or by their models, and in places the text is problematic. M. Dolbeau and his colleagues in Paris have made numerous acute emendations—and have left a number of cruces still to be considered.[5] Some mistakes may go back to the shorthand writers who took the sermons down at the time of delivery. Probably they were able to derive some income out of selling copies to less eloquent bishops elsewhere in Numidia where the possession of fluency in Latin was far from universal. Augustine (*Ep.* 84.2) expressly says that in Numidia the preaching of the gospel was much hindered by the widespread ignorance of Latin. From the Divjak letters (16 and 23A) we know that at Carthage also there was a demand for copies of his sermons, since one letter mentions a request from the primate, Aurelius of Carthage, for some sermons which he could use. Augustine agreed, on the understanding that the source would be acknowledged.[6] Those homilies were evidently to be prepared written texts in the form in which they reached Aurelius. But that was unusual.

Augustine normally preached extempore, not from a carefully prepared written text which he had before him at the ambo.[7] His sermons normally follow the manner of those homilists whose discourse is determined by their stream of consciousness as their mind circumambulates round the texts given by the proper lections, and who therefore do not have clear-cut and particular points to put to the congregation in the hope that at leisure they may recall what was said and meditate further thereon. His usual method is to expound the psalm, or epistle, or gospel, or, on the feast of a martyr, something taken from the Passio of the saint which has also been read.[8] The readings of the lector were not always what he had asked for

---

5. In M 54.6 (REAug 27, 1991, 276) line 184, where the question discussed is the familiar theme of the mind's superiority to the senses of which it is judge, the word *sensus* stands where one expects *mens*. Perhaps Augustine's phrase was *sensus mentis,* cf. *Retr.* i.1.2: *est enim sensus et mentis.*

6. *De doctrina Christiana* IV.29,62 allows the use of another's sermon as long as it is 'offered in the person of the author'.

7. Besides the classic book of Van der Meer, there is now a notable survey of Augustine the preacher in the great work by Alexandre Olivar, *La Predicación cristiana antigua* (Barcélona: Herder, 1991), 330–389, with many references to detailed studies.

8. Canon 47 of the third council of Carthage rules that the one exception to the exclu-

and, because he was accustomed to improvise, he still preached on what had actually been read even when the lector produced something wholly unexpected. In M 12. 1 he remarks to the congregation that the choice of reading 'was not mine but the Lord's'. A well-known parallel occurs in the homily on Psalm 138:1.

For high festivals the lectionary was predictable and reliable. For baptisms it was common to have Psalms 41 (42) and 4—and it is surely not accidental that these psalms provide important citations in the *Confessions*. On the vigil of Pentecost the expected psalms were 117 and 140 (M 20–21) as in *Sermo* 29 in the Maurist edition. M 21 takes the text from Psalm 117 'Confitemini Domino . . .' which, according to *contra Adimantum* 13, 4, was 'chanted in the Church every day', and uses it to explain that *confessio,* commonly understood to mean the admission of faults, has the other meaning of praising God.

Because his usual procedure was to improvise, he could not avoid repeating himself, even if he had wished to do so. Once (*S.* 125.1) he defends repetition in sermons as being like familiar Bible stories, which serve to remind the congregation of valued truths. In consequence a fairly high proportion of the content of the newly found sermons can be located in homilies already in print, and this, of course, helps to settle any arguments about authenticity. The hands and the voice are familiar. The normal pattern is a combination of expounding the lections read, laced with some doctrinal point which seldom receives more than a single paragraph, and then some direct and fervent exhortation. Those of the congregation who liked what Augustine said were impassioned in their admiration, and some came along merely to see this great sight: 'Do not suppose that I stand here for you to gaze at (*ad spectaculum*)' (M 12.16); 'Some come here merely on my account' (55.1). In at least one north African church, whether beside or (less likely) instead of the lections from scripture, either the lector or the bishop had started reading passages from the writings of Augustine, thereby giving the impression to his people that the works of the wise bishop of Hippo virtually ranked as edification alongside the biblical canon (M 27.15). Similar passages disowning authority appear in a number of Augustine's works, normally in the form that he makes no claim to be achieving more than progress in understanding (e.g. *Tract. in ev. Joh.* 53.7, or *Ep.* 143.2 to Marcellinus, or the striking text in *Conf.* XII.25,34 that God's truth is shared by all believers and

---

sive reading of canonical scripture in church is the Passio of a martyr on the anniversary; also the Council of Hippo of 393, canon 5, p. 21, Munier.

is never the property of one individual). To elevate his writings to the status of canonical scripture was, he felt, bringing down to the merely human level a Bible in which, by God's grace, there was nothing untrue or mendacious to lead one astray (48.3).

Most of the Mainz sermons belong to the period between his consecration as bishop of Hippo in 395 and the year 410. One sermon (M 51) touches on the doctrine of grace, and might belong to the early stages of the great debate on that issue. But since that question was already raised in the *Questions for Simplicianus* of Milan and in several places in the *Confessions,* there is no imperative necessity to put this sermon late. The sermon has the special interest of offering the earliest text to distinguish between *credere Deo, credere Deum,* and *credere in Deum,* where the last of this triad means to love Christ and to be incorporated in him, not merely to believe him to teach truth or to be predicted by the prophets. If Christ had been no more than human, he could never have imparted justification to us, but would be with us in needing it. In becoming human he remained what he was, so that in him we have both our way and our destination (*et qua iremus et quo veniremus*). And if he is in us, then the bread which he gives is not distasteful but a delight and a source of strength. Salvation is deification (13.1).[9]

The sermon preached on the following Sunday (M 53) betrays that some of the congregation, which was noted as being numerous, found the discourse on faith and justification burdensome to follow (*molesta quaestio*) (51.10, line 228). 'I preached as I did because of those who think it sufficient to believe but then live evil lives.'

As we should expect there are a few attacks on Manichees, either for their denial that the Old Testament has any significance for Christianity (42.6) or for their belief that Christ's human body was not real, and that he was not really crucified—the cross bring a symbolic myth (54.12). But insofar as the Mainz collection can be taken as representative of their situation, Manicheism seems not to have been any serious threat in the churches where they were delivered.

It was otherwise with Donatism. Several of the sermons contain attacks on Donatists combined with pleas to them to show charity and restore unity with the Catholica. Two of the sermons (M 9.3 and 62.45) refer to the occasion, known from the *Enchiridion* (v. 17) and from Possidius (*Vita* 12), when the circumcellions set an ambush intended to silence Augustine forever and

---

9. On this frequent theme see Gerald Bonner, 'Augustine's Conception of Deification', *JTS,* NS, 37 (1986), pp. 369–86.

stop his evidently influential attacks, and providentially the guide took him by the wrong road so that he escaped their murderous intentions. Like Pope Symmachus at the end of the fifth century, after he had escaped unhurt from a rain of hostile stones hurled by the supporters of the rival candidate for the papacy, Laurentius,[10] Augustine understood his escape as a divine act of deliverance, vindicating both his work and his theme of the unicity of the Church Catholic. Augustine did not believe in chance in this or any other matter.

The collection contains the familiar gravamen of complaints against the Donatist puritan separatists. They are deficient in *tolerantia* (M 45.7). When receiving converts from the Catholic Church, they repeat the holy sacrament of baptism; yet they do not rebaptize members of their own connection who have received this sacrament from clergy polluted by acts of criminality or adultery (M 7.14, line 209). M 7, a sermon for the Nativity of John the Baptist on 24 June, inveighs against the Donatist understanding of baptism, and has an ironic reference to their thug bishop—a kind of mafioso 'godfather'—Optatus of Thamugadi, who had actually been dead for about nine years but long remained a valued weapon in Augustine's arsenal.[11]

The same sermon, M 7, ends with a significant warning to the Catholic congregation, which evidently included a number of native Punic speakers (7.7), that drunkards would be excluded from heaven no less than heretics.

Every time a Donatist lector reads from the Bible in their liturgy, the schism stands refuted; for the Bible foretells a universal worldwide church, not one confined to Africa. (How providential it was for Augustine's argument that Donatism did not spread beyond Africa and a handful of expatriate African congregations in Spain or in Rome.) God's promise to Abraham was that all nations would be blessed. Therefore the real tussle with the Donatists is not about what did or did not happen at Carthage when Caecilian was consecrated bishop to the anger of the Lady Lucilla and the Numidian episcopate: *Non quaeramus antiqua quae gesta sunt* (M 60.4).[12] Admittedly Augustine found it necessary to undertake scrupulous investigation of municipal archives to discover the documents of the time. But the authoritative

---

10. Symmachus, *Ep.* 10.7, p. 702, Thiel; critical edition by E. Schwartz, *Publizistische Sammlungen zum Acacianischen Schisma* (Abh. Bayer. Akad. NF 10, 1934), 154: *Inter imbres lapidum tutus euasi: iudicavit deus.*

11. In view of Augustine's express statements that Optatus had some association with the rebellion of Gildo (*c. litt. Petil.* ii.83, 184; *c. Crescon.* iv.27, 34), I believe some of Professor Frend's suggestions on this deserve more sympathy than they have received.

12. Similarly *En. in Ps.* 57.7; *c. litt. Petil.* i.14, 15.

records which prove Donatists schismatic—and schism persisted in passes into heresy[13] (*incipiente malo schismatum quae postea errore hominum confirmata sunt*) (M 61.4)—are not in the files at public offices but in the scriptures.

A passage at the end of the long sermon for the Kalends of January (M 62.52) restates the objection to the Donatist bishop of Carthage, Parmenian, that according to his ecclesiology the bishop is an indispensable mediator between God and the laity—a doctrine which in his reply to Parmenian's letter he denounced as 'the voice of Antichrist, intolerable to Christian ears'.[14] The same sermon contains what might well be an implied attack on a saying of Petilian, Donatist bishop of Cirta, that while the clergy pray for the laity, they are the mediators of holiness to the people and have no need to ask the congregation to pray for them (M 62.54; *c. litt. Petil.* II. 105, 240–241). Augustine often asks the laity for their prayers.

The sustained campaign against Donatism, in which Augustine took a prominent role, lies in the background of M 5, a sermon rebuking the congregation at Carthage assembled on 23 January, the day after a well-attended celebration of the Spanish martyr St. Vincent of Zaragoza, martyred at Valencia.[15] Augustine and Prudentius both possessed a grisly narrative of the inhuman tortures to which he was successively subjected, and perhaps fascination with the gruesome, gory details contributed to the popularity of the feast which was widely celebrated beyond Spain, at least in the West. A few months previously, during the autumn, Augustine had been preaching in Carthage on four successive days to state the Catholic case for unity. Presumably at that time all passed off peacefully. But in January, on St. Vincent's day, disorder erupted. When preaching against Donatism in the autumn Augustine had delivered his discourses standing by the altar, but for St. Vincent's homily he went to the foot of the apse. Midwinter journeys were not good for Augustine's health (he has a pointed reference to very cold winds). All probability favours the view that his voice was particularly weak.[16] A crowd of women surged forward to hear him better, and some seem to have asked him to move to the altar further down the body of the basilica. Impatient members of the congregation began to shout that it was time for the catechumens to be sent away: *Missa fac, missa, missa fac* (5.20).

13. So also *c. Crescon.* ii.7, 9.

14. *c. ep. Parm.* ii.8, 15.

15. V. Saxer, 'La Passion de S. Vincent diacre dans la première moitié du Ve siècle', *Revue des études augustiniennes* 25 (1989), 275–97.

16. On Augustine's dread of winter travelling cf. *Ep.* 124.1; *Ep.* 22.1.1, Divjak; weak voice—*S. Mai* 126.1, p. 356, Morin; *S.* 154.1.

Augustine had abandoned any serious attempt to be heard. Perhaps he failed to communicate at this point with the primate Aurelius. At any rate, rumour immediately began to circulate that between him and the primate there was tension over the affair.

So at a church service on the day after St. Vincent's day he explained how wrong this rumour was. That he had come to Carthage at all in mid-winter was explicable only by the mutual affection between Aurelius and himself. Strictly he ought to have been attending the provincial synod of Numidia summoned by the old Numidian primate, Xanthippus of Thagora, to meet at Constantine, where the bishop Fortunatus was an old friend, a former presbyter at Thagaste. But Aurelius's invitation had pressed him with such warm declarations of regard that he had agreed to come to Carthage for the popular festival of the Spanish martyr. And now his discourse must be on obedience. He tactfully praised the people for their good following of their bishop, and singled out for approval the prudence of Aurelius, who had acted to protect the women from loutish jostling and lecherous whistles by appointing different entrances for the two sexes and then segregating them in the basilica. In Roman theatres the sexes were often segregated as they were not in the amphitheatre.[17] But in the church the people were not to behave like audiences at the theatre. (It is safe to deduce that a Carthaginian theatre audience was noisy, and no doubt included many of the *eversores,* the Wreckers, who were among the students mentioned in the *Confessions* as disrupting Augustine's classes.)[18]

The sermon for Peter and Paul on 29 June (M 9) is the complete form of a homily first printed by Mai, but only in a truncated version (*S. Mai* 19, Morin p. 307 = PLS II. 462). It contains one of the two references in the Mainz collection to the unsuccessful circumcellion ambush designed to silence Augustine. It appears from this full form of the sermon that after his escape some considerable time elapsed during which Augustine preached no anti-Donatist discourses. Unkind gossip said that he had been scared into keeping his mouth shut. The sermon for the glorious apostolic martyrs replies that he would have been only too willing to join the company of those who had been the seed of the church's mission (9.7). The sermon goes on to encourage his congregation by speaking of the beneficent imperial legis-lation which was now enforcing the concealment of images of the old gods

---

17. The main texts are Suetonius, *Augustus* 43f. and Ovid, *Tristia* 2.280ff.; the best dis-cussion is by Elizabeth Rawson in *Papers of the British School at Rome* 55 (1987), 83–113.

18. *Conf.* V.8, 14.

of polytheism (9.8, cf. 60.8), and by referring to the mixture of Babylon and Jerusalem in this world.

As one would expect, Augustine's anti-Donatist polemic is insistent that there is, and can be, only one Catholic Church. Some people seem to have been arguing that because the apostle Paul wrote epistles to several churches there could be more than one body so entitled. In reply Augustine contends that, if one counts the region of Galatia as a single church, Paul's letters to churches add up to the symbolic number of seven, which signifies completeness (62.51). Again he is emphatic that the one church is symbolized by the seamless robe of the Lord. He concedes that there may be other garments of Jesus symbolic of more fissiparous and independent bodies, but at least these bodies cannot be called the church (54.18). The Catholica is the whole, never merely a part of some larger grouping (54.17), and Christ is the head of this body, so that with the church he and his people are the *totus Christus*.

The sermon on Psalm 21 (M 55) states a principle of biblical exegesis that one must distinguish statements referring to Christ as God, statements referring to him in his incarnate state as man, and those which speak of him as head of the church. This distinction is inherited from the first of the seven rules of Tyconius. The discussion is then embroidered with an allegory of esoteric improbability interpreting the rods with which Jacob increased his flock. The passage on the incarnation answers a difficulty: how could the Word be with God and also in the Virgin's womb? The reply is that the question presupposes that God, who is incorporeal, can be divided into different pieces. The omnipresent Word is no more divided than a human word (*totum ubique*) (55.8, line 208). 'When I am speaking, it is not the case that one person hears one word, another person a different word. The entire sentence reaches everyone listening.' Or take the example of *Iustitia,* found in both East and West. It has no difficulty in being in two places at once.[19]

Augustine's discourse apparently puzzled some of his hearers, since he had to ask them to stop talking to each other and to listen to him (55.9). They may have been baffled by his juxtaposition (55.7) of an affirmation of the Trinity with the admission that 'if we little people (*parvuli*) wish to say anything worthy of God, we should say nothing at all'.[20] Some of the questions remind him of issues raised in the Arian controversy which were

---

19. M 59.7 has an attack on the notion that justice is merely social convention.

20. This reverent agnosticism is not infrequent in Augustine; e.g. *Conf.* XIII. 11,12 (of the Trinity): *rara anima quaecumque de illa loquitur scit quod loquitur. De ordine* ii.44: *Deus qui scitur melius nesciendo* (cf. Porphyry, *Sententiae 25*). *c. Adimantum* 11: *humani conditionem sermonis feramus ut ad divinum perueniamus silentium.*

'disturbing to the weak but conquered by the catholic faith' (55.12). Yet the old questions are not yet dead, the old serpent is still whispering, and trying to eject the church from paradise by the promise of a certain *scientia*. There is still trouble with the Johannine text 'The Father is greater than I', but all difficulty is removed by the exegetical rule that references to the inferiority of the Son are to his incarnate state as man.

Again it is an exegetical principle that whatever in scripture sounds absurd or superfluous has hidden meaning, discoverable to those who seek.[21] Scripture has *magnum pondus auctoritatis*. People despise 'They two shall be in one flesh', and ask if God cares about sexual intercourse. It suggests, they say, that Moses had a mediocre mind (55.22).

The Bible resembles a nut hard to crack, but with a delicious kernel once one has penetrated to the heart of its meaning. So the allegorical meaning of Jacob's rods in Gen. 30:37–38 is presented with the evident motive of illustrating the way in which a most unlikely story can symbolize the incarnation and redemption by Christ. Jacob is a figure of Christ. He chooses three different kinds of wood[22]—a nut tree signifies the incarnation and the cross, for as the husk is the medium through which the kernel is available, so Christ does not feed us (reading *pasceret* for the MS *portaret*) unless we come to his body through the wood of the cross. The perfumed storax or gum tree signifies the inviolate virginity of Mary. The plane tree means the Holy Spirit, 'but it would be more difficult to show how'. The answer is its very broad shade protecting people resting from the heat, suitably symbolizing Mary conceiving Jesus not in the heat of sexual desire but in the coolness of faithful chastity and uncorrupted virginity by the overshadowing of the Holy Spirit. The variety of offspring refers to the Gentile converts after the Jewish doctors of the law, who discerned something of the mystery of Christ but failed to enter in themselves.

The illustration of the hard nut is presented as likely to evoke a smile (*ut aliquid hilariter dicamus*). The sermon had become something of a lecture on principles of interpretation, and needed a light touch. The conclusion reflects that any profit from this homily has its criterion in the congregation's good works, and they can show this by fasting during pagan festivals and praying not only for pagan worshippers but in particular for some Christian brethren who on the previous day took part in a heathen celebration.

An early witness to M 55 is found in a florilegium contained in the Ve-

---

21. On this principle see *De utilitate credendi* 7, 17; *En. in Ps.* 77.26; 118.31.5.

22. The trees of the Old Latin here correspond to the Septuagint, not the Vulgate.

rona codex LIX (57) of the late sixth or early seventh century. The fragment of 55 there quoted has a rubric, and the text was printed by Morin in the appendix to his supplement to the Maurist sermons (*Miscellanea Agastiniana* I, 1931). The rubric says: *Item eiusdem beatissimi ex tractatu de tribus modis in deum Christum dictum in Basilica Restituta dixit pridie idus decembris.* That is to say, the sermon was preached on 12 December at Carthage in the Basilica Restituta, information more likely than not to be correct. Early in December was a normal time for *munera*—shows at the circus and the amphitheatre. The Mainz sermons contain more than one defensive reference to the temptation which these riveting entertainments constituted. The year is more delicate to determine. M 55 refers to a visit to Rome by the emperor Honorius shortly beforehand, *temporibus nostris.* He might have visited the great imperial tomb of proud Hadrian, but he went instead to the sepulchre of the fisherman to ask for his intercession with the Lord, such as no proud emperor would be able to obtain (55.4). M. Dolbeau argues persuasively that M 55 cannot have been preached before December 405, but could be assigned to later years, with the proviso that times are excluded when Augustine is known to have been elsewhere than Carthage.

It is intriguing to note that M 55.19 appears to provide the text otherwise unidentified to which Alcuin refers, *Contra haeresim Felicis* 72.

Two themes appear to be recurrent. The first is that true religion is inward and a matter of the heart—outward acts are secondary and a means to a spiritual end; Christian custom is to turn east for prayer, but the movement of the heart to God is the important thing (M 5.12). Of the fans excited at the races, or of a man madly in love, people say 'he is beside himself' (*non est secum*). There is analogy to the love of God. When you begin to love God, you are also loving your self. Loving God has no limit but is *sine modo.* If you loved the shows with wild beasts on a *dies muneris,* you would rise early and rouse your neighbour to come to the amphitheatre, for which he may even be grateful to you that you molested him. That is the kind of passion that Augustine would like to see for God. 'Love the source of your love and you are loving God.' The question is put, how can one reconcile the two commandments of Matt. 22:37–40 with the one commandment of Rom. 13:9? The answer is that after you have understood the two, one is then enough. The faith which seeks to keep the law is a form of love. Forgiven for our sins in baptism, we are never weary of our 'bread' and know that nothing imparts satisfaction except God (M 40).

Accordingly, 'everyone prays truly when the prayer is inward' (62.14). 'My sounds reach your ears, and if good results, that is only because *deus intus agit'* (62.27). 'You wish to be happy, but then look in the wrong place, not seeking *idipsum,* the unchanging' (M 46–47). May the Son of God, God's Word, be present to your hearts, *intus vobiscum* (M 7.6).

A second prominent theme is that true faith will issue in a reformed moral life. Many Christians think it enough to have faith but then live unregenerate lives. They believe but produce no good works (M 51–52). Augustine was painfully aware of the problems of marital infidelity among his people. Tolerating an unfaithful husband is a mark of the noble and chaste wife (41.6). The Lord foretold scandals, and some of these are found within the church itself (12.6). Augustine had his share of scandals, as the letters first printed by Divjak richly illustrated. The morale of his clergy and people had been disturbed by the homoerotic affair between the presbyter, Boniface, and Spes, the monk in Augustine's monastery (*Ep.* 78), leading Augustine to remark that when a lay person is involved in sexual scandal, it is no nine days' wonder, but when a charge is laid against those who profess a holy name, it immediately becomes a matter for general gossip, and people guess that it is true of all the clergy.

Rich Christians were made anxious by some gospel sayings, and needed reassurance that if they used their wealth rightly, they could be saved. They were reminded that in all their fine clothes they were merely human, of the stock of Adam and Eve, and when naked they had no marks for ostentation (12.12). So also, when it is their duty to punish a delinquent slave, let them remember divine mercy, and be sure that in the inflicting of discipline there is no touch of cruelty and hatred. It is a principle that such a slave should not be punished more harshly than a naughty son (54.4). M 54.5 illustrates the three orders of God, soul, and body by the analogy of a master, his slave, and, in third position, the slave of the slave—the slave-owning slave being called *peculiosus,* i.e. he manages money or property virtually as his own, though incapable of legal ownership, this money being a *peculium.*

The moral standard asked of believers, especially but not only in sexual matters, deterred many catechumens from giving in their names for baptism (M 44). They preferred to guide their life by consulting their favourite astrologer (44.7). Indeed Augustine knew some who would turn to their astrologer for a decision whether or not it was a good day for becoming a Christian (61.27). That a *fidelis* was expected to give up such sources of guidance was a hurdle too high for many. Augustine warned the catechumens that by providence the day of their death was unknown, and M 44 pleads with them to come forward for baptism. M 63, which is not strictly a homily but a case in canon law, rules against allowing the burial among the baptized faithful of the child of well-to-do parents, who had been enrolled as no more than a catechumen. There were evidently tears over this question. In the *Confessions* (II.3,8) Monica herself is described as a worldly Christian still living in the suburbs of Babylon. That description could have been applied to numerous members of north African churches. Believers came to the church in quest of happiness, and supposed this would mean temporal goods and success in their career. Eternal things were not on their horizon.

Augustine was concerned to encourage private Bible study—which presupposes a degree of literacy in his congregation. Biblical codices were openly for sale in the shops (12.14; 62.20; cf. *En. in Ps.* 66.10). But this book was never less than puzzling. The precepts of the Old Testament law appeared like an impenetrable jungle, though thankfully Christ had reduced everything to a single brief command (40.2). Inquiring and thoughtful believers found it difficult to accept biblical language about hell and the end of the world (12.3).[23] The appeal to fear as a motive for conversion needed some explanatory unction (51.5). People thought it an apostolic confession of failure when in Rom. 11:33 the apostle frankly abandoned the attempt to give a rational explanation of the mystery of election. Augustine agreed that the matter was incapable of reasoned exposition: 'I do not explain the inexplicable, but I commend what the apostle says' (54.1). Some remained puzzled by the difference between the Old and New Testaments. They should remember that just as a physician may prescribe one medicine at one stage of a sickness and another as the patient's condition changes, so too God's precepts can differ at different ages (42.6; *S.* 82.10; *Conf.* III.7,13).

The Epiphany sermon (M 59), of which *S.* 374 is a medieval recension, faces the question whether, since miracles do not occur now, biblical miracles occurred. Augustine resorts to the classical contention, familiar since Justin Martyr, that the miraculous events are vindicated by the prophecies which they fulfil—an argument as useful for convincing pagans as for internal queries in the congregation.

The defence of Christianity before educated pagan criticism was important if inquiring members of the congregation were not to be unsettled. Porphyry had criticized the Apostle Paul for inconsistency, professed in his programme of being a Jew to Jews and a Gentile to Gentiles, in circumcizing Timothy and yet denouncing Peter for observing Jewish customs at Antioch.

---

23. Disbelief in Hell: *S. Frangip.* 2.9, p. 200, Morin; *S. Guelf.* 30.4, p. 555; *De civ. Dei* 20.30. Pelagius on Rom. 2:8, p. 87, Souter, deplores doubters. The theme was a target for much pagan mockery.

The dissension at Antioch was taken out of that kind of debate by Jerome's explanation that the apostles were playacting, a solution which notoriously offended Augustine by undermining apostolic veracity.

The conduct of St. Peter at Antioch was embarrassingly appealed to by those who argued that there are situations and circumstances where a lie can be proper and honourable. In *De Mendacio* 43 of 395, his last work written while still presbyter, this issue is mentioned as delicate to determine. At least in that work he felt confident that in the cause of religious truth no lie can ever be justified (ibid. 17), and the Pauline programme of being all things to all men is expressly defended as meaning sympathetic understanding rather than unprincipled mendacity (ibid. 42). In M 27 Augustine feels a need to answer those whose reading of Galatians 2 leads them to assume that St. Peter was in the wrong. He observes that negative criticism is always an easy thing, and Peter merits credit for taking Paul's criticism so well. 'Never have I seen a person bearing criticism with equanimity' (27.3). (He was no doubt self-conscious of his own inability in that respect, with his admitted weakness for self-justification.[24]) A judicious estimate would say that in practice Peter was right that ethnic Jews becoming believers in Jesus as Messiah are perfectly entitled to continue keeping Mosaic customs, even if one cannot say it is an obligation. Augustine's defence of Peter sounds like the kind of reply that would have made much sense early in the second century, but would have surprised his congregation early in the fifth. A different impression would be derived from *De utilitate credendi* 9 or *Ep.* 82.15 or *De baptismo* II.1,2.

In M 27 it is explicit that some in the congregation are being unsettled by external critics sniping at Paul for lack of integrity—admittedly a charge brought against the apostle in his lifetime. Augustine has to deal with the issue 'not merely for your sake but also for those who hear both me and you' (27.5). And then there was a related question about apostolic integrity raised by the famous chapter on celibacy and marriage in 1 Corinthians 7, discussed in M 41. In this chapter, so Augustine says with perhaps a quiver of apprehension, Paul as a holy man ventures to enter bedrooms to tell married couples what they may do. But was he consistent to say that marriage is no sin when he had also declared that sexual intercourse within the marriage relation is a matter for pardon, *venia?* Did not the latter statement imply something to be forgiven, some pollution therefore contracted by the act? The answer has to be that what needs pardon is conjugal intercourse going beyond the intention of procreation. But how very venial that may be is

24. *Conf.* X.37, 61.

shown by Augustine's belief that it is a fault included in the daily forgiveness granted in answer to the Paternoster.

The question would always have a rather sharp point for Augustine who was bound to affirm against Manichees the essential goodness of the divinely implanted procreative impulse, but against the Pelagians asserted that in concupiscence there was a link between sexuality (uncontrolled by reason) and sin. His conviction that sexual intercourse is 'natural' when the act is for procreation was a proposition common to Plato (*Laws* 839a, 841d) and Stoics such as Musonius Rufus, and was explicit in the Emperor Julian (153b, 359c).

Moral pressures towards ascetic renunciation could hardly be resisted by a man dedicated to the establishment of monasteries among the African churches. But in M 41 he is insistent that no married person may make a unilateral decision to withhold conjugal relations. Experience showed what disasters might follow.[25]

At the same time he regretted family pressures deterring young idealists from following or testing an ascetic vocation.[26] Parents used to say: 'Is a young man not to marry? Must he always be fasting? Is no property to be bought?' (M 12.8). The theme is surely an undercurrent in M 42 on those situations where the judgement of parents should be set aside. The sermon is given for the feast of a martyr—M. Dolbeau gives good reasons for thinking St. Catulinus on 15 July (Possidius, *Indiculus* X[6] 124, ed. Wilmart), and suggests that it was preached at Carthage in 397 in the Basilica Fausti where Catulinus was buried. The Passio evidently recorded his successful resistance to the pleadings from his parents and other relatives, especially his wife. Spouses can hinder the path to glory. A man on the way to martyrdom fears his wife may be an Eve, a wife fears her husband may be a serpent (42.13). But in the hierarchy of virgins, widows, and married women, there is no suggestion that the last named are excluded.

The Mainz sermons have discourses with other martyr festivals in mind: M 9 for Peter and Paul, M 50 for bishop Quadratus of Utica, M 45 for the martyrs of Maxula south of Carthage. The self-denying heroism of these martyrs may move Christians, living in the age after persecution has ceased at least in its old form, to realize what discipline they are called to exercise.

---

25. In the case of Ecdicia (*Ep.* 262) both partners agreed on abstinence, but the husband could not keep it up and lapsed into adultery.

26. *S. Denis* 20.12, p. 23, Morin, speaks of parents who deter daughters wishing to take vows.

And Catholics will know that it is the cause, not the physical pain or death, which is the necessary condition of martyrdom. There is no glory for criminals enduring torture or Donatists subjected to a flogging (5.17; 45.7–8).

After the imperial decree of 405 enforcing unity, there were some reluctant conversions of sullen Donatist congregations in rural areas. Maximin, Donatist bishop of Siniti in Hippo territory, was converted to the Catholica; anyone accepting communion at his hands was to have his house torched.[27] Maximin himself must have found it a life-threatening experience to remain there. This is no doubt the bishop Maximin of M 63, seen accompanying Augustine in *City of God* 22.8, in the Mainz sermon going with him to a forcibly converted ex-Donatist plebs which resented the government's coercion. Augustine's discourse cites the Psalm: how good and pleasant to dwell in unity—'all grant that unity is good, not all agree that it is pleasant' (63.5). But Mother Church presses food on her sickly children (63.6). In the city of Hippo reconciliation has already been achieved, but in the rural areas of the territory the rustics have been slow to understand (63.2). Now at long last we can share bread and peace (63.3).

Controversy with educated pagans is prominent in more than one sermon, and homilies with pleas to Donatists to recover unity are often also evangelistic attempts to convert thoughtful, critical adherents of polytheism. The Lorsch collection consists of a group of discourses preached not at Hippo but in various towns, suggesting that Augustine had gone on a tour in Numidia and Proconsularis. The evangelization of some areas was recent. Preached at Tignica, M 54.16 observes that all his congregation were children of pagan parents. A comparable remark occurs in *En. in Ps.* 96.7: 'everyone here had a pagan grandfather or greatgrandfather'. Augustine has to confess that he has found himself unable to move educated pagans to conversion (M 13.7), and that the better educated they are, the less willing they are to listen (M 62.13).

M 61 was preached in the town of Boseth, the site of which is unidentified but was somewhere in Proconsularis, probably early in 404. It is the second of two discourses (the first not extant) given when a group of educated pagans came to hear what Augustine had to say. Presumably they had been specifically invited to attend. The sermon expounds at length the Neoplatonic ascent of the soul beyond visible and material objects, much in the manner of the vision at Ostia described in the *Confessions*. The Neoplatonic aspiration is qualified by the two Christian theses that the soul is less

27. Augustine, *Ep.* 105.4.

than divine because it is mutable—up one day, down the next—and that the way of the philosophers is a reliance on human pride. Admittedly there have been philosophers like Pythagoras with whom Christians can feel affinity. M 60.8 remarks that while some are members within the church, there are also fellow travellers who are 'in the vicinity' of the church. Augustine is kind to philosophers who do not value sacrificial rites. Yet they rely on their own morality to achieve a level which needs divine grace.[28] The main polemic in M 61 is against pagans who hold that while the soul admittedly needs purification, this purging can be achieved only by the rites of theurgy. Thereby the powers are placated, and ascent to the supreme deity is facilitated. The powers are the old gods, and once placated they act as mediators. And why, asked the pagans, should Christians object to that? They too give a mediatorial role not only to Christ but also the martyrs in their calendar, and they also invoke angels. Educated Christians scorn uneducated people (*imperiti*) who believe that the god resides in the wood or stone idol. But uneducated Christians worship the columns and pictures in the church buildings.

This last point of the pagan criticism of Christian behaviour is capable of more than one explanation. Augustine's reply makes the assumption that the pagans were asking the same question as Marius Victorinus put to Simplicianus, reported in the *Confessions* (VIII.2,4): do walls make Christians? Why should Christians suppose that God can be properly worshipped only in a church building? His answer is effectively in terms of the warmth generated by the fellowship of the community singing and praying together, just as oarsmen in a boat are encouraged to keep going by the *keleuma* of the boatswain or other voice. In the sermon on Psalm 57:23 he met the question: why should I go to church when people who attend every day fail to act on what they hear? The pagan question, if Augustine correctly understood its force, was in effect concerned with the localization of worship in a particular place when good Platonists knew that God occupies no space.

Two other possible interpretations of the pagan critique seem worth a mention. That the churches of north Africa had pictures on the walls is certain (*S.* 316.5). They had pictures of Christ (*De fide et symbolo* i.7,14), of Peter and Paul (*Cons. Evang.* i.10,16), and of Adam and Eve decently covered (*c. Julianum* V 6), and the early Augustine of *De Moribus* I.34,74 expressed anxiety about the superstitious attitudes of those who worshipped martyrs at their shrines and holy pictures. *De Trinitate* VIII.4,7 comments on the

---

28. *Conf.* X.23,33: a Christian cannot judge of pagans whose moral struggle lacks grace, since one cannot know who will come under grace.

variety of portrayals of Christ. The observation that a Christian cannot be certain what the Virgin Mary looked like surely presupposes icons of her. None of this is surprising when one recalls Paulinus's churches at Nola. The reference then to columns and pictures being venerated could be explained on the hypothesis that the pictures were attached to the columns of the basilica, and that casual pagan observers supposed veneration of the icon to include some veneration of the column to which it was affixed.

A third possibility must be that Punic peasants, with a long ancestral background of Phoenician religion and the cult of Tanit, understood stone columns to be the natural habitat of divine beings. One has only to recall the prohibitions of the Old Testament against the asherah to be sure that such cultus penetrating ancient Israel could be reconciled with the worship of Yahweh. What might not have gone on in southern Numidia?

That new converts expected the externals of Christian worship to have some affinity with the ceremonial forms of the past may perhaps be illustrated by the surprise which seems to have been felt at the absence of incense, mentioned by Augustine in M 59.18. This evidence coheres with the well-known text, *En. in Ps.* 49.21, that God asks for the sacrifice of praise, so Christians do not go to Arabia to look for incense. (That search had begun.)

Augustine would have felt that celebrating the Kalends could be open to Manichee criticism. Faustus the Manichee specifically accuses ordinary church members of celebrating pagan festivals such as Kalends and Solstices (*c. Faustum* 20.4).

M 62 also presupposes other pagan complaints. 62.38 stresses that Melchizedek and Job were not of Jewish race, implicitly replying to a sophisticated pagan complaint that belief in only a single god of the entire world seemed in scripture to be simply in the God of the Jews with no interest outside his own chosen people—tribal rather than universal.

Christian assurance of total remission of sins by baptism, however dreadful those sins have been, did not sound to pagan ears like moral seriousness (M 44.6; 61.20). The continual cry, 'Believe, believe' (M 61.14), pushed reasoning aside. The accusation that pagans worship the material idols in temples showed ignorance of true worship, which is of what these images symbolize. This last claim was a gift to Augustine's polemic. Images of Neptune, Juno, or Mercury symbolize sea, air, and intelligence. To worship sea, air, sun, and moon is to honour merely physical objects, and to worship intelligence forgets that clever intellectuals make mistakes (61.23; 62.24). Intelligence is a neutral power which can be directed to evil ends as well as to good (62.24). This pagan treatment of the church resembles those patients who physically assault their good physicians (61.18).

The tenacity with which pagan landowners kept to the old religion is well attested in various texts of Augustine, such as *Confessions* VIII.4,9 or *Ep.* 136.3 of 412. M 62 makes it evident that some of Augustine's educated pagans in Proconsularis had a class problem with the prospect of conversion. One is quoted as asking: 'Am I to be like the slavegirl who guards my front door and not like Plato and Pythagoras?' (62.55). Wealthy senatorial landowners were disinclined to share the faith of uneducated fishermen (61.24). If, as the Christians boast, their God chose fisherfolk, was not that rather ostentatious?

Augustine's reply to the class argument appeals to the emperor himself. Honorius's visit to Rome, mentioned above, was a grand refutation of all the reservations of opulent senators who felt that Christianity was really very un-Roman and at best a faith for the lower classes. Today's emperor is 'wearing a cross on his forehead' (61.24). And in any event, from time to time God has chosen saints of high ability like Cyprian.

A few quotations from the poetry of Virgil are scattered about the Mainz sermons. 27.3 has an unmarked reminiscence of *Eclogue* 3.95; 59.15 quotes *Aeneid* VI; 62.34 quotes the same passage from *Aeneid* VIII which is familiar in *Confessions* VIII.2,3. Hippocrates appears in 61.17, and a fable from Aesop in 21. So any cultured persons in the congregation would not be in doubt that in coming to the church they had not left their great literature behind them. As in his correspondence with Nectarius (*Ep.* 104.3), Augustine was aware that the Bible had been no part of his education, and that the literature which he knew by heart was pagan (M 59.19, cf. *En. in Ps.* 102.25).

The humility of Christ, his birth, and especially his horrible death were in pagan eyes repulsive (61.17). The Christians might proudly say that now they lived in Christian times, but almost all the allusions in Augustine to *Christiana tempora*[29] are answering complaints of pagans that since the old gods were abandoned, things have become bad: buildings are collapsing, theft and rapine never so widespread, the crowd of adulterers and fornicators massively increased (M 13.15). To live in Christian times seemed like a curse.

---

29. G. Madec, 'Tempora Christiana: Expression du triomphalisme chrétien ou recrimination païenne?' in *Scientia Augustiniana, Festschrift Adolar Zumkeller* (Würzburg, 1975), 112–36. Augustine thought food shortages caused by wicked or incompetent men, not by the weather (*S.* 25.4). What made times bad was the oppression of the poor, corruption in the lawcourts, perversion of the laws—all matters for which human beings are responsible (*S.* 311.8; *S. Denis* 24.11, p. 151, Morin).

Augustine replied that the criticism took no account of the large increase in the number of consecrated virgins (13.15). In any event times were not bad because Christ has come; he came because times were and are bad. ('It is not times which are bad, but we who live in them', *S.* 25.4; 80.8. It is delusion to think that calmer and better times will come, *En. in Ps.* 96.20.) So let pagans read their own histories and there find incessant wars and unending crises (13.13). Admittedly the world is senile and in a condition of serious decrepitude (12.14). The end is surely near (41.2).

By contrast with this doom and gloom, M 61.9 includes significantly positive statements about the life of the *civitas,* stressing its beautifully cultivated fields, the good ordering of the officers of state, the fine architecture, different arts, languages, the depths of human memory, and the overflowing richness of eloquence. And in M 13.9, what dignity has the image of God in humanity! Yet it is defaced by sin: 'If you smashed the emperor's statue, you would be liable *legibus publicis'*, and the charge (which Augustine clearly thought a misnomer) would be sacrilege.

Imperial legislation created problems for intransigent pagans. Questioned by a police officer in uniform (*birratus stationarius*) as to whether sacrifice had been offered, a pagan would deny—a contrast with the martyr who bravely confesses (9.8). Many pagans remained unreconstructed after the government had banned sacrifices and closed temples—some being dismantled, others adapted for use by Christian congregations (*S.* 163.2; *Ep.* 232.3). But Augustine was painfully aware of the need for reeducation. People were now coming to the church in large numbers, especially at high festivals, but 'there is no advantage in the closure of temples if you fabricate an idol in your heart' (viz. by an anthropomorphic image of God), *En. in Ps.* 138.8. Adherence to the church in no way reduced the popularity of divination and astrology; amulets and sortilege were almost universal. *Ep.* 98.1 concerns Christian parents who sought healing for their sick child by offering sacrifice to pagan deities; the child had already been baptized without the therapeutic effect that had evidently been hoped for. Augustine felt the church to be swamped by a multitude whose morals were very unholy (*Tract. in ev. Joh.* 122.7): 'Many come into the Church whom we do not want, and many leave whose exit we regret' (*En. in Ps.* 147.9).

There remained resentful pagans, whose loathing of the church was particularly felt when Christians fasted at the time of traditional pagan festivals. Pagan priests were no longer allowed to offer sacrifice and had to perform their rites in secret (62.28). The evangelist's task remained that of removing idolatry not merely from the temples but from the hearts of people (60.8).

But when pagans complain of bad times, what they really mean is that they want more material luxuries, the cruelty of the amphitheatres which is the delight of the demons, the pornography of the theatres, the uncontrollable irrationality of horse racing at the circus.[30] Contentiousness is the natural state of unredeemed society with all the animosity of litigation, rival claims for actors and charioteers, and those who fight wild beasts going 'over the top' with absurd excitement. What a paradox that pagans become passionate partisans of this or that actor or jockey, and yet these are occupations which they despise; the last thing they wish to be is an actor or jockey themselves (62.3; cf. *Conf.* IV.14,22). It qualifies their complaints of hard times that they still have costly public shows (12.14). If times really were hard, that would teach us not to love earthly pleasures, and should be welcomed as providential therapy (12.16). It is no bad thing that amphitheatres are collapsing (13.13).

If there was a *dies muneris* with a show at the amphitheatre, then Augustine knew what temptations and dissensions this would bring to many of his congregation. It divided families when he asked them to observe a fast on the Kalends of January (62.7). Significantly the very fact that the church was demanding a fast made them resistant and unwilling to fast (62.6). One recalls Priscillian's troubles in Spain when he recommended fasting on 25 December.[31] Moreover, Augustine was disturbed to meet some Christians who thought pagan religion a possible and legitimate alternative route to the transcendent deity and defended it for others (60.10). Evidently there were echoes of Porphyry and of Symmachus's plea to Gratian that to so impenetrable a mystery there cannot be only one road. An embarrassed author of *Retractationes* found that he had said much the same himself in the inexperience of comparative youth.[32]

The sermon for 1 January shows how anxious he was to persuade his people that at the celebrations of martyrs' anniversaries they were not trying

---

30. Similarly *Ep.* 138.14 to Marcellinus: distorted human hearts reckon prosperity by fine buildings, theatrical shows, actors living in 'luxury' (no doubt meaning immorality). Ovid, *Tristia* 2.280ff., draws a picture of the Roman theatre closely resembling Augustine's. M 62.7 observes that few pagans are now attending the theatre.

31. Turibius of Astorga complained to Pope Leo I that Priscillianists fasted on the day of Christ's Nativity (Leo, *Ep.* 15.4, *PL* 54.632A; critical edition in B. Vollmann, *Studien zum Priszillianismus* (St. Ottilien, 1965). The first council of Bracara echoed this grumble.

32. Augustine, *Retractationes* i.4.3. This defence of polytheism as a possible path to the sublimity of God appears in the correspondence of Longinianus with Augustine (*Ep.* 234) who also defended theurgy.

to placate the holy saint, to persuade and cajole him or her into interceding for them. All our prayers are to God, not to the martyrs (62.47). And of course we never pray for martyrs (50.1). It is very wrong to suppose that the angels who are invoked, especially Gabriel and Michael, are like corrupt court officials who demand a douceur as the price of furthering one's petition or cause (62.48). The tough realities of the way to get things done in the political world deeply influenced attitudes to the angels and saints. In the *City of God* (21.27) fear is expressed that people who make little effort to behave with righteousness think the saints will compensate for their defects.

A few other texts of Augustine referring to the eucharistic sacrifice (notably the most important of all in *Contra adversarium legis et prophetarum* i) show sensitivity to the need to avoid the notion of worshippers using Christ's sacrifice as a kind of bribe to the Father to gain mercy.

The New Year sermon (M 62) is insistent that all Christian prayer is offered to Christ and, in the sacraments of the church, is directed on to the Father (62.49). The eucharist participates in Christ's heavenly intercession with the Father (62.57). Although bishops are given the title of priests, *sacerdotes,* in truth Christians have in Christ their one and only priest (62.49). And his mother Mary herself, by virtue of her relationship to Elizabeth, was of priestly descent (62.50).

François Dolbeau's momentous discovery has greatly enriched our knowledge of Augustine and his time.[33]

---

33. An admirable general survey of the Mainz collection is given by F. Dolbeau in *CR Acad. Inscr.,* 1993, pp. 153–71.

A new sermon on physical health is now printed in REAug 40 (1995), 279–303 from a codex in Heidelberg University library.

On Re-reading the *Confessions*

In this notable conference we commemorate a momentous event in the life of Augustine, his ordination to the presbyterate, for which at the time he felt no enthusiasm. Augustine wanted to be a monk, not an urban priest or diocesan bishop, and during his years as a layman he made a systematic point of not visiting churches which were looking for a suitable bishop.[1] The coercion of Valerius's little congregation at Hippo was not unusual at that time and place as a route to the priesthood. Augustine himself tells us that most clergy in North Africa had been ordained *violentia populorum.*[2] In his *Questions on the Heptateuch* he has occasion to observe that ordination is a call of the Church which cannot be refused without forfeiting the respect of the community.[3] To refuse would be to declare oneself the man entrusted with a single talent who selfishly buried it in the earth.[4] Nevertheless, candor requires note of the facts that the clergy of the North African churches were far fewer than the pastoral needs of the people demanded,[5] that it appears

1. *Serm.* 355.2.
2. *De coniugiis adulterinis* 2.22 (*CSEL* 41.409.15). It would be unsafe to use the riot of the Hippo poor which was intended to force ordination on the wealthy Pinianus as a basis for arguing that Augustine also came of a rich family, and so was economical with the truth in describing his family estate as relatively poor, "a few acres" (*Epist.* 126.7). However, the fact that Augustine recalls the admiration people felt for his renunciation of his inheritance no doubt implies that the farm was more substantial than a peasant's small holding. It was simply not comparable with the great estates of his patron Romanianus.
3. *Qu. in Hept.* 4.54.
4. *De fide et op.* 32; cf. *Serm.* 339.
5. Aurelius of Carthage at a council of 16 June 401 bewailed "the great shortage of clergy, many churches being so deserted that they are found to have not even one deacon, and that illiterate" (*Conciliae Africae,* ed. C. Munier, *CCSL* 149, p. 194). Augustine (*Trac.*

frequently to have been the case that the plebs, whose voice in an election could be considerable, were more inclined to look for a bishop to answer their temporal concerns than for one whose ministry might so make them weep for their sins as to get them to heaven,[6] and that Augustine utters misgivings at the practice of seizing laity to be priests and bishops against their will.[7] The method did not always produce ideal results.

In the Western Church we have become influenced by a pietist expectation that the initiative in offering for ordination will lie with the postulant, who decides to be a candidate because his heart has been strangely warmed, because he, or indeed she, feels a sense of inward calling by an incommunicable divine monition, which the overt and public act of prayer and laying on of hands by a bishop in Catholic communion hardly does more than acknowledge as an almost inherent right. In the Eastern Orthodox churches there is perhaps a more obvious belief that the initiative lies with the Church: the individual receives the divine call by and through the community, which may use some pressure on an apparently qualified but reluctant candidate who is morally obliged to submit and may be dragged before the bishop by large men resembling wrestlers.

The classic ancient instance in the Greek world is the contemporary narrative of the ordination to the priesthood of the stylite saint Daniel, whose pillar stood on the European shore of the Bosporus (by Rumeli-Hisar) during the reign of the emperor Leo, twenty-five years after Augustine's death. At the emperor's order the ecumenical patriarch solemnly proceeded to the foot of the column; but the holy man refused leave for the ladder to be placed so that the patriarch might ascend for spiritual conversation. The day became hotter. After several hours the exhausted patriarch raised his hands and ordained Daniel from a distance and in defiance of his reluctance. Daniel bowed in submission, allowed the patriarch to ascend, and concelebrated

---

Joh. 57.5 and *Epist.* 22+, Divjak) bears this out. The Catholic community in Numidia was painfully short of Punic-speaking clergy who could be entrusted with ex-Donatist congregations: hence, the dreadful affair of Antoninus, consecrated for such a church at Fussala on the edge of the Hippo diocese and then turning out to be a disaster. On the desperate need for Punic-speaking clergy, see Augustine, *Epist.* 84.2; 209.3.

6. This attitude is strikingly expressed to Sidonius Apollinaris by a church which desired a new bishop "more competent to intercede with an earthly judge for our bodies than with a heavenly judge for our souls" (*Epist.* 7.9.9). Augustine observed that the mass movement to join the Church in his time was motivated by hope for temporal aid, not for eternal life (*Enarr.* 46.5). Cf. *Trac. Joh.* 122.7 on mass conversions with unreformed morals.

7. *Epist.* 173.2; *Sermo ad Caesariensis ecclesiae plebem* 8 (*Bibliothèque Augustinienne* 32.443).

with him at the top of the column.[8] (Pillar saints had a flat platform on top of their column, but two celebrants may well have been a little precarious.)

Reluctance to be ordained was not universal. Constantine the Great had worries about keen candidates whose main motive in seeking ordination was to be free of curial duties.[9] As Church resources grew, the social rather than the pastoral and sacramental duties of a bishop made the position attractive. The office of bishop or even of presbyter was held in honor; unlike the deacon, the presbyter had a seat in the apse and acted as assessor in the bishop's court.[10] The bishop naturally had a prestige which a presbyter did not, and at Hippo there were those who misread Augustine's tears at the moment of his ordination to mean that his ambitions to be a bishop *per saltum* were being disappointed.[11] A bishop had an apostolic commission: he was the source of order, and thereby embodied visibly and tangibly the continuity, universality, and legitimacy of the community and of the sacraments entrusted to him. It was distinctly unusual for a presbyter to do much preaching, if he were attached to the cathedral where the bishop was the normal teacher,[12] just as he was also the regular minister of baptism and president of the eucharistic synaxis. Presbyters who baptized and celebrated were likely to be assigned to rural congregations, or to the suburbs of large cities.

Bishops enjoyed some perquisites of office. One of Cyprian's letters (65.3) speaks of ambitious men wanting to be bishops "for the fees and presents and profits, the grand dinners and banquets," and an alarming chapter of his *De lapsis* (6) describes some bishops as principally using the office

---

8. See the *Life of Saint Daniel the Stylite* 42. Text in H. Delehaye, *Les Saints Stylites* (Brussels: Société des Bollandistes, 1923), 38f.; English translation in Elizabeth Dawes and Norman H. Baynes, *Three Byzantine Saints* (Oxford: Blackwell, 1948), 31f.

9. *Cod. Theod.* 16.2.6 of 326, a law which proposed the impossible rule that a man could be ordained only as a replacement for one who had died. Basil the Great had to cope with men wanting to be subdeacons to avoid military conscription; they did not want to be deacons or presbyters (*Epist.* 54).

10. Cyprian (*Epist.* 39.5.2) speaks of "honorem presbyterii"; cf. 1.1.1: "conpresbyteri nostri qui nobis adsidebant".

11. Possidius, *Vita Augustini* 4, following Augustine, *Epist.* 21.

12. For sermons by presbyters, see *Serm.* 20.4; 137.11 and 13; *Epist.* 41; 63.2–5; 65; 251. In the absence of the bishop, the presbyters would preside at the eucharistic offering (*Serm.* 227). Possidius (*Vita Augustini* 5.3) records that until Augustine was ordained by Valerius in 391, it was quite contrary to African usage for a presbyter to preach in his bishop's presence. Pope Celestine (*Epist.* 21, *Patrologia Latina* 50.528–29) warns the bishops of Provence against presbyters taking on themselves unauthorized teaching roles, forgetful that the disciple is not above his master.

to feather their own nests. Augustine once wrote to warn a newly elected Donatist bishop to beware of the silk coverings on his throne and the choir of nuns singing him into his seat: *Transit gloria mundi.*[13]

Augustine the ascetic was speaking in that letter. At heart he was always, after July 386, a monk on his guard against the pleasures of the senses, the hollow crowns of honor and wealth, the insidiousness of flattery. His biography might be summarized as that of a bookish but highly sexed man who painfully brought himself to renounce marriage and a secular career to become a contemplative ascetic, but who was then dragged from his quiet quasi-monastic life to serve a troubled and turbulent church which needed him as a pastor and defender of the faith. The *Confessions* tell the first stage in some detail, and explain how the young man, who took to his bed a low-class but Catholic girl-friend at Carthage,[14] nevertheless joined the sect of the Manichees for whom procreation was a forbidden act, and who thought of sexual intercourse as a diabolical invention.[15] They go on to tell how he lost confidence in Manichee mythology, became drawn toward Neoplatonic mystical quests for which, once more, sexual acts were not thought to be desirable,[16] and finally returned to the Catholic faith and practice of his mother having made the surprising discovery that the Catholica had room for lay ascetic communities. The *Confessions* do not directly record anything of his reaction to the ordination of 391, six or seven years before the composition of the book. Yet the book reveals obliquely a number of things about his understanding of ordination, and in this paper I hope to submit evidence to support that proposition.

In the first place, we may remind ourselves that the work popularly thought of as a candid catalogue of moral transgressions, publicly coming clean about a too colorful past, is in effect an essay in self-defense rather than

13. *Epist.* 23.3. Cf. *Serm.* 23.1.

14. That it was common for a young man to take a consort from the lower classes but then to separate from her is attested explicitly in Firmicus Maternus's handbook of astrology (*Mathesis* 5.3.16). Cf. the attack on the practice by Caesarius of Arles, *Serm.* 43 (*CCSL* 103.190f.).

15. *De moribus* 2.63; *C. duas epist. Pelag.* 4.4 (all procreation is the work of the prince of darkness). The Manichee demand for sexual continence was admired by Alypius who felt revulsion from sex after an adolescent experience (*Conf.* 6.21f.). To Hearers, however, sexual intercourse was allowed during the "safe" period of the menstrual cycle (*De moribus* 2.65).

16. Porphyry's maxim was that, for the higher life, "one must flee from everything bodily": *omne corpus est fugiendum* (*De regressu animae* cited in *Civ. Dei* 10.29; 12.27; 22.12.26–28; *Serm.* 241.7; criticized in *Civ. Dei* 13.17). Porphyry's principle is stated in his letter to his wife Marcella (35) quoting a Pythagorean maxim "Never use your bodily members merely for pleasure" (paralleled in the *Sentences* of Sextus 232).

in self-accusation. The double sense of the Latin *confessio,* meaning both admission of fault and praise, helped Augustine here. He can praise his Maker not only for the redeeming grace which has rescued him from a life alienated from God, but also for the splendid personal endowments of a good memory, facility in the use of the Latin language, and a rare gift for friendship.[17]

As all students know, the autobiographical sections are not quite a simple record. Important theological theses are being illustrated by the autobiographical matter: the theme that the soul here is a pilgrim which has wandered from its true home in God and is, by grace, finding its way back again—and in this regard is a microcosm of the entire created order; the grinding theme that the only thing wholly his own which sinful man can contribute to salvation is sin.[18] At one point he even states this last point in the surely exaggerated form that sin is all that he imparted to his clever natural son Adeodatus.[19]

At the same time, there is a continual awareness of critics who thought a poor training for pastoral ministry a past life of sexual irregularity,[20] Manichee heresy, skeptical philosophy, and highly secular employment—teaching pagan literature soaked in idolatry and fornication, and purveying to the young the meretricious arts of rhetoric for a remunerative career in the law courts.[21]

When he became a presbyter, Augustine asked Bishop Valerius for time off to study the Bible, of which he felt too ignorant.[22] The study of Holy Scripture, so repellent to him at the age of eighteen, now had an extraordinary effect once he had assimilated Ambrose's principle of spiritual interpretation.[23] His excellent memory was an ideal tool for bringing together texts from very remote parts of the Bible and from different contexts. How deep an effect ordination brought to his mind is writ large in his writings. When he himself drew up his own reckoning of his published works in the *Retractationes,* he not only recorded no comment on anything written before

17. *Conf.* 1.31; 4.30–31.

18. *Trac. Joh.* 5.1 (cited by the Council of Orange, 529, canon 22); *Enarr.* 58.1.19; 44.7; 126.4; *De doctr. christ.* 2.25.39; *Serm.* 32.10 (remove sin and what you see remaining in man is of God); *Serm. Denis* 18.2 (p. 92, 11 Morin) "Non esse in nobis nostrum nisi peccatum"; *Serm. Mai* 101.2 (p. 352, 25, Morin) "Homo sine Deo nihil potest nisi peccare." *Civ. Dei* 14.4.1; and elsewhere.

19. *Conf.* 9.14.

20. *Enarr.* 36.3.19: "People know my evil past, especially here in Carthage" (probably preached at the end of 403).

21. *Conf.* 1.26.

22. *Epist.* 21.

23. *Conf.* 6.6.

his conversion (such as the study of aesthetic theory, *De pulchro et apto*), but also divided the reappraisal into two sections. The point of division comes at his ordination as a bishop. Ordination, first as presbyter then as bishop, came to mark watersheds in his life as a Christian.

His letters give a vivid portrait of the endless distractions to which the life of an urban priest and bishop was vulnerable. Augustine never resented the provision of help for orphans, foundlings, those whose names were on the church list for receiving financial support. (The *matricula pauperum* is a phrase which Augustine first attests.)[24] In his preaching, the duty of almsgiving is a prominent theme.[25] In *The City of God* we find the observation born of experience that the problem of poverty was too great to be solved by private charity and could be met only by state action and some measure of redistributive taxation.[26] So the fostering of works of mercy was part of the vocation of the clergy, never to be grumbled at. The more secular aspect of the calling, however, was less congenial. The writing of recommendations to get good jobs for supportive members of the congregation was faintly distasteful, though it was the accepted system.[27] (He liked to quote a wise man's saying: "I have too much regard for my own reputation to vouch for that of my friends.")[28] The worst part of a bishop's task, to which the presbyters acted as assessors, was the Monday morning court for arbitrations between quarrelling members of the flock.[29]

The duty of episcopal arbitrations arose from the apostle's stern precept that the Corinthians must never take their disagreements before the secular

24. For orphans (*De pecc. merit.* 3.13.22; *Serm.* 176.2). Foundlings (*C. duas epist. Pelag.* 2.11; *Epist.* 98.6). *Matricula Pauperum* (*Epist.* 20.2, Divjak). On later developments, see M. Rouché in Michel Mollat, *Études sur l'histoire de la pauvreté* (Paris: Publications de la Sorbonne, 1974), 83–110.

25. The best discussion of Augustine on poverty remains that of H. Rondet in the volume *S. Augustin parmi nous* (Le Puy, 1954). Typical exhortations are *Serm.* 25.8; 178.4; 259.5 (share in a common humanity). I discuss patristic notions of "humanity" in the *Reallexikon für Antike und Christentum,* article "Humanität" (1993).

26. *Civ. Dei* 5.17.

27. *Epist.* 151.2 to the prefect Caecilian; cf. 155.11 to Macedonius.

28. Possidius, *Vita Augustini* 20.1 "... quod multa suae famae contemplatione amicis non praestitisset." I am not aware that the maxim is otherwise attested. The saying cited in *Vita Augustini* 19.2 is found in, e.g., *Gnomologium Vaticanum* 150, ed. Stembach (Berlin: de Gruyter, 1963), 65. Its occurrence in Diogenes Laertius i 57 is noted by M. Marin in *Vetera Christianorum* 17 (1980), 119–24.

29. On Monday arbitrations (*Didascalia Apostolorum* 2.47, p. 111). Connolly = *Apost. Const.* 2.47. The bishop's judgment was regarded as invalid unless confirmed by the presence of his clergy (*Statuta Ecclesiae Antiqua* 14, p. 81, Munier).

magistrates, whose authority "counts for nothing in the Church" (1 Cor. 4:6). If the dispute was between rich and poor, there was especially high tension. God, cries Augustine in the *Confessions* (12.34), is the very life of the poor. A bishop was expected to be a voice for the powerless, voiceless, landless, oppressed, destitute, whose perpetual temptation was to solve the problem of their hunger by stealing.[30] Admittedly Augustine would note that the number of truly destitute were few, but relative poverty was a considerable social factor,[31] and the clergy were expected to exercise bias in favor of this category. Yet, the rich man in the bishop's court could be entirely in the right in terms of the law of private property, and to decide against him was sure to incur anger and resentment against the arbitrating bishop. "Mercy to the poor is not justice."[32] In the sermons on Saint John he recalled a painful case between father and son where he had decided for the son.[33] Ambrose found the experience of arbitrating between disputing members of the same family particularly awful, and in his work *On Duties* he advised bishops to decline money disputes.[34]

There were also delicate issues when property was bequeathed to the church and aggrieved heirs wanted to dispute the legacy.[35] Augustine as bishop found himself the object of obloquy in his congregation because of his reluctance to accept for the church chest legacies which left the children short of resources.[36] In the church at Hippo he found himself surrounded by detractors,[37] though there were certainly impassioned admirers, too, for whom no sermon by their bishop could go on too long.[38]

Politically delicate situations could arise when asylum was sought at the church by slaves on the run from cruel punishments or by pathetic debtors

---

30. *Enarr.* 61.16; cf. 72.12.

31. *Serm.* 14.5.

32. *Enarr.* 32.2.12. A bishop became cordially hated by whichever party lost the case under his arbitration (*Serm.* 125.8).

33. *Trac. Joh.* 30.8.

34. Ambrose, *De officiis* 2.24.124ff.

35. Bishops were instructed by African canon law that if Church property was claimed by someone else, the clergy were not to yield (evidently in the hope that abdication of rights might make the Church more popular); see *Conciliae Africae,* ed. Munier, p. 49. Augustine regretted that the plebs expected the clergy to neglect their pastoral office, even to the extent of being absent for a year or more, so as to combat attempts to deprive the Church of its due revenues for feeding the poor (*Epist.* 21.5).

36. *Serm.* 355.

37. *Epist.* 124.2.

38. One lengthy sermon includes a prayer that God would give them physical strength to hear him to the end (*Enarr.* 49.29).

being hunted by the authorities. Augustine did not defend inviolable asylum for known criminals and perjurers, but otherwise he thought it socially justifiable.[39] For those who experience secular society as violent and unjust, sanctuary is a lifeline. In the *Confessions* he writes of the obligation to "rescue a person suffering injustice from the hands of the powerful and provide the shelter of protection by the mighty force of just judgment" (13.21). A bishop was expected to be the advocate if one of his flock was in trouble with the magistrate or the taxman. As we should expect, civil governors could be deeply irritated by episcopal interventions. Both Basil and Augustine record how ineffective their intercessions often were.[40] In one famous sermon Augustine rather bitterly reminds his congregation how long he was kept waiting at the governor's office before he was coldly granted a hearing for an intercession on their behalf.[41] "No one who has not been a bishop would ever believe what people expect us to do."[42]

39. There is a partial collection of Augustine's evidence in Jean Gaudemet's article, "Asylum," in the *Augustinus Lexikon*. Asylum in churches was not legally recognized at the time of the writing of the *Confessions,* but was nevertheless respected by the authorities: so *Serm. Denis* 19.2 (p. 99, 28ff., Morin). Augustine defended the necessity of this kind of sanctuary (*S. Guelf.* 25, p. 529, Morin) but not inviolable asylum for acknowledged criminals and perjurers (*Epist.* 1+, Divjak). He was sad that the intervention of the Church was seldom effective: only "very few" cases were successfully defended (*Epist.* 22+, Divjak). On runaway slaves (*Trac. Joh.* 41.4). In the case of the debtor who sought the "help" of the Church (*Epist.* 268.1), Augustine paid out seventeen solidi for which he asks reimbursement. In 399 the Council of Carthage sent two bishops to ask the emperor Honorius to enact the right of sanctuary in churches (*Reg. eccl. Carth.* 56, p. 194, Munier).

40. Basil, *Epist.* 72–73; *Epist.* 112 requests the release from prison of an admitted criminal, and perhaps the letter survives because the improbable application was successful. Augustine, *Epist.* 22+, Divjak. Too many judicial decisions were determined by class or improper influence and bribery, as Augustine complained (*Trac. Joh.* 27.10). He held up the model of Alypius's integrity in *Conf.* 6.16. It was a delicate matter when Macedonius, vicarius Africae 413–414, responded to Augustine's intercession on a man's behalf by saying that he felt able to be lenient only when asked by entirely reliable intercessors and that interventions by bishops could prevent justice being done (see *Epist.* 152–54). Synesius (*Epist.* 121) refused intercession for an adulterator of wine.

41. *Serm.* 302.17. Synesius, writing as a layman, found excessive and burdensome the crowd of petitioners asking for his intercession with the governor Pentadius, and wrote to Pentadius telling him to shut the door in his face when he came on behalf of the petitioners. Only so could he and the governor have any respite (*Epist.* 29). *Epist.* 30 shows him being more positive. As bishop he was sharply rebuffed by the governor Andronicus (*Epist.* 42, Garzya = 58 Hercher). At Milan, Macedonius, Master of the Offices to Valentinian II, resorted to locking his door to repel intercession by Ambrose. He was to regret that when he himself sought asylum after Gratian's murder (Paulinus, *Vita Ambrosii* 37).

42. *De opere monachorum* 29.37. Augustine there observes that his social and secular

The high profile of the bishop of Hippo was enhanced by the acclaim accorded to his writings, at least after the publication of the *Confessions,* which rapidly became a best-seller, though the book had some severe critics. The lead which he took in organizing the rebuttal of the Donatist majority in Numidia and his repute as a preacher and disputant brought him constant demands to visit other churches, to be the "keynote" speaker or visiting preacher,[43] e.g., if a wealthy benefactor had provided a new basilica,[44] or if a disagreement had to be settled in an episcopal election where the congregation wanted the son of their former bishop translated from a nearby see and where the consecrating provincial bishops thought this choice strikingly inappropriate.[45] The time-consuming and exasperating affair of Antoninus of Fussala brought him to threaten resignation if the Roman see were to support this criminous clerk whose diocese found his rule insufferable.[46] Truly, ordination brought him a heavy burden of duty far beyond that of pastoral and sacramental ministry, the *sarcina episcopi.*[47]

"By this book I am confessing to you who I now am, not what I once was" (10.4), and how "you brought me to preach your word and dispense your sacrament" (11.1). The *Confessions* answer accusations. At the time when the elderly primate of Numidia Proconsularis, Megalius of Calama, was asked by Valerius of Hippo to consecrate Augustine to be his coadjutor bishop, Megalius initially wrote a letter expressing consternation at the proposal.[48] The African churches too well remembered Augustine's combative

---

responsibilities left him no time for his real tasks. *Epist.* 213.5 records how the plebs at Hippo solemnly undertook in writing to allow him five days a week for study and failed to keep to the agreement. He used to work far into the night (*Epist.* 139.3; Possidius, *Vita Augustini* 24.11: "in die laborans, et in nocte lucubrans").

43. Possidius, *Vita Augustini* 9.1.

44. The consecration of new churches is mentioned in several passages of Augustine, e.g., *Enarr.* 29.2.6–9; *Serm.* 27.1; 116.7; 163; 336.1. Ancient evidence on the consecration of buildings is gathered in J. Bingham, *Antiquities of the Christian Church,* book 8, chap. 9, and E. Martène, *De antiquis ecclesiae ritibus* III, book 2, chap. 13; M. Andrieu, *Les Ordines Romani du haut moyen âge* 4 (1956), 359–84; P. Puniet in *Dict. d'Arch. Chrét. et Lit.* 4 (1921), 374–404.

45. *Epist.* 22+, Divjak; summary in *Journal of Theological Studies,* n.s., 34 (1983), 445. The Divjak letters are translated into English by R. B. Eno in *Fathers of the Church,* vol. 81 (1989).

46. *Epist.* 209.10 to Fabiola, whose support Antoninus was enlisting.

47. On *sarcina episcopi,* see M. Jourjon in *Recherches de science religieuse* 43 (1955), 258–64.

48. Possidius (*Vita Augustini* 8.2) says that Valerius first obtained clearance for Augustine's consecration not from the primate of Numidia but from Aurelius, primate of Carthage. The move may reflect anxiety on some of the matters which Megalius was to raise.

Manicheism, humiliating half-educated bishops with his criticisms of the Old Testament.[49] His activities encouraging the founding of monastic communities in Africa aroused widespread alarm: were they Manichee cells in disguise? The ascetic movement, with which Augustine was fully identified, was under severe criticism in the 380s and 390s from Christians who thought it Manichee infiltration. Augustine claimed to have been baptized by Ambrose at Milan. Custom prescribed that a bishop should write to the home church from which a candidate for baptism came, inquiring into his good character and conduct. Had Ambrose written to Thagaste or to Carthage? An unpleasant report said that, to a distressed lady who had become part of a "triangle" and whose marriage was in trouble, Augustine had responded by giving some blessed bread which had been interpreted as a love-charm to foster her adulterous desires.[50]

So in the *Confessions* Augustine will describe how he came to be enrolled for baptism, together with Alypius and his natural son Adeodatus. Characteristically, the *Confessions* do not specifically mention Ambrose as the baptizer, though that was certainly so.[51] He will describe how his liaison with his son's mother had been one of mutual fidelity, ended because of her inappropriateness as consort for an aspirant to be governor of a minor province and because, in a world where all public offices were for sale, his ambition could be realized only with the dowry of a rich wife. So he will use his autobiographical record to show how, in astonishing ways of which at

---

The Numidian primate may have felt himself diminished and slighted by Valerius's resort to Carthage; it was generally acknowledged that the bishop of Carthage was primate over all the African provinces (see *Concilia Africae,* ed. Munier, pp. 269–70, citing a council of Hippo in 393). Megalius's letter fell into Donatist hands (*C. litt. Petil.* 3.19; *C. Cresc.* 3.92 and 4.64). Petilian used it to flog Augustine at the Catholic/Donatist conference at Carthage in 411 (*Gesta coll. Carth.* 3.243–247, ed. Lancel, *Sources Chrétiennes* 224, 1181–87; and Augustine, *Brev. coll.* 3.9). In 397 news of Megalius's death led Augustine to reflect on his need to sublimate anger lest it turn to hatred (*Epist.* 38.2). Megalius's withdrawal and apology for his letter and willingness to consecrate Augustine at Hippo had not wholly healed the scar.

49. See *Serm.* 51.6, which is paralleled in part in *Conf.* 9.11. *Conf.* 4.26 records his harassment of uneducated Catholic Christians.

50. Much of the third book, *Contra litteras Petiliani,* deals with these "calumnies." On questions about his baptism, see *Enarr.* 36.3.19; *C. Cresc.* 4.54; *C. litt. Petil.* 3.28. Even if it were true that Augustine was baptized in Italy, that would not commend him to Donatists for whom the Church in Italy was polluted by compromise. That clergy were occasionally invited to perform like sorcerers to further amatory affairs is also attested in Augustine (*De continentia* 27), and in Jerome's *Life of St. Hilarion* 21.

51. Augustine's *Epist.* 147.52 and *De nuptiis et concupiscentia* 1.40 are explicit that "by Ambrose's priestly office I received the washing of regeneration."

the time he was unaware, long before his conversion and baptism at Milan, God was preparing him to be a dispenser of the word and sacraments to the people of God.

It follows that the *Confessions* are being misinterpreted if we start complaining about episodes that Augustine may have omitted.[52] The episodes recorded are there to illustrate one or other of his central themes, and above all aim to justify himself against those critics who judged him unsuitable for the episcopate. He saw a mysterious hidden providence in the succession of events which brought him to Ambrose at Milan. He left Thagaste because every street corner vividly recalled the memory of the dead young friend to whom he had been deeply attached (4.12). He left Carthage because the students were turbulent (3.6; 5.14). He found Rome uncomfortable because the students there were not honest about paying him their proper fees (a dishonesty precisely paralleled for the pagan Palladas at Alexandria at the same time).[53] He got the post at Milan because influential Manichee friends put his name to the militantly pagan city prefect Symmachus. Symmachus gave him an audition and no doubt satisfied himself that Augustine was no Catholic Christian and could safely be recommended for the appointment in close contact with the imperial court of Valentinian II. The moves which he had made were not in the least motivated by a desire to serve God and his Church. Yet that was how it had fallen out. "At Milan I came to Ambrose the bishop . . ." (5.23).

Repeatedly in the *Confessions* Augustine stresses that what is to our human minds mere chance is not fortuitous at all. In retrospect a wise providence is discernibly at work. By chance in a lecture at Carthage attended by Alypius, Augustine (at that period still a Manichee Hearer) happened to include a scornful aside about people addicted to the low pleasure of the circus; the words felt like an arrow in the mind of Alypius. How providential, too, that when Alypius was falsely accused of attempted theft by the Carthaginian silversmiths, he had the luck to be seen by an influential friend, the city architect, who had often met him at a senator's soirées, and then to run into the slave-boy of the real thief. "The future dispenser of God's word and examiner of many arbitrations in God's Church went away with increased experience and wisdom" (6.15).

Just as the adolescent Augustine was carried off by the other boys at

---

52. *Conf.* 9.17 is explicit that he has omitted much.

53. *Conf.* 5.22. Palladas, in the *Palatine Anthology* 9.174, complains that his pupils would suddenly leave as they were due to pay their yearly fee of a single gold solidus.

Thagaste to steal pears, an act which "alone he could never have done," so, too, Alypius would learn the power of the gang and the intoxication of an excited crowd when he was captivated by the blood-lust of the amphitheater. "He was not now the person who had come in but merely one of the crowd." That was eventually to teach him that without God's help the human will can be swept into irrationality and surrender to inebriating pleasures that diminish one's humanity (6.13).

Because the one and only source of real goodness is grace, if someone is reformed in character, the reformation does not result from the clever rhetoric of the preacher but from a hidden divine power (9.18). Human life apart from this saving grace is an experience of incoherent mess, of a chaotic sequence of events where the best laid plans can be suddenly overthrown, where storms of meaningless events tear one's thoughts to pieces. Augustine the bishop knew in what bewildering times he was living; inward security and unity would come only at that final day when "purified and molten by the fire of God's love, I flow in a single stream which merges into God himself" (11.39, cf. 10.39).

Augustine understood his mastery of Latin rhetoric and his facility in expressing himself as a gift of natural endowment, not implanted or even much fostered by the rotten teachers he encountered at Thagaste, Madauros, or even Carthage. From this perhaps comes his skepticism as to whether skill in public speaking was something capable of being imparted to somebody not possessing the innate gift for it (8.13). This secular school of oratory and literature was assuredly corrupt, a meretricious business of selling the arts of flattery and deception. All the emphasis was on a well-turned elegance of style indifferent to moral content: *integritas verborum* mattered far more than *veritas rerum* (*Trin.* 14.11.14). It was therefore understandable that some Christians are put on their guard if polish and high style are employed to present truth; insofar as a fine style does not make anything true, they are right (*Conf.* 5.10). Yet provided one is deploying verbal skill on the side of truth, not in opposition to it, that is good (*C. Faustum* 14.9).

Accordingly, the story of Marius Victorinus's conversion, which fills some pages of Book 8 of the *Confessions,* is more than a model for the conversion of a leading intellectual like Augustine himself, and no doubt like some of the readers he hoped to address. The paradoxical welcome given by Rome's outstanding teacher of rhetoric and logic to the emperor Julian's prohibition of Christians from teaching literature and oratory showed Victorinus's complete dedication of his skills to a higher and sacred end, the communication of divine truth (8.7).

The extent to which Augustine thought of his preaching task as an extension of a pedagogic vocation may be illustrated by remarks in a letter he wrote to his friend in the government service, Marcellinus (*Epist.* 138.10): "Church congregations are like comprehensive public schools where the pupils are distinctive in being of both sexes and of all ages and social classes. In this school the less intelligent need a teacher with skills in communication; they need not only to be taught but persuaded."[54] For the stupid therefore, rather than for the highly educated élite, there is an ancillary and supportive function for eloquence, which Augustine tersely defines as the use of language appropriate to the subject, the audience, and the circumstances.[55]

The *Confessions* insist that in the Church rich and poor, noble and low-born, are all equal (8.9). On no account may slaves be scorned or treated with inhumanity (13.22). In mind and intellectual power men and women are entirely equal, even though the woman's biological destiny is physically determined and gives her a subordinate and less public role (13.47). Moreover, spiritual judgment is exercised no less by spiritual laity than by the clergy. The perception of God's will for his Church is not only granted to the ordained but to all spiritual members (13.33). Congruent with this proposition is Augustine's profound antipathy toward a clericalized conception of the Church. Though usage applies the word *sacerdos* to bishops and presbyters, all Christians share in the one priest who is Christ (*Civ. Dei* 20.10). The name *pastor,* Shepherd, provokes equal coolness: there is only one shepherd, Christ himself, who is "bishop of bishops" (*Trac. Joh.* 123.5; *S. Guelf.* 32.8). Augustine censures Donatist language about the bishop in apostolic succession as exclusive mediator to God (*C. epist. Parm.* 2.8.15f.) or about the holy clergy obtaining for unworthy laity gifts they could not obtain for themselves (*C. litt. Petil.* 2.105.240f; *Enarr.* 36.2.20).

The truth of the preacher's message is grounded in the word of God conveyed, not exclusively, but in a special degree (*Serm.* 12.4) through the Scriptures which the Church accepts as its guiding rule or canon. The numerous difficulties which the sacred texts present are a signpost to the hidden mystery which they contain. That inner meaning is found only by grace, and therefore the young but undocile Augustine, stirred by his readings in Cicero's *Hortensias* to pick up his Latin Bible, found that once he had put it down, he could not pick it up again, repelled by the barbarous style and the translationese of the Old Latin version (3.9). Even at the time of his conver-

54. *De ordine* 2.13.38.
55. *C. litt. Petil.* 2.73.

sion at Milan he found incomprehensible the prophet Isaiah recommended to him by Ambrose: "I put it on one side to be resumed when I had had more practice in the Lord's style of language" (9.13).

Ordination required deeper study. During his five years as a layman he had continued writing on the liberal arts; the Cassiciacum dialogues censured in the *Confessions* (9.7) for the literary tone which some readers found too sophisticated and élitist (*De gen. c. Manich.* 1.1), too reminiscent of his old lecture room (though they were more Christian than Alypius thought appropriate); his first attempt at an anti-Manichee exposition of Genesis on creation; his assimilation of much from Porphyry in *De vera religione.* His direct engagement with the exegesis of Scripture remained superficial, and he knew it. His non-literal exposition of Genesis picked on two points important in the Manichee debate—first, that *In principio,* "In the beginning," is not to be taken in a temporal sense, but refers to Christ, and secondly that the matter created by God was "unformed," form being imparted as a second stage. Both themes were to be restated in the *Confessions.*

The African churches included many simple believers who took Genesis to be a handbook of creation science.[56] They were uncomfortable if they were told that the first chapter of Genesis was not intended to bear any literal sense. So two years after his ordination to be presbyter Augustine began an unfinished literal commentary, composed with more than half an eye on literalists in the Church. The stress of the commentary lies on the uncertainty of the precise meaning of the creation narrative, and on the caution which is necessary in the interpretation of the text, provided that, where the essentials of the faith are concerned, there is no skeptical suspense of judgment. Even so, Augustine was also confident in this commentary that the matter created originally by God lacked form.

In the *Confessions* (12.17f.) we meet sharp polemic against Catholic critics of his exegetical work. The critics evidently thought that the clever presbyter of Hippo had expelled the Manichees at the price of inviting in the Platonists. Augustine retained lasting gratitude for what he had learned from the books of the Platonists. But he discerned a special hidden providence in the fact that he had read the Platonists first, before turning to his codex of Saint Paul. Had he read the Bible first and then gone on to study Plotinus and Porphyry, the experience might have disturbed his faith—for the Neoplatonists were in effect proposing an alternative and rival metaphysic which in Porphyry was intended to exclude Christianity. But the Platonists who saw the goal

---

56. *De genesi ad litteram* 1.19.38–39.

from a great distance did not know the road that gets one there. They knew nothing of "the price of our redemption" (Augustine's regular phrase for the eucharist)[57] nor the need for humility and confession (*Conf.* 7.26–27).[58]

Neoplatonism was an important bridge in his conversion from a Manichee understanding of the problem of evil, which Mani had solved by limiting divine power to eliminate it. Neoplatonism helped him toward a Catholic acceptance of the world as a manifestation of divine power and goodness stamped with rationality and mathematical order. In the last four books of the *Confessions* Augustine would no longer look back on the path which had brought him to conversion and the realization of Monica's hopes and tearful prayers. He reached the point of describing his state of mind in the present, when he is writing as a recently consecrated bishop. Astonishingly there are few writings of Augustine more deeply impregnated with Neoplatonic themes, even to the extent of incorporating at one point a substantial piece of Neoplatonist exegesis (perhaps Porphyry's) of the last section of Aristotle's categories, discussing the multivalent concept of priority (12.40). Many Platonizing assumptions are made about the relation of mind and matter, which affect his evaluation of the sacraments in Book 13. At the same time he restates his exposition of the first chapter of Genesis, insisting against his critics that there is room for more than one correct interpretation of the sacred inspired text, subject to the proviso that the essentials of the apostolic faith are affirmed (12.27).

The duties of a city presbyter or bishop are not conducive to the contemplative life after which Augustine's soul always yearned. Rachel and Leah, Mary and Martha, symbolize the contemplative and the active; and in this life we are all Marthas who have to wait for the life to come to join Mary sitting at the Lord's feet. The nature of the pastoral ministry, however, means that if no time at all is devoted to meditative contemplation, the task becomes an intolerable burden.[59] So something of the monk's longing came through in the practical vision of the urban clergy.

Monks and urban clergy were frequently at odds; yet, they shared important concerns. The narrative in the *Confessions* leaves the clear impression

---

57. E.g., *Conf.* 10.70.

58. The revulsion with which cultivated Platonists regarded the Christian penitential system may be seen in the remarks of Celsus quoted by Origen (*C. Cels.* 6.15), contrasting its humiliations with Plato's serene words about humility in *Laws* 715e. Tertullian (*De paenitentia* 11) shows that many Christians recoiled from the public shame.

59. *Serm.* 169.17; *Trin.* 1.10.20; *S. Guelf.* 29.543–49, Morin; especially *C. Faustum* 22.52–54.

that by a series of providential accidents Augustine ended up unmarried. When he was young Monica had done nothing to encourage him to find a wife, not in the least because she foresaw a future bishop in her gifted son but because the wrong partner—perhaps the only class of wife that could be expected for the son of a small-time farmer in rural Thagaste—might obstruct the success of his secular career (2.8). So she tolerated his cohabitation with Adeodatus's mother as a temporary way of containing his sexual drive. The time came at Milan when Augustine's partner blocked his ambitions and had to be sent back to Carthage. Monica found for him a well-to-do bride, but providentially she was too young for a wedding to take place. Chest pains enforced resignation from his Milan teaching post, the work which he in any event had come to find mountingly uncongenial. The decision in Verecundus's garden at Milan in July 386 was to abandon his pursuit of a secular career financed by his bride's dowry—a reversal of intention which would have made him a very unattractive son-in-law in the eyes of his fiancée's parents.

There is a temptation to suggest that it is part of Augustine's justification of his decision for celibacy that he consistently represents his relation with Adeodatus's mother in very carnal terms, as merely self-indulgent lust in which thoughts of disciplined responsible parenthood played no part. The bond of love which both parents of Adeodatus felt for their originally unwanted son (4.2) suggests that there was more to the relationship than physical appetite. And the deep pain of their separation also suggests that the cohabitation was congenial even if her lack of education meant that she could not be his sparring partner in scintillating conversation[60]—a pleasure for which Augustine turned to his male friends like Nebridius. The portrait of his sexual relations with her looks part and parcel of his picture of his past life as so alienated from grace as to partake of the very nature of sin. For Adeodatus "the son of my sin," as for himself and Alypius, baptism at Easter 387 washed all this soiled past away (9.14).

The monk and the presbyter shared the Bible, but it was more his pastoral calling in ordination which taught him to devote himself to Scripture studies with a vehement dedication. This can only have seemed extraordi-

---

60. *De genesi ad litteram* 9.9. Nebridius, well-to-do son of a freedman with an estate near Carthage, was with Augustine at Milan and an intimate friend—"a most rigorous examiner of very difficult questions" (*Conf.* 6.17). He was not at Cassiciacum, but on returning to Africa brought his entire household over to Catholic allegiance. After his premature death, Augustine published their correspondence as a memorial to him (*Epist.* 3–14). A biography of Nebridius is given by A. Mandouze, *Prosopographie chrétienne du Bas-empire* 1 (Paris: Editions du Centre National de la Recherche Scientifique, 1982), 774–76.

nary to his former secular colleagues, offended by his renunciation of literary pursuits (1.22) which, on the opposite wing, were offensive to puritan Christians (9.3). One recalls Ponticianus's amazement at finding a codex of Saint Paul on the table of the city professor of rhetoric and literature (8.14). Augustine's confession of praise to his Creator includes the line "You are not irritated by the burning zeal with which I study your Scripture" (11.28). We may reasonably deduce that, though God was not irritated, some human contemporaries were. Are they to be understood as those Catholic exegetes to whom Augustine's expositions of Genesis were hard to take? or pagan *literati?* The latter are perhaps more likely.

If so, we may suggest that in the *Confessions* there is an undercurrent of apologetic addressed to a critical pagan intelligentsia, in whose eyes the Church was a collection of largely uneducated people. In the preface to *De doctrina christiana* Augustine frankly observes that the intellectual capacities of bishops in North Africa are low.[61] Congregations often consisted largely of elderly women.[62] A powerful court official like Ponticianus who often spent time praying at the church was surely exceptional (*Conf.* 8.14). The plebs whose voice was still influential in the choice of their bishop preferred wealthy candidates with low educational and spiritual qualifications rather than poor men with high qualifications (*Epist.* 167.18, written to Jerome). Admittedly, important cities liked bishops whose sermons showed rhetorical abilities.

No work by Augustine is composed in a more sophisticated Latin than the *Confessions*. Without being obsessed with rhyme, he certainly liked assonances and indulged himself with antitheses. It seems characteristic that in this prose-poem the passage most like poetry and least like plain prose is the "Tolle Lege" scene in the garden (8.29), when a major turning point in his life is written up in high style with literary echoes of Persius's *Satires* and Plotinus's *Enneades.*

The pagan intelligentsia who mocked the Christians for their lack of high culture were assuredly infuriated by the conversion and then the ordination of the most acute intelligence in the Latin West of their time. Augustine's writings are not normally decorated with literary allusions to Vergil, Terence, Sallust, and Cicero unless he is expecting to be read by readers who

---

61. Similar warnings that uneducated Catholic bishops and presbyters who cannot cope with Manichee attacks are not to be taken as representative occur in *De moribus* 1.1.

62. *Serm. Denis* 18.6, p. 96, 18, Morin, quotes as an insult hurled at a Christian who confesses he has just been to a church service: "Are you not ashamed to go where widows and old women go?"

would appreciate these allusions. I would therefore submit that there are latent in the *Confessions* elements both of self-vindication in relation to anxious Catholic critics needing reassurance about his past life and also of protreptic exhortation to conversion. By his ordination (as he was abrasively to inform the young Dioscorus who asked him for instruction in philosophy), he abandoned his teaching of those "arts which pagans call liberal and Christians call secular."[63] Ordination liberated him to be blissfully independent of the patronage system, the humiliating toadying of the powerful which was the only route to any considerable office of state, and even the toadying route had to be oiled with cash. He could view with a touch of detachment his old ambition for a career dependent on rich senators who could easily fall from power at the next palace revolution. That very precariousness was one of the factors that induced disillusion about a secular career (*Conf.* 8.15: "In that position what is not fragile and full of dangers?"). He despised the worldly values which priced a racehorse far higher than a skilled slave[64] and confused ends with means.[65] The *Confessions* speak always in an idealized way about clergy and about the ascetic "servants of God," and express scorn and accusation of the values of pagan society.

By implication, therefore, no work by Augustine reveals more about his understanding of the high calling of the priesthood, even though ordination is never a subject under discussion in the book.

63. *Civ. Dei* 6.2 The testy letter to Dioscorus (*Epist.* 118) is a fascinating document of cultural confrontation: a clever young man (Augustine's term for that is "a Greek") who is not a Christian turns to the bishop of Hippo to answer some questions on philosophical points in Cicero's dialogues, so that he is not put to shame when he goes to Greece and meets experts. After a lengthy and regrettably pompous rebuke to Dioscorus for asking such questions of a bishop, Augustine concludes by actually answering his questions arising from Cicero's *De natura deorum,* but refuses to consider Cicero's *Orator* and *De oratore* as unsuitable topics for a bishop to discuss.

64. *Civ. Dei* 11.16; *Enarr.* 143.10.

65. The perversion of humanity is to use ends and to enjoy means (*De diversis quaes.* 83.30; *Serm.* 21.3; *C. Faustum* 22.28).

Providence and the Problem of Evil in Augustine

With a few exceptions found among those who thought all religion superstition (*vera rel.* 69ff.), the predominant consensus of intellectual and educated people in Augustine's age held to belief in divine providence, both in the general order of things and in the particular, looking (through divination or charismatic figures) for individual guidance. Atheists, he once remarks, are as rare as Christians of very great devotion (*s.* 69, 3; cf. *en. Ps.* 52, 2). The existence and providence of God were grounded on universal consent (*Io. ev. tr.* 106, 4), based on the order and beauty of the cosmos. Popular theology pointed to design and order. Philosophic minds could argue from the imperfection and contingency of the world to the existence of perfect and necessary Being (*lib. arb.* 17, 45; *trin.* VIII, 4–5).

In an intellectual climate dominated by Neoplatonism, its assumptions about the coincidence of existence and value, of being and goodness, could even provide an outline of the ontological argument, such as we get in the 54th of the *83 Different Questions.* The extent of educated assent to belief in God and divine providence may be deduced from *The City of God,* a work principally conceived as apologetic to educated people not yet Christians, like Firmus. In the tenth book (X, 18) he expressly declares that he is not addressing those who deny God and providence.

Nevertheless, he felt it necessary in the *Confessions* to repeat twice (VI, 5, 7; VII, 7, 11) that in all his wanderings, whatever sceptical books he might have read, he never lost his belief in the being and providential care of God. This, it seems, had remained with him not only through his long Manichee decade but even through the briefer flirtation with radical scepticism. No doubt the protestations in the *Confessions* reflect the way in which the man who had now become bishop of Hippo felt about his own past.

It is evidently no accident that he records no high motivation in the successive decisions which took him from Thagaste to Carthage, thence to Rome, and finally to the encounter with his true vocation at Milan. He moved to Carthage because Thagaste was full of associations with his unnamed dead friend; to Rome because at Carthage students were turbulent; to Milan because at Rome they failed to pay and because Manichee friends and a most illustrious pagan prefect used influence on his behalf. Yet through it all the watchful hand of the unseen *custos,* the *tutela* invoked upon him by Monica when as a baby he was made a catechumen, was silently at work. In retrospect he discerned special and individual providences, in which decisions, made with a worldly motive or made possible by entirely uncatholic agencies, brought him to where God wanted him to be.

I suppose that, despite the immense thoroughness and penetration of such modern studies as Professor Feldmann's investigation of his relation to Manicheism, we cannot now know with certainty exactly what it was in Manicheism which attracted him, and then had the power to hold him for so many years. He mentions the pull exercised by the impressively bound and beautifully written codices, evidently superior to anything at the church in Thagaste, and the solemnity of their music. We now know that the Manichees had sensitive and poetic Psalms to sing. Something deep inside him seems to have shared the view that sexuality is diabolical, even through the years when he lived faithfully with the mother of Adeodatus. The character and content of Manichee mythology, repellent in his later representations, may not have seemed to him at the time so bizarre. The sect claimed to offer a more plausible account of the origin and present power of evil; of the relation of faith to higher knowledge; of the determinism which explained why some are elect and others not. Moreover, on a deterministic basis it might seem a consolation to know that one could not really sin (*en. Ps.* 140, 10; *c. Fel.* II, 8). In the *Confessions,* however, his adherence to Mani is represented as an indirect result of his reading in Cicero's *Hortensius,* and as a consequence of his disillusion with the Bible after Cicero set him on fire with desire for truth and happiness. Negative criticisms of the morality of the patriarchs and of the gospel genealogies were combined with the un-Ciceronian style of the Latin Bible, and seemed to make his mother's religion impossible for him.

To us the mythology of Mani seems very unphilosophical, though no doubt a Plutarch could have given it a metaphysical interpretation as coherent as the myth of Isis and Osiris. The assumption is easily made that so long as Augustine remained an adherent of this sect, he must have been rather like

Faustus of Milev, who is dismissed as an elegant phrasemaker rather than a coherent thinker. How could one follow reason and believe such a farrago of fantasy? Augustine was educated in a culture quite accustomed to combining polytheistic religious practice with a total disbelief in the myths. No contemporary pagan would have been disturbed by contradictions between his myths. In his twenties Augustine was familiar with Aristotle's *Categories* and his readings in Cicero certainly extended beyond the orations to the philosophical dialogues. Moreover at Carthage aged 26 or 27 he had composed *De pulchro et apto,* "on Beauty and Proportion". Like the *Soliloquia,* its literary form was an internal dialogue with his own mind *(contemplatio).* The thesis, that one must distinguish the beauty of the whole from the proportion between the constituent parts, is reinforced with Neopythagorean material. One may deduce that something akin to Neoplatonism lodged in his mind before he arrived at Milan. He made much of the Pythagorean antithesis between the Monad as principle of goodness and the Dyad as principle of multiplicity and evil. The essential argument of the work recurs in his maturity (*ep.* 138, 5; *civ.* XXII, 24). Only, in his Manichee period he combines the aesthetic approach to evil, that the parts must be considered in relation to the whole, with the Manichee conception that *divine power is limited by matter.*

As philosophical sophistication increased, above all after the catalytic effect of Neoplatonism dragging him away from rhetoric to philosophy—a move reinforced by his asthmatic pains—Augustine could no longer accept the weakness of the Manichee light-power, imprisoned in matter and unable to act without grave restriction. The difficulty in the concept of a limited weak God was one that Nebridius had urged upon him when they were together at Carthage (*conf.* VII, 2, 3): The weakness of God is no voluntary self-limitation but is in the very nature of the case. Nebridius's difficulty may be put to the twentieth-century exponents of process theology, who dissolve the problem of evil by seeing the evolutionary struggle and the technical progress of humanity as beset by setbacks and blind alleys, yet nevertheless disclosing the essentially limited power of God.

Conversion to Christian Platonism entailed the consequence that now he would uphold the absolute, unlimited power of God, qualified by the subordination of power to goodness and freedom. This demanded an interpretation of evil as being *either* not really evil *or* as capable of transformation into an instrument to achieve a higher end.

A Christian theologian might like to say that this great change in his mind resulted from meditation on Romans 8, or even on the significance of the Cross as Augustine turned to his Redeemer in penitence and faith and sought cleansing through the sacraments. The historian has to report that the depth of religious reflection implied by this theme did not visibly penetrate his thinking until some years after conversion and baptism. Despite Ambrose and *O felix culpa,* it is not at once that Augustine came to think of sin and redemption as invested with higher value than an innocence which allows of neither sin nor redemption. More immediately the influential books were Cicero's *Tusculan Disputations* and Plotinus. The first book of the Tusculans would naturally have been an important source of consolation to the young Augustine shaken by the strain and stress of losing a close friend at Thagaste. Cicero argued that death is no evil: either the inner self perishes with the body or, as the Platonists teach, it enjoys immortal bliss in heaven. The alarming myths about Hades are simply incredible. In any event, nothing can be evil which is the universal pattern of nature. In his last tractate Plotinus says the same (I, 7, 54, 3). In the second book of the Tusculans, on pain, Cicero contended that, while the Stoics exaggerate in denying pain to be evil at all, it is much less evil than people often assume. It may have to be an accompaniment of medical therapy, but its role is not unconstructive. The fourth and fifth books of the Tusculans tell us that virtue is sufficient for a happy life; certainly not honour or riches or sex (IV, 68ff.; V, 106).

The pastor of Hippo found it necessary continually to warn his flock against supposing that the purpose of Christian faith was to ensure secular success, whether in marriage, or commerce, or agriculture, or in a career in the imperial service. Poverty required strong remedial action when it became absolute; that is, when the poor starve and are destitute of the bare necessities of life. Augustine knew the inadequacy of charity from the church chest, and advocated welfare financed by redistributive taxation (*civ.* V, 17). But poverty is mainly a relative term. The relatively poor have illusions about the extent to which money and property confer freedom. In reality the wealthy have to expend huge efforts defending their property *against* thieves, and lose their freedom if they need bodyguards and have to build their mansion like prisons. Worst of all is the corrosive effect of lust for yet more property: the more the rich have, the more they seem to need (*en. Ps.* 29, II, 17; *s.* 50, 4, 6). A property owner calls himself possessor when he is in fact the one possessed (*en. Ps.* 48; *s.* 1, 1). A conscious decision for frugality is an essential ingredient in happiness (*civ.* IV, 3). If you wonder how attached you are to worldly goods, the simple test is to sell for the sake of the poor (*conf.* X, 37, 60). If the loss of external things causes distress, you care more than they are worth (*s.* 311, 13).

And how uncertain life is! A merchant can lose his entire fortune by a single storm at sea (*s. Morin* 12, 3, MA, p. 639, 10) We have to remember that in this life we are only tenants on a short lease (*en. Ps.* 148, 11). Nothing in the 'river' or 'torrent' of human history (*en. Ps.* 143, 2; 109, 20) is constant, everything is transient. The religious mind finds joy in the *pulchra mutabilitas temporum* (*vera rel.* 40; *nat. b.* 8). History has its ups and downs, like a very long epic poem, a *pulcherrimum carmen* (*civ.* XI, 18; *ep.* 138, 5; *vera rel.* 43).

The young Augustine could be cheerfully optimistic about the *Christianum imperium,* the *orbis Christianus* under the godly emperor, bringing the security of *Christiana tempora.* The political struggles and the sense of the impending demise of the empire in the West gave him more detachment in his maturity. People heard the disastrous news and said *Christiana tempora, mala tempora.* Like any other preacher and moralist, Augustine could not resist the temptation to urge that disasters like the sack of Rome were divine judgment on residual paganism or the low moral quality of professing Christians. Once, astonishingly, he suggests that the nuns raped at the sack of Rome may have had secret sins and therefore deserved it; but this is part of his general thesis that the most dedicated fall short and can never think they do not deserve whatever God sends (*civ.* I, 27).

But his detachment, if that is an acceptable word, never meant that he encouraged passivity. The faithful may be by the waters of Babylon, but they are not to sit and weep; they are to be active participants in the efforts to keep justice in society (*en. Ps.* 136, 2). The letters, perhaps especially the Divjak letters, show that Augustine was far from unconcerned about social issues, such as slavetrading. Most of his attacks on usury concentrate on the tragic consequences when loans were taken out on the security of houses or small-holdings, ending in evictions.

Jerome (*Com. Is.* XVI, CCL 73A, 690) specifies such evictions as a major cause of urban riots. Nevertheless, it is characteristic of Augustine to look to deeper causes, that is to "the inner war in the heart of man", in the restlessness and endless cupidity of human greed (esp. *s.* 25, 4). In the *Confessions* the theme is repeated that the desires of alienated man are insatiable. Augustine was impressed by Sallust's picture of Catiline as above all the man with an unending desire to explore and carry out new acts of iniquity—he liked cruelty not merely to achieve a deterrent effect but *gratuito* (cited *conf.* II, 5, 11; *en. Ps.* 108, 3; from Sallust, *Catil.* 16).

So in the *Confessions* Augustine paints a portrait of himself in his unregenerate youth as exemplifying Catiline's delight in evil for its own sake.

Many homiletic utterances show Augustine insisting that when disaster strikes, what creates resentment is sin within us (e.g. *vera rel.* 43). Alternatively, the catastrophe contains divine judgment: a bad harvest has come because of Christian compromises (*s.* 25, 4). Times are bad because of sin in the Church (*s. Caillau* II, 19, 7, MA, p. 270). The world is a millstone which slowly but surely grinds to powder those who love it (*en. Ps.* 132, 4). Sin is rooted either in cupidity or in fear (*en. Ps.* 38, 2). Its insidiousness is shown by the way in which human virtues are quickly distorted into faults: married men caring for their family become avaricious. Clever commercial dealing is under overwhelming pressure to pass over into fraud. Upholding honour reclines into petty revenge. Zeal for truth and salvation can engender a persecuting spirit. One is justified in using force in self-defence or to recover stolen property; but war in actuality becomes an angry affair, leaving deep resentment and the seed of future conflict.

Ambition for high office is beset by dangers both in achieving it and in holding on to it (*conf.* VIII, 6, 15). Success is transitory, haunted by the knowledge that eventually one will fall (*conf.* X, 28, 39). The higher the honour, the more precarious (*en. Ps.* 32, 2; *s.* 2, 24). To little people the fall of great personages brings an ill-judged delight (*en. Ps.* 50, 3). The fall of Stilicho seems to have created a deep reverberation in North Africa (*en. Ps.* 45, 2). If you fall from power and suffer exile, remember that the place which is prison to you is home to those who live there (*en. Ps.* 141, 17; cf. Seneca, *ep.* 24, 17; Boethius, *Cons. Phil.* II, 4, 17).

Adversity is good for the wise soul. Beware *fallax felicitas* (*en. Ps.* 128, 1; *s.* 105, 8). "If you have experienced no bereavement, no drought or hail has attacked your vineyards, your wine casks have not grown acid, your cattle have not failed, you have not been ejected from a high office, your friends retain their regard for you, your children are obedient, your slaves tremble, and your wife harmonias: then find tribulation somehow if you can, to teach you to call on the Lord" (*en. Ps.* 136, 5).

Augustine saw that many things people count as evils are inconveniences arising from conflicts of interest. We should not think this world designed to maximise our material comfort (*civ.* XII, 4). Gnats restrain our pride (*Io. ev. tr.* 1, 15; *en. Ps.* 148, 10). The scorpion's sting may be bad for us, but it is vital to the scorpion (*mor.* II, 8, 11). As for wild beasts, the lion in the forest is a noble sight (*c. ep. Man.* 38).

Thus far we have seen mainly Stoic arguments being deployed to show that things reckoned evil may not be as destructive as people think when they fail to consider the whole or the long term. As in Plotinus, the injection of Platonic metaphysics changed the framework of discussion. The Stoics taught endurance of the inevitable with nobility: "what is laid on you by necessity, do of your own free choice". The Platonic school held the cosmos to derive from an all-powerful and perfect goodness: how then could there be such imperfections or at least inconveniences?

Platonism deployed three types of argument in answer to this question:

(1) Errors derive from mistaken free choices of the soul. A perfect providence could not logically have programmed the inferior creation invariably to choose the good, if there is also to be true freedom of choice. Being set midway between spirit and matter, between the divine and the beasts, humanity does not easily choose the right and the good.

(2) Matter and the body exercise a downward pull and, once the soul begins to neglect higher things, tends to make the soul forget its true destiny.

(3) The created order is a vast continuum of graded entities. The perfect unfolding of the cosmos is seen in the completeness of this chain of being. Different levels of being are also levels of value. A defect of goodness is only a function of occupying an inferior grade on the ontological ladder. "Evil" is no positive quality, but merely the absence of being-and-goodness, just as darkness is lack of light and silence lack of sound.

All three arguments are plentiful in Augustine's pages, though conversion to Catholicism made him insistent that the body is beautiful, not evil. *De vera religione* 20, 40 tells us that the body is not evil, but to love it is sin. But *retr.* I, 26 affirms that the body should be loved. The positive evaluation of the body is also found in Porphyry.

In Plotinus Augustine found a powerful statement of the aesthetic argument that 'evils' are the dark colours in a picture enhancing the whole. Do not look at isolated parts (Plot. III, 2, 3; III, 2, 11, 10ff.). Consider not the transitory present, but past and future as well (III, 2, 13).

In Porphyry's edition of Plotinus, the first of the two tracts on Providence (III, 2–3), which perhaps were originally one tract, contributed further propositions which Augustine was glad to make his own:

1. "To the good nothing is evil; to the evil nothing is good" (III, 2, 6).
2. "The supreme power can use evil for a noble end, and is capable of transforming shapeless things to give them a new form" (III, 2, 5, 23).
3. One should not ask *why* an autonomous being decides for the worse rather than the better. An initially slight deviation begins an ever-increasing gulf (III, 2, 4).

Augustine, however, had an explanation of why the deviation of will is *possible,* namely, that the soul is created ex nihilo. To emerge from non-existence is to be contingent, not to be necessary and eternal, but essentially liable to the flux of change which, to the Platonist, means imperfection.

The young author of *De ordine* liked Plotinus's remark (III, 2, 17, 87) that the public executioner's function is hateful but necessary. He adds that prostitution contributes to the stability of the institution of marriage (*ord.* II, 4, 12).

So also criminals sent to the mines suffer terribly, but serve society by their toil (*s.* 125, 5). Even the devil is turned by God to serve a useful end (*civ.* X, 17).

> God would not have created a being, whether angelic or human, whose sin he foreknew, unless he also foreknew what good he would bring out of it. (*civ.* XI, 18; *cf.* XXII, 1–2)

But he did not easily make his own Plotinus's notion that evil is a necessary counterpart of good—expressly rejected in *civ.* XIV, 17. The Augustine of *De libero arbitrio* had sympathy for the view that perfection is not to be expected of immature creatures, beset by ignorance of what is good and difficulty in performing it (*lib. arb.* III, 22, 64 of infants).

As he grew older, he became inclined to the doctrine of a hard rather than a soft Fall—the disharmony of nature, the storms of human history, ignorance and difficulty, the peculiar intractability of Christian division; all these elements showed pervasive, radical evil. So, refuting Julian in the *Opus Imperfectum,* he gave those stern catalogues: the ghastly waste and apparent purposelessness of physical deformity and mental deficiency in infants, the needless nausea of pregnant women and the pains of childbirth, the misery of grinding poverty, grief for partners or children whom we have loved and lost. None of these, Augustine triumphantly adds, is the consequence of the least moral fault. On the Pelagian hypothesis it is all inexplicable (*c. Iul. imp.* II, 87; III, 154, 160; VI, 31).

There can be no undeserved suffering in God's world (II, 87; cf. *conf.* VII, 16; *civ.* XX, 2). But by grace it can be transformed.

Augustine runs together the retributive and the remedial doctrines of punishment. "There is no sin that goes unpunished" (*en. Ps.* 44, 18). Therefore it is better to suffer now than hereafter (*en. Ps.* 33; *s.* 2, 20; 85, 9). By an exact retribution, sin brings its own destructive effects (*conf.* XIII, 17, 20; *doctr. chr.* III, 17). Our punishment is no emotional reaction in God; we make it for ourselves. God's punishments are like fire, beautiful in the proper place, but painful otherwise; beneficial to those disposed to be healed, penal to those alienated from him (*civ.* XII, 4).

How far can the instrumental view of evil go? At the heart of his conversion was the renunciation of marriage and the saeculum. Yet Catholicism required a positive value in sexuality; it is the Creator's good gift to be rightly used. In *The City of God* (XI, 23) Origen is criticised for saying that the physical world was created not to produce good, but to restrain evil. Yet *De peccatorum meritis* (I, 29, 57) declares that the instinct to unite with a loved member of the opposite sex is an evil thing, which in marriage and procreation is turned to a good purpose. The theme is twice repeated in *De nuptiis et concupiscentia* (I, 24, 27; II, 21, 36).

Similarly slavery is an evil. But order is better than anarchy; and the slave in a good house is better fed, clothed, and housed than a free wage-labourer (*s.* 159, 5).

Likewise Augustine observed that greater satisfaction is given when the prize has been hard to achieve. We value things by what it costs us to gain them. Joy is greater when the preceding pain has been worse (*conf.* VIII, 3, 7–8). The four cardinal virtues are possible only if the opposites are a threat (*civ.* XIX, 4; *trin.* XIV, 9, 2—from the *Hortensius*).

To sum up: Augustine's approach to the problem of evil uses many Stoic and Platonic elements. The biblical heritage led him to lay greater stress on the penal nature of human distress. We suffer because we deserve it. Nevertheless, the retributive emphasis is ultimately overlaid by the remedial. Hence his evident sympathy for the idea of purification after death, of advance in sanctification hereafter, whereby evil is purged away and God is all in all.

The Attractions of Mani

Antonio Orbe has done as much as any living person to make intelligible both the gnostics and their orthodox opponents. The mutual antagonism was strong. Yet inevitably if the controversy was to be seriously possible, the orthodox and the heretics had to share many attitudes and ideas in common. It was only because gnosticism was so like orthodox Christianity that it had the power to attract adepts and devotees. Nevertheless, both sides in the debate were anxious to distinguish themselves from their opponents. The gnostic criticisms of orthodoxy were principally directed against what seemed the inadequacy of catholic tradition, its incapacity to answer convincingly the urgent questions of uncertain believers who began reading their Old Testament and wondered how some of its stories of deception, adultery, polygamy, and murder could be made edifying for the Christian community, or who read New Testament texts about the renunciation of marriage such as 1 Corinthians 7 or Matthew 19:12 and concluded that a serious and full commitment to the Gospel of the new covenant demanded celibacy of every baptised believer, not merely of individuals or travelling missionaries or even resident clergy needing to be pure for the daily eucharist.

The portraits of gnosticism provided by the orthodox writers were never intended to depict anything very attractive or even comprehensible, and the refutations leave the reader with the painful question how such a farrago of nonsense could be seriously believed by a number of not un-educated people. For the general level of education and culture presupposed by several gnostic texts is far from low. Their minds may have been foggy but were not stupid or illiterate. What made gnostic belief and practice attractive and credible? The high social position occupied by a number of Manichees does not easily support the view that gnostics were predominantly drawn from disillusioned, overtaxed, middle-class people unhappy at the developments of urban life.

It is no doubt commonly observed that converts are seldom the most reliable sources of accurate and just information about the religious body which they have abandoned. There is almost always some element of self-justification, some urge to vindicate the very negative view of the past community which in many (not all) cases characterises those who move from one group to another. Nevertheless, it would be instructive to gather evidence for converts from gnosticism to orthodoxy, and vice versa, and to consider their portrait of the group which they abandoned.

Among ancient converts to orthodoxy, one stands out for the richness of his information and the force of his argument against the beliefs and practices of his own past. That is Augustine of Hippo, whose conversion and baptism at Milan were far from his native North Africa and therefore not regarded with complete confidence by the Catholic communities of Numidia. It became indispensable for him to refute the Manichees, not merely because Manichee cells were active in recruiting on the fringes of the local churches, but also because the committed and orthodox Catholics were long suspicious that he had not fully shed the rags of his Manichee decade.[1] His anti-Manichee tracts, among which the *Confessions* deserve to hold the supreme place, had to perform two antithetical tasks, not easily reconciled. They had to represent Manichee belief and practice as pitiful, ridiculous, repellent, irrational, distastefully erotic, and incoherent; so they provided an arsenal of argument for orthodox clergy needing guidance on the intricacies of a sect about which some of them may not have been well informed, but which was always capable of carrying off an elderly subdeacon in Mauretania, or a Catholic layman who thought the flies of a hot summer could be created only by the devil, not by a benevolent Creator.[2] At the same time the anti-Manichee tracts also had to defend Augustine's decade of adherence to a belief so implausible. On the one hand the tracts had to show the sect to be teaching a nightmare of mythological nonsense. On the other hand, they

---

1. Aug., *C. litt. Petil.* III 17,20. The Numidian primate Megalius of Calama expressed grave hesitations when Valerius of Hippo asked him to make Augustine a bishop, and his letter enumerating Augustine's shortcomings fell into Donatist hands. Cf. *C. Cresconium* III 80,92. The issue was raised by the Donatists at the Colloquy at Carthage in 411: *Brev. Conl.* III 7,9; *Gesta Conl. Carth.* III 247. The news of Megalius's death (not very long after Augustine's elevation to the episcopate) led Augustine to reflect on his struggle to prevent just anger passing into hatred: *Ep.* 38,2, to Profuturus of Cirta.

2. *Ep.* 236; *Tr. in Joh.* I 14.

had to suggest ways in which it was possible for even a man as intelligent as Augustine to be led astray. Because of the second latent under-current, the tracts reveal something of the power and effectiveness of Manichee propaganda. Augustine himself more than once observes that human beings may wish to deceive, but cannot endure being deceived.[3]

Manicheism presented itself as the authentic form of Christianity, essentially distinct from the account of the faith found in the Catholica. Mani entitled himself 'apostle of Jesus Christ',[4] and claimed the authority of the Paraclete for his teaching—the Paraclete being his heavenly alter ego or guardian angel, in the Manichaean Psalm Book indentified with Christ.[5] From this position it followed that the force of Mani's appeal must lie exclusively in being addressed to Christians or to people much influenced by and attracted to Christianity. Manichee belief and practice could hardly draw anyone from a pagan background, and the polemic of Faustus against the Church contains many passages which attack the compromises of the Catholic Church with an older and polytheistic religion.[6] Yet Mani offered a universal religion, for both East and West.[7]

The central thrust, therefore, of Manichee propaganda towards members of the Church, or at least to catechumens on the fringe of the Church attending services infrequently, was to argue that the religion of Jesus was ascetic as the majority of baptized Christians were not.[8] Manichees renounced marriage and family ties if they were admitted to the number of the Elect. They adopted poverty, surrendering all gold and silver.[9] They were strict

3. *Conf.* X 23,33; *De Doctr. Chr.* I 36,40; *De Civ. Dei* XI 27.

4. Aug., *C. ep. fund.* 5,6.

5. See the evidence collected by A. Henrichs and L. Koenen, 'Ein griechischer Mani-Codex', in *Zeitschrift für Papyrologie und Epigraphik* 5 (1970), pp. 161–89.

6. E.g. *Contra Faustum* XX 3–4.

7. Mani opened his book dedicated to king Shapuhr of Persia, son of Ardashir, with the claim that different regions of the world have had different messengers from God: Buddha in India, Zoroaster in Persia, Jesus in the West, and now Mani in Babylonia. The text, from Al-Biruni, is conveniently in A. Adam, *Texte zum Manichäismus* (Berlin, ²1969), pp. 5–6. H.-C. Puech, *Le Manichéisme* (Paris, 1949), p. 62.

8. Augustine's friend Alypius was moved to admiration by the Manichaean espousal of continence: *Conf.* VI 7,12. His rich friend Cornelius (Romanianus) was at least temporarily converted from a lifelong habit of seduction by becoming an adherent of the Manichees for a time; he later became Catholic again and relapsed into old ways: Aug., *Ep.* 259. For the identification of Cornelius with Romanianus (CIL VIII 17226) see A. Gabillon in *Revue des Études Augustiniennes* 24 (1978), pp. 58–70, accepted by A. Mandouze, *Prosopographie de l'Afrique chrétienne* (Paris, 1982), s. v. *Romanianus,* pp. 996f.

9. *Sermo* 50,8; *C. Faustum* V 1; *Mor. Eccl.* 35,78.

vegetarians and teetotalers;[10] meat and wine formed no part of the diet of the Elect.[11] Concessions were made for vinegar and mead.[12] They had no baths.[13] Particularly strenuous Manichees slept on rough mats on the floor, not in comfortable beds.[14] Their ideal was the homeless travelling missionary, enduring persecution from governments and hostility from the 'half-Christians' of the Catholic Church.[15] For these celibate wandering missionaries the model was provided by the portraits of the apostles in the Manichee canon of five apocryphal Acts of Paul, Peter, Andrew, Thomas, and John.[16] The Manichaean Psalm Book edited by Allberry contains a psalm with a long catalogue of saints who have suffered persecution, from Jesus to Mani himself.[17]

Various forms of social activity were forbidden for the Manichee Elect. They could not own land or practise agriculture. Because of the part played by an apple in Adam's Fall, no Elect person could pick an apple, still less eat it.[18] Usury, however, was surprisingly allowed.[19] And Augustine answers Faustus's snide attacks on Catholic worldliness and laxity by observing that he has known Elect Manichees who ate meat, drank wine, visited the baths, reaped harvests, gathered in the vintage grapes, engaged in trade and occupied high offices of state.[20] As for the strict Manichee sex ethic, Augustine's confidence in the sect was in part shaken by the discovery that there were Elect whose celibacy was nominal, who might share their bed with a *subintroducta* and were occasionally discovered by the pregnancy resulting, or whose profession of renunciation of sexual activity went with occasional forays in which they were a hazard to any women in the market-place.[21] So at least Augustine claims, admittedly in passages where he appears to be

10. *C. Faustum* XXX 1; cf. XVI 3.

11. *C. Faustum* XVI 31; XX 13; *Mor. Man.* 14,31.

12. Aug., *Mor. Man.* 47.

13. Aug., *Mor. Man.* 68; Hegemonius, *Acta Archelai* X, 4, p. 16, 10 Beeson: 'If anyone washes himself, he solidifies his soul into water'.

14. *C. Faustum* V 5; *De Haeres.* 46: mattarii.

15. *C. Faustum* I 2–3 semi-christiani.

16. *C. Faustum* XXX 4.

17. C. R. C. Allberry, *A Manichaean Psalm-Book* II, pp. 142f.

18. Aug., *En. in Psalm.* 140, 12; *Opus Imperf. C. Julianum* VI, 23.

19. Ibid.

20. Aug., *C. Faustum* XX 23. A substantial proportion of anti-Manichee polemic in Augustine is given to the argument that in practice they are often inconsistent with their principles, which are impressive.

21. *Mor. Man.* 19,68ff.; *De Haeres.* 46. The Elect man who made his partner pregnant lived in the Figsellers' Street; her brother's associates expelled him and beat him up.

painting as lurid a picture as he can and is willing to admit that his information is second-hand.

Some forms of public entertainment were disapproved by Manichee ethical principles; circuses and gladiatorial shows in the amphitheatre were forbidden. Augustine records, however, seeing Elect persons at the theatre.[22]

Catechumens or 'Hearers' were not expected to observe equally strict rules. Their prime function was to serve the Elect in matters that the Elect themselves were forbidden to touch. Their first duty was to provide the Elect with food of the prescribed kind. Manichee myth included special doctrines that the diet of the Elect was one principal means by which the divine element within them could hope for liberation from matter. Chastity, prayers, and psalms were other means of purification.[23] Hearers were encouraged to be vegetarian and teetotal, but abstinence from meat and wine was not imposed on them with absolute rigidity. For them also marriage and concubinage were frowned on but tolerated, with the proviso that all reasonable steps should be taken to avert the conception of a child, since this would incarcerate more divine substance within the material body.[24] The body is, not only in its lower half, a product of diabolical design and origination.[25] Accordingly, Manichee Hearers were encouraged to confine conjugal intercourse to safe periods of the monthly cycle.[26] The arrival of Adeodatus was not welcome to Augustine initially, though the experience of fatherhood soon led him to take a very different view.[27]

The criticism of the Catholic Church for allowing married people to be baptized members in good standing was a major theme in Manichee recruiting. They contended that the Church simply had not taken the teaching of Christ seriously. What was new about the gospel of the New Testament if it were not that the new covenant required abstinence from marriage and sex? The main theme of the apocryphal Acts of the Apostles, for which the Manichees had high regard, was the apostolic proclamation of the necessity for virginity. In Manichee eyes orthodoxy was uxorious. Catholics read in their lectionary of Jacob's wives and slavegirls competing for the honour of

---

22. *Conf.* VI 7,12; *Mor. Man.* 72.

23. *Mor. Man.* 36.

24. *C. Faustum* XV 7 (coitus interruptus); *De Natura Boni* 47 (abortion). A distinguished discussion in John T. Noonan, *Contraception* (Cambridge, Mass., 1965), pp. 107–39.

25. Aug., *De continentia* IX, 22; gender differentiation is of the devil, X, 24.

26. *Mor. Man.* 65.

27. *Conf.* IV 2,2.

his bed, and of womanising on a gargantuan scale by Solomon. David seemed a bloodthirsty and licentious bandit.[28]

On the other hand, Faustus was aroused to particular scorn by the Catholic zeal for persuading young girls to take vows of lifelong virginity when they were still at a tender age. He scathingly suggested that in Catholic churches there were almost as many virgins as married women. He did not admire this.[29]

Another manifestation of Manichee austerity, contrasting with Catholic practice in North Africa by Augustine's time, was their refusal to use any pictures to portray their myths.[30] Later, in Central Asia, it was very different.[31]

On the other hand, they did not eschew the study of the liberal arts. Faustus of Mileu had no knowledge of the mathematical sciences, and no skill in logic, and Augustine who possessed these skills could afford to be superior about him. But Faustus certainly possessed eloquence. He had studied Cicero and Seneca, and had late in life applied himself to the acquisition of a good education, damaging his health by the overzealous hours of reading.[32] There was no suggestion that these studies were incompatible with Manichee asceticism and renunciation of the secular world. Augustine scorned him for being only half-educated, but did not criticise him on this score for being inconsistent with a proper Manichee attitude to worldly matters. Coherent with a positive Manichee attitude to culture is their claim to be supported by Plato and 'Hermes in Egypt'.[33]

Manichees gave a prominent place to the sun and moon, which they venerated, if not as actual gods, at least as supernatural staging posts on the route up to heaven and reception points for purified particles of divine Light, including Jesus himself.[34] In Mesopotamia and Persia the theme no doubt

---

28. *C. Faustum* XXII 5.

29. *C. Faustum* XXX 4.

30. *C. Faustum* XX 10.

31. See J. P. Asmussen, *Xuastvanift, Studies in Manicheism,* Acta Theologica Danica 7 (Copenhagen, 1965), pp. 10–11.

32. *Conf.* V 3,3–4; V 6,10–11; *C. Faustum* XXI 10 (XVI 6 on Faustus's lack of skill in handling logic).

33. *C. Faustum* XIII 1 on Hermes, Sibyl, and Orpheus as surpassing Old Testament prophets. Ephrem Syrus reports that according to the Manichees 'Hermes in Egypt, Plato among the Greeks and Jesus who appeared in Judaea, are heralds of the good (Mani)': C. W. Mitchell, *S. Ephraim's prose refutations of Mani, Marcion and Bardaisan* II (1921) XCVIII. Severus of Antioch, *Hom. Cath.* 123 (Patrologia Orientalis 29/1, 1960, pp. 176f.), says that the Manichees claimed the agreement of Plato.

34. Alexander of Lycopolis, p. 7, 27ff. Brinkmann. On Alexander there is now a good

added to the plausibility of the myth, and can hardly have been a disadvantage or liability in a Neoplatonic milieu. The Manichee openness to astrology was congenial to the young Augustine as he turned away from the Bible in appalled disillusion.[35] But they did not think the Saviour's birth could be controlled by a star, and regarded the star of Bethlehem as evidence of the legendary character of the birth narratives of the Gospels of Matthew and Luke.[36] (In general Mani approved of St. John's Gospel, of whose authenticity he felt sure.)[37]

Faustus of Mileu's ignorance of the mathematical sciences, including astronomy, seems to have been particularly influential in his failure to retain the Manichee allegiance of the inquiring and doubting Augustine. So in the *Confessions* Augustine prominently emphasises the incompatibility between Mani's account of eclipses and the views held by the most eminent scientific students of astronomy.[38] Mani held that eclipses occur when the sun or the moon wishes to hide its face from the ghastly sight of cosmic battles between the forces of light and the hosts of darkness.[39] It was a *vera causa* of Augustine's loss of confidence in the Manichee system that competent investigators of celestial phenomena did not hold anything remotely resembling this mythological opinion.

Nevertheless, one may wonder if one of the attractions of the sect lay in a strong claim to provide scientific explanations of natural or indeed supernatural phenomena. In a world which wanted to be both Christian and scientific, Mary Baker Eddy owed much success to the title of her new religion, Christian Science. The Manichees offered their recruits something which was Christian at least in the sense that in their entire scheme Jesus was a redeemer figure of the first importance.[40] They also claimed to provide a knowledge which was rationally grounded and contrasted with the submission in mere faith to the authority of the Catholic Church. Moreover, if Augustine ended by being disappointed to discover how pseudo-scientific

---

French translation and commentary by André Villey (Paris: Cerf, 1985); on the cult of sun and moon, Villey, p. 182; *C. Faustum* XVI 10; XX 2.

35. Aug., *Conf.* IV 2,3.

36. *C. Faustum* II 5.

37. *C. Faustum* XXIII 2; Titus of Bostra IV, 34, p. 145, 23 Lagarde.

38. *Conf.* V 3,6. Alexander of Lycopolis (p. 29, 26ff.) similarly appeals to the astronomers to refute Mani.

39. Simplicius, *Comment. in Epictet.* 34, p. 167 Salmasius (Leiden, 1640) = 27, p. 72 Dübner (Paris, 1877). Cf. *C. Faustum* XVIII 7; XXII 12. The theme was evidently suggested by the gospel story of an eclipse at the Passion of Jesus. See the Manichaean Psalm-Book 196,8.

40. E. Rose, *Die manichäische Christologie* (Wiesbaden, 1979).

Manicheism was, it nevertheless seems to have taken him some considerable time to find that out. When he joined the sect, it was far from obvious to him. Probably the enormous majority of Manichees, even if well educated as some were,[41] liked to think of their prophet as an inspired source of truth about the mysteries of sun and moon, and did not further pursue investigations. The pseudo-science may have been a help rather than a hindrance to the sect's successful diffusion.

The sacramental rites of the Catholica were regarded by the Manichees with considerable reserve. To drink wine, which was the invention of the princes of darkness, seemed impossible.[42] If they received the eucharistic species, they would receive in only one kind and pass the cup by.[43] Above all, they rejected any particular sacredness in the eucharistic offering, with the formula that Catholics ascribe to the eucharist a holiness which Manichees discern in everything.[44] This contrast of universal against particular expressed their negative view of the reality and particularity of the crucifixion of Christ.[45] Not only did Christ not suffer in the flesh (flesh being in any event a product of the powers of darkness), but the crucifixion is a universal myth about the suffering of the faithful Elect. 'Christ is crucified in the entire world'.[46] The particularity of Catholic eucharistic belief suggested to Manichee critics an infiltration of pagan idolatry into the Church, a worship of Ceres and Bacchus in the forms of bread and wine.[47] Augustine was uncertain if the Elect had any eucharistic rite.[48]

Baptism was also for the Manichees altogether superfluous, not commu-

41. Alexander of Lycopolis, p. 8, 5 Brinkmann, remarks that there are 'educated Manichees not ignorant of Greek traditions'. Some of those who studied philosophy with him have become Manichees (p. 8, 14). According to Faustus (*C. Faustum* XV 6) Mani 'left no problem unsolved' in the interpretation of Scripture.

42. Aug., *Mor. Man.* 44. On Manichee rituals see H.-C. Puech, *Sur le Manichéisme* (Paris, 1979), pp. 235-394.

43. Leo Magn., *Tract.* 42,5 (p. 247 Chavasse).

44. Faustus in August. XX, 2 . . . et nobis circa universa et vobis similiter erga panem et calicem par religio est.

45. *C. Faustum* XXVI-XXIX. For the Manichees the crucifixion was a symbol of the painful involvement or mixture of the divine power with matter; without being any kind of reality in the actual world, it expressed a universal truth.

46. Aug., *En. in Psalm.* 140,12; *C. Faustum* XX 2. Augustine's Manichee friend Secundinus tells him that if Christ took real flesh, all hope of salvation is lost: *ep. ad Aug.* 4 (Bibl. Aug. 17,518). He saw Christ 'crucified in all the world and every soul' (ibid. 3,514).

47. *C. Faustum* XX 13.

48. *Acta Contra Fortunatum* 3 (Bibl. Aug. 17,136).

nicating any advantage or grace to the recipient.[49] To use water to cleanse the soul was simply ridiculous, and even the symbol was dangerous if someone might understand it as a means of grace. Accordingly Manichee texts that speak of baptism[50] are surely to be interpreted as figurative. If they used the rite, it can only have been on the understanding that it was in no sense necessary to salvation.

On the other hand, the Manichees attached value to the confession of sins.[51] The spring Bema festival in solemn memorial of Mani's execution and death was preceded by a fast for thirty days on the part of the Elect, and was an occasion for penitence.[52] Augustine says that the Manichees took it more seriously than observance of Holy Week and Easter.[53] Sin mattered intensely to them.

The theme that Catholicism was infiltrated by survivals of polytheistic practice emerges in the Manichee criticism of the unruly feasting and drunkenness commonly associated with the celebrations at martyria.[54] It is texts such as these which explain how the learned Lutheran Beausobre (1734) could present Mani as a Protestant before the time, an unsuccessful attempt to liberate the Church from vulgar Catholic superstitions. For Beausobre's view it was congenial that Manichees did not make the sign of the cross,[55] or set any value on sacraments.[56]

---

49. Aug., *C. duas epist. Pelag.* IV, 4–5. See also the Coptic *Kephalaia* 33,29–32, and a good note by L. Koenen and A. Henrichs on the Cologne Mani codex (84,9–12), n. 206 in *Zeitschrift für Papyrologie und Epigraphik* 44 (1981), p. 144. An ex-Manichee Hearer became a Catholic nun and finally a Donatist at Cirta where her confession misled bishop Petilian about Manichee baptismal practice: *C. litt. Petil.* III 17–20.

50. Aug., *C. Faustum* XXIV 1.

51. The subject receives masterly treatment in J. P. Asmussen, *Xuastvanift . . .* , cf. n. 31.

52. Aug., *Conf.* V 3,4.

53. Aug., *C. ep. fund.* 8,9. Augustine there says that the Bema or tribunal had five steps and was adorned with precious coverlets. Solemn confession was made before an enthroned icon of Mani giver of absolution (Psalm Book 16,28). The Bema ceremony was in March (*C. Faustum* XVIII 6) and effectively replaced Easter (*C. ep. fund.* 8). C. R. C. Allberry, 'Das Manichäische Bema-Fest', in *Zeitschrift für die neutestamentliche Wissenschaft* 37 (1938), pp. 2–10, made it very probable that the festival had a ritual or sacramental meal with bread. As a Hearer Augustine would not have been admitted to this; cf. *Acta C. Fortunatum* 3. See further J. Ries, 'La fête de Bema dans l'église de Mani', in *Revue des Études Augustiniennes* 22 (1976), pp. 218–33, and 'Le prière de Bema dans l'église de Mani', in *L'Expérience de prière dans les grandes religions* (Louvain-la-Neuve, 1980), pp. 375–90.

54. *Mor. Eccl.* I, 34,75; *C. Faustum* XX 4.

55. *C. Faustum* VI 9.

56. This is not inconsistent with granting that the Bema festival included a ritual meal

With the aid of a critical faculty developed by some degree of liberal education, the Manichee critique of Catholic orthodoxy turned its principal guns on the Church's acceptance of the Old Testament. How could the Old Testament be regarded as divinely inspired scripture when it contained shockingly unedifying narratives such as Abraham's treatment of his wife Sarah, Lot's intercourse with his daughters, Moses' murder of an Egyptian?[57] The Old Law required animal sacrifice. The God of the Jews was venal, a demon thirsty for blood and sacrifices.[58] Circumcision was disgusting; sabbaths were unnecessary and a dangerous veneration of Saturn, besides being based on the absurd notion that the supreme God can become weary and need a rest.[59] The ceremonial laws contained in Leviticus were merely trivial.[60] In a word, Catholic orthodoxy fails to acknowledge that the Old Testament is a frankly unedifying collection of writings, largely contradictory of the teaching of the New Testament. One of Mani's twelve disciples, Adimantus or Addas, wrote a book to catalogue the contradictions between the Old and New Testaments and to bring out the essential newness of the Christian gospel, obscured by the judaising circles responsible for editing the New Testament books accepted by the Church as canonical.

The Manichees claimed to accept the epistles of the apostle Paul, though suspecting interpolations by judaisers, as in the text of Romans where Jesus is entitled 'Son of David',[61] and loved to quote Romans 7 to prove that there is a cosmic conflict of good and evil continuing in humanity.[62] It was a major thesis of Mani that Catholic orthodoxy got itself into an impossible and even blasphemous position by making the supreme God of light responsible for the creation of a world which manifestly included

---

of bread. Faustus of Mileu makes it clear that the Manichees did not think of this in the way Catholics understood the Eucharist; above, n. 44. See G. Widengren, *Mani und der Manichäismus* (Stuttgart, 1961), pp. 104–7. The Cologne Mani codex (35,8, in *ZPE* 19, 1975, 35) mentions 'religious meals' of the Elect.

57. *C. Faustum* XXII 5.

58. *C. Faustum* XVIII 2; XXII 2; XXXII 2.

59. *C. Faustum* XXV 1; VI; XVIII 2; XVI 28.

60. *C. Faustum* VI.

61. It is particularly instructive that the Manichees rejected as interpolation the text of Romans 5 from which Augustine deduced the transmission of original sin: Aug., *Retract.* I 9,6; *de dono perseverantiae* 26. The point enabled Augustine to deny that his notion of hereditary sinfulness was of Manichee origin, and was a controversial godsend to him. On Rom. 1:3 see *C. Faustum* XI 1.

62. See Mani's letter to the Persian lady Menoch in *Opus imperf. c. Julianum* III 80; text in Adam, *Texte zum Manichäismus* 12, pp. 31–33.

much evil.[63] To Mani it was indispensable to affirm that evil comes from a separate and altogether alien force, utterly opposed to God, and that the present situation of the world in which evil continually launches deeply dangerous attacks on the good reflects a deadlock between the opposing cosmic powers. Romans 7 showed the battle at work in the human heart. It proved that there are 'two souls', one good and the other evil, contending for the prize of possessing the person.[64]

The Manichee Elect could be utterly assured of their ultimate salvation. This proposition might suggest that Augustine was right in concluding that sin was simply out of their power.[65] Yet it stands side by side with many Manichee statements that even within the Elect the cosmic conflict of light and darkness is present and continuing. The Manichee penitential texts published by Henning and Asmussen do not suggest that an Elect was never in need of absolution or wholly immune from solemn excommunication. It was intrinsic to the Manichee picture of the world and of human nature that the divine element was not so potent that it could in all circumstances put to flight the powers of darkness. The possibility of 'a bit of God' being permanently imprisoned and incapable of purification is expressly found in texts of Augustine describing the Manichee system.[66] If admission to the number of the Elect signified the possession of true gnosis, it also marked the conferring of the gift of free will; and that freedom of the will could be wrongly used. Secundinus the Manichee protests against Augustine's caricatures of Manichee determinism; 'The soul is not punished because it sins but because it does not grieve when it has sinned'.[67] Impenitence is the deadly fault that must be overcome by the annual Bema solemnities, and it is inward, not merely externalised.

The Catholics, on the other hand, seemed to Manichees 'Pharisees'[68] with external rites and a calendar of festivals. Their New Testament must

63. In Hegemonius, *Acta Archelai* 5, pp. 5–8 Beeson, Mani explains in a letter that he has been sent to correct the error that good and evil both derive from one source or principle.

64. See Aug., *De duabus animabus; Conf.* VIII 10,22–24. The Manichees themselves did not speak of two souls so much as of two natures.

65. Aug., *En. in Psalm.* 140,10. The claim to be unable to sin is attributed to the Manichees by Severus of Antioch, *Hom. Cath.* 123 (Patr. Or. 29/1, 180).

66. Aug., *C. Adimantum* VII 1: any divine elements still mixed with the race of darkness will suffer condemnation at the last judgment. *Ep.* 236,2; *C. Felicem* II 7. Simplicius reports Manichees as saying that it is like a general sacrificing part of his army to gain victory with the rest (in Epict. p. 165 Salmasius = 27, p. 70 Dübner).

67. Secundinus, *ep. ad Augustinum* 2 (conveniently in Bibl. Aug. 17,512).

68. Aug., *Op. imperf. C. Julianum* I 75.

have been corrupted in the interest of proving the continuing validity of the Hebrew scriptures for the Church. Happily the interpolators were unsuccessful. No sensible reader of the prophets would naturally take them to be speaking of Jesus; and if there were any plausibility in the claim that some among the prophets prefigured the coming of Jesus, there can be none in the notion that Levitical sacrifices had such a role.[69]

In combat with orthodox church members, bellicose Manichee propagandists loved to press the question, *Unde malum?*[70] Their theme was not the incompatibility of human experience of evils with belief in a supreme being, but rather an attack on the orthodox proposition that God the Creator of all things is both all-powerful and infinitely good. If the orthodox proposition were true, that would make the almighty, beneficent Creator responsible for making Adam and Eve so constituted as to be capable of being overthrown by a snake and an apple, and that would argue for a fault in the planner and designer of human nature.[71] Evil may be described as darkness, but if God is light there can be no darkness in a creation where he is omnipresent. 'How can the soul sin if created by omnipotent goodness?'[72]

Admittedly, at first sight there is some inconsistency in the Manichee attack. On the one hand, they resolved the problem of evil by denying divine power rather than divine goodness. On the other hand, the God of the Old Testament record seemed to them seriously deficient in goodness—ignorant, envious, greedy for blood, jealous, ill-tempered, liable to destroy men for relatively trivial offences.[73] In other words the Old Testament was itself part of the problem of evil. What was abhorrent to Mani was to make God responsible for evil, and that abhorrence he shared with orthodox Catholics, and with the Platonists who were no less vocal than the orthodox Christians in rejecting the Manichee account of nature, man, and God. But the Manichees thought it absurd to follow the Platonic way of reducing the evil of Evil to vanishing point by treating it as a privation of good. Evil seemed to

69. *C. Faustum* XII-XXIII and XVI.

70. *De utilitate credendi* 36, and *Conf.* VII.

71. To Mani, Adam and Eve were not created by the good God of light, but were the offspring of the princes of darkness, Saklas and his spouse Nebroel (Aug., *Mor. Man.* 73; *Nat. Boni* 46; *De Haer.* 46,14; Coptic Kephalaia LV-LVII), the differentiation of gender being a particularly diabolical invention. Mani's Fundamental Letter speaks of their origination as a deep mystery (Aug., *C. ep. fund.* 12,14). For, though created by princes of darkness, Adam had much light in him (*Mor. Man.* 73).

72. Aug., *Conf.* IV 15,26.

73. *C. Faustum* XX 4; XXII 4 and 14; *C. Adimantum* VII 4.

Mani a fixed point in the discussion, a certain and ineluctable fact. A Platonic philosopher stung by a scorpion could not plausibly claim that it was not a bad experience.[74] Stinging creatures and such pests as flies in hot climates were in Manichee eyes evidence of diabolical creativity, like the humiliating and undignified processes of human reproduction.[75] If therefore evil was a fixed term in the discussion, the only remaining alternatives were to diminish either the divine power or the divine goodness. Mani diminished the divine power, which had the merit perhaps of explaining why particular providences and miraculous interventions in special situations do not occur. The question remained how so weak a deity could properly be worshipped.[76]

Manichee propaganda was continually confronted by a difficulty. The religion of Mani was going to be attractive only to those who were at least touched by Catholic communities and wanted some form of Christianity. It was therefore necessary to emphasise how Christian Manicheism is, how explicit the Manichee confession of the divinity of Christ,[77] how Trinitarian is their belief in the equality of Father, Son, and Holy Spirit,[78] how sure they are that their own community is the bride of Christ.[79] With the orthodox conceptions of the Last Things, they had more difficulty. But then belief in the resurrection of Christ's body, which enlightened persons of that age found as difficult as belief in the Virgin Birth,[80] was simply eliminated by the Manichee discernment that Jesus did not really die and that the story of the crucifixion is no more than a symbolic statement about the tragedy of suffering humanity. One who did not die did not need to endure human birth;[81] a divine being

74. *Mor. Man.* 11.

75. *Tract. in Joh.* I 14; *C. Faustum* XXIV 1.

76. *Conf.* VII 2,3; *Mor. Man.* 12; *C. Secundinum* 20. The Manichees remained unmoved by the argument, since they thought the existence of *evil* on so great a scale must presuppose either incomplete power or incomplete goodness, and they preferred to reduce the power than to qualify the goodness. In their eyes, the mixing of the divine Light with the darkness was the redemptive method by which the powers of Evil were tricked.

77. *C. Faustum* XXII 3. Cf. E. Rose, *Die manichäische Christologie* . . . , cf. n. 40.

78. *Conf.* III 6,10; *C. ep. fund.* 8. Secundinus's letter to Augustine, reacting to his reading of the *Confessions,* begins with a Trinitarian formula.

79. *C. Faustum* XV 1. The Life of Mani in the Cologne codex (111,16) has 'the Church of the saints' for the Manichee community: *ZPE* 44 (1981), p. 219 with n. 393.

80. Among many texts in Augustine, see *Ep.* 102; *Ep.* 135,2; *C. Faustum* XVI 20; *De civ. Dei* XXI 5; XXII 5; *Sermo* 51, 3f. Augustine's defence of the virgin birth as fact depends on the general supernatural character of the gospel attested by its worldwide extension, and on particular faith in the reliability of scripture as divinely given.

81. *C. Faustum* XXVI 1; XXVII 1.

could not have been insensitive to 'the horror of a virgin's womb'.[82] 'Reverence for Christ' was regarded by Faustus as a prime principle,[83] compelling belief in his words but also eliminating from the record of his words and acts anything Faustus found incompatible with divine dignity. At one point Faustus's polemic against Catholic orthodoxy observes that both Manicheism and orthodoxy involve belief in what is 'contraria naturae', but Manichee belief is decent and respectable whereas Catholicism is shameful and indecent.[84] Accordingly, Manichee missionary propaganda constantly claimed to offer not only Christianity but the one authentic form of it, specifically authorised by God's inspired prophet Mani to correct the gravely mistaken and misleading account of the matter put about by the 'pharisaic' Church. This entailed the difficulty that Manichee claims had to be made plausible not merely by trumping Catholic asceticism with greater austerities or by pointing to evident moral problems in the Old Testament, but also by presenting a religion essentially distinct from Catholicism, itself coherent and self-consistent, yet asserting the authority of the scriptures. To deny to Manichees the title Christian was as painful to them as it is to twentieth-century Mormons.

The Manichee ethical teaching stressed the duty of love to God and one's neighbour; only they denied that this was taught in the Old Testament.[85]

Mani had provided a rationale for his entire system with a richly coloured mythology, revealed to him by a visitation of the Paraclete his heavenly twin,[86] concerning the utter antithesis between Light and Darkness and the primaeval conflict between them resulting in the present mixture of fragments of light within a world of darkness. To know the myth is to know oneself, to understand one's personal nature and ultimate destiny, to realise that we sin involuntarily and under an inward coercion from hostile and external forces. This is the realisation which brought self-knowledge to Fortunatus, the Manichee priest in Hippo with whom Augustine had a public disputation in the baths of Sossius on 28 August 392.[87] The recognition that sin is imposed on the unwilling led Fortunatus to know whence he had come, what was the nature of the evil in which he found himself, and how his faults could be corrected by good works. Fortunatus even went so far as

---

82. Manichaean Psalm-Book 52,23ff.

83. *C. Faustum* XVI 8.

84. *C. Faustum* XXIX 1. That some matters of Manichee theology lie beyond reason is affirmed by Secundinus: *ep. ad Augustinum* 6 (Bibl. Aug. 17,520f.).

85. *Mor. Man.* 22.

86. See the Coptic Kephalaia I, p. 14.

87. *Acta Contra Fortunatum: PL* 42,111–30; *CSEL* 25,81–112; Bibl. Aug. 17,132–92.

to claim that one could accept the Manichee faith without the least conflict with the 'auctoritas fidei christianae'. What seemed to him impossible was to attribute to the Creator-God, source of all power and goodness, responsibility for the irrational urges that beset normally sexed human beings, and that are experienced as their 'nature', not as a distortion of nature which they themselves have brought about by selfish or morbid choices. Manicheism has at its heart the claim to provide a way of liberation from the tyranny of sexual impulse, and is the classic expression of the view that the repression of sexual activity is the royal road to heaven. Soul and body are therefore utterly disjunct, the soul a fragment of the very substance of God, the body diabolical in its most central urge to reproduce itself: the supreme conflict of ego and id, of new man and old man, is acted out in the struggle for abstinence from conjugal self-indulgence. But this inward conflict is but a microcosm of the grand cosmic struggle between Light and Darkness, the myth which explains that humanity is not what it was in origin. Manichee practices are the way by which the original divine condition may be recovered, and are designed to separate out the commixture of incompatible elements coexisting in empirical human nature. The function of vegetarianism and teetotalism is to reduce the force of the sexual impulse by which the divine element is further imprisoned in diabolical matter.

Accordingly, the Manichee is taught to observe the three seals of mouth, hands, and breast; that is, the prohibitions (1) of meat, wine, lying, and blasphemy (2), of any action that could hurt the 'Living Soul' or 'Cross of Light' ubiquitously suffering in matter; and (3) of any act of procreation.[88]

Such prohibitions and the language of cosmic struggle reflected in inward experience by humanity might lead one to expect that the Manichee system would include a careful analysis of the freedom of the will and of the destiny of those who, in Mani's own phrase, 'neglect to purify themselves . . . and fail to observe the law given by their liberator'.[89] The Manichees had so powerful a sense of determinism that they hardly conceived of the will as possessing any significant capacity to extricate itself from the toils of bodily appetites. The will (for them) was granted freedom by the powers of Light, but was not understood to be an organ by which liberation could be

88. *Mor. Man.* 19 and 27. Manichaean Psalm-Book 115, 31–33: 'The seal of the mouth for the sign of the Father, the peace of the hands for the sign of the Son, the purity of virginity for the sign of the holy Spirit'. More detail in Kephalaia LXXX, pp. 192–93. A general account of Manichee morality is given by P. Alfaric, *L'Evolution intellectuelle de S. Augustin* (Paris, 1918), pp. 126–43.

89. *Acta C. Felicem* II,5.

attained. In any event, full liberation was the privilege of the Elect. Hearers in the catechumenate were destined to experience a series of reincarnations, in each of them dependent on the Elect for any hope of ultimate salvation. A very good Hearer hoped to return as one of the Elect.[90]

The orthodox language of resurrection as the ultimate expression of salvation presupposed an utterly unacceptable idea of the harmony of soul and body, though even from the body in death some elements might ascend to purification in the moon and sun. As for the judgment, the Elect would join Christ as assessors, while the sheep and goats among the Hearers were placed respectively in salvation or in hell.[91]

The Manichee texts show that the mythological elements were important within the internal life of the community. But the myth belonged to the secrets of the cosmos which were first disclosed to those who penetrated far into the mysteries of the society. Augustine expressly records that the missionaries never started by revealing the Manichee cosmogony to those whom they had targeted for recruitment.[92] Their initial moves were to attack the embarrassing texts of the Old Testament, asking by what authority Christians could accept Old Testament authority and then decline to observe the ceremonies which the Law enacted. They went on to ridicule the willingness of the Church to accept for baptism married couples cohabiting and procreating, when the personal example of Jesus and the clear teaching of the apostle in 1 Corinthians 7 showed renunciation of sexual activity to be necessary to salvation. Only at a late stage would the agonising problem of evil be brought into the conversation and the Manichee explanation of its present power and future elimination could then begin to be unfolded. That a purged New Testament had authority was very right in Manichee eyes, but study showed how unscrupulously the biblical texts current in the Catholic Church had been interpolated partly by judaisers mendaciously pretending that the Old and New Testaments contained an identical and unchanging faith, partly by stupid people who supposed that Jesus the saviour experienced birth and death. Their stupidity was fortunately obvious to the Manichee critic from the simple incompatibility of the Matthaean and Lukan genealogies, the authors of which were not ingenious enough to cover their tracks.

At what stage the missionaries produced the canon of Manichee sacred

---

90. *C. Faustum* V 10; XX 21; *C. Adimantum* XII, 2; Hegemonius, *Acta Archelai* 10, pp. 15f.
91. See the Coptic Manichee Homilies, II.
92. *De agone christiano* 4.

texts it is impossible to say. In the disputation with Augustine in August 392 the Manichee presbyter Fortunatus made no appeal to his sect's sacred books, but forcefully cited St. Paul's saying that 'Flesh and blood will not possess the kingdom of God'. Augustine, however, comments that this text itself was a breach of the rules of debate, which required an exclusive recourse to reason and excluded any appeal to authority on either side. One cannot therefore safely deduce that the Manichee canon of books was kept in the background. Indeed, Augustine informs us that one of the great attractions of the sect lay in its impressively large books, finely bound.[93] They certainly possessed their own independent places of worship, with elaborate ritual forms, vestments, and clothes with distinctive insignia to mark off the Elect from the Hearers. If one supposes the ceremonies to have some resemblance to those of freemasonry, perhaps that may help the modern reader to envisage the solemnity of the forms. Moreover, they had fine music and beautiful psalms.[94]

One recalls what an important role the psalm-chants of the church at Milan played in the conversion of Augustine in 386. More than a decade earlier perhaps Manichee chanting and psalmody had helped to gain his allegiance for the sect at Carthage.

A problem concerning the conversion of Augustine to Manicheism lies in his consort, Adeodatus's mother. He had taken her to his bed before he became recruited by the Manichee group in Carthage. One scrap of evidence suggests that she was a member of the Catholic community and did not accompany Augustine to meetings of the Manichee conventicle.[95] In the ninth book of the *Confessions* where Augustine looks back with mingled pride and grief on the brief life of his son, he has occasion to remark that the boy was brought up by his parents in God's way of discipline: 'nutriebatur a nobis in disciplina tua'.[96] In other words, the child was nurtured in Catholic teaching, presumably by his mother and grandmother rather than by his Manichee father. The context in the *Confessions* indicates that there was something remarkable about this fact, as if one might have expected some very different course to be pursued. If the boy and his mother were at least intermittently at the Catholic mass, it is perhaps reasonable to suppose that the sceptical Augustine might sometimes have attended the liturgy of the catechumens.

93. *C. Faustum* XIII 18; *Conf.* III 6,10.
94. Manichaean Psalm-Book 168,20; *Mor. Man.* 46.
95. An independent Manichee meeting house is attested in *Conf.* VIII 10,13.
96. *Conf.* IX 6,14.

It has been suggested by Schmitt that Augustine felt able to take a consort to his bed because Manichee doctrine discouraged marriage but tolerated liaisons, and that his ceasing to be a Manichee had something to do with his decision to send the woman back to Carthage from Milan.[97] This suggestion is hard to endorse. The Manichees opposed procreation; they tolerated sexual contact provided that steps were taken to avert conception. At least for the Hearer a sexual partner was tolerated, but this partner could be a legal wife as well as a concubine. Moreover, there is no hint in the *Confessions* that he had any reason to dismiss his consort other than the secular necessities of his career. He had high ambitions to become a provincial governor. To achieve that end (as Monica saw clearly) he needed a respectable and well-connected wife. A partner in bed and board from the lower classes of Carthage would hardly be acceptable at the governor's residence as hostess. More important than respectability, perhaps, was money. In the later Roman empire desirable posts were not awarded to deserving persons merely on the ground of objective consideration of their quality of mind. Fourth-century imperial courts were no simple meritocracy. The mere history of the word *mereor*, virtually losing all sense of 'merit' and becoming a synonym for 'obtain', may be significant in this connection. Anyone ambitious to become a provincial governor needed money to provide splendid hospitality for the high court officers, to make suitable presents to them to enlist their favour in the competition for places, to flatter their power of patronage. The woman from Carthage brought no money. The young—too young—bride found by Monica would bring a dowry with which ambition might be realised. No other motive was needed than ambition in the secular world. The parting with the Carthaginian concubine had nothing to do with loss of confidence in Mani as a prophet and teacher.

Earlier there had been a time when the quasi-masonic brotherhoods of Manichees in Carthage and Rome had been able to foster and further the young Augustine's ambitions. Although Augustine speaks of Manichees as 'hiding' in society,[98] and of occasions when they were delated to the authorities as illegal practitioners of forbidden cult,[99] he also mentions Manichees holding high positions in government and society: 'publicos honores administrent'.[100] Manichee associates in Rome brought pressure to bear on Sym-

---

97. E. Schmitt, *Le mariage chrétien dans l'oeuvre de S. Augustin* (Paris, 1983), p. 27.

98. Aug., *Ep.* 64,3; *Conf.* V 10,19 (plures enim eos Roma occultat).

99. *Ep.* 222,3. The penalty imposed was mild. A well-known letter of Libanius (*Ep.* 1253) intercedes for Manichees in Palestine as harmless sun-worshippers.

100. *C. Faustum* XX 23.

machus, the pagan prefect, persuading him to write in support of Augustine for the teaching post at Milan.[101] He certainly found congenial company in the Manichee Constantius at Rome who established a community of Manichee ascetics in his own house until it broke up in a split.[102] Moreover, his own high culture was shared by his friends Alypius, Honoratus, Secundinus, and his wealthy supporter Romanianus, all of whom were attached to the Manichees in Africa and in Italy. Though the presbyter Fortunatus at Hippo is described as being, like Faustus of Mileu, eloquent rather than learned, the Manichee Felix, one of the Elect, was reckoned cleverer than Fortunatus, even if lacking in extensive literary culture on Augustine's level. In other words, to be among the Manichees was not at all to be associated with a group of uneducated fools, and Augustine might well have found a number of them to be both wealthy and prudent in the affairs of the world. Possidius records Augustine's conversion of a wealthy Manichee merchant named Firmus.

In the tract 'On the Two Souls' Augustine expressly observes that he was drawn into the Manichee circle by the personal influence of friends.[103] And few things in this life were more important to Augustine, at any time of his life, than friendship. 'Human life is so full of misery and misunderstanding that only the confidence and love of true friends make it bearable'.[104] In the same general context he pleads in self-defence that he was young and immature in judgment, but adds that he loved the combat of debate, and the crushing in argument of 'imperiti Christiani'—presumably a reference to the Manichee attacks on the Old Testament which were so powerful a weapon in their arsenal for making Catholics uncomfortable.

Our discussion has suggested that Manichee propaganda was not as absurd as the converted Augustine would have liked his readers to think. There were weaknesses in the Christian acceptance of the Old Testament and rejection of its ceremonial law; it was not clear that this was not an arbitrary choice by orthodox interpreters for which no self-evidently valid defence was forthcoming. Again, the argument from the fulfilment of ancient prophecy in the gospel history and the mission of the universal Church depended

---

101. *Conf.* V 13,23. Roman Manichees could not have influenced Symmachus unless they were themselves rich and aristocratic.

102. *C. Faustum* V 5; *Mor. Man.* 74.

103. *De duabus animabus* 9 (11).

104. *De civ. Dei* XIX 8. See M. A. MacNamara, *Friendship in St Augustine* (Fribourg, Switzerland, 1952); W. Geerlings, 'Das Freundschaftsideal Augustins', in *Theol. Quartalschrift* 161 (1981), pp. 265–74.

on the prophecies being clear, which perhaps relatively few seemed to be. Manichee myths could be prudently kept in the background until the person being recruited was already captured. The sect's high moral tone could appeal to all those who felt their sexual impulses and their religious aspirations to be pulling them in contradictory directions. The segregation of the Elect from the Hearers and the demand that the Elect keep the rule of celibacy also had an appeal; for to be celibate was to be the bearer of a certain kind of authority, of a priestly separateness, of a visible detachment from secular patterns of living.

The close similarity and proximity of Manichee belief and practice to Catholic orthodoxy made the local churches the natural prey to the sect's missionary persuasiveness. On the other hand, Augustine was far from being the only ex-Manichee to turn away from the sect in disillusion. The unnamed bishop, mentioned at the end of the third book of the *Confessions,* who counselled the distressed Monica to continue praying for her son's conversion and to exercise patience, had been brought up by his own mother as a Manichee. He had even been a copyist of Manichee sacred books. Profuturus and Fortunatus, who both became bishops of Cirta, had at one time been Manichees,[105] as also Alypius bishop of Thagaste. Accordingly, the direction of the traffic was probably more from Manicheism to orthodoxy than the other way round.

One argument, however, cannot seriously be used to explain the attractions of Manicheism for Augustine, namely that the Manichees already had monasteries, and Augustine was a man with a profound inner aspiration to be a monk in community. The evidence of Constantius's failure to gather a Manichee monastery in his house at Rome is powerful evidence that the idea of a separate community of Elect and Hearers living together under rule was not at home in the Manichee ideology.[106] That, however, is not to say that Manichee attitudes to sexuality left him unresponsive. Nothing became more characteristic of Augustine's interpretation of sexuality than his repeated insistence that the involuntary nature of sexual arousal is a manifestation of a morbid and corrupt condition consequent upon the Fall of Adam and Eve, for whom, in paradise, union was controlled by reason and will. Julian of Eclanum could crow with delight on discovering virtually the identical doctrine in Mani's letter to the Persian

---

105. Aug., *De unico baptismo* 29 (Bibl. Aug. 31,730). Fortunatus's Donatist rival Petilian was able to exploit the charge of a Manichee past against him (*C. litt. Petil.* II 18,40).

106. Above, n. 102. See also a wide-ranging note in J. P. Asmussen, op. cit., p. 260.

lady Menoch.[107] This is only the most striking sign that some themes and assumptions of his Manichee decade succeeded in remaining with Augustine, even after his renunciation and sustained polemic in anti-Manichee treatises. Mani originally won his allegiance through the effectiveness of his attacks on the Old Testament and through his austere asceticism. The Manichee mythology was what Augustine renounced. Something in Manichee ethical attitudes was to stay in his bloodstream.[108] The attraction of Mani was never quite lost.

107. *Opus imperfectum contra Julianum* III 167. The citations from Mani's letter are in Adam, *Texte . . .* , cf. n. 62, p. 32.

108. The question of persisting Manichee influences on Augustine has been put in a fresh light by the work of E. Feldmann, *Der Einfluss des Hortensius und des Manichäismus auf das Denken des jungen Augustinus von 373* (Diss. Münster, 1975). Cf. also Christoph Walter, *Der Ertrag der Auseinandersetzung mit den Manichäern für das hermeneutische Problem bei Augustin* (Diss. München, Kath.-theol. Fakultät, 1972). On social factors in the diffusion of Manicheism see Peter Brown, 'The Diffusion of Manicheism in the Roman Empire', in *Journal of Roman Studies* 59 (1969), pp. 92–103, reprinted in his *Religion and Society in the Age of Saint Augustine* (London, 1972). Other studies important for the question here discussed are A. Adam, 'Das Fortwirken des Manichäismus bei Augustin', in *Zeitschrift für Kirchengeschichte* 69 (1958), pp. 1–25; W. H. C. Frend, 'The Gnostic-Manichaean Tradition in Roman North Africa', in *Journal of Ecclesiastical History* 4 (1953), pp. 13–26; 'Manicheism in the Struggle between St Augustine and Petilian of Constantine', in *Augustinus Magister* 2 (1954), pp. 859–66; P. J. de Menasce, 'Augustin Manichéen', in *Freundesgabe für E. R. Curtius* (Bern, 1956), pp. 79–94; A. Escher di Stefano, *Il manicheismo in S. Agostino* (Padova, 1960); F. Decret, *Aspects du manicheisme dans l'Afrique romain* (Paris, 1970); S. N. C. Lieu, *Manicheism in the Later Roman Empire and Medieval China* (Manchester, 1985); R. Merkelbach, *Mani und sein Religionssystem* (Opladen, 1986).

Augustine's Ethics

Augustine's ethical teaching especially on specific questions of conduct is widely scattered through his writings. A few treatises directly deal with moral issues, for example arguing that asceticism is both catholic and scriptural and does not imply a Manichee dualism; or we have two widely separated treatises on lying, the early tract of 395 conceding that while one may never lie to anyone's hurt, there can be circumstances where, if it were to save someone's life or honour, it could be justifiable to be economical with the truth; the late tract of 420 allows for no exceptions to the requirement of absolute truth telling. Even in the early tract he insists that one can never solve a problem in this life if it risks losing one's soul in the next (*De mend.* 38). His final position is Never deceive: one is not obliged to say all that one knows (*Serm. dom. in monte* 2.67f.) Several tracts on marriage and sexuality were elicited by the Pelagian controversy. A tract 'On Faith and Works' he directed against clergy who told converts and catechumens that the qualification for baptism was simple faith, and sorting out tangles in their moral life could come gradually afterwards; for if in the sacrament they laid the foundation of Christ's name, any combustible chaff would be purged by the fire of divine love hereafter. He wrote a treatise 'On the Good of Marriage', mainly to combat Jerome's extreme and offensive opinions. (Jerome is never mentioned.) Near the end of his life he wrote against allowing remarriage after divorce, seeking to rebut the opinion that such rigorism is lacking in humanity.

Paper dated 2.12.1991. The standard German monograph on Augustine's ethics (Mausbach 1909, 2nd ed. 1929) runs to almost 900 pages. I shall leave a lot out. I select three themes: means and ends; intentions; moral values beyond the frontiers of the Church.

About 411 Augustine received an inquiry from an old friend named Hon-oratas who had once shared his Manichee beliefs. Now he faced a variety of questions, one of which concerns the moral situation of an infant. Augustine replies: The baby makes no choices; necessity is all in its life. But soon the child learns to avoid what hurts and to do what brings pleasure. In self-pres-ervation, seeking pleasure and avoiding pain are essential to survival. As reason develops, the child discovers that some pleasures are harmful and even evil. (The point is already in Aristotle, *EN* vii.12.) The child begins to exercise a choice between bodily and mental pleasures. Bodily pleasures are transient; mental felicity lies in being directed towards more distant, long-term achievements, indeed towards eternal and divine things. That is not to say that physical and temporal things may never be indulged in; only they are to be used rightly—that is, with a certain detachment, treating them as *means,* never as *ends.* To use means as ends is a neglect of the Creator who alone is our true end (*Ep.* 140.3–4).

The distinction between means and ends goes back to Plato and Aris-totle. Plato's *Lysis* acknowledges that all our choices are part of a process; we choose X for the sake of Y, Y for the sake of Z. But Socrates denies that the process is infinite. The supreme good is desired for its own sake, not as a means to an end beyond it (220b). The ultimate good is the final criterion for evaluating our choices and priorities (*Euthydemus* 280–321). Therefore, concludes Plato, *this supreme good stands outside the temporal process.*

Aristotle's *Ethics*—a work probably not known to Augustine—assumes that people know what ends they want to achieve. The interesting philo-sophical questions all concern means where choice has to be exercised. Yet Aristotle grants, like Plato, that among the ends, one end is final, the su-preme Good (*EN* i.7, 1097a 28). If we pursue honour, pleasure and even virtue itself, we do so as means to this final end of the Good sought for its own sake (1097a 1), and without such a criterion or reference point, our desires become vain and empty (i.1, 1094a 18–22). In the 8th book the dis-tinction between means and ends is applied to people. Some simply enjoy their friends' society; others love them because of the benefits they receive from the relationship. Some people are liked for their money, others for their witty conversation. But a perfect friendship is grounded exclusively in moral virtue, giving a permanence which never belongs to the merely useful (which changes as circumstances change).

Augustine translates means and ends into what is used and what is en-joyed. Cicero had contrasted what is morally right and what is expedient (*honestum, utile*), and argued that nothing morally right can ever be inexpedient, nothing morally wrong can be expedient. Augustine commented on this that there is, nevertheless, a distinction of importance between what is sought for its own sake and what is sought as a means towards something else. To use as means what ought properly to be enjoyed as an end is the definition of vice, so too it is wrong to enjoy as an end in itself what ought only to be used as a means. True joy is not in physical pleasure and beauty but in the mind. Food and sex are enjoyed by healthy animals. The rational being uses such pleasures as means to a higher end, for procreation or health, but not what lies beyond what is necessary for these ends. Nothing in the physical order, nothing in space and time, is a proper final end. Our only ultimate joy should be in our Maker, and other fellow human beings we may use insofar as society is essential to life (*DQ* 83, 30).

Here Cicero's language is being overlaid by (a) a Neoplatonic doctrine that the non-physical is alone a proper object of aspiration; (b) a biblical doctrine of the gulf between Creator and creature—to love the creature when one ought to love only the Creator is idolatry.

Somewhere indirectly at the back of Augustine's language lies Aristotle's distinction between friendship which is enjoyed and friendship which is a means or tool. Augustine was a man with a genius for friendship, and it mattered to him at a profound level. Friendship is the gift of God which makes life between birth and death bearable (*CD* 19.8). Good health and good friends are the supreme natural goods (*S. Denis* 16, p. 75; *Ep.* 130.18). We share a common bond of humanity (*B. Conj.* 1.1). To see the goodness of all God's creatures is a divine gift (*Conf.* xiii 31.46). But friends can let one down. Only in heaven we shall neither fear an enemy nor lose a friend (*Tr. Joh.* 20.7). Moreover, friendship can lead one into mistaken or even tainted decisions (*Conf.* ii.5.10). There are cases where it is unequal between the two parties, the weaker feeling more love for the stronger than the stronger partner returns (*Cat. rud.* 4.7; Cicero, *Lael.* 71ff.). Physical expression by one partner may have a negative repellent effect on the other who asks for no more than good will (*Conf.* iv 8.13). The only friendship that is impregnable is in God, and among humans is grounded on mental, not physical rapport (*Tr. Joh.* 32.2). But in human life, many kindnesses to our friends have mixed *motives.* Unrequited love can suddenly turn into hatred (*Tr. Joh.* 32.3). So human love requires purification by grace. A love which uses a friend becomes moral if it is referred to God and is an expression of love to God (*DDC* 1.22.21). 'He truly loves a friend who loves God in that friend, either because God is in the friend or in order that God may be in the friend.' (*S.* 336.2)

Rightly to love a human being, indeed even one's spouse, one must love in him or her the creation of God (*Ep.* 258.21; *Serm. dom. in monte* 1.15.41).

In his dialogue on Benefits Seneca insisted that the moral value of an act is not only in the act but also in the intention with which it is done (*Benef.* vi.10–11). Plato (*Euthydemus* 280b–282e) wrote of the importance of a right *use* of any good thing one possesses. Good things are ambivalent; the manner in which they are used determines how good they are. Aristotle composed an exhortation to the study of philosophy (*Protreptikos,* ed. During). There we are told that the body is 'a tool which may be used rightly or wrongly'. 'Philosophy is the possession and use of wisdom'. Stoics were specially interested in matters neither good nor bad but indifferent, *adiaphora*. Something capable of being used well or badly is not in itself a good; wealth and physical health are not good in themselves (*SVF* 3.117). What lies in our power is the way we use these things, and that is a moral issue (*Epict.* 2.5.1–8).

In many texts Augustine is emphatic that the moral value of an act is never independent of intention and circumstances, and never has value in God's sight unless it is grounded in faith. 'Virtues are distinct from vices by the ends or intentions, not by the acts in themselves' (*C. Jul.* iv.20f.). Virtues can easily slide into faults: constancy into obstinacy (*C. Jul.* iv.20; *Qu. an.* 51), righteous indignation into hatred (*Ep.* 38.2), prudence into mere cleverness (*C. Jul.* iv.20). 'Love and do as you like' is a principle of restraint in discipline, where the therapy of correction depends on inner attitudes in both punisher and punished.

It is not wrong to be rich, only to be obsessed and controlled by one's possessions (*S.* 17.5) and to fail to use them in relief of the poor, feeding the hungry, clothing the naked, offering a roof to orphans or foundlings or travellers, comforting prisoners (*En. Ps.* 83.7). In Matt. 25 hell is not for the adulterers and murderers, but for those who fail to feed the starving (*S.* 60.9: cf. John Chrysostom similarly *ad hoc*). When you give alms do not do it for show or just to rid yourself of an inconvenient beggar (*En. Ps.* 71.3). In feeding and clothing beggars freezing in winter, you are doing it to Christ (*S.* 25.8; 95.7). Rich people should not imagine they can grind the faces of the poor and then salve their consciences by allocating a tiny sum to feed them (*CD* 21.27; *En. Ps.* 103.iii.9–12). The misery of the rich is that the more they have, the more they need (*En. Ps.* 29.ii.17; *S.* 50.6; *CD* 7.12). They live in perpetual anxiety about their estates (*CD* 4.3). And the sole motive for acquiring wealth is to have power over others (*En. Ps.* 48.3). Take away pride, and wealth does you no harm (*S.* 39.4). Use it for God. Bequeath to the church chest for the poor the proportion that would go to an additional child (*S.* 86.13; *En. Ps.* 48.i.14). Society values people by what they have; God values them by what they are (*En. Ps.* 51.14).

Augustine's stress on intention entails the corollary that the context and circumstances need to be considered. Nudity is acceptable at the bath-house, not in the forum, not when lascivious dancing provides entertainment at a dinner party (*Nat. Boni* 23; *DDC* 3.12.18). Transvestism is both disreputable and against both Roman law and the Bible (cf. *Mus.* 6.4.7, citing Deuteronomy 31:5), but in war a man might clothe himself in female dress and so save his country, or if the weather turned bitterly cold and nothing else was available, there would be no impropriety (*Solil.* 2.16.30).

Epicurus the hedonist recommended marital fidelity on the ground that infidelity entails so many inconveniences and embarrassments but he did not pretend fidelity had any moral merit (*Nupt.* 1.3.3). The criterion of every act is whether its motive is love (*Enchiridion* 121; *En. Ps.* 70.1). You are not morally innocent if you tried to commit adultery and found the door locked so that you failed in the attempt.

There is no merit in fasting if its motive is to give yourself an appetite for an imminent feast (*En. Ps.* 43.16). In Syria the prefect at Antioch put a debtor under sentence of death, but the poor man's wife paid off the debt getting the money by sleeping with a wealthy lover (*Sermo dom. in monte* 1.16.50; *C. Faust.* 22.37; *CAG* xx 142.9): Augustine could not say she did wrong. On the other hand, to sleep with one's lawful spouse in a lascivious or even unnatural way is indefensible. (Augustine was not among those who have thought a wife obliged to agree to everything her man might do, by the mere fact of being legally married: *Contra Mendacium* 18.)

Intention is constant, circumstances vary. But the negative *Golden Rule* is absolute: Do not do to others what you would not have them do to you. It is innate in the human heart to know what justice is (*Trin.* 8.6.9). Good people can agree on the definition of justice and still disagree on particular cases (*Ep.* 153.22). One criterion of whether a person is just is whether he or she loves other people agreed to be just (*Trin.* 8.6.9). No Christian will dispute the virtuousness of the cardinal virtues, prudence, self-control, courage, justice, and of these justice is part of goodness and so inherent in the very being of God. Christians want a merciful, humane society, in justice, helping the weak, orphans, widows; Augustine's nuns rescued foundlings, his monastery took in orphan boys.

Despite St. Paul (1 Cor. 11:7) Genesis makes it clear that women and men are alike in God's image (*Trin.* xii.7.97; *Gen. Litt.* iii.22.34). Paul's command that women must cover their head in prayer is such obvious absurdity it must bear hidden sense (*Trin.* 12.7.11). In the marriage relationship, husband and wife are in private equal, especially in bed; but in public the wife's role is supportive. In the street, however, husband and wife should walk side by side (*Bon. Conj.* 1)—a remark probably directed against the custom still in force in Arab countries where the wife walks a few yards behind her husband with the children. (If you see the wife walking 5 yards in front, that might be a sign that landmines are suspected.)

Equality extends to responsibility for fidelity. Augustine deeply disapproved of the ancient double standard, which expected a wife to be faithful, but not the husband, a double standard based on the axiom that fathers and sons need to be sure of their blood relationship to one another. The wife is differentiated from the female slavegirl in a pagan household by the fact that her children legally inherit (*S.* 51.26).

The married state is good, but the dedication of the monk or nun is superior. The ascetic vocation calls for a heroism characteristic of the celibate missionaries who carry the gospel round the empire and beyond. The married Christian man has domestic responsibilities that preclude heroism on that scale. But even he will fast in Lent, be more generous in almsgiving, will avoid all litigation, and by Lenten abstinence from legitimate sexual relations with his wife discipline himself to avoid infidelities at other times of the year. The gospel imposes *commands* which all must keep; but there are also *counsels,* to sell all, to be celibate, which it is not given to everyone to follow.

As for a public social ethic, Augustine hated torture and capital punishment; under torture people confess to crimes they have not done and innocent people come away maimed for life. Against capital punishment, it is sufficient to observe that it cannot be remedial, and that mistakes are made. But Augustine wanted Christians to serve as magistrates, governors, prefects, as they also served as emperors. The 'taxman is not a dragon, but serves the community.'

On usury (loans at interest), which, surprisingly, the Donatists seem to have allowed, Augustine did not think this right; it encouraged little people to take out loans beyond their means, ending in eviction and destitution (*Ep.* 153.25; *S.* 239.4; *En. Ps.* 39.26; 36.iii.6). It was a terrible indictment of society that in the lawcourts justice was commonly for sale.

Augustine's views on war are that all war is miserable (*CD* 19.7) whether just or not, and civil wars are the bitterest of all (*CD* 3.29). But good men may find it necessary and believe it right to resist aggression (*CD* 19.17), in self-defence, or to recover stolen property. The purpose of war is to recover peace; treat vanquished with dignity.

Military victory had been a reward for Constantine's faith. Why orthodox emperors like Jovian and Gratian lost their lives to be succeeded by emperors less supportive of orthodoxy is mysterious (*CD* 5.25). But Augustine rejoices that Christian emperors are closing pagan temples (C. *litt. Petil.* 2.131); that in Rome St. Peter's basilica is honoured more than Romulus's temple (*En. Ps.* 44.23; 86.8; 140.21).

The Christian aspiration is for a 'just empire' which cares more for the poor than for splendid buildings (*Ep.* 138.14 Marcellino). They want to see power subject to justice (*Trin.* 8.13.17). A society in which people take the law into their own hands with avenging violence would rapidly become intolerable; and therefore Augustine is wholly opposed to private resort to violence (*CD* 3.17).

Augustine applied his division of means and ends, use and enjoyment, so as to make God the only proper end; everything in this temporal life is no more than means. But the right intention can refer everything to God. What is done, even in secular administration, for God's sake is morally good. Nevertheless, Augustine cannot allow that good works done without faith have moral value. Good works preceding faith and baptism are vain (*Mor.* 1.17; *C. Jul.* iv.25–6).

The two cities, Jerusalem and Babylon, symbolise two loves, the people of God and the impious (*VR* 50). Augustine's reading of history leaves most of the human race outside the walls of Jerusalem, though only God knows who is on which side of the walls. Within the church itself many live evil lives, and are in the line of Cain, Esau, Judas, and Simon Magus (*Bapt.* 1.25). There are many sheep outside, many wolves inside. So the Church both is and is not the city of God.

And Babylon both is and is not the Roman empire, its power structure and army enforcing dominion at the point of a sword. It is a corrupt society; and its end is power and glory in this world. Yet the peace of the Roman government is a faint reflection of the peace of the heavenly city (*CD* 15.4; 19.23 and 26). Admittedly earthly peace is short-lived; sooner or later the conquered peoples get liberty (15.4). Peace on earth is a temporary truce; the natural state of human societies is rivalry, competition, not cooperation.

Many virtuous pagans feed the hungry, clothe the naked, house the homeless, visit the sick, comfort prisoners, and live in faithful chaste matrimony (*Contin.* 12.26; *Nup.* 1.4; *C. Jul.* 4.16; *En. Ps.* 83.7). There is a natural theology held by those who share Christian admiration for Socrates, for wise men both Jewish and Roman, Orpheus, Hermes Trismegistus and sages who belong to our common humanity before Europe, Asia, and Africa became divided (*Ep.* 234). There are non-Christians who have never broken the Commandments, and who are little impressed when Christian traders think themselves entitled to rip them off because they are pagan. They think the world has become more unsafe since Christian emperors came to power. 'Christiana tempora, mala tempora.'

Can such people be saved? All who have lived rightly will be saved (*Ep.* 102.12). But humanity without Christ is flawed by sin, original and actual, and needs grace. Of those who are not elect the virtues are really *vitia,* flawed actions. In one letter to his friend Evodius (*Ep.* 164.4) Augustine agonises over the splendid people, thinkers and heroes, for which he can find no room in the city of God.

Yet the Incarnation is God's assertion of human value (*En. Ps.* 148.8). Christ fulfils the longings of all humanity (*Ep.* 155.4). So to give to the destitute, whatever his beliefs, is to give to Christ. The Christian's moral duties are not concerned only with the specifically sacred, not only with fellow members of the body of Christ, but extend to all human life, individual as well as social.

The Originality of Early Christian Ethics

Lord Bryce was born 150 years ago, and died in 1922. His widow gave a benefaction to Somerville to commemorate one of Ulster's greatest gifts to Oxford and to Britain. A scholar and then fellow of Trinity, he became Regius Professor of Civil Law but left Oxford for the political and diplomatic work of cabinet minister and ambassador.

Four problems that mainly occupied him 100 years ago have a very familiar ring: Ireland, South Africa, the national responsibility of the universities, comprehending the American constitution. Lord Bryce was a major and embattled figure in the struggle for getting university education for women in Victorian England, and became a founding member and lecturer of Girton in the days when it was first founded at the safe distance of Hitchin. A pioneer in winning higher education for women, he was to his dying day equally passionately opposed to giving them a vote. Like many Gladstonian liberals, he combined the high-minded belief that politics is a rough and dirty game from which the fair and gentle sex should be protected, with the low-minded fear that most women would vote Tory and so end Liberal power in Parliament, a fear which the event justified. An Ulster presbyterian of unshakable conviction, he was alarmed at the left wing opinions common among the parish clergy of the Church of England, and even found among some of the bishops. His liberalism made him unsympathetic to any denominational or religious tests in higher education, and his Ulster background reinforced that dislike. He wanted Oxford to be open to all classes of society merely on ground of merit, and sharply attacked the Royal Commission on the ancient universities of 1881 for doing nothing either to provide opportunities for women or to widen the social mix in the colleges. He acidly wrote that the Commission did admirably if its task was understood to be the entrenching of vested interests and the ensuring that no important changes would occur (*Fortnightly* 33, 1883, 382ff.). He deeply loved Oxford but did not want to see it out of touch with social change. Not every undergraduate prize essay becomes a best-seller repeatedly reprinted and translated as was his work on the Holy Roman Empire. Warden Fisher of New College (who did much for Somerville) recalled how in 1898 some Italian academics met Bryce in the Alps he loved to climb, and on discovering his identity doffed their hats in awe with the reverential words 'Holy Roman Empire'. The archives of his papers in Bodley and in Illinois remain an only partly tapped mine of information.

Bryce was a convinced and undoubting Christian believer who was bored by philosophical speculation. I hope a historian's remarks about early Christian ethics are no unfitting way of remembering him and of saluting a great College.

To ask what is original or distinctive in early Christian ethical teaching is inevitably to enter a field scarred by some controversy, and certainly to embark on an inquiry which looks the more daunting and difficult the longer one reflects upon it. We had better begin by setting aside two not uncommon answers to the question. The first is a popular notion that used to be maintained by some writers on Christianity and that embarrasses the informed believer by its naivety: this notion is that the first missionaries brought a brilliant light and radiant purity into the Stygian darkness of a polytheistic society, the supreme values of which were nothing but power, honour, wealth, and sex. (Witness Sallust, Petronius, Juvenal, Tacitus, all of whom could be called to witness to the depravity of Roman society.) In the phrase of Jowett, Christianity stopped the moral rot of the empire: the obscenities of the ancient theatre, the unspeakable cruelty of gladiatorial combat in the amphitheatre (where the average expectation of life among the fighters seems to have been about that of subalterns in the front line at Gallipoli in 1915), the lust for domination impelling Rome to empire, the paederasty of the Greek world, the virtually universal assumption that the master of the house slept with the slave girls as well as his wife whose distinction lay only in the fact that her children were free and legitimate, and (one must add) that the mistress of the house could and often did sleep with the male slaves at her whim.

No one familiar with the ancient texts would deny that this and a lot more went on. But then the lust for power, honour, wealth, and sex is a permanent characteristic of human nature in all centuries, past, present, and no doubt future. It would be utterly unhistorical to suppose that there was much more vice in the world before the time of St. Paul or Constantine the Great or even St. Benedict and St. Francis than there was after their time. We cannot, of course, quantify how many people in antiquity were regularly unfaithful to their spouses. St. Augustine, who was in general more severe to men than to women, once remarks that infidelity is a particularly common 'male disease', and as bishop found himself the recipient of many sad confidences from married women among his flock. Admittedly he also encountered women with an unstoppable urge to break up other people's marriages. The managers of ancient theatres, much as their modern counterparts, well knew that to fill their seats they had to put on something fairly outrageous or no one would come. Christian influence might affect civic and public affairs, could impose pressure for the ending of the murder and blood-lust of gladiatorial combats, and tried to clean up the streets, but could not so easily change the pattern of private life.

Occasionally one meets the obverse of the argument that Christian morality cleaned up the ancient world, with the contention that before Christian missionaries arrived people enjoyed much freer attitudes to sexuality, and that the missionaries introduced a blight of guilt and the notion that sex is something rather dirty. There is amazingly little evidence to help this opinion. In the pre-Christian world it would not be at all easy to find a writer with any romantic idea that unrestrained freedom in this department of life is a source of liberation and psychological fulfilment. In general, restraint is a precondition for any real significance to attach to the experience. But in any event, almost all ancient writers on the subject think it a very problematic area of human experience. The arch-hedonist Epicurus and his disciple Lucretius adopt a distinctly negative position, namely that it is a source of more pain than happiness. And Virgil's picture of poor Dido does not suggest the contrary.

The second common but, I think, mistaken interpretation of early Christian ethics claims that they had nothing new to say at all, no word that in this department of reflection can be regarded as an advance on the moral wisdom of Plato, Aristotle, the Stoics and Epicurus. In evaluating this claim it is necessary to observe at once that Christians in antiquity avowed deep sympathy for some Stoic authors. Tertullian's *Seneca saepe noster* ('Seneca often speaks like one of us') is echoed by his fellow African Lactantius a century later. In Augustine, admittedly, echoes of Seneca are relatively few and far between; he once shows knowledge of the letters and only one or two traceable (or at least hitherto traced) allusions to the moral essays, a restraint surprising in a man who knew Cicero's writings intimately and almost by heart. Epictetus was certainly read with appreciation by many more people than the élite who knew their way about Plato's dialogues, and the reason for his popularity is expressly recorded as his beneficial influence on personal moral life (Origen, *c. Cels.* vi.lf). The *Enchiridion* or handbook of Epictetus survives in a Christianised version, which presupposes far-reaching sympathy on the part of the editor. At the same time Christian writers frequently distanced themselves from two characteristic features of Stoicism, namely the Stoic convictions that justice is polluted if judgment is ever mitigated by mercy or compassion, and that suicide was not only an assertion of personal freedom which one is entitled to exercise but even in certain circumstances a duty (Cic., *fin.* 3,16; Plutarch, *repugn. St.* 18, 1042D). The main body of classical philosophy rejected this view, and, with Euripides, regarded it as an act of cowardice (Eur., *Herc. f.* 1347f.) or a failure to accept public obligations (Aristotle, *EN* 5,15; Cic., *rep.* 6,15). Perhaps it might be justified in the case of an unsuccessful military leader or a noblewoman threatened in her honour.

The Christians thought suicide wrong, because they believed life to be a gift of the Creator to be used in service until the Creator himself gave a discharge. Epictetus, Stoic though he was, exhorts to stay on sentry duty until relieved (1,19,29; 2,15,4–20); 'until God gives the signal' is his phrase.

In short, the distance between Christianity and Stoicism can be reduced even further than is often supposed, and perhaps that fact helps to explain the remarkable historical phenomenon that the emperor Marcus Aurelius is the last Stoic writer. Everything the Stoics had said about ethics was taken over either by the Platonists or by the Christians and notably, of course, by the Christian Platonists.

Sometimes a contrast is drawn between the Greek ethic fitted to make citizens good members of a *polis,* or the Latin ethic fitted to make citizens qualified to govern an empire, and the New Testament ethic where, at least in the Gospels, the *polis* is well over the horizon, and indeed is not located on earth at all. Our *politeuma,* says the apostle, is in heaven. Here we have no continuing City. Paul taught his converts the duty of obedience to legally constituted authority in society, and at the same time the paradoxical antithesis of this, that so far as internal matters within the Church are concerned or internal disagreements between believers, the magistrate 'has no authority whatever' (1 Cor. 6:3, a sentence correctly rendered in the NEB and its recent revision, but often given more Erastian and chicken-hearted translations especially by Protestant translators). Yet a large part of the moral exhortation in the tradition of Plato and Aristotle is concerned with the individual, whereas a large part of the emphasis in Christian moral recommendations lies in social questions. Take, for example, the sermons preached by John Chrysostom at Antioch and then at Constantinople, and you find a stress, meriting the epithet 'intense', on questions of slavery, wealth and poverty, class divisions, the duty of humanity and *philanthropia* which requires mercy to all in need and misery, irrespective of their religious belief, and without scrutiny of the personal merits of the recipient of aid.

Much of John Chrysostom's preaching is directed towards the creation of a greater sense of shared humanity between people separated by race or class or wealth, and especially to persuade the well-to-do to act in such ways that the poor and their domestic slaves did not have reason to resent their existence.

One of his favourite words is *homotimia,* equality of respect. He could lambast the rich for having slaves whipped for quite trivial offences, and asked Christian slave-owners not to beat their slaves at all, and never to separate married couples, as some masters assumed the right to do (*H. 1 Thess.*11,3). A number of passages show the same awareness as we find in Augustine, that a slave in a reasonable household was far better housed, clothed, and fed than a free wage labourer whose plight might be desperate (*H. 1 Cor.* 20,5; *H. Heb.* 11,3; *H. Matt.* 56). Plutarch was outraged at the austere inhumanity of Cato whose principle was to sell a slave cheap as he or she got old, so that he did not have to feed useless and unproductive mouths. Plutarch, who was certainly a man of much moral sensitivity, was embarrassed to record such behaviour on the part of so great a man. John Chrysostom likewise expected masters to care for their servants, and, unlike Aristotle who thought friendship between master and slave was impossible, John thought it both practicable and much to be desired (Arist., *EN* 8,11,1161b; *H. Col.* 10,1).

To read much of John Chrysostom is to be aware that often he is baptising themes one can find in pre-Christian writers (he especially liked the discourses of Dio of Prusa who acquired, as he came to do, the same nickname of Chrysostomos, golden-mouthed), but at the same time to see him giving a Christian framework. His many pleas for humanity and generosity to the poor and starving can rise to passionate heights as he cites the judgment scene in Matthew 25. How astonishing, he remarks, that those going to hell are not the adulterers and other social delinquents, but those who failed to lift a finger to help those in great need and destitution.

A feature of John Chrysostom's moralistic preaching may stand for a great body of Christian exhortation, namely that he expects a very high ethical standard from his people, and at the same time knows perfectly well that he will spend much of his time coping with the great number who have failed, and perhaps dismally failed, to achieve even an approximation. The same phenomenon appears in Augustine in the Latin world. This may serve to point us towards the beginning of an answer to our initial question about the distinctiveness of Christian ethics, namely that it is not necessarily located in a set of specific recommendations the like of which the ancient world had not heard before from pre-Christian moralists, but in the conception of divine grace. The characteristic stress on humility is the correlative of that.

So far, in this lecture I have been at some pains to bring out continuity rather than discontinuity, the sense very commonly found in early Christian moral writing that the gospel is a fulfillment, a making actual, of that which has been an aspiration or even a dream; but the aspiration is not in itself very new or distinctive. If one is looking for continuity, one obvious place to look is the treatise *On Duties* composed by Ambrose of Milan in the late 380s, and expressly presented as an adaptation and correction of Cicero's famous treatise on the same subject, itself modelled on a Greek work of the 2nd century BC by Panaetius of Rhodes. Panaetius and Cicero understand the term duty, *officium*, as implying that individual self-interest is set aside for the sake of the survival of the group – the *patria,* the family, one's friends, one's neighbours. To fail them is treachery, and duty overrides private interest. It is therefore an *officium* to accept public responsibilities, 'office' in fact. And there is a hierarchy of duties: the *patria* comes first, for if that is destroyed, no family can exist; then duty to parents and children in one's household, including dependent slaves, neighbours and friends, in that order. But even duty to the *patria* is qualified by the consideration that there are acts so vile that they cannot be done even to save one's *patria* (Cicero, *off.* i.,159).

Just as Cicero wrote primarily to direct upper class governors and magistrates, so Ambrose wrote his adaptation mainly to guide the clergy. Whereas Cicero wanted to make this world a success, Ambrose had his eye on the next. The *fides* which in Cicero means loyalty becomes faith for Ambrose. Ambrose was writing not long after the catastrophic invasion of the Balkans by the Goths with the Huns prodding them from behind, and he was oppressed by the consequent social chaos bringing refugees pouring out of Dalmatia into Italy. People had been driven off their estates and farms, and Ambrose felt that distressed gentlefolk had a claim on the church chest, their indigence being made more painful and shaming by their inability to sustain the style associated with their family. The times had also generated many beggars, some of whom exploited and conned the clergy, telling mendacious stories; to them Ambrose was unsympathetic.

Like Cicero, Ambrose thought that the four cardinal virtues were the recipe for troubled times, with fair dealing, truthfulness, and generosity to the needy ranking high in the scale of values. So much of Ambrose is happy to be a restatement of Cicero, but with interesting differences. Cicero wanted to teach one how to talk eloquently and impressively, whereas Ambrose begins his treatise by commending the virtue of silence. In the disorder of the times we see the first beginnings of the phenomenon that the clergy replace the civic authorities as the social linchpin, because the civil authorities are no longer in evidence. But Ambrose was anxious that this prominence was making some clergy walk rather too tall and others rush about as if they were beset with affairs. Some clerics tried to impress people by adopting an effeminate voice instead of speaking in public with rhythmic strength. (The passage is the earliest text known to me to complain about the parsonical voice.) Let them beware of worldly dinner parties where they would hear risqué stories and have their glass repeatedly filled.

The third and last book of Ambrose's work illustrates once more the characteristic Christian concern for humanity, with an attack on corn merchants who stored grain to keep the price artificially high, and a sharp critique of cities (happily not his own beloved Milan) which in tough times had expelled foreigners.

Augustine once remarked in a letter to Jerome (of 405, *Ep.* 82,21) that Ambrose was one of the very few Christian writers who had spoken of duty. The statement is something of an exaggeration, but certainly Ambrose was the one and only writer of Christian antiquity to write a treatise expressly on this subject. In any event the observation may serve to remind us (and sad experience suggests that the reminder is not unnecessary) that the early Christians had not read Kant. They talked about duty and conscience a great deal less than many have supposed, though there is the forever startling sentence in John Chrysostom that the starry heavens above and the moral law within are the two main signposts to the knowledge of God (*Anna* 1,3; *PG* 53,636). It was natural that a community sprung from a Jewish matrix which did not understand the Levitical ceremonial law to be now binding would think conscience an important guide to right and wrong; that step had been taken as early as the first epistle to the Corinthians, chapter 8, i.e. the discussion whether an enlightened Christian who knows that evil spirits and pagan gods have no existence can eat meat that has been offered in sacrifice at a pagan altar. Epicurus had taught his pupils never to do anything if it left them feeling uncomfortable about it; 'always act', he said, 'as if Epicurus were watching you'. The apostle is much less individualistic: his principle is that one should not act in ways which other members of the community think wrong even if one does not regard the act as defiling the conscience. But in general, Plutarch or Philo of Alexandria have more to say about conscience than Christian writers of the first three centuries, though the Christians were of course aware that a bad conscience is a driving psychological force of intense power. Augustine once compares a bad conscience to a man married to a shrew who prefers to walk the streets rather than go home to be greeted by a biting tirade.

The Christian conscience did not merely draw the line at idolatry. Themes especially prominent in the early Church's social critique are the wickedness of usurious moneylenders giving credit to the poor on the security of their house or small holding, and then evicting them; the corruption and bribery without which no one could achieve anything at the court and which pervaded the lawcourts and tax departments; the amphitheatre with its blood-lust, of which in the sixth book of the *Confessions* Augustine painted a brilliant word-picture of mingled fascination and horror. The early Christians were markedly reserved toward eroticism on the stage or at the music hall. On prostitution they speak with more hesitant voices. Naturally they knew it to be a great evil. But they could be remarkably compassionate to the harlot as opposed to those exploiting her, and they were aware of the paradox that the existence of prostitution can contribute to the stability of the institution of marriage which would be far more dangerously threatened by general promiscuity. Abortion they held in abhorrence; they did not think one could defend abortion except by arguments equally valid for infanticide and the exposure of unwanted children, usually girls I fear. (Perhaps I might insert a polemical observation that in John's Gospel, 16:21, the joy of a mother delivered of her child is that a human being, not necessarily a male human being, is born into the world; the Greek is *anthropos*.)

The question is sometimes put whether Christianity improved the condition of women. It made the survival of female babies a matter of principle. It declared with intense emphasis that wives had as much right to expect fidelity and loyalty from their husbands as husbands had from their wives. The Christians, I should add, were not the only people in the ancient world to say that, but they orchestrated the theme for the brass with an ear-splitting fortissimo, and elsewhere it was usually only a flute-like sound. The Christians, said Justin in the middle of the second century, stood for stable marriages and honesty in commerce. Justin, it is only fair to add, is also our source for the misery of a Christian wife married to a beast of a man whom she divorced and who took his revenge by accusing her to the prefect of being a Christian, which cost her her life.

Women of today who think the institution of marriage a polite name for a not too open prison will not think Christianity did much for them. Those for whom the family is the seedcorn of society (a phrase of Cicero's, approvingly borrowed by Augustine in the *City of God*) will not take so negative a view.

Asceticism has had a much larger place in other religions than in Christianity, and is in no sense distinctive of Christian ethical attitudes. The social ethic of Christianity, on the other hand, is nearer the heart of the matter. The ransoming of prisoners captured by the barbarians was always a cause for which the churches thought it appropriate to sell even sacred vessels of gold and silver presented by well-to-do benefactors. During the frequent wars on the eastern frontier between the Roman and Persian empires, the bishop of Amida once cause a considerable frisson by selling his church plate to redeem not Roman citizens captured by the Persians, but Persian prisoners whom the Roman soldiers were refusing to release (Socrates, 7.21). It was a principle that charitable aid to the poor should not be confined to church members, but must be for those in need whatever their religious allegiance (Socr, 7.25). That was acting out the lesson of the parable of the Good Samaritan with its defiance of racial prejudice.

The emancipation of slaves in bad households was accounted a proper cause for subsidy from the church chest. A runaway slave might find asylum in a church; but it was not then easy for the bishop to defend him against the arm of the law. A programme for complete abolition of slavery was announced in the fourth century in a utopian sermon by Gregory of Nyssa; but for reasons I have mentioned earlier, namely that the free poor were generally much worse off than the domestic slave, the best that one can say is that monasteries were not allowed to have slaves.

A programme for the emancipation of women in ancient society would surely have appeared to be dangerous laxity, as indeed such a programme appears in our own time in high class Moslem society. There an unmarried young woman of good family and reputation cannot imaginably live on her own in a bachelor flat in a city. The Lord chose no women to be among the apostles; but women play a very substantial role in the story of Christian origins, and the absolute equality of access of both women and men to the sacraments of salvation is a principle that in antiquity no one questioned.

A matter on which the ancient Church did not achieve consistency is coercion, military force, capital punishment. Capital punishment is almost consistently rejected by the Church Fathers, a fact which I find to be little known but which the texts sufficiently demonstrate. That some Christians thought any participation in war forbidden to them is certain. It is also certain that soon there were Christians serving in the Roman army, and the Church did not tell them to resign, but only that war must not be aggression. It is justified to defend oneself or to recover stolen property and land, but should be so conducted that afterwards victor and vanquished can live in mutual respect, and the wounded or the prisoner treated with every humanitarian care. But it was not a distinctively Christian principle that the object of war is to achieve peace and justice. Others said that too.

One obvious difference between Christian and Greek ethics is that the former possesses a prophetic mark. It is a declaration of the good as the revealed will of God. The Platonic ethic of purification depends on a hypothetical imperative (saying: if you wish to be this kind of person, then follow this method). The Christian imperative is categorical. It does not tell us 'if you wish to take your inquiries further, then repent and believe'. It says rather, 'Because you are who you are, you stand under a moral demand that can be evaded only by being false to the end for which you are made.' Hence the evident fact that while religion and morality are not identical, and while morality needs no religious sanctions or rewards to impart authority to it, in the Christian tradition the nexus is very intimate. If and when morality is divorced entirely from religion, it becomes easier for its authority to be set aside, because the sense of awe so central to monotheistic religion is no longer integral. In an ethic formed by the Gospels, the moral life is not merely a prerequisite for acceptable worship but is of the very substance of worship.

A second point of difference lies in that in Greek ethics, and especially in the Neoplatonic school, there is a drive towards individualism, to 'the flight of the alone to the alone', to an understanding of the inner life as 'escape' (to use Plato's word in the *Theaetetus*). That individualism has certainly influenced some forms of Christian asceticism and mysticism but not the most central, characteristically social expressions of Christian moral conviction.

In trying to evaluate distinctiveness (or originality) in Christian ethical attitudes, unreality is introduced if we forget a major point: some substantial element of that which sets Christian morality apart in the Greek-Roman world is derived from the Jewish matrix and the Hebraic background of the Torah and the prophets. Among the Jews we can find a stricter attitude towards sexual licence; one has only to read Philo's treatise *On the Contemplative Life* to see how he regards the acceptance of paederasty as a blight on the high culture of classical Greece. The Jews, like the Christians, would not participate in polytheistic cult. And the Jewish/Christian affinity does not lie merely in a few extra prohibitions but in positive precepts, acts of benevolence and works of charity. The Rabbis held it a duty within the Jewish community to be hospitable to strangers, to care for orphans, to ransom prisoners, to visit the sick, to bury the dead.

The universalist Christian ideal took these precepts out to a wider world without frontiers.

Sometimes we are told that the Sermon on the Mount represents a radical critique of traditional Jewish morality, and sets out a new ethical programme. Sometimes it is urged that good in that sermon can be paralleled in the Talmud, and nothing which cannot be thus paralleled is any good.

Both views are grinding axes. It is evident that by making love the supreme value the Christians were bound to end by refusing to identify morality with a specifiable code of rules, just as they were also sure to feel uncomfortable with the self-satisfaction of Aristotle's magnanimous man.

In a word, ultimately the specific individuality or distinctiveness of early Christian ethic derives from the call to imitate Jesus of Nazareth.

Pachomios and the Idea of Sanctity

To talk of saints is hardly free of controversy. The subject of sanctity and of the means by which it is normally achieved, namely asceticism and renunciation, cannot be altogether a suitable topic for an urbane dinner-party conversation. We have decided that it is all right for an academic symposium, since historically the ideal is of vast consequence; but it may be well if we begin with some recognition that the topic can be divisive.

To most men and women life is beset by noise; and the possibility of chosen silence comes to be felt as a divine gift, at least to that large number of us whose daily round is a succession of trivialities punctuated by frustration, rage, envy, and the rest. ('Telegrams and anger', as E. M. Forster put it.) The pain of ascetic renunciation lies in the forgoing of natural goods, in a deliberate choice that puts the normal activities of human society on the far side of a wall.

But the shining portrait is also felt to have a dark shadow, which we can see depicted in eloquent prose in the pages of Gibbon's chapter on the monastic movement.[1] To Gibbon and the Enlightenment all monkery is synonymous with superstition of which, if not the creator, it is a fanatical fosterer—fanatical in the sense that it requires a devotion that is impervious to rational consideration. For Gibbon the ascetic life is a religion of 'children and females', a refuge for those who have failed or blundered in this world and seek solace for their misfortune and healing for their remorse. As monasteries came to be recruiting grounds for the episcopate, so the profession was entered by ambitious men hungry for power, who realised how celibacy enhanced their authority. The discipline of the monasteries, Gibbon thinks,

1. *The Decline and Fall of the Roman Empire*, ch. 37.

is one of repellent, inhuman austerity — the disgraces, confinements, fastings, and bloody flagellations, executed in the name of a religious obedience which is tyranny. 'A cruel unfeeling temper has distinguished the monks of every age', writes Gibbon (in a surely dreadful and gross sentence), a stern indifference inflamed by religious hatred, a merciless zeal put to the service of intolerance and the Holy Office. With all this goes the resentment of lay people when popular monks insinuate themselves into noble households, and vast public and private wealth becomes absorbed in the maintenance of unproductive persons useless to society and enjoying a sacred indolence in the name of holy poverty; a body whose aggressive and useful military spirit is suppressed in the cloister but then reemerges to fight bitter, futile ecclesiastical controversies with implacable hostility. To monks pleasure and guilt are synonymous; and, as for their style of life, 'every sensation offensive to man is acceptable to God'. But for Gibbon they do not falsify the Christian spirit; rather do they supremely exemplify it by acting out the ultimate logic of 'the preaching of patience and pusillanimity'.

Gibbon evidently enjoyed writing his savage indictment. One recalls Porson's famous review of *The Decline and Fall*:

> An impartial judge, I think, must allow that Mr Gibbon's History is one of the ablest performances of its kind that has ever appeared [. . .]. Nor does his humanity ever slumber, unless when women are ravished or the Christians persecuted [. . .]. He draws out the thread of his verbosity finer than the staple of his argument [. . .]. A less pardonable fault is that rage for indecency which pervades the whole work, but especially the last volumes.[2]

Even when one has discounted Gibbon's vehement prejudices, which add such power to the elegance of his mannered prose, modern studies of the Byzantine saint have to recognise that for us modern men the subject can be one of peculiar complexity. Whatever our personal standpoint, we of 1980 do not share many of the assumptions that produced their manner of setting themselves on the road to sanctity. In consequence we are tempted either to tell the stories of their mortifications and then, as was said of Lytton Strachey, ostentatiously refrain from laughing, or we go in search of trendy non-religious explanations of the social needs that created them. It is of course certain that Byzantine saints fulfilled social needs, and it is a proper question to ask how that worked out. I am also sure that a stripping away of

2. *Letters to Mr Archdeacon Travis [. . .]* (London, 1790), preface.

their religious motivation will leave the historian with a distorted picture. So in this paper opening the conference, I venture to put some initial questions about the religious presuppositions that underlie the saintly man's role.

Early Christian Attitudes

The early Church was a tiny, persecuted body, and the experience sharpened its sense of having different values from the surrounding society. Its ideal was the martyr whose allegiance to his crucified Master was so strong that he preferred death to apostasy. But the second- and especially the third-century churches enjoyed long periods of peace during which their numbers grew to an extent that embarrassed those concerned to maintain standards. Many texts of Origen comment on the to him appalling fact that the churches are packed out with passengers, who come from a mixture of motives, who sit in dark corners of the building reading secular literature while the preacher seeks to expound the word of God, who prefer bishops to be easygoing in the discipline of the laity. In large cities bishops are becoming persons of social consequence cultivated by ladies of wealth and refinement, so that the office comes to be sought for non-religious reasons. Several third-century texts disclose strong debate about the compatibility of office and power with the Christian profession. On the one side, there stand the biblical examples of Joseph and Daniel, holding high office, yet keeping their conscience undefiled. On the other side, a Roman magistrate cannot escape idolatrous pollution and punitive duties; and to Tertullian (*On Idolatry* 17–18) the exercise of power and authority is simply incompatible with humility; that is the axiom which already in the fourth century led many 'secular' clergy to withdraw to monasteries and a quiet life. In the seventies of the second century the pagan Celsus was calling the Christians to shoulder public office and to serve in the army (Origen, *C. Cels.* viii.75). The third-century Christians did just that, and the more they did so, the greater the pagan apprehension that they aroused.

Already by the middle of the third century two ethical standards were being if not advocated, at least acquiesced in. Origen's 26th homily on Numbers (26.10) distinguishes within Christ's army the front-line troops who fight Satan hand to hand and the many camp followers who support the combat forces but do little or no fighting themselves. A generation later Eusebius of Caesarea (*Dem. Evang.* i.8. 29–30) marks a distinction between (a) those who keep the moral commands of the Decalogue while pursuing trade, farming, soldiering, political life, marriage, and attend church services on special occasions, and (b) those who go beyond what is commanded to keep themselves unencumbered by marriage ties, practise poverty, renounce the world of Vanity Fair, and devote their whole life to God's service.

So the Christians even before Constantine's revolution provide a blueprint for the scene realised after Constantine's conversion, both for the world-renouncing ascetics and for the world-affirming ethic which identifies the *res Romana* with God's purpose at work through the Church. In either case they are operating with a basic contrast between the Church and the *kosmos* or *saeculum,* the earthly city under the dark god of this world (even if only temporarily so), standing in antithesis to the heavenly city of God's Kingdom. Thereby the ascetic Christians create the concept that this world, in its daily business of getting and spending, of political power and social organisation, is a 'secular' entity apart from and perhaps hostile to the true calling of God; certainly going on its way in indifference to and independence of the divine purpose.

'Secularisation' is a complex word for a complicated and ambiguous idea. Its modern use comes from the mid-seventeenth century to apply to the transfer of property from clerical to lay hands; then from being first used for the expropriation of property, it comes to be used of a deeper attempt at expropriation of minds: *non licet esse vos,* Tertullian quotes the pagans as saying.[3] We should be on our guard against suggestions that secularisation is a modern concept. Both the concept and the vocabulary stem from the ascetic drive in quest of holiness in the pre-Constantinian Christian tradition, which sought to erect an invisible wall between the Church and the world.

Pachomios's Wall

If we ask who first made this invisible wall into a visible entity, we are brought to Pachomios.[4] To him more than to any other single man we owe

3. *Apol.* iv.4.

4. The earliest Greek Lives with the letter of Ammon and *Paralipomena* are edited by F. Halkin, *Sancti Pachomii vitae graecae* (SubsHag 18 [1931]), the Coptic translated into French by L. T. Lefort (1943), the Arabic into French by E. Amélineau (*Annales du Musée Guimet* 17 [1889]); Jerome's Latin version of the Rule and Letters edited by A. Boon, *Pachomia Latina* [Bibliothèque de la Revue d'histoire ecclésiastique Fasc. 7] (Louvain, 1932); Dionysius Exiguus's Latin version of the Life, akin to the second Greek Life, by H. van Cranenburgh (1969). Pachomios's *Catechesis,* Coptic text edited and translated by Lefort (CSCO 160 [1956]). New material in Hans Quecke, *Die Briefe Pachoms* (Regensburg, 1975). See

it that the word 'monk', literally a 'solitary', is one we naturally associate with a community and not with a hermit withdrawn in isolation. Everyone knows that this ex-soldier peasant Copt from upper Egypt, converted from paganism by the impression made on him by Christian charity without regard to membership of the Church, created the *koinobion* or community of monks and the concept of an 'order' with many monks in several linked houses living under rule. His houses were mainly located in or around the loop of the Nile in the neighbourhood of Dendera (ancient Tentyra). To say 'created' is not actually quite true, of course. From the earliest of the Greek Lives of Pachomios we know that, at the time when he first became a Christian and put himself to school with the laconic hermit Palamon, there were already little groups of semi-anchorites living near one another or together, mainly in twos, though we also hear of a group of five and another of ten. There is high probability that all these were groups of disciples gathered round some master of the path to sanctity. In the earliest Greek Life of Pachomios (cited below as G¹) we learn of an otherwise unknown Aotas, remembered for his unsuccessful attempts to form a *koinobion,* his failure being contrasted with Pachomios's success (G¹ 120). The Coptic tradition recalls how Pachomios too had his initial setback.

But Pachomios is differentiated from all contemporaries and predecessors by the sheer scale of his operations, designed to incorporate large numbers of monks within his society and to subject them to strict discipline. So far as our information goes, Pachomios first makes the enclosure wall of the monastery a physical and not merely a mental fact. The wall was the first building operation to be undertaken; and we learn that his brother John disapproved of it and tried to dismantle it, since he could see that it spelled the end of anchoritic life as hitherto understood.

The wall had evident consequences for the development of the commu-

---

also his lecture 'Ein Handvoll Pachomianischer Texte', *XIX Deutscher Orientalistentag 1975* (Wiesbaden, 1977), 221–29, promising yet further Coptic texts from the Chester Beatty library. H. Bacht edits with commentary the *Liber Orsiesi* in *Das Vermächtnis des Ursprungs* (Würzburg, 1972). Pachomian scholarship has not welcomed A. Veilleux, *La liturgie dans le cénobitisme pachômien au quatrième siècle* (*Studia Anselmiana* 37 [1968]); Veilleux summarises his argument in *Bibliotheca Sanctorum* x (1968), 10–20, and meets rejection from A. de Vogüé, *RHE* 69 (1974), 425–63, and D. J. Chitty, *JTS* 21 (1970), 195–99. Cf. J. Vergote, 'La valeur des vies grecques et coptes de S. Pachôme', *Orientalia Lovaniensia periodica* 8 (1977), 175–86. Much of the recent bibliography is in Philip Rousseau, *Ascetics, Authority, and the Church in the Age of Jerome and Cassian* (Oxford, 1978).

nity.[5] It greatly facilitated the control of the monks within at the same time as it limited access to outsiders, such as members of their families and members of the opposite sex who might distract them from their high purposes. No doubt the wall also served to mark out the frontiers of the monastery in face of encroaching farmers. Above all the wall made a very visible, public statement not merely about the division from the pagan world outside but also about the compromises besetting the normal life of the churches lived out in a pagan world.

One cannot assume that life in the Thebaid in A.D. 320 was so untroubled by Blemmyes or other nomadic marauders that the wall was not intended to serve any defensive purpose. But the Pachomian texts give no hint of this. The likelihood is that Pachomios's wall was simply a self-evidently natural thing for him to build, familiar as he was, after his pagan upbringing, with the walled *temenos* characteristic of unnumbered Egyptian temples going back to Zoser's funerary complex at Saqqara early in the third millennium B.C. Within his wall Pachomios planned buildings to serve various purposes: houses for groups of monks (each with their distinctive marks), a chapel, a guest house near the gate for visitors, a bakery and cookhouse for preparing food, a depository for the library of codices, another store for clothing. It can hardly be accidental that this general type of organisation is exemplified by pagan complexes in the Nile valley, such as the marvellously preserved Ptolemaic temple at Edfu. So nothing could have seemed more obvious to Pachomios than that his community should be enclosed, and that the wall should be provided with gates and door-keepers to control ingress and egress. If not intended as a fortification wall against marauding tribesmen, the barrier was evidently of sufficient height to deter anyone from going in and out without due authority; and before many years had passed its merits as a defence against barbarian raiding parties seeking prisoners to sell in the slave-markets must have been evident.

The Pachomian Lives

In this paper I shall not discuss at length what everyone knows, namely the sharp controversies of modern scholarship concerning the complex sources

---

5. H. Torp, 'Murs d'enceinte des monastères coptes primitifs et couvents-forteresses', *Mél Rom* 76 (1964), 173–200, has seen the disciplinary, juridical, and *temenos* significance of the wall.

for the history of the Pachomian foundations. The Greek, Coptic, and Arabic Lives have each in turn enjoyed zealous advocates of their primacy. After consideration and comparison of the various documents and of the writings of their respective advocates, I believe we ought to conclude that the Arabic tradition and its advocate Père Veilleux have the least claim to be held in awe, though there are assuredly places where the Arabic text includes good matter. As for the old battleground between the Greek and the Coptic, the subject of hard jousting between Derwas Chitty and L. T. Lefort, scholars to whom all students of the Pachomian texts owe a large debt, there is no very simple choice to be made. Both sets of texts draw on the same pool of tradition, which was originally Coptic and oral, but I do not think it likely that the Greek *Vita Prima* drew on a prior written Coptic Life. It is composed from a very Greek and Alexandrian viewpoint. Of the Greek and Coptic Lives each preserves good tradition neglected in the other strand. Lefort was evidently right in urging that the Coptic merits deep attention. The Coptic biographers offer early strata in the transmission for which we look in vain in the Greek Lives.

The consensus of sensible men is that the Greek *Vita Prima* is a priceless witness from within the Pachomian monastic tradition, but naturally from its Greek-speaking minority perhaps from the Pachomian house at Canopus (Metanoia) mentioned by Jerome in the preface to his Latin version of the *Praecepta*. The *Vita Prima* may be dated with reasonable confidence in (or very soon after) A.D. 390–400. The name of Origen is a bogy (G¹ 31). Moreover there is an emphatic statement (G¹ 94) that the incomparable honour of the patriarchate of Alexandria, whose occupant the Pachomian monks see as Christ's representative, is not actually personal to Athanasius himself but, by virtue of office, belongs to his successors. This looks like a reflection of Theophilos's well-known struggle to retain archiepiscopal authority in relation to the many monasteries within his jurisdiction, where offence had been caused by his initial indications of sympathy for Origen and Evagrios and of hostility towards 'anthropomorphites' who wanted to picture God in human form in their prayers.

The *Vita Prima* is of course more than a Life of Pachomios (though that is the simple title of the manuscript tradition). It includes also the story of his first three or four successors. In particular it is at least as much interested in a biography of his devoted pupil and eventual (perhaps to the regret of the *Vita Prima,* not immediate) successor Theodore. Pachomios's death may be confidently assigned to 9 May 346 (G¹ 114–16 and 120), that of Theodore to 27 April probably of either 368 or 371. Much of the dramatic force of the Life turns on the contrast between these two superiors of the order, and on the assertion of an ultimate harmony triumphing over a succession of painful episodes between them.

The author of the *Vita Prima* is acutely conscious that things are not now what they used to be; in his time there is moral and spiritual decline, and the readers need warnings of the perils of negligence (G^1 118). Some monks have an open ambition to be higumen or even to be promoted to the episcopate (G^1 126, 118). The old discipline requiring a stern renunciation of family ties has evidently undergone some relaxation (G^1 24, 67–68, 74, 80). The portrayals of the intense severity of Pachomios and of the self-extinguishing humility of Theodore are sermons addressed to a generation where discipline has fallen off, so that monks now actively seek posts of honour and leadership which, in the earlier period, they would have accepted only as an act of obedience to their superior.

There are also other indications of the post-Pachomian concerns of the biographical tradition. The author of the *Vita Prima* is anxious that Pachomios's *koinobion* (his name for the entire order of monasteries) be ranked on a par with the achievements of Anthony, so sweetly sung by Athanasius. This biography of Pachomios is intended to do for the founder what the *Vita Antonii* had done for Anthony. Moreover, the Pachomian houses, it is stressed, had a warm place in Athanasius's heart. How widely known this love was is shown by the fact that the refugee archbishop was vainly sought in the monasteries by the dux Artemius (G^1 137–38). In 346 Pachomian monks called upon Anthony who expressed warm approbation of the *koinobion* as a re-creation of the apostolic *koinonia,* and added how much he himself would have liked to enter a *koinobion* had such a thing existed when he began to follow the ascetic life (G^1 120). Again, Pachomios once says that 'the three most important things in Egypt are Athanasius, Anthony, and this *koinobion*' (G^1 136). It is stressed that Pachomios and especially Theodore act constantly in reverence for and in harmony with the bishops (G^1 27, 29–30, 135, 144), and indeed that when Athanasius came up the Nile on his visitation of the Thebaid Theodore (not at that time superior) laid on a noble reception for him from the monks (G^1 144).

Twice the author of the *Vita Prima* seeks to explain why no contemporary of Pachomios wrote a Life at the time (G^1 46 and 98), and is clearly aware of sceptics who will ask how authentic his portrait is, so that he must assure them of the valued traditions from the old fathers he has consulted. These two texts appear to assume that the earliest Greek biographer has no written material before him in either Coptic or Greek. On the other hand, the oral tradition has surely shaped the portrait in important directions; and in recent times the question has been increasingly put whether in the tensions between Pachomios and Theodore depicted in the *Vita Prima* and in the Coptic Lives there may have lain some fundamental conflicts of principle about the nature of the Pachomian ideal and its attachment to the Church. In particular does Theodore represent, in contrast with Pachomios, a tightening of the disciplinary rules (necessitated perhaps by the increasing size of the community), a stronger insistence on obedience within the *koinōnia* in antithesis to an older anchoritic freedom? And is there any possible link with a greater theological freedom in the earlier stage of development?

Pachomios's Orthodoxy

The so-called gnostic library of Nag Hammadi was found in the mountain within sight of the Pachomian monastery nearby. John Barns thought that letters and receipts used as filling for the bindings of some of the codices are likely to have come from the Pachomian houses.[6] His suggestion has not yet been either vindicated or disproved, but in principle it has obviously inherent probability. Athanasius's Festal Letter announcing the date of Easter for 367 lists the books of the Bible canon, and forcibly forbids the reading of secret books. Perhaps the cache was made in consequence of this or some similar later 'crackdown' by authority. That the codices were read in the nearby monastery is surely as good as certain. Several Nag-Hammadi texts are not so much gnostic (though many may be so labelled) as encratite: they are to justify celibacy, and hence the presence of a piece from Plato's *Republic* (588–89), and a Coptic version of the Sentences of Sextus. On the other hand, the libertine wing of gnosticism is virtually unrepresented (other than in ambiguous allusions such as logion 61 of the Coptic Gospel of Thomas, where the couch of Salome on which Jesus is said to have rested is more naturally located in her dining-room than in her bedroom).

It is not inherently probable that Pachomios was interested in the niceties of orthodox doctrine as a theological system. Except for the Origenists, early monks are seldom concerned with theological refinements which they

6. John Barns, 'Greek and Coptic Papyri from the Covers of the Nag Hammadi Codices', in *Essays on the Nag Hammadi Texts in Honour of Pahor Labib,* ed. M. Krause [Nag Hammadi Studies vi] (Leiden, 1975), 9–18. See the preface to the recent volume of the Nag Hammadi Codices in Facsimile (on the cartonnage) by J. M. Robinson (1979).

regard as having intellectual pretensions conducive to pride and as generating dissensions. Pachomios's links to the ordinary life of the Church may have gradually grown as local bishops either came to assert jurisdiction over his houses or, as at Panopolis, saw how useful monks could be in a missionary situation and encouraged them to build a monastery as an assertion of a Christian presence in a predominantly pagan city (G¹ 81). But initially such links will have been few and weak. It is worth asking whether the various early strands of tradition attest any tendencies to sympathise with doctrinal themes that could have aroused alarm in an orthodox bishop's breast. This is not a matter of naively setting out to 'discover' Pachomios to have been a heretical ascetic subsequently covered in orthodox plasterwork, but rather of asking to what extent it is reasonable to think the early Pachomian tradition largely indifferent where dogma is concerned, content to make use of a diversity of gifts so long as they all encourage renunciation of the world.

In the *Vita Prima* the resurrection of Christ is first affirmed as a historic redemptive fact; and nothing can be less gnostic than that. But when the theme is reinterpreted of the 'spiritual resurrection' which means that we should exercise patience and not revile others (G¹ 57), such language is reminiscent of the dualistic heretic Hierakas, a Greek-speaking Copt of Leontopolis in the Delta about 300, whose influence provoked Epiphanios of Salamis in 375 to compose some pages of refutation (*Panarion* 67).

According to one Pachomian narrative (Letter of Amnion 12), when Pachomios desired to become a monk, he was first invited to join the schismatic Melitians and the heretical Marcionites; but a vision assured him that Christ stands with the bishop of Alexandria. The same source (26) speaks of an influential monk in one Pachomian monastery, named Patchelphios, who taught a young man to disbelieve in the resurrection of the flesh but was brought to conform to the teachings of the Church.

In the second Greek Life there is mention of demonic assaults on Pachomios's orthodoxy,[7] but without success since he hated Arians, Melitians, and Origen.[8]

On one occasion (*Paralipomena* xiv.33) heretics in hairshirts challenged Pachomios to walk on the water of the Nile, a charism attributed to several holy men, and once in the *Vita Prima* credited to Pachomios himself.[9] But Pachomios angrily rejected the suggestion as being both foreign to God and

---

7. G² 17; Halkin, 183.
8. G² 27 and 88; Halkin, 268.9–10.
9. G¹ 21; Halkin, 13.21.

also thought ill of by secular persons; in other words as a well-known trick of sorcery. (Lucian, *Philopseudes* 34, tells us that in the caverns of Memphis sorcerers professed to teach one how to do this trick.)

In all our texts Theodore appears as a pillar of orthodoxy explicitly attached to the authority of the episcopate. That there was tension between Pachomios and Theodore over the succession is certain (G¹ 106). One can only speculate (and therefore go beyond the authority of the texts), but it seems inevitable to ask whether or not the tension between the two heroes originated in Theodore's wish to link the *koinōnia* more closely with the local churches and their clergy, whereas Pachomios represented the desire to keep the old independence and freedom of the initial colony of anchorites.

When the news came that Athanasius was coming south on his visitation of the Thebaid, Theodore was responsible for hastily rushing monks north to meet him before he reached Hermopolis (on the left bank opposite Antinoopolis). A hundred monks lined the banks of the great river, with Theodore holding the bridle of the ass on which Athanasius rode when he came to visit the Pachomian houses, honouring the primate with a torchlight procession and chanting. Theodore, we are told, won Athanasius's approval for the internal arrangements of the monasteries, the chapel, refectory, cells with the little stools on which the monks rested (it was not their way to lie down for sleep) — everything evoked the primate's praise. But Horsiesios, still in office as superior of the *koinōnia,* did not appear, and Athanasius was persuaded to send him a letter by Theodore's hand (G¹ 144).

The Pachomian Rule

According to one strand of the Coptic tradition, Pachomios's first attempt to establish a community of disciples under his personal direction was a failure. He gave a rule to the brothers gathering round him, namely to share all their earnings for a common purse to supply the group's material needs and for food. Pachomios acted as treasurer. But they would not accept his authority and insulted him, indulging in mockery and laughter. After five years he abandoned his efforts and dissolved the community. The dissident monks in vain complained to the bishop of Dendera, Saprion, who, after listening to them stating their complaints, decided that Pachomios was getting it right (VC 68–69).

The Greek *Vita Prima* suppresses or ignores this false start in which the founder is insulted, and reports that the scheme for founding the *koinōnia* was formed in response to an angelic message calling Pachomios to a life of service to the human race, evidently in contrast to his personal and private interest. Then follows an account of Pachomios's Rule for the community laying down that dress, food, and sleeping arrangements are all to be uniformly observed by every monk without distinction. All recruits are to be admitted after a test of some kind; then they are clothed in the habit, required to make formal renunciation of the world and of any contact with their kinsfolk. They are set to learn parts of the Bible, especially the psalter and the gospels. If illiterate, they are to be taught letters.

The mature Rule translated from Greek into Latin by Jerome at the end of the century shows how many permanent monastic customs originate in the Pachomian houses: the weekly roster of duty in church, refectory, and kitchen (*Praecepta* 13); the weekly catechism; the reckoning of seniority from the date of profession, not by age or dignity (31). Monks should act with consideration for their brothers, not entering another's cell without express leave (112), never physically touching another (95).

Neither Greek nor Coptic tradition knows of expulsions for homosexual practices (the Coptic has dark allusions that might be so construed but do not require this interpretation).[10] On the other hand the Rule forbids joking or playing games with young boys in the monastery.[11]

Pachomios's initial rule was not to admit any clergy to his *koinōnia*, on the ground that ambition for office produces envy, strife, and faction (G[1] 27). The community in each monastery attended the liturgy on Saturdays and Sundays; on Saturdays at the nearest village church, on Sundays in the monastery itself, the local presbyter being invited to come and celebrate. Attendance at the synaxis is compulsory (G[1] 74; *Praecepta* 22). The communities meet for prayers in the evening and at dawn. The monks have a duty of service to one another and to the weak, the old, the sick, the young (G[1] 28; cf. 24). Their employment is to weave baskets and spin ropes for sale, and to cultivate vegetables on adjacent land belonging to the monastery.

Expansion of the *Koinōnia*

Pachomios's community rapidly grew in numbers, and this came to require the division of each monastery into constituent houses, each ruled by a

---

10. VC 156f., 185, 397.
11. *Praecepta* 166; Boon, 66.10–15.

housemaster and his assistant or second. Soon other monasteries beside the upper Nile were impressed and asked to be incorporated into the *koinōnia.* Although a number of bishops in the Thebaid distrusted Pachomios and virtually put him on trial at the synod of Latopolis *c.* 344 (below), he was vindicated; and as we have seen, the bishop of the pagan stronghold Panopolis (Akhmim) actually invited the Pachomian monks to come to his diocese to found a house. At first local opposition dismantled by night whatever walls were erected by day, but eventually, with miraculous aid and angelic fire, the monks succeeded in constructing their enclosure wall as a fortress of Christian protest in a militantly pagan environment (G¹ 81).

By the year 345 the federation of the *koinōnia* numbered no less than nine houses. The great monastery at Pbau had 600 monks in 352 (Letter of Ammon 2), twenty of them being Greek-speaking (ibid. 7). The figures given by the fifth-century writers seem to be rounded up to an impressive size without any reliable precision, and one can conclude only that the total numbers continued to grow in the second half of the fourth century. Jerome's figure of 50,000 seems a wild exaggeration, Sozomen's 500 a grave underestimate. John Cassian speaks of 5,000. Palladios offers both 3,000 and 7,000.[12]

Pachomios's Successors

A crisis of leadership occurred on Pachomios's death. The support for Theodore had been set aside by Pachomios himself, who designated Petronios to succeed him (G¹ 114). But plague was removing many of the brothers by death, and Petronios was soon among them. Before death he nominated Horsiesios as superior, despite Horsiesios's protests that it was beyond his powers. This proved to be the case. The monasteries were so growing in numbers that they could put more land under cultivation with their large labour force. Already in Pachomios's time it was the rule for the superior to summon the heads of all his monasteries twice a year, at the August meeting going carefully through the accounts (G¹ 83). They acquired numerous boats for transporting their produce (G¹ 146), in contrast to the early days when the entire *koinōnia* possessed only two boats (G¹ 113). Apollonios the abbot of Monchosis (Temouschous) was among those who had associated his house

---

12. Jerome's preface, Boon, 8; Cassian, *Inst.* iv.1; Sozom. iii.14; Palladius, HL VI.6.xxxii. Cf. G. M. Colombás, *El monacato primitivo* i (Madrid, 1974), 97, whose pages on Pachomios are particularly well done.

with the Pachomian *koinōnia*. Apollonios wanted the agricultural industry of the monks to increase still further, probably by the taking on of additional labour from lay persons, perhaps even women, outside the monastery. At the parent house of Pbau, Horsiesios agreed with Apollonios's expansionist economic policy. But Theodore saw in it a serious threat to Pachomios's overriding religious purpose. A dramatic crisis ensued in which Horsiesios suddenly retired by night to Chenoboskeia, and Theodore succeeded him as superior. For a time Apollonios wholly withdrew his monastery from association with the *koinōnia* but was eventually won back by Theodore's diplomacy, with some compromise formula of which we are not given the text. Even Horsiesios who had moved outside Theodore's jurisdiction to join Apollonios at Monchosis was eventually charmed by Theodore to move back to Pbau, a transfer that Theodore stage-managed with an evident sense of high dramatic style (G¹ 145). But the disagreements certainly went deep. Both the Greek and the Coptic traditions seek to gloss over them, and only the Arabic Life frankly explains the essence of the matter.

Theodore, in a word, feared the secularisation of Pachomios's ideal. It is no doubt true that the Pachomian monasteries were solving a social and economic problem for many peasants in the Nile valley, put out of work by the inflation of the second half of the third century so well attested in the papyri. Both Tabennisi and Pbau are described as deserted villages.[13] A peasant was more secure economically inside the monastery than outside.[14] Inside his life would be simple and frugal. The food would not be rich, but sufficient for life without any temptation to excess (G¹ 53, 55). Wine and meat would be very infrequent unless one were to fall sick. Except for the two nunneries (134), there was virtually no contact with women, which spared the monks emotional stress, and no doubt contributed something to the common achievement of great longevity among the old men. The dilapidations of old age were cared for by the young recruits. All this is enough to explain why the monasteries attracted large numbers. But the magnetic attraction seems to have been Pachomios himself and his unconditional obedience to his own uncompromising ideals.

13. G¹ 12; Halkin, 8.1 and G¹ 54; Halkin, 36.4.
14. *Liber Orsiesi* 47; Boon, 140.5ff.

The Call to Obedience

The Greek *Vita Prima* once contrasts Theodore's gentleness and charm with the 'mournful and fierce austerity' of Pachomios (G¹ 91) who never allowed himself to forget the souls in torment and felt himself responsible for seeing that his monks did not join them. It is easy to think of Pachomios as resembling the Pantokrator at Daphni. He inspired fear in his flock — in contrast to Samuel, who combined abstemiousness with characteristic cheerfulness of character (G¹ 81). The founding father of the *koinōnia* expected his monks to give him that unconditional obedience that a disciple wished to give an anchorite in the desert.

Pachomios's discipline is hostile to all excessive mortifications (G¹ 69) and especially to ostentatious proposals such as ordeal by fire (G¹ 8). The monk who proposed to him this test of faith ended, by a terrible irony, in throwing himself on the hot coals of the furnace of the bathhouse at Panopolis. Perhaps he was trying his luck at fire-walking once too often rather than committing suicide. (G¹ 96 mentions suicides among the Pachomian ascetics.) Excess, however, is a relative term. Laughter and gossip in the bakery (cf. *Praecepta* 116) or working during an hour appointed for meditation brought unpleasant consequences.[15] An ex-actor Silvanos began his novitiate by strenuous mortifications. But he then relaxed his rigour until one day his conversation suddenly reverted to entertaining his brother monks with the old indecent jokes of the stage.[16] Before all the brothers Pachomios demanded that he remove his habit, resume his lay clothing, and submit to expulsion. 'Forgive me, just this once more', pleaded Silvanos. 'But how much have I tolerated and rebuked already, how many beatings have you received and ignored?' (a reply which is important evidence for monastery discipline).[17] But then senior monks took the evidently high risk of speaking on behalf of the delinquent Silvanos, an act of intercession which, as the *Liber Orsiesi* shows, could easily land one in as much trouble as the delinquent himself, making one a partaker of his sins.[18] Pachomios relented, Silvanos stayed. His weeping was so uncontrollable as to make him distressing company in the refectory. After eight years of the severest penitential life he died, and Pachomios assured the community that he had heard flights

---

15. G¹ 89 of Tabennisi; cf. 121 of Pachoum near Latopolis=Esna.
16. Cf. *Praecepta et Inst.* 10 (Boon, 56.5): '*qui [. . .] plus ioco quam honestum est deditus*'.
17. Cf. *Praecepta* 163; Boon, 65.6.
18. *Liber Orsiesi* 24; Boon, 125.14–16.

of angels singing him to his rest.[19] A delinquent monk ran the risk of being refused a cortège singing psalms at his funeral as his body was borne up to the mountain caves three miles away.[20] The Rule lays down a strict control over the psalm-singing at a funeral (*Praecepta* 127).

Pachomios is a seer who is granted visions, not (he says) of his own will but when the Lord so grants (G¹ 112). And some of his visions of things to come predict fearful decline after his departing, penetration of the monasteries by heresies, and lax discipline (G¹ 71).[21] At the synod of Latopolis *c.* 344 serious charges were brought against Pachomios's claim that he could see the demons (G¹ 112). Happily the synod included two bishops who had at one time been Pachomian monks and who helped to defend him. Like other holy men, he can discern the hearts, and can detect innocence and guilt (G¹ 42–43, 122). A bishop sends a man accused of theft to Pachomios for judgement (G¹ 76; cf. 92). His diacritic power also enables him to diagnose illness (52). He possesses clairvoyant powers of knowing things happening at a distance (89). He has a criterion for distinguishing divine from demonic spirits, namely that in divinely given visions the recipient's personal thoughts wholly disappear together with any self-consciousness of receiving the vision, whereas in demonic visions the recipient knows he is seeing it and can still retain the power to think and deliberate naturally (87). It is a criterion that has a strongly Montanist ring about it. The old orthodox complaint against Montanist prophecy protested that orthodox prophets always retain their natural rationality when delivering their prophecy, even if that may be suspended while they are receiving its revelation.

A fundamental requirement in the Pachomian *koinōnia* is obedience to the superior. Provided that the superior himself is the first to keep the rules, this principle holds the society together. The coherence of the congregation therefore depends intimately upon one man. The superior is responsible for his monks as shepherd of their souls, as their intercessor when they fall sick (G¹ 132–33). Pachomios has to teach Theodore obedience by the hard way. He is arbitrary, unreasonable, jealous of his personal autocracy, at the borderline of cruelty, until Theodore has learnt that Pachomios will never share his authority with anyone else (G¹ 50; cf. 126). At the same time the Lives record anecdotes of Pachomios's humility and self-effacement. I do

---

19. *Paralipomena* 2–4; cf. G¹ 104–5. The power to hear the angelic choir receiving a departing soul is possessed also by Theodore (G¹ 93).

20. G¹ 103; cf. *Paralipomena* 5–6.

21. Cf. G¹ 146 on Theodore.

not think much will survive of recent suggestions that in the cenobitic tradition the begetter of paternal autocracy is Theodore, and that the authentic Pachomios had much more democratic and fraternal conceptions of his role than his successors found practicable.

Pachomios communicated with the heads of his monasteries with the help of a strange alphabetical cipher whose code remains unbroken. Even though a major recent discovery by Fr Quecke has unearthed the Coptic and Greek originals of several letters hitherto known only in Jerome's Latin, it remains the case that no cryptographer has yet been able to penetrate their arcane method of communication. I venture to suggest that the cipher will never be broken because its intention is not actually to communicate in the ordinary sense of that word; it has the purpose of being obscure, and therefore of surrounding its author with an aura of mystery and authority.

The Pachomian Heritage

In this paper I have tried to sketch out an outline of Pachomios's achievement. The ideal of sanctity is a noble end; the means by which it is to be realised are beset by thorns and brambles on the pathway. Pachomios realises some important Christian aims: identification with the poor, restraint of lust for power and clerical domination, creating a *koinōnia* of the Spirit bound together by the common prayers and meals and labour and by a personal obedience to the superior which is seen as a way of following the Lord himself. Simultaneously Pachomios does more than any other single person to create rules and wise customs necessary for the good order of a religious community, a remarkable number of which remain in use even now. Nevertheless, there is another side to the coin. The enclosure wall that symbolises the separateness of the community from the world also accentuates the secularisation of the created order.

To busy university teachers beset by committees and administration the monastic ideal of withdrawal and reflection can provoke to envy. And even university teachers can easily operate with a mental wall separating their college or their campus from the outside world, in some cases with a physical barrier as well. The enclosure wall fulfils several roles, some beneficial, others not so. When Pachomios created the enclosed religious community, something was lost at the same time as something was gained.

Christian and Roman Universalism
in the Fourth Century

Adherence to Christianity was no doubt a matter of religion rather than political calculation to the emperor Constantine the Great. But there is an element of unreality to the old contrast between the saintly emperor 'canonized', so to speak, by a grateful Church and the ambitious, power-hungry military commander who, in Burckhardt's eyes, could not have decided to worship the God of the Christians unless he had carefully calculated that this would be to his political advantage. Calculation or no, he needed something the Church could provide, namely legitimation. There is paradox in this. For the emperor, already under question for usurpation in 306, to be identified with a body so un-Roman as the Church cannot prima facie have assisted him in acquiring wider recognition of his legitimacy. Might rather than any form of right had been decisive in his meteoric rise of 306. His admission to the second tetrarchy with the rank of Caesar was accepted by Galerius in 307 surely in recognition of the legions which Constantine commanded. Any reluctance that Galerius may have felt would have been far stronger if, following the opinion of T. D. Barnes, Constantine's identification with Christianity was already a public fact as early as 306.[1] In 312 the lightning war against Maxentius made necessary the justification that a religious ideology

---

1. T. D. Barnes, *Constantine and Eusebius* (Harvard University Press, 1981). Lactantius (*De mortibus persecutorum* 24.9 and in the addition of 324 to *Div. Inst.* 1.1.13) says that Constantine's first act on being invested with the purple was to restore freedom of worship to the Christians. This text is insufficiently explained away by Barnes's critics, e.g. Thomas Grünewald, *Constantinus Maximus Augustus: Herrschaftspropaganda in der zeitgenössischen Überlieferung* [Historia Einzelschriften, 64] (Stuttgart, 1990), p. 80. I am not able to follow Barnes in his refusal to find any tendency to tolerate non-Christian cults or any syncretism in Constantine, and would be inclined to discern polemic against syncretism with sun-cult

could provide, and he won the battle *instinctu divinitatis, mentis magnitudine,* as the triumphal arch would declare.[2] The anonymous orator who in 313 delivered a panegyric in his honour included cautious words about the divine power which had moved Constantine to launch his attack 'against the advice of men, against the warnings of the haruspices'. The panegyrist felt sure that the amazingly successful Constantine possessed a private line of communication to 'that divine mind which delegates the care of us to inferior divinities and deigns to disclose himself to you alone'.[3] The highest god was on his side; and none knew more about the worship of the highest than the Church.

That Constantine did not identify himself with the Church to impress the citizens of the empire seems certain. Eusebius of Caesarea's oration for Constantine's thirtieth anniversary mentions the way in which scornful people laughed at him for supporting the Church.[4]

Constantine both consulted the haruspices and ignored their advice: it encapsulates the ironic problem of his religious allegiance. To consult them and then to do the opposite of what they told him was a kind of assertion that he had a higher power to guide him, namely the 'supreme Creator of the world who has as many names as there are peoples', and whose preference among these names we humans cannot know—a power immanent in the visible world and transcendent beyond and above it.[5]

The audience for an imperial panegyric in 313, or for that matter in 321, was largely pagan, and the terms used by the panegyrist cannot be squeezed to force the conclusion that not only the emperor but the selected singer of his praises was already Christian. The panegyric of 313 nevertheless presupposes that Constantine was a man for whom the highest deity had a grand purpose to fulfil, and that to achieve this end he needed special protection.

The God of the biblical record was held in awe and respect by pagan intellectuals. Porphyry himself praised the piety of the ancient Hebrews in worshipping 'the great and true God who is terrible even to the other deities', and thought it correct to distinguish among the inferior powers benevolent angels in the ethereal realm from the daimones inhabiting the air

---

in Eusebius's interpretation of the Logos as the Sun (*Laus Const.* 6.19–20). Averil Cameron's remarks (*Journal of Roman Studies* 83 (1983), p. 197) are surely judicious.

2. Dessau, *Inscriptiones Latinae Selectae* 694.

3. *Paneg. Lat.* 12.2.4.

4. *Laus Const.* 11.3, 224,15 Heikel.

5. *Paneg. Lat.* 5.26.

whose benevolence could not be taken for granted.[6] Nothing in the panegyric of 313 goes beyond what Porphyry could have approved. Indeed Porphyry himself wrote words which indirectly might have influenced Constantine away from a syncretism of Christianity with the worship of the unconquered Sun. Porphyry is quoted by Augustine as declaring on the authority of the Chaldean oracles that the rites of the sun and moon, acknowledged to be the principal divinities among the gods, are incapable of purifying a man.[7] Porphyry felt sure that there must be some universal way of salvation, valid for every soul, but could not identify it.[8]

In the fourth century there were potent attractions, for an emperor trying to hold things together, in a religious policy which accepted all cults not obviously immoral as equally valid ways of venerating the deity. In the last book of Apuleius's *Metamorphoses,* Isis informs Lucius at his initiation into her mysteries that she is the one divinity 'worshipped under different forms, with a diversity of rites, and under many names by the entire world'. A list of goddesses follows, concluding with the Egyptian claim that Isis is her true name.[9] That all religions follow different routes but aspire to attain one and the same destination was a widespread view, receiving from Symmachus its most famous formulation during the argument with Ambrose over the altar of Victory, but also found elsewhere as a conventional pagan opinion.[10] In the east Themistius urged the mystery of God, impenetrable by the human mind, to be the ground for mutual toleration; the fact of religious diversity is for Themistius evidence of the relative character of all human religious assertions.[11]

The Christians found it impossible to take an optimistic evaluation of

---

6. Cited by Augustine, *De civitate Dei* [= *DCD*] 20.24.1; 10.9.

7. *DCD* 10.23.

8. *DCD* 10.32.

9. Apuleius, *Metam.* 11.5.

10. Symmachus, *Relatio* 3.10 (p. 40 ed. Barrow, 1973); Augustine, *ep.* 104.12 (Nectario); Porphyry in Eusebius, *Pr. Evang.* VIII 9.10 and XIV 10.

11. Themistius, *or.* V addressed to Jovian in 364, tells the emperor, confronted by high tension between pagans and Christians in the aftermath of Julian and by frenetic rival factions in the Church demanding his support, that because the essence of religion lies in freedom of conscience, state authority is useless; that because there are many different ways to God who actually likes diversity, controversy is coterminous with religion; and that a policy of religious toleration will help to keep the newly found peace with Persia. (Had Constantius regarded his eastern wars as imposing Christian civilization and stopping the Persian custom of incestuous marriages?) Themistius receives a masterful study from G. Dagron in *Travaux et Mémoires* 3 (1968), pp. 1–242, and is edited by G. Downey (Teubner edition, 1965).

any form of pagan cult. The gods of the heathen nations are 'daimonia', declared the Psalmist (96.5).[12] In Christian eyes polytheistic worship was, like sorcery, hanky-panky with evil spirits. Christians were glad to discover in pagan writers of the third century, like Cornelius Labeo and even Porphyry, that in the pantheon of polytheism some of the powers are not friendly tribal spirits but malevolent forces who have to be placated and propitiated.[13] The Christians did not wish to mix their myths. Augustine was not enthusiastic when a priest of Cybele assured him that Attis, the kindly god nursing his sheep, was a Christian now.[14]

Religion is simultaneously the most uniting and the most dividing force in human society. Roman society had a large number of local cults, and the maximum of social cohesion was achieved by serene toleration. Augustine once drew a sharp contrast between the cohesiveness of a society that juxtaposed a large number of polytheistic cults, each with incompatible myths which no one took very seriously, side by side with the quarrelsome Christians, whose rancour and mutual hatred had devastating effects on North African social relations.[15] Donatist and Catholic were utterly agreed in being wholly negative to pagan cult. Before the rabid bands of Donatist Circumcellions turned their ferocity on Catholic churches and clergy, they acquired a fearsome reputation by their unstoppable charges on the orchestral players providing music for pagan festivals.[16]

12. Cited by Origen, *contra Celsum* 3.3 and 37; 4.29; 7.65; especially 7.69 where Origen proves his point from the magical spells that compel a god to reside in his or her image. On this art I gather some of the principal texts in my note on *contra Celsum* 5.38. Cf. also Augustine, *DCD* 21.6.1. For rejection of the Christian thesis that all pagan cult is sorcery cf. Themistius V 70b. He even defends Maximus of Ephesus, VII 99dff., whose magical skills had enthralled the emperor Julian. Pagans protested to Augustine that they worshipped angels, not demons: *En. in Ps.* 85.12.

13. Labeo in Augustine, *DCD* 2.11; 3.25; 8.13; Porphyry, *De Abstinentia* 2.58, and as quoted by Philoponus, *De opificio mundi* 4.20. Porphyry was also willing to grant that when gods inspired oracles, that was a compulsion imposed upon them by magic (Eusebius, *Pr. Evang.* 5.8 and 6.5).

14. *Tract. in ev. Joh.* 7.6: a priest of Attis used to say *Et ipse pileatus Christianus est.* Did he mean that a temple of Cybele had lately been transformed into a church, on the analogy of Jerome, *Ep.* 107.2: *Iam et Aegyptius Serapis factus est Christianus*? Augustine did not so understand him. Ambrosiaster (*Quaest.* 84.3, *CSEL* 50 p. 145) reports a pagan opinion that the Christian Good Friday memorial was plagiarized from the expiation spring ceremony of Attis and Cybele, and therefore that both religions were saying the same thing.

15. *De utilitate ieiunii* 9 (*PL* 40.712–13; CChr.SL 46.237–38).

16. Augustine, *Ep.* 185.12; *Sermo* 62.17; *c. Gaudentium* I 28, 32; 38, 51. Augustine grants that some Circumcellion attacks were directed against very bad people: *ep. ad Cathol. de*

Therefore, a Christian universal religion could not possibly be achieved by treating all cults as equally valid, all equally relative.

Constantine had a strong consciousness of possessing a mission from the highest God.[17] The intercession of the Church's bishops would be potent to secure heavenly favour for his military ventures and for the prosperity of his empire. Dissensions in the Church, on the other hand, were not only socially divisive on earth but also vexatious to heaven. The squabbles in North Africa and then at Alexandria were a source of distress and alarm that the displeasure of heaven would be provoked, with grim consequences for the defence of the frontier, the avoidance of famine and plague, and all the many threats to the survival of his rule. Pagan opinion was to interpret his adhesion to Christianity as a flight on the part of a guilt-ridden conscience, haunted by the memory of dreadful acts of inhumanity, especially the murder of Crispus and Fausta in 326.[18] Constantine needed absolution before he died to show that the highest deity had not only been the cause of his political success but also accepted him among his Friends.[19] So in its own way the quest for absolution by baptism at the end of his life was also a contribution to his search for legitimacy. God had forgiven him even if some human beings had not.[20]

But by his adhesion to the Church, Constantine identified himself with a society which did not think of itself as bound to the particularity of the Roman empire. His 'conversion' was hailed by his Christian panegyrist Eusebius of Caesarea in terms of fulfilling Old Testament prophecies that the earth would be filled with the glory of the Lord as the waters cover the sea.[21]

---

unit. ecclesiae 20.54, commenting that it is unwise to use illegal means to deter illegal acts. Compromise with paganism was not a Donatist characteristic (*En. in Ps.* 88, ii, 14). A degree of rivalry between Catholic and Donatist seems presupposed by *c. Gaudentium* I 38, 51: *pagani quorum certe ubi potuistis templa evertistis et basilicas destruxistis, quod et nos fecimus.*

17. Eusebius's oration in honor of his thirtieth year as emperor mentions his pride in being 'God's servant' (7.12). The self-consciousness appears strongly in the bizarre letter to Arius and his supporters where Constantine tells God 'I am your man': H. G. Opitz, *Urkunden zur Geschichte der arianischen Streites* (document 34), 71,20. In *Vita Constantini* I 25 Constantine's campaigns against Germans on the Rhine and then in conquering Britons are fought to impose civilized gentleness, the savage and ineducable being expelled.

18. Zosimus II 29,3-4.

19. For Constantine as admitted to the circle of God's Friends cf. Eusebius, *Laus Const.* 2.3 p. 119,7 Heikel.

20. The erection at Constantinople of the Church of the Apostles as a mausoleum for himself and his dynasty provided a Christian version of Alexander the Great's apotheosis as the Thirteenth god: John Chrysostom, *Hom. in 2 Cor.* 26.5 (*PG* 61.581f.).

21. On the importance of the universal expansion of the Church in fulfilment of prophecy, see H. Berkhof, *Die Theologie des Eusebius von Caesarea* (Amsterdam, 1939), pp. 49f.

Could it be that the Christian emperor's role was not simply to ensure that, under the right worship of the true highest Deity, there would be security and prosperity for the Roman world but, further, to diffuse the values of a Christian society, governed under the rule of law to which every citizen had equal access,[22] beyond the frontier to embrace all the barbarian peoples? Could it then be that the economic, political, and military success of the empire was destined by providence to be an instrument in the service of an ultimately spiritual end of which the prime agency would be the ecclesia catholica? This universal Church did not sacrifice its universality by being anchored to a visible and ordered community structured round an episcopate with focal points of authority in its great sees, and perhaps in particular in the cathedra Petri at Rome. Among jurists it was established convention to hold that, in all the diversities created by local decisions, one could be confident of having a sound basis for action if one inquired how the matter in question had been decided in the city of Rome.[23] So too a Christian Roman emperor could come to see in the episcopate, focussed in the great patriarchates and especially in the Roman see, an agency for maintaining discipline in an international order.

Ancient polytheistic religion was attached to particular places and peoples. Notoriously the Christian Church was distinctive in ancient society for being a body emancipated from attachment to ethnic divisions. Unhappily it turned out to be harder to stop civil war within the Church than to quell it in the secular world. The Donatist schism in Africa was assuredly a civil war.[24] In 313 it cannot have been a foregone conclusion that the see of Rome, with the churches north of the Mediterranean, and ultimately the emperor himself were going to support Caecilian rather than Donatus. It may simply have been inconceivable in 314 that the Council of Arles would come to a conclusion other than that the Pope's council of the previous year had been right. Donatus's appeal from the two councils to the emperor himself met

---

22. Ambrose, *Hexaemeron* V 21.66. Ambrose generally has a less pessimistic portrait of the justice administered in the courts than one finds in, e.g., John Chrysostom or Augustine who are frank and sharp about the prevalence of bribery. But Ambrose was aware that the powerful often put improper pressure on judges (*De officiis* II 24,125) and that prisoners in chains may be innocent men (*in Ps.* 118.20.23, *CSEL* 62). He could write that every secular dignity is under the power of the devil (*in Luc.* iv.28). Themistius (I 14d, 15a) also stresses equality before the law as crucial to Roman civilization.

23. *Digesta* I 3:32 (Salvius Julianus).

24. *Bellum civile:* Augustine, *c. Gaudentium* I 19,21.

with frustration, and thereafter the government had a long and peculiarly intractable schism on its hands.

*   *   *

The ideological background of Constantine's vision of himself and of the Church lies in much earlier attitudes within the Church. In the Pauline epistles, as in Romans 13 and 2 Thessalonians 2, the Roman empire was understood to have a providential part to play in the divine plan for human history. It is presupposed in the Acts of the Apostles that the apostle Paul's final arrival in Rome, after a reasonably successful mission to the intellectuals in Athens, has symbolic significance.[25] Melito of Sardis was to see the pax Romana as divinely granted to foster the progress of the Christian mission.[26] But mission is always intimately bound up with unity, and the Christians did not find unity easy to preserve. Augustine was sadly to record that the mutual hatred between Donatist and Catholic in North Africa was driving many of the recently converted peasants back to their old polytheistic ways.[27]

In the seventies of the second century, the anti-Christian pamphleteer and Platonic philosopher Celsus made observations about the Christians which prima facie appear contradictory and antithetical. He was aware that round the body which he calls 'the great Church', or 'those of the multitude',[28] there was a large penumbra of sects in utter disagreement not only with the great Church but with one another. 'They attack one another with dreadful and unrepeatable terms of abuse; they are willing to make not the least concession to reach agreement, but hold one another in total detestation.'[29] The sects to which Celsus refers turn out to be the followers of Marcion, and various gnostic groups about which he was reasonably well informed— Valentinians, Ebionites, Simonians, Carpocratians, and Ophites, the last named being noteworthy for adapting a Mithras liturgy to their syncretistic purposes. On the other hand, 'the great Church' of the majority is presented

---

25. How deep the significance is portrayed in Acts by the narrative of successive hindrances to his arrival in Rome which the apostle surmounts—the storm and the snake-bite being only the most dramatic.

26. Melito in Eusebius, *H.E.* IV 27.7-11.

27. Augustine, *Ep.* 20* Divjak (*CSEL* 88.105). How recent the evangelization of Numidia was can be judged from Aug., *En. in Ps.* 96.7: 'Everyone present had a pagan grandfather or greatgrandfather.'

28. Origen, *contra Celsum* [= *CC*] 5.59 and 61.

29. *CC* 63.

by Celsus as a tightly coherent body whose most striking characteristic is 'agape', the mutual love bonding the Christians together 'more powerfully than an oath'.[30] This coherence struck Celsus as a phenomenon calling for some explanation, since on the face of it such unity was a most surprising thing, and indeed on closer examination he suggested it was no more than a façade. For what Celsus could not discern in the church was any serious principle of religious authority. Because they are a breakaway body from the national religion of the Jews, a spirit of dissidence and fissiparousness is inherent in their very being. By instinct, by the law of their origin, the Christians are people wanting to defy authority.[31]

It is a leading theme in Celsus's political and religious ideology that ethnic religious cults possess an authority to be respected, even if, as he thought was the case with Judaism, some of the attitudes and practices are bizarre and highly peculiar.[32] Christianity is distinctive as a religion in ignoring ethnic frontiers. Therefore to Celsus it appears to be essentially a *stasis,*[33] a revolt, a conscious counter-culture of barbarian origin (and how barbaric Celsus will demonstrate in some detail), scornful about great Greek literature and philosophy.[34] The scorn reflects the low level of education in the community. Moreover, the Christians appear dangerously alienated from giving proper support to the emperors, to the laws of the empire, to the defence of the frontier against the attacking barbarian tribes whose sole aim is to burn and destroy.[35] Above all, they seem outrageous in their negative attitude to the gods, the givers of all fertility on the land[36] and of all military success for the legions.

Celsus asks the Christians to abandon their dangerous innovations and to resume a stand upon the old paths of polytheism, philosophy, and due respect for public office. They appear to treat as their authorities sacred books of the ancient Hebrews, full of obscurities and even absurdities (like the seven days of creation) which only sophisticated allegories can twist to give a rational meaning.[37] On such a frail foundation their

30. *CC* 1.1.

31. *CC* 5.33 and 51. Celsus (3.9) was acutely aware that the Christians would be horrified if they succeeded in converting everybody.

32. *CC* 5.25. In 5.41 Celsus mocks the Jews for arrogantly thinking their religion superior to that of others.

33. *CC* 3.5; 5.33; 8.2; 8.49.

34. *CC* 1.9.

35. *CC* 8.73 and 75.

36. *CC* 8.55.

37. *CC* 1.27; 4.37; 6.60.

exegetes, not surprisingly, merely succeed in producing a mass of inconsistent doctrines.

In these circumstances, Celsus discerns within the great Church a seething debate with parties forming 'each with its own leader'. And yet this condition of somewhat acrimonious debate internal to the Church is in amazing contrast to the unanimity of their initial history. 'When they were beginning, they were few and of one mind; but since they have spread to become a multitude, they are divided and rent asunder, and each wants to have his own party.' The result is that now 'the only thing they seriously have in common is the name of Christian, which they are unwilling ever to abandon'.[38] But this name covers an astonishing diversity of opinions.

At the time when Celsus was writing, the emperor Marcus Aurelius was busy making an example of the poor Christians in the Rhône valley at Lyons, subjecting the Church there to ferocious and inhuman attack.[39] Celsus felt that persecution must be the external force imparting coherence to so heterogeneous a body. The cohesive power holding Christians together must be nothing other than the pressures of a hostile society surrounding them. Celsus has no misgivings about the emperor's policy of drastic harassment. Persecution to death is the appropriate penalty for those who insult the images of the gods, and the magistrates who impose the death penalty are only the instruments of divine vengeance.[40] At the root of the unity manifested by the Christians there lies but a single cause, 'the fear of outsiders'.[41]

Nevertheless, Celsus also knows that the squabbling Christians nurse a dream of incredible unity. Among them he finds an alarming ambition to conquer society, to become 'masters of the world',[42] to convert emperors to their faith and so to be the instruments of a providential design which is to 'unite under a single law the inhabitants of Asia, Europe, and Africa', including in this monolithic polity 'not only Greeks but the most remote barbarians'.[43] In other words, the normal barriers of ethnic difference and divergent cultural levels are, for the Christians, to be transcended. What is particularly strange is that the Christians do not think their dream will be realized through a military conquest, and yet their vision of a supra-national United Nations includes a large role for the Roman emperor. Celsus has

38. *CC* 3.10 and 12.
39. Eusebius, *H.E.* V.1.
40. *CC* 8.41.
41. *CC* 3.14.
42. *CC* 8.69.
43. *CC* 8.72.

heard Christians—a community known to have its reservations about war and military service—asserting that were the emperor to become a Christian, the thorny problems of defence would be altogether transformed.[44] The cause of the empire would then be defended, not by the unsatisfactory gods of the polytheistic tradition, but by the one true God. And his minister would be a believing Christian world-ruler uniting not merely the existing empire but all races of humanity under a benevolent polity, turning the *res Romana* into a theocratic world-state with centralized universal control to restrain crime and sin and to fill the inhabited world with the knowledge of the Lord.

This kind of language confirmed the pagan's worst anxieties. Were any such nightmarish scenario ever to be realized, would not the barbarians merely pour across the Rhine and the Danube and the Euphrates, destroying civilization unhindered?[45] The notion that Christianity has the potential to contribute to the social cohesion and prosperity of the empire is dangerous nonsense and fantasy. If the Church's internal coherence depends on external persecution, is it not implicit that the removal of harassment with the coming of a Christian emperor will only open the flood-gates of latent dissension and mutual intolerance which Celsus has detected in this ambitious community? In a word, nothing seemed to Celsus less likely to impart consolidation and strength to civilized society (i.e. the empire) than a fulfilment of the Christian aspiration to conquer and to bond together Roman and barbarian under one polity and moral code.

Celsus could see in polytheism a principle essentially tolerant of religious diversity. He liked to quote Herodotus who long ago saw diversity of moral and religious custom to be instinctive among the variety of the human race, where 'each tribe thinks its own customs the truest and the best'. Against biblical monotheism, inherited by the Jews and Christians from Moses the magician and sorcerer, Celsus laid down that 'each nation makes no mistake in observing its own laws of worship'.[46] To respect tribal diversity is to affirm polytheism, the cults of which are essentially local and regional. A cosmopolitan Christian monotheism is essentially intolerant and asks for an unrealizable degree of uniformity.

It follows for Celsus that the Jews were merely inconsistent. If they up-

---

44. *CC* 8.69. Cf. *Scriptores Historiae Augustae, Probus* 20, 4–5.

45. *CC* 8.68. The fifth-century barbarian invasions were blamed on the Christians by pagans (e.g. Aug., *Ep.* 111 and especially 138.9ff. to Marcellinus).

46. *CC* 5.34 and 41. Herodotus was also congenial to the programme of toleration advanced by Themistius (II 27d).

held their own customs on the principle that Moses was legislating only for his own race as instructed by the God of the Jews, there would be no ground for reasonable criticism, however peculiar their practices might be. But Celsus found it strange of the Jews to maintain an ethnic form of worship and at the same time to affirm a monotheism which, as they understood it, entailed the invalidity of all other cults which were no more and no less tribal than their own.[47]

Celsus's hostile but informed portrait of the Christian mind of his time shows how even in the second century there was a blueprint in the Church for the Constantinian revolution. In reply to him Origen (writing about 248) defended the hope of an eventual universal unity of all souls, but conceded that 'for those still in the body' it is 'probably' impracticable and will not be realized until the life to come.[48] In a much earlier work[49] Origen contrasted the large variety of human law codes, Greek and barbarian, each valid for its own limited race and region, with the one universal law under which all Christians are happily united. Moreover, in his commentary on the epistle to the Romans, Origen understood both magistrates and bishops as complementary instruments for restraining transgression of divine moral law. The secular magistrate, he says, is God's minister to punish such elemental crimes as murder, adultery, theft, homosexual assault, that is 'the greater part of God's law', whereas bishops have to see to the finer points and must correct more private moral failures.[50] Here even so ascetic and world-renouncing a writer as Origen could echo the language of a blueprint for a coming Christian society in which magistrates and bishops would engage in a cooperative enterprise of social control.[51]

The success of the bishops, however, would inevitably depend on the maintenance of unity in the Church. In answering Celsus Origen sharply dismisses as malicious the suggestion that Christian unity is the result of external hostility. But in other works addressed to a Christian readership or audience, he can be found expressing nostalgia for the old days when under persecution one could be sure of the authenticity and integrity of believers, contrasting that with the secularity and compromise which have now come to invade the community, with clergy of low quality and many laity

---

47. *CC* 5.41.

48. *CC* 8.72.

49. *De principiis* 4.1.1.

50. *Comm. in ep. ad. Rom.* 9.28 (*PL* 14.1228).

51. Jerome (*in Michaiam* I 2.9–10, p. 457 Vallarsi) regarded the cooperation of bishops and magistrates as repressing the legitimate human concerns of the poor.

repairing to the Church's weekly eucharist only very intermittently.[52] Origen records that some converts apostatized soon after their baptism because of their disillusion with the dissension and faction in the churches.[53] Conflict seemed endemic. Yet 'if only the Church were really united, the walls of Jericho would fall'.[54] 'Those who conquer on the battlefield may lose all if they then fall to quarrelling'.[55]

The double concern for unity and mission becomes prominent with Constantine the Great.

Constantine's concern for the inter-related themes of Christian mission and Christian unity is writ large in the writings of Eusebius of Caesarea. Eusebius's panegyrical language about his hero, both in his *Laus Constantini* (including his speech for Constantine's thirtieth anniversary) and in the unfinished *Vita Constantini,* has not improved his reputation with modern historians. Funerary or royal panegyrics of any age tend to reticence about the dark side. In antiquity too panegyrists were notorious for being less than wholly veracious.[56] But it is certain that no panegyrist ascribes to his living imperial hero attitudes other than those he would wish to possess. The oration of 336 offers an ideological programme for a universal world order bonded and led by a Christian Roman monarch. It moves a step beyond the emperor's *Oratio ad sanctos* (I assume the text is an official translation of a Latin discourse, designed to imply that no emperor responsible for persecuting worshippers of the true God can be deemed to possess legitimacy). In the *Oratio* the emperor explicitly claimed that his mission from God is to convert the entire empire to the right religious faith.[57] In Eusebius's *Vita Constantini* the point is made indirectly as the panegyric passes (apparently without betraying any awareness of the contradiction) from praise of Constantine's toleration to an account of his moves against pagan cult, the latter being given a moral justification. In the oration of 336 the emperor is emphatically told that legitimate sovereignty depends on true religion, and no pagan ruler

---

52. Among many texts cf. Origen, *Hom. in Num.* 10.2; *Hom. in Jerem.* 4.3; *Hom. in Gen.* 10.1; 11.3; *Hom. in Levit.* 9.5.

53. *Comm. in ep. ad Rom.* 9.41.

54. *Hom. in Jesu Nave* 7.2.

55. *Hom. in Num.* 26.2.

56. Plotinus V 5.13.14; Augustine, *Conf.* VI 6,9, comments that mendacity was regarded by the audience as a virtue in such circumstances. There was no praise for a panegyrist who told the truth.

57. Eusebius, *Laus Constantini* 11.1 (p. 223 Heikel), i.e. in the opening chapter of the treatise which Eusebius attached to his oration of 336.

can be legitimate (4.1; 5.3) The argument rebuts critics of Constantine's liquidation of successive superfluous colleagues, who did not share his faith. Indeed, the emperor's special divine calling is manifest in his liking for the title 'God's Servant' (7.12). Polytheism stimulates national dissensions and is productive of conflict (9.2; 13.9; 16.2). We meet here the Christian theme that error is associated with diversity, truth with unity. The authentic religion of peace is bringing such conflicts to an end (8.9).

Through a monarchical government, which is the image and earthly counterpart of God's heavenly monarchy (4.3, p. 203.17 Heikel), all peoples in North, South, East, and West can now live under a single law (10.6).[58] The acknowledgement of one God brings recognition of the unity of all humanity (16.3). By the universal power of Rome, the knowledge of the one God is diffused (16.4). So the sign of the cross protects Roman power (9.8), and through this agency there will be brought to completion what is in part already achieved, namely, the uniting of all nations in a single polity with freedom and security of travel anywhere (16.6). So on the Lord's day all tribes and peoples will offer a united worship to the one true God (17.13–14). The universal moral law brings an end to idolatry, defiled by the barbaric custom of human sacrifices (13.7; 16.10), cannibalism, incest and the gross homosexual practices and harlotry at the temple of Aphaca in Phoenicia, lately dismantled by Constantine's express order (8.5–6; *Vita Constantini* III 53). The attack on pagan cult is justified by concern for morality.

The ideological vision in the *Vita Constantini* is less universalist and more specifically Roman than that in the Tricennalian oration. The stress lies on the supremacy of the Roman empire as the home of law and civilization, acknowledged by the stream of barbarian ambassadors pouring into Constantine's court with their gifts and tribute—Britons, Scythians, Sarmatians, Blemmyes, Indians, Ethiopians—all remote barbarians untouched by high culture and respect for legal institutions. It must be doubtful whether Constantine's letter to Sapor, telling the Great King that the Persian capture of Valerian in 260 was caused by his persecution of the Christians, and that

---

58. Themistius also sees the emperor as God's counterpart (n. 61 below) and therefore the bond uniting East and West in a single harmony of soul and judgement (XV 198b). The Christians thought this required one religion. The theme appears in Eusebius, *Pr. Evang.* I 4.6f. (picking up a theme from Bardaisan of Edessa), and VI 6.70f.; *Dem. Evang.* I 2.14. The distinguished monograph of T. D. Barnes, *Constantine and Eusebius* (1981), treats Eusebius with much understanding and sympathy, especially on this last point. Augustine (*DCD* 18.22) writes of God's design to unite the whole world in a single respublica enjoying peace under one system of law. Cf. *Conf.* XIII 34,49.

he is now commending them to the king's protection,[59] would have had the effect intended. The Persians would have observed that the Christianization of Armenia had brought the Armenians under strong Roman influence and authority. Although Constantine said not a word to suggest that a contiguous kingdom with a large Christian population might one day be incorporated within a wider orbis Christianus et Romanus, it would not have been difficult for the Persian king to envisage this possibility and to dislike the prediction.

Eusebius is surely correct in portraying Constantine as moving to the judgement that his one empire should come to have one law, one religion. The universalist ideal, however, could still be accepted by those who did not want pagan cult suppressed and felt the programme of suppression to be socially divisive and bad for the empire.[60] Themistius was to be their spokesman. He fully accepted the universalist language of a world empire; of an emperor who is the earthly image and counterpart of the divine monarch[61] and whose heart, as 'the Assyrians' said (i.e. *Proverbs of Solomon* 21.1), is in the hand of God;[62] of God as the source of all legitimacy and the Giver of victory to the emperor's armies.[63] Themistius was very aware of the mounting immigration of barbarians, especially the Germanic tribes of the north, into the empire, and of the crucial decision of Constantine in 332 to incorporate the Goths within the empire by making them foederati with responsibility to defend the frontier.[64] As the immigrants increased in number and became indispensable for the army, tension rose. The frontier was no longer an effective barrier, and in 375 the Danube defences crumbled, with consequences leading to the catastrophic defeat of Valens and the Roman legions in 378 at the battle of Adrianople, leaving the road to Constantinople wide open. Themistius interpreted the emperor's universalist ideology to entail the conclusion that war on the frontier was a mistake,[65] and that the barbarians should be peacefully settled and turned into good Romans.[66] The barbarian

---

59. Eusebius, *Vita Constantini* IV 9–13. The letter has an undercurrent of threat, especially in the opening observations that Constantine's zeal for true religion has overthrown tyrants.

60. Themistius V 70b. The reference to Empedocles in this passage was explained by Petavius as Themistius's coded name for Christ.

61. Themistius I 9b, cf. XI 143a.

62. Themistius VII 89d, XI 147c, XIX 229a.

63. Themistius XI 143a, XIX 229a Victory: II 39a.

64. Themistius VIII 119c. Date: Mommsen, *Chronica Minora* I 234.

65. Themistius VI 75d, XVI 212a, especially X.

66. Themistius XIII 166c. Themistius claimed Jovian a true son of the Constantinian

tribes he once compares to the *thumos* in the Platonic soul, a vast emotional force which needed to be harnessed for constructive ends by being made subordinate to reason and law.[67] They are to be Romanized, which for Themistius must involve making them more than helots to do the inferior and menial jobs and means that they will have a serious stake in Roman society.

Romanization, however, means incorporation in a society that enjoys equality before the law and at the same time affirms freedom of worship and conscience in religion. There are many paths to God, who is pleased to see much disagreement about theology and religion since it is an indirect testimony to the mystery and transcendence of the divine.[68]

Themistius's understanding of imperial universalism was not generally shared. In Ambrose and Synesius we meet Christians who deplored the weakness of the government towards the barbarian immigrations and who thought the emperor was neglecting his first duty, the defence of the frontier. The barbarians threatened civilisation and public order, and the Church was a buttress of order in society. The experience of the Gothic invasion of the Balkans in the 370s was one of cruel inhumanity. Ambrose regarded the invaders as showing no mercy and no spark of human feeling, unless their prisoners could command a price in the slave market.[69]

Nevertheless Ambrose was sure that the pax Romana made possible the spread of the gospel far beyond the frontier, the mission of St. Thomas in India and of St. Matthew in Persia, and adds: 'All have learnt by living under the authority of a single earthly imperium to confess in faithful words the rule of a single almighty God.'[70] He could tell Gratian (much as Themistius could also) that he was Augustus not of one race alone but of the entire world.[71]

The universal extension of the Christian gospel becomes fused in fourth-century ideology with the limitless claim to authority by the Roman emperors of the age. Already in the third century 'ruler of the world' *(kosmokrator)* is attested in inscriptions as an imperial title for Caracalla and Gordian.[72] Ammianus Marcellinus, however, felt it to be absurd vanity that the em-

---

dynasty, in effect a new Constantine reestablishing the line after Julian's death (V 70d), but needing to be less bellicose.

67. Themistius X 131c.

68. Themistius V passim.

69. Ambrose, *De officiis* II 15, 71.

70. *In Ps.* 45.21.3 *(CSEL* 64.344).

71. *De fide*, prol. 1 *(CSEL* 78.4). Cf. Themistius XIII 163c, 169b.

72. E. Peterson, *Heis Theos* (Göttingen, 1926), p. 173 n. 1.

peror Constantius liked to sign himself *totius orbis dominus.*[73] In contrast, Themistius was normally content to say that the emperor ruled over 'almost all the world'.[74]

The immigration of the Germanic tribes transformed the empire and in the West substituted several small barbarian kingdoms—which Augustine thought a much more satisfactory form of organization for government than the huge unwieldy Roman empire.[75] The Christians did not think the barbarians fell outside the kingdom of God.[76] But incorporation in the ecclesia catholica was also integration into a society respectful of Roman law. As civil authority declined under the hammer blows of barbarian invasion, bishops emerged as the defenders of their flock and so of their cities. Bishops, Augustine once remarked, are becoming *principes super omnem terram,*[77] in an international Church which embodied unity and universality through the episcopate that transcended all frontiers whether ethnic or imperial.

For the Greek East the linchpin of order, and the embodiment of unity and universality, was seen in the emperor at Constantinople, and that ideal is already present in Themistius's pages in the 370s. In the Latin West the stronger sense of reserve towards interference by government in the independence of the Church left the path open for the authority of the Roman see, enhanced further as barbarian invasion and the dangers of travel made episcopal synods harder to hold. The Eusebian and Constantinian dream of a universal society acknowledging a single law and one authority came to be realized in the western Church in a manner distinct from that of the East.

---

73. Amm. Marc. XV 1.3. John Matthews, *The Roman Empire of Ammianus* (1989), p. 235, comments that 'Ammianus' objection is a curious one. Apart from its triviality as an instance of the point of principle at stake, he must have known that the style to which he refers was commonplace in imperial pronouncements of the times'. He later (p. 431) explains it from XX.3.12 where Ammianus again writes of the earth as tiny in comparison with the whole universe.

74. Themistius XIII 169b; XVIII 217cd; XIX 227b.

75. *DCD* 4.15.

76. Augustine (*DCD* 20.11) rejects the exegesis of Gog and Magog attacking the holy city (Apoc. 20) to mean northern barbarians invading the empire, as in Ambrose, *De fide* II 16; Jerome, *Heb. Qu. Gen.* 10.2, *PL* 23.1009; *in Ezech.* XI praef., *PL* 25,1, 341.

77. *En. in Ps.* 44.32. Augustine could speak of the empire as being 'Christian by God's mercy' (*De gratia Christi et de pecc. orig.* II 17.18) and even of *imperium Christianum* (*c. Faustum* 22.60). But for him the saeculum was at a great distance from God. 'The emperors have become Christian, the devil has not' (*En. in Ps.* 93.19). His estimate of the actualities of the empirical Church is one of individual failures on a dreadful scale, striking among such bishops as Antoninus of Fussala.

Oracles of the End in the Conflict of Paganism and Christianity in the Fourth Century

The conflict between paganism and Christianity in the fourth century was not an ideological battle with which Father Festugière could have been entirely happy. No twentieth-century scholar did more than he to illuminate the aspirations of the highest and best minds on both sides of the divide. As his book on Antioch shows, he himself would surely have found equally delightful the company of Libanius and the prayers of the ascetics in the Syrian desert, but he was not unaware that there was strong mutual disapprobation between the parties among whom he would have wanted to find friends. The Christians were sure that the pagan cults were paying homage to inferior and evil daemons; far from being beneficent powers capable of giving earthly success and fertile lands or spouses, the gods should be estimated as malevolent spirits. They were pleased to find in the pages of Porphyry the acknowledgement that the daemons presiding over oracles and local shrines requiring sacrifices are not very exalted cosmic powers, but merely regional deputies. In his tract "On the Decline of Oracles" (*De defectu orac.* 17ff.) Plutarch had allowed that there are inferior daemons, some of whom are actually evil (though he would hesitate to go so far as to say they are all responsible for natural catastrophes), and that the local daemon is sufficiently vulnerable to flattery to enjoy being given the name of the superior god that he serves (21, 421 E). If, Plutarch argues, there is a cosmic Love flowing out from the creative goodness of the supreme god, there must be inferior gods to be objects of this love (24, 423 D). In his treatise "On the Philosophy derived from Oracles", Porphyry allowed that the divine powers responsible for oracles and divination are of a lowly and earthly level or milieu (Philoponus, *De opif. mundi* iv, 20).[1]

1. The fragments of Porphyry's book on Oracles survive exclusively through Christian

The collection of oracles made by Porphyry included some given in his own time which had a strongly anti-Christian content. He had a special interest in these. Eusebius of Caesarea (*Demonstratio Evangelica* iii, 7, 1) and Augustine (*De Civitate Dei* xix, 23, 2) preserve some striking pieces so obviously hostile to Christianity that Porphyry's naiveté in quoting them as if they were genuinely inspired cases of oracular possession justly occasioned some tart comment from Augustine. A passage remarkably similar in tone occurs in *De Civitate Dei* xviii, 53–54, and it is very probable that John J. O'Meara is right in suggesting that this also is derived from Porphyry's book on Oracles. Here Augustine quotes some Greek oracle "composed by a learned man" using verses to declare that, by means of sorcery, St. Peter established that the name of Christ would be worshipped for a period of 365 years, and then end. St. Peter achieved this, said the pagan source, by killing a boy one year old, dividing up the corpse, and then burying him with occult rites.[2] Augustine offers a calculation based on his belief that Christ died on 25 March of the consulship of the Gemini (A.D. 29), bringing the supposed end of Christianity to the year 398; a date he delights to contrast with the fact that in March 399 the pagan temples of Carthage were officially closed on imperial authority by Gaudentius and Jovius, sent from the emperor Honorius. Obviously Augustine has miscounted: the correct year would be 394;

---

writers mainly engaged in refutation: Eusebius of Caesarea, *Praeparatio Evangelica;* Augustine—mainly *De Civitate Dei;* Philoponus, *De Opificio Mundi;* and more appreciatively by the Tübingen *Theosophia* found by K. Neumann and first edited by K. Buresch, *Klaros* (1889) and reedited by H. Erbse (1942) in a book as rare as the gold of Ophir and not accessible to me: *Fragmente griechischer Theosophien,* Hamburger Arbeiten zur Altertumswissenschaft 4 (1941).

J. J. O'Meara, *Porphyry's Philosophy from Oracles in Augustine* (Paris, 1959), sought to show that Porphyry's book is identical with *De regressu animae.* The monograph is a most valuable study of Porphyry, even if the main thesis is not established.

2. The employment of a murdered infant for divination is a conventional accusation against distinguished figures who have lost power: see for example Dio Cassius, 73, 16; SHA Heliogabalus 8, 1–2; Dionysius of Alexandria on the emperor Valerian, quoted by Eusebius, *HE* vii, 10, 4; Eusebius, *Vita Constantini* i, 36, on Maxentius. The historian Socrates, iii, 13, 11–12, reports that at the time of the Julianic revival of paganism sorcerers at Athens and Alexandria slew infants to study their entrails for divination; cf. Joh. Chrys., *in Matt.* 28, 2–3.

The accusation was brought against the Montanists, but roundly disbelieved by Jerome, *Ep.* 41, 4, 1.

See F. J. Dolger, "Sacramentum Infanticidii", in *Antike und Christentum* 4 (1934), 188ff.; J. Hubaux, "L'Enfant d'un an", in *Collection Latomus* II (1948) = Hommages à J. Bidez et à F. Cumont (Brussels), 143–58; Id., "La crise de la trois cent soixante-cinquième année", in *L'Antiquité classique* 17 (1948), 344–54.

that would have offered a less dramatic juxtaposition for North Africans, but not for the emperor Theodosius who, in 394, conquered the pagan uprising of Eugenius. If the pagan oracle predicting the end of Christianity in 394 had anything to do with the pagan revolt of Eugenius, that would give a sharper point to Augustine's observation that, at the time of Maximus's rise to power in the West and the civil war of 377–78, Theodosius consulted no pagan oracle before his campaign but sent to the hermit John in the Egyptian desert, from whom he received assurance of victory. The campaign of 394 was likewise a holy war, in which the emperor's opponents were pardoned on condition of becoming Christians (*De Civ. Dei* v, 26). Before embarking on so hazardous an enterprise, it was obvious that the emperor needed a special prophecy from a charismatic figure, if only to trump the pagan opposition with their oracles.

In view of Augustine's great interest in Theodosius's defeat of the pagan uprising led by Eugenius, it is surprising that he seems not to see any special significance in the year 394 as the 365th anniversary of the Crucifixion. He may have been influenced by the high excitements of the year 398, and failed to notice that to set 398 as the terminal point of the Great Year would presuppose a different starting point, in 33 rather than 29. In his famous sermon on the fall of Rome to Alaric in 410, *De excidio Urbis,* he records the extraordinary memory (of which he has evidently had an eye-witness account) of an earthquake and terrifying natural portents at Constantinople in the time of the emperor Arcadius. The quaking earth and stormy sky convinced the entire population that the End was imminent; everyone; including the imperial family, left the city in a panic, and people did not even stop to bolt their doors. The Arian historian Philostorgius similarly looked back on the catastrophes of the time as the signs of the coming end consequent upon the Church's apostasy from the great truths stated by Arius, and devotes many lines to a catalogue of woes (xi, 7 p. 137 Bidez).

Learned antiquarians (as Hubaux pointed out) could easily have recalled Camillus's observation that the year in which the Gauls captured Rome in 390 was the 365th year since the foundation of the city (Livy, v, 54, 5). Claudian's repeated comparison of Camillus with Stilicho may conceivably have stimulated the consciousness that the year in some way marked an epoch in the divine dispensation in history.

Be that as it may, the pagan hopes for an end to Christianity after 365 years could derive reinforcement from the ancient axiom, to which the Christians themselves made eloquent appeal when arguing against the eternity of the world, that whatever has a beginning in time will also have an end. Surprising as it may at first sight seem, the pagan contention that after a fixed term of years the Church on earth would meet some transforming catastrophe was strikingly paralleled by the hopes entertained by the Christians themselves. Believers also expected Antichrist to come with attendant disasters to presage the final revelation of the man of sin sitting in the very temple of God.

In the 380s the bishop of Brescia in Northern Italy was Filastrius, who had been elected there after ascetic wanderings about the Mediterranean, during which his inquiring mind had taken special note of heretical deviations and unusual exegetical traditions. Augustine commented that Filastrius was rather too inclined to confuse the latter with the former; *Haeres.* 80 "Et alias quidem ipse (Philaster) commemorat, sed mihi appellandae haereses non videntur." Among his list of bizarre eccentricities Filastrius reports (106) a belief that the End would come 365 years after the first advent of Christ, an exegesis supported from the text of Isaiah 61:2, "Adnuntiare annum dei acceptabilem et diem retributionis". Filastrius's refutation of this exegesis rests on the observation that 400 years or more have passed since the time of Christ. Later this figure becomes enlarged to 430 years (112). The figures look puzzling at first sight, since it is certain that Filastrius was present at the council of Aquileia in 381 and that Augustine met him at Milan between 383 and 387 (Aug., *Ep.* 222, 2). The figures therefore suggest either that a copyist revised the text about 430 or, perhaps more probably, that Filastrius had only a limited capacity to count. His misdating of the apologist Tatian by approximately a century (48) makes chronological incompetence an entirely possible explanation.

The political disasters of the 370s and 380s conspired to give many in the Empire an impending sense of doomsday. The shattering impact of the emperor Valens's defeat and death and the loss of two-thirds of the army at the appalling battle of Adrianople in 378, a drama which gives the climax to the history of Ammianus Marcellinus (xxxi, 13), would surely give impetus to contemporary futurologists. If the pagans were baffled, perhaps the Christians could find a clue in the apocalyptic obscurities of the prophet Daniel, especially the interpretation of King Nebuchadnezzar's dream (Dan. 2:31–45) and the prophet's vision of four beasts (= kingdoms), the fourth of which has ten horns (= kings), after whom another king would rule "until a time and times and half a time", i.e. for three and a half years. The mystery contained in this period of time found an echo in the Apocalypse of John (11:2) where the holy city is to be trampled under foot by the heathen for 42 months, i.e. three and half years. Moreover, the Lord's witnesses, slain by the Beast, are to lie in the streets of the "city where the Lord was crucified, spiritually called Sodom and Egypt" for the space of three and a half days. Thereafter they will be revived and ascend to heaven (Rev. 11:9–11). Who, moreover, are the alien nations Gog and Magog who in the last times come to lay siege to the camp of the saints and the beloved city (Rev. 20:8 from Ezekiel 38:2ff.)? Ambrose (*De fide* ii, 16) believed them to be the invading barbarians from the north pouring unstoppably across the Danube into the Balkan peninsula after the massive push of the Hun migration in 375. This exegesis was to be rejected both by Jerome (*in Ezech.* xi, *PL* 25, 372) and by Augustine (*De civ. Dei* xx, 11), but certainly retained advocates convinced by the living fulfilment of prophecy before their eyes.

Augustine himself was ready to see prophecy in process of being acted out in the emperor Theodosius's edicts closing down temples and forbidding pagan sacrifices. (See, for example, *De Divinatione Daemonum* ix, 13; *S(ermo) Guelf.* 33, 2 p. 578 Morin; *S. Morin* 13, 4 p. 643).

Early in the fifth century, Sulpicius Severus in Aquitaine wrote his chronicle of world history,[3] about four-fifths of which offer a summary of biblical history leading up to a list of nine persecutions ranging from Nero to Diocletian. These herald a tenth horror at the coming of Antichrist, to whom Nero redivivus will be forerunner. Severus sees Antichrist's dark foreshadowings in the Arian controversy; in the socially disruptive entry of unassimilated barbarians who, like the Jews, do not keep Roman customs; and in the deplorable secularity manifested in the reaction to Priscillian of Avila. Severus could apply to the Church of his time the embittered, sad language used of the Roman state by Sallust and Tacitus—language which he mingles with exegesis of the prophecies of Daniel (ii, 3) and the Apocalypse of John, for whose canonical status he hotly contends (ii, 31, 1). He thought it a deplorable inconsistency in those who accepted the fulfilment of prophecy in the past that they did not wish to see it being fulfilled in the shape of things to come.

That the contention provoked by Priscillian's ascetic and occult evangelicalism was a sign of the coming end was held by Priscillian himself (*Tract.* ii, p. 35, 6–7 Schepss).[4]

The three and a half days of St. John's Apocalypse or the years of Dan-

---

3. G. K. van Andel, *The Christian Concept of History in the Chronicle of Sulpicius Severus* (Amsterdam, 1976).

4. H. Chadwick, *Priscillian of Avila, the Occult and the Charismatic in the Early Church* (Oxford, 1976), p. 10.

iel invited bold interpreters to look for the End 350 years after the Lord's birth or death. In North Africa we find an echo of this exegesis in the *Regulae* of Tyconius, the excommunicate Donatist theologian who appalled his fellow-sectaries by insisting that the Church must be world-wide and by denying that holiness can be a matter of merely subjective individual taste. In his Regulae he set out to formulate hermeneutic principles to guide the biblical exegete, and thereby impressed and lastingly influenced the mind of Augustine on the other side of the ravine separating Christian brothers in North Africa.[5]

Tyconius devoted his fifth Rule to times and numbers in Scripture. Biblical times, he explains, always have a mystical meaning. This world's age lasts 6,000 years, and the Lord was born and died and rose again in the sixth millennium. But in Scripture a day symbolises not only a thousand years but, in some cases, only a hundred. So it is written that the Church lies in the city where the Lord was crucified for three and a half days, and that the resurrection of the Son of Man comes after three days. These figures are for Tyconius profound clues to the expected End.

Among the North African Christians of the fourth century, millenarianism was common belief shared by Catholic and Donatist alike. In a well-known passage of the *City of God* (xx, 7, 1) Augustine looked back on a time (as we find him in *S.* 259, 2 or *S. Mai* 94, 3–5) when he himself had held the very literal expectation that after six thousand years from the creation, the Lord would return and the saints rise to celebrate a sabbath rest for a seventh period of a thousand years.[6] Some Christians, however, believed that there would be banquets of exquisite dishes to eat. Others, of whom

---

5. Tyconius's *Regulae* were edited by F. C. Burkitt in Texts and Studies III, 1 (Cambridge, 1894), and best studied by T. Hahn, *Tyconius-Studien* (Leipzig, 1900; reprinted Aalen, 1971). Augustine was surprised that after his excommunication Tyconius did not become a Catholic, but remained hoping for restoration to his own community. Hahn eloquently pointed out the strength of his Donatist convictions as expressed in his commentary on the Apocalypse, of which the Church is the central theme. And this theme is taken further by J. Ratzinger, "Beobachtungen zum Kirchenbegriff des Tyconius im Liber regularum", *Revue des études augustiniennes* ii (1956), 173–85 = Memorial G. Bardy. Ratzinger stresses Tyconius's statements that the visible church may be the sphere of operation for either Christ or the Devil, and that Antichrist is present as much as Christ in the empirical visible Church, no separation being made before the Last Judgment (p. 63, 10ff. Burkitt). To this doctrine Augustine took exception (*De doctrina Christiana* iii, 45). He may, however, have owed something to Tyconius's theme of the organic unity of Head and Body (e.g. p. 7, 24 B.).

6. G. Folliet, "La typologie du sabbat chez Augustin: son interpretation millénariste entre 389 et 400", *Revue des ét. aug.* ii (1956), 371–90.

Augustine was or came to be one (e.g. *Ep.* 36, 5, 24. 31) preferred to think the delights purely spiritual, but were then confronted by the complaint that without good food, sex, and above all the fun of bargaining in the market, the millennium would surely be very dull (*S.* 362, 28; cf. *S. Guelf.* 8, 2 p. 466 Morin). From the view that the delights of the millennium will be spiritual it was a negligible distance to a third, more radically allegorising position, that, if the joys are those of the spirit, perhaps the thousand years are symbolic language for the eternal presence of God, transcending the successiveness and flux of this transitory, material order.

Augustine ended in this last position; but exactly where we ought to locate Tyconius on this interpretative scale is not obvious. He writes in a quietly subdued but decisive independence from the vulgar Donatist thesis that because, in Scripture, the Devil's dwelling is in the north while the Bridegroom of the Song of Songs rests in the south, the true Church is in Numidia alone. Tyconius believed that both Christ and the Devil may be found in both north and south (*Reg.* vii p. 74 Burkitt). This opinion did not prevent him from thinking it deeply significant that the providence of God, by which Christianity began in one province of the empire, had chosen Africa to be the field on which was being fought out the conflict between Christ's holy Church and the Antichrist embodied in the persecuting imperial Church of secular Roman glory. Tyconius found a way of reconciling his belief in the extension of the universal Church with the recusant spirit of the Numidians. In at least large parts of his commentary on the Apocalypse (which can only partially be reconstructed from the eighth century commentary of Beatus of Liébana who often copied him)[7] Tyconius's exegesis was in general symbolist. The commentary lay before Gennadius of Massilia who expressly remarked: "nihil in ea carnale sed totum intelligens spiritale" (*Vir. Inl.* 18). Nevertheless a spiritualising interpretation of the millennium was not incompatible with a less poetic understanding of the six thousand years of temporal history preceding heaven.

In short, Tyconius may easily have believed that the millennial reign of Christ and his saints is a symbol of the eternity beyond the bloody flux of history and simultaneously held to a Donatist expectation that Antichrist, perhaps preceded by Nero redivivus, would arrive 350 years after either Christ's birth (would not this virtually coincide in date with the "tempora Macariana" under Constantius II when the Donatists were subjected to fe-

---

7. Beatus, first edited in 1770 by Florez, was reedited by H. A. Sanders (Rome, 1930; reprinted at Madrid by Edilan, 1975).

rocious harassment and many preferred suicide to surrender?) or the crucifixion and resurrection. In the latter event, one would be brought to the
390s and to the age of Augustine's mobilization of Catholic forces against
the Donatist communities.

To sum up, a lot of people in the fourth century continued to expect
the End to come, and looked to oracles to tell them when it would be.
The pagans found in Porphyry an oracle proposing a term of 365 years for
the Christian faith. Filastrius reveals that there were Christians who held
a similar opinion. Tyconius tells us that the prophecies of Daniel and the
Apocalypse of John offered a slightly shorter alternative of 350 years. As
the forecasts failed to be realised, it was not beyond scientific futurology to
propose alternatives. The author of the Tübingen Theosophy, calculating
that Christ was born in the year 5500 from the Creation, risked the prediction that the world would end 500 years thereafter, i.e. during the reign of
the emperor Anastasius in A.D. 507. Augustine regarded all calculations of
the date of Antichrist's coming as *curiositas* or inquiring into hidden cosmic
secrets which God has not intended us to know (*S. Morin* ix, 3 p. 622). His
correspondent Hesychius bishop of Salona was sure both that the End was
imminent and that Scripture gave no decisive basis for calculating in exactly
what year it would come. Augustine's reply to him (*Ep.* 199) suggests that
even this is claiming too much; that people well read in history may laugh
at Christians who see the final catastrophe in the barbarian invasions when
many worse things have happened in the past (*Ep.* 199, 39); and that the
only certain conclusion from Scripture is that the end will not come before
the Gospel has been preached in all the world—"and in Africa innumerable
barbarian tribes have not yet heard the Gospel" (199, 46). Augustine cannily
concludes that while adventist expectation is productive of excellent devotion, it runs the risk of provoking mockery as the hope is not realised, and
therefore that the wisest and most edifying position is to believe that the
Lord will return and the End come, but not soon. It is better to be surprised
by joy than humiliated and disappointed (199, 54).

Credits and Permissions

Apart from minor stylistic changes, we have tried as much as possible to preserve each article in its original form.

———

"Ministry and Tradition." First published in *Telogia del Sacerdocio* 21 (1990).

"Episcopacy in the New Testament and Early Church." First published in *Today's Church and Today's World: With a Special Focus on the Ministry of Bishops: the Lambeth Conference 1978 Preparatory Articles*. London: CIO Publishing, 1978.

"The Role of the Christian Bishop in Ancient Society." First published as the *Protocol of the 35th Colloquy*. Center for Hermeneutical Studies in Hellenistic and Modern Culture: Protocol Series of the Colloquies of the Center 35. Berkeley: Center for Hermeneutical Studies in Hellenistic and Modern Culture, 1979. Reprinted with permission of the Graduate Theological Union, 2400 Ridge Rd., Berkeley CA 94709; 510-649-2400; www.gtu.edu

"Bishops and Monks." First published in *Historica, Theologica et Philosophica, Gnostica*. Studia Patristica, vol. XXIV. Leuven: Peeters Press, 1993. Used by permission.

"The Origin of the Title 'Oecumencial Council.'" First published in the *Journal of Theological Studies* XXIII, no. 1 (1972): 132–35. Used by permission.

"Faith and Order at the Council of Nicaea: a Note on the Background of the Sixth Canon." First published in *Harvard Theological Review* 53, no. 3 (July 1960): 171–95. Copyright © 1960 President and Fellows of Harvard College. Reprinted with the permission of Cambridge University Press.

"Ossius of Cordova and the Presidency of the Council of Antioch, 325." First published in the *Journal of Theological Studies* IX, no. 2 (1958): 292–304. Used by permission.

"The Chalcedonian Definition." First published in *Actes du Concile de Chalcedoine: Sessions III–VI*, translated by Andre-Jean Festugiere. Cahiers d'Orientalisme IV. Geneva: Patrick Cramer, 1983. Used by permission.

"The Circle and the Ellipse: Rival Concepts of Authority in the Early Church." Inaugural Lecture, University of Oxford, 5 May 1959. Oxford: Clarendon Press, 1959.

"St. Peter and St. Paul in Rome: The Problem of the Memoria Apostolorum Ad Catacumbas." First published in the *Journal of Theological Studies* VIII, no. 1 (1957): 31–52. Used by permission.

"The Power of Music." First publication.

"New Letters of St. Augustine." First published in the *Journal of Theological Studies* XXXIV, no. 2 (1983): 425–52. Used by permission.

"New Sermons of St Augustine." First published in the *Journal of Theological Studies* XLVII, no. 1 (1996): 69–91. Used by permission.

"On Re-reading the *Confessions*." First published in *St Augustine the Bishop*, edited by Fannie Lemoine and Christopher Kleinhenz, 139–62. New York: Garland, 1994. Copyright © 1994 From *St Augustine the Bishop* by Fannie Lemoine and Christopher Kleinhenz. Reproduced by permission of Taylor and Francis Group, LLC, a division of Informa plc.

"Providence and the Problem of Evil in Augustine." First published in *Congresso Internazionale su S. Agostino nel XVI centenario della conversione (Roma 15–20 sett. 1986). Atti*. Studia Ephemeridis Augustinanum 24. Rome: Institutum Patristicum Augustinianum, 1987. Used by permission.

"The Attractions of Mani." First published in *Pléroma: Salus Carnis: Homenaje a Antonio Orbe*. Edited by Eugenio Romero-Pose. Santiago de Compostela, 1990.

"Augustine's Ethics." First published as chap. 13 in *Studies on Ancient Christianity*. Burlington: Ashgate Valorium, 2006.

"The Originality of Early Christian Ethics." James Bryce Memorial Lecture, Somerville College, 1988. Oxford: Somerville College, 1990.

"Pachomios and the Idea of Sanctity." First published in *The Byzantine Saint: University of Birmingham Fourteenth Spring Symposium of Byzantine Studies*, edited by Sergei Hackel. Studies supplementary to Sobornost 5. London: Fellowship of St. Alban and St. Sergius, 1981.

"Christian and Roman Universalism in the Fourth Century." First published in *Christian Faith and Greek Philosophy in Late Antiquity: Essays in Tribute to George Christopher Stead*, edited by Lionel R. Wickham and Caroline D. Bammel. Leiden: Brill, 1993. Used by permission.

"Oracles of the End in the Conflict of Paganism and Christianity in the Fourth Century." First published in *Memorial Andre-Jean Festugiere*, edited by E. Lucchesi and H. D. Saffrey. Cahiers d'Orientalisme X. Geneva: Patrick Cramer, 1984. Used by permission.

Index of Names and Subjects

Index of Ancient Sources